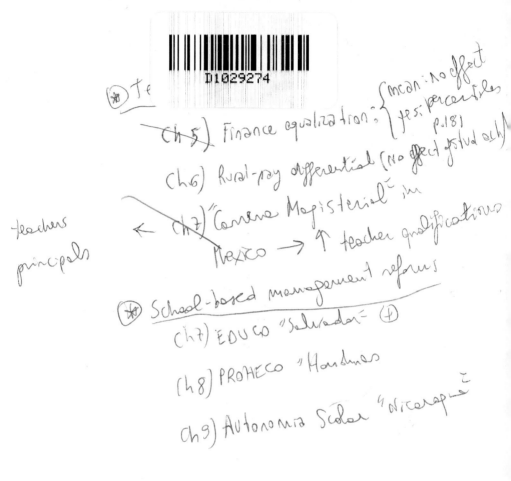

(*) Te

(Ch 5) Finance equalization: { mean: no effect
                                yes: percentiles
                                p.181

(Ch 6) Rural-pay differential (No effect of stud ach)

← (Ch 7) "Carrera Magisterial" in
        Mexico → ↑ teacher qualifications

teachers
principals

(*) School-based management reforms

(Ch 7) EDUCO "Salvador = (+)

(Ch 8) PROHECO "Honduras

(Ch 9) Autonomia Scolar "Nicaragua =

WITHDRAWAL

Cheap tutoring program
  ↳ Chile (p.250)
     Umpula (2003)
     Chay
     McEwan

Incentives to Improve Teaching

Lessons from Latin America

Emiliana Vegas
Editor

THE WORLD BANK
Washington, D.C.

Library of Congress Cataloging-in-Publication Data

Incentives to improve teaching : lessons from Latin America / Emiliana Vegas, editor.
    p. cm. — (Directions in development)
    Includes bibliographical references and index.
    ISBN 0-8213-6215-1
    1. Teachers—Salaries, etc.—Latin America—Cross-cultural studies. 2. Rewards and punishments in education—Latin America—Cross-cultural studies. 3. School improvement programs—Latin America—Cross-cultural studies. I. Vegas, Emiliana II. World Bank. III. Directions in development (Washington, D.C.)

LB2844.L29I53 2005
331.2'813711'0098—dc22

September 23, 2005

2005047500

Contents

7   Teacher and Principal Incentives in Mexico **213**

Patrick J. McEwan and Lucrecia Santibáñez

**8   Decentralization of Education, Teacher Behavior,
        and Outcomes** **255**
The Case of El Salvador's EDUCO Program

Yasuyuki Sawada and Andrew B. Ragatz

**9   Teacher Effort and Schooling Outcomes in Rural
        Honduras** **307**

Emanuela di Gropello and Jeffery H. Marshall

**10   Teacher Incentives and Student Achievement in
        Nicaraguan Autonomous Schools** **359**

Caroline E. Parker

Figures

Preface

This book is about one of the most pressing challenges in improving education quality in Latin America: designing and implementing effective incentives for enhancing teaching practice as a means for raising student learning outcomes. The various evaluations presented in the volume tackle this issue using the best available data and latest methodological approaches to provide insights into why and how education reforms can affect who chooses to enter and remain in the teaching profession and how effective are teachers in fostering student learning.

By providing well-researched evidence on diverse education reforms affecting teacher incentives in the region, the book makes an important contribution to the literature on teacher incentives in general and, especially, to the education literature in Latin America. Perhaps more important, the lessons on teacher incentive reforms from this research can be useful to policy makers in Latin America and in the rest of the world.

The research in this book provides evidence that teachers respond to incentives, and that these vary in nature: some incentives affect who decides to enter and remain in the teaching profession, while other incentives affect the work teachers do in classrooms. How well teachers are paid relative to similar workers in other professions affects teaching quality. Additionally, changes in the structure of pay—in which teachers are rewarded for doing specific things, such as mentoring new teachers or having students perform better in tests, can lead to higher student learning. But pay incentives appear to be more powerful when teachers can lose their jobs as a result of poor performance. As in most policy reforms, in the case of teacher incentive reforms, too, the devil is in the details. The cases in this volume show that clarity in the behaviors that are being motivated, as well as real differentiation in the rewards to teachers who adopt the desired behaviors and those who do not, can have a big impact on the effectiveness of teacher incentive reforms.

Changes in other aspects of teacher contracts can also have a great impact on teaching quality and student learning. Education reforms, even those not specifically designed to affect teachers, can influence—and sometimes have even greater effects than changes in compensation—the characteristics of those who choose to enter and remain in teaching and, importantly, their work in classrooms. For example, school-based management reforms that devolve decision-making authority to the school were found to have had an important impact on teacher performance and student learning.

Although Latin American countries are continuously reforming their education systems, it is rare to find examples in which findings from sound evaluations inform reform design. This study is an important contribution to fill this void.

Guillermo Perry   Ariel Fiszbein
Chief Economist   Lead Economist
Latin America and the Caribbean   Human Development
  Region   Department
The World Bank   Latin America and the Caribbean
                                           Region
                                         The World Bank

Acknowledgments

This publication is possible thanks to the collaboration and support from many colleagues and friends. I am indebted to Beth King, who first envisioned this project with me, and with whom I co-authored the initial proposals to obtain funding for this research. For their constant support throughout the various stages to produce this book, I am grateful to Ariel Fiszbein, Marito Garcia, Guillermo Perry, Luis Serven, and Eduardo Velez Bustillo.

Special thanks go to the authors of each of the chapters, including: Luis Crouch, Emanuela Di Gropello, Nora Gordon, Werner Hernani-Limarino, Jeffery Marshall, Patrick McEwan, Alejandra Mizala, Carrie Parker, Andy Ragatz, Pilar Romaguera, Lucrecia Santibáñez, Yasuyuki Sawada, Ilana Umansky, and Miguel Urquiola.

Many individuals contributed to improve the research, and its presentation, with very helpful comments and suggestions. Among them: Charles Abelmann, Jishnu Das, Andrea Guedes, Gustavo Ioschpe, Peter Moock, Richard Murnane, Vicente Paqueo, Harry Patrinos, Jeff Puryear, Alberto Rodríguez, Halsey Rogers, Jaime Saavedra, Carolina Sánchez Páramo, Luis Serven, Sergei Soares, and Kristian Thorn. As usual, only the authors and the editor are responsible for any remaining errors.

1

Improving Teaching and Learning through Effective Incentives

Lessons from Education Reforms in Latin America

Emiliana Vegas and Ilana Umansky
The World Bank

As a region, Latin America faces tremendous challenges, particularly those of development, poverty, and inequality. Education is widely recognized as one of the most critical means of defeating those challenges. Democratizing education—by improving both its coverage and its quality—is critical to overcoming the social and economic inequality that plagues Latin America. Ensuring that all children have the opportunity to learn critical skills at the primary and secondary level is paramount to overcoming skill barriers that perpetuate underdevelopment and poverty.

Although most people recognize the importance of improving the quality of education systems for reducing poverty and inequality and for increasing economic development, how to do so is less clear. A growing body of evidence supports the intuitive notion that teachers play a key role in what, how, and how much students learn (see, for example, Hanushek and others 2005; Park and Hannum 2001; Rivkin, Hanushek, and Kain 1998; Rockoff 2004; Sanders and Rivers 1996; Wright, Horn, and Sanders 1997). Attracting qualified individuals into the teaching profession, retaining those qualified teachers, providing them with the necessary skills and knowledge, and motivating them to work hard and to do the best job they can is arguably *the* key education challenge.

This book, *Incentives to Improve Teaching—Lessons from Latin America*, focuses on the effect of education reforms that alter teacher incentives to achieve teaching quality and to enhance student learning. The goals of our book are, first, to broaden and deepen our conception of how education reforms affect teachers in Latin America and, second, to shed light on how reforms can be designed and implemented to maximize their beneficial effects on teaching and learning. We hope to demonstrate which teacher incentive reforms have been most successful at improving teaching and learning in the region, as well as to shed some light on the importance of how reforms are negotiated in the larger society, particularly by looking at the important role of teachers' unions.

The reforms explored in this volume represent efforts by several countries in the region to increase teachers' accountability and to introduce incentives to motivate teachers so they raise student learning. Some countries—such as Bolivia, Chile, and Mexico—have established salary differentials, thereby rewarding teachers for working in rural areas, or have introduced salary structures that reward teachers for improved performance and student learning. Brazil changed the resources available for education generally and for teacher salaries more specifically, as well as the mechanisms by which the resources are made available to municipality and state-level education systems. El Salvador, Honduras, and Nicaragua devolved their authority to communities, thus granting professional autonomy to schools and teachers in the belief that the increased accountability would lead to higher teaching quality and student outcomes.

Policy options to improve teaching quality can be grouped into three main clusters: (a) policies to improve teacher preparation and professional development, (b) policies that affect who becomes a teacher and how long he or she remains in the field, and (c) policies that affect the work that teachers do in the classroom. This volume focuses entirely on the second and third options, both of which can be understood as policies that create incentives to positively affect teachers and their work.

Teacher training and professional development have received attention in the past from educators, policymakers, researchers, and the international donor community.[1] In contrast, the literature on policies that generate teacher incentives in Latin America is not very extensive. Although previous studies have addressed questions related to teaching quality and incentives in Latin America,[2] ours is the first study that we are aware of in which researchers sought to learn about the effect of various policy *reforms* affecting teachers on teaching quality and student achievement in multiple Latin American countries.

Because teacher incentive reforms are frequently politically contested and are difficult to implement, many countries have shied away from changing their prevailing structures of teacher incentives. The selection

---

1. For a review of the literature and assessment of current teacher preparation systems in Latin America, see Villegas-Reimers (1998); for a review of recent trends and innovations in teacher preparation programs in the region, see Navarro and Verdisco (2000).

2. See, for example, Navarro (2002) for various case studies that describe many aspects of teacher contracts and teacher characteristics in several Latin American countries.

of case studies in our volume was largely determined by the presence of a reform affecting the teaching profession. Our methodological approach entails using existing data and econometric techniques to shed light on the effect of such reforms on teaching quality and incentives. Our analyses have been limited by the quality of the data available, and we have used alternative econometric and statistical techniques in an attempt to overcome some of the shortcomings of existing data.

Why and How Do Incentives Matter?

A substantial amount of the literature on incentives in firms has emphasized that the interests of workers (teachers) and their employers (principals, education authorities, or school boards) are often not aligned. For example, although school administrators and education authorities may be interested in attracting more students to their schools, teachers may want to keep some difficult-to-teach students out of their classrooms. Compensation contracts may be designed to include incentives that will lead workers (teachers) to operate in the interest of the firms (schools).[3] In the example above, school administrators could devise incentives (such as extra pay or promotion possibilities) so that teachers will keep all students in their classrooms.

Evidence suggests that changes in teacher incentive structures can affect who chooses to enter and remain in the teaching profession, as well as those teachers' daily work in the classroom. For example, in the United States, where there is growing concern about the declining quality of teachers, recent research shows that the increase in labor market opportunities for women led to a decrease in the pool of qualified applicants for teaching positions.[4] At the same time, research suggests that teacher salary scales in the United States are so compressed that the best teachers are likely to leave the profession for higher-salaried jobs in other occupations.[5]

In less industrial countries, recent research indicates that teachers respond to incentives. For example, an evaluation of a randomized teacher incentives program in Kenya found that teachers increased their effort to raise student test scores by offering more test-preparation sessions (Glewwe, Ilias, and Kremer 2003). In this program, a financial bonus was

---

3. For a review of the literature about providing incentives in firms, see Prendergast (1999).

4. Corcoran, Evans, and Schwab (2004) and Hoxby and Leigh (2004) present evidence that the quality of teachers in the United States has declined over time because of changing labor market opportunities.

5. Hoxby and Leigh (2004) present evidence that the decline in teacher quality in the United States is a result not only of increased opportunities for women outside of teaching, but also of the highly compressed structure that deals with teaching wages.

offered to teachers whose students achieved higher scores on a standardized examination. Although student test scores of teachers who were candidates for the bonus did increase in the year it was applied, the learning
gains disappeared once the application of the financial bonus ended and
teachers had no longer a chance of earning additional pay. More promising,
a recent evaluation of a performance-based pay bonus for teachers in Israel
concluded that the incentive led to increases in student achievement, primarily through changes in teaching methods, after-school teaching, and
teachers' increased responsiveness to students' needs (Lavy 2004).

Because teachers respond to incentives, education policymakers can
improve the quality of teaching and learning by designing effective incentives that will attract, retain, and motivate highly qualified teachers. But
how teacher incentives are designed—and implemented—also matters.
In various cases, teachers have been found to respond adversely to incentives by, for example, reducing collaboration among teachers themselves,
excluding low-performing students from classes, cheating on or manipu-
lating the indicator on which rewards are based, decreasing the academic
rigor of classes, or "teaching to the test" to the detriment of other subjects
and skills (see Cullen and Reback 2002; Figlio and Getzler 2002; Figlio
and Winicki 2002; Jacob and Levitt 2003; Murnane and Cohen 1986).

Incentives as a Broad and Complex Concept[6]

Many people think of teacher incentives exclusively as salary differentials and other monetary benefits. Indeed, differences in pay can act as an
incentive to attract and retain qualified teachers or, conversely, can discourage qualified applicants and talented practitioners who are already
in the profession. But many other kinds of incentives exist, both monetary and nonmonetary, including—among others—adequate school infrastructure and educational materials, the internal motivation to improve
children's lives, the opportunity to grow professionally, pensions and
other nonsalary benefits, and job stability. Figure 1.1 displays many types
of incentives that may exist for attracting highly qualified teachers and
for motivating them to be effective in their jobs.

Teacher Effectiveness and Student Performance

Who is a good teacher? What makes a good teacher? Everyone who has
been through school can remember a great teacher. People usually provide
a variety of reasons for what makes that teacher great—from being "loving

---

6. We are grateful to Jeff Puryear, whose comments at the conference titled, "Learning to
Teach in the Knowledge Society," which was held in Seville, Spain, in June 2004, greatly
informed this section.

Figure 1.1 Many Types of Teacher Incentives Exist

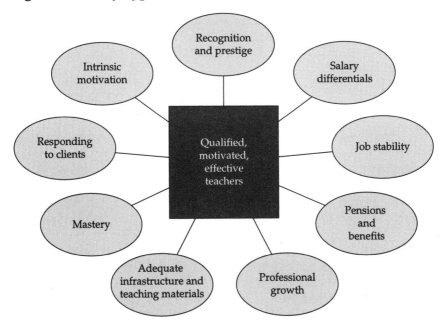

and caring," "knowledgeable," or a "good communicator," to being "tough" and "pushing me to work hard and expand my horizons." These complex behaviors are not easily measured. In fact, measuring the factors that effective teachers have—or that ineffective teachers do not have—has proved imprecise, technically difficult, and expensive. This measurement problem creates one of the challenges for designing effective teacher incentives.

Ultimately, what society should care about is whether teachers are generating learning within their students. In other words, although having the teachers show affection for the student and command knowledge of the subject they are teaching are behaviors that are likely to stimulate students to learn, not all teachers who are affectionate or knowledgeable are also effective teachers.

In our study, we use a specific definition of teachers' effectiveness. We consider a teacher to be effective when there is evidence that his or her students have acquired adequate knowledge and skills. To measure the effectiveness of teachers, we rely primarily on available indicators of student learning from national assessments of subject-matter (usually language and mathematics) knowledge. Because student learning takes multiple forms and is difficult to measure, and because tests are an imperfect measure of learning, we recognize that test scores are an incomplete and imperfect proxy for teaching quality.[7] However, given the absence of a better understanding of what factors make a good teacher and given the paucity of systematic and comparable data on student learning, national assessments are our best option for shedding light on the quality of teaching and learning.

A Wide System Affecting Teaching and Learning

Although teacher incentive reforms are a promising option to improve teaching quality and student learning, they do not operate alone but instead are part of a broader system that affects teaching and learning. As a result, reforms to teacher incentives may be more effective in raising student learning when other parts of the broader system affecting teaching and learning are in place. For example, tying salary increases to teacher performance may be effective only in raising student achievement when teachers have clarity about what knowledge and pedagogical skills are needed to improve student learning. Similarly, the benefits of increased teacher accountability reforms are possible only when teachers know to whom they are accountable and when those individuals, in turn, have authority to reward and sanction teachers on the basis of their performance. In short, effective incentives are a necessary, but not sufficient, condition for ensuring teaching quality and student achievement.

Education Reforms, Teaching Quality, and Student Learning

Just as there are many types of teacher incentives, various education reforms may affect teachers even if not originally planned as teacher incentive reforms. Policy changes in the level or structure of compensation, as well as changes in teachers' professional autonomy, can significantly affect the teaching profession. The chapters included in our volume approach the question of the effect of teacher incentive reforms on teaching quality and on student learning from various angles. Each chapter explores one or several aspects of a teacher incentive reform in Latin America and attempts to identify its effect on teaching quality and student learning.

Conducting impact evaluations of education programs is challenging given the impossibility of knowing what would have happened to those affected by the program if the program were not present. For example, to understand the effect of school attendance on labor market outcomes, we

---

7. Kane and Staiger (2001) and Koretz (2002) provide evidence of the multiple problems in assessing the knowledge of students.

would need to compare two identical individuals at the same time in the same place, one who attended school and one who did not. Because this comparison is impossible in practice, a challenge for the impact evaluation is to construct groups of individuals who can be convincingly compared. In this sense, for evaluation purposes, all participants of education programs should ideally be selected in a randomized fashion. Although, in many cases, randomized assignment to participate in education programs is not possible, creative ways of analyzing good data about education programs can yield results that are of comparable quality to those from randomized trials. This approach is the one we took in the chapters of our volume.

Review of Chapters

The second chapter in our book, by Ilana Umansky, reviews the earlier literature about teacher incentives. Incentives, in general, and teacher incentives, in particular, have been the subject of much academic and policy debate. It is clear that "Incentives do matter, for better or for worse" (Prendergast 1999). That is, incentives have direct implications on teachers' characteristics and behavior. However, it is much less clear how incentives work and under what conditions teachers create the types of changes desired. Similarly, it is intuitively clear that teaching quality affects student learning, but it is less evident what qualities make a good teacher or what precise behavior composes good teaching. Chapter 2 provides a review of the literature on incentives as they relate to teaching quality, characteristics, and behavior, as well as their relationships to student development and learning. It also presents the various arguments and findings on many of the types of incentives that teachers frequently face.

Because differences in salary between teachers and nonteachers can have a great effect on who chooses to enter the teaching profession, the third chapter, by Werner Hernani-Limarino, addresses the question of how well teachers are paid relative to comparable workers in other occupations. As in other parts of the world, people in Latin America have a widely held belief that teachers are not well paid and that, in general, teachers earn less than they would in other professions. Yet, previous research has found that, in many cases, teachers in Latin America may be paid more than workers with similar characteristics in many countries (see Liang 1999, for example). In his study of teachers' salaries in 17 Latin American countries, Hernani-Limarino, however, demonstrates that relative salaries for teachers vary widely across Latin America and depend largely on to whom teachers are compared and what methods are used to make those comparisons.

He finds that teachers in Argentina, Chile, Colombia, El Salvador, Honduras, Panama, Paraguay, and Peru are, on average, paid more than comparable workers in other occupations. Teachers in Nicaragua earn lower average wages than do workers in other fields. But in Bolivia, Brazil, Costa Rica, the Dominican Republic, Ecuador, Mexico, Uruguay, and Venezuela whether teachers are well paid varies depending on the comparison group used in the analysis. Hernani-Limarino develops several comparison groups but finds that when compared to workers in office, technical, and professional occupations—arguably the most appropriate comparison group because the workers tend to have similar educational levels as teachers—teachers do not have a pay advantage in any of those eight countries.

Chapter 3 also compares the structures of teachers' salaries with those of workers' salaries in other occupations. In the 17 Latin American countries examined, the teachers' wage structure is flatter and begins at a higher level than the salary structure of nonteachers. Although teachers throughout the region receive higher base salaries than do comparable workers in other occupations, teachers receive lower returns than do nonteachers when we compare their improved characteristics, such as higher education or training plus additional years of experience. In practice, then, teachers earn comparatively higher salaries than they would outside of teaching when they are at the lower end of the wage distribution (that is, have less education and experience), while teachers with more education and experience earn the same or less than they would in other professions.[8]

Chapter 4, by Alejandra Mizala and Pilar Romaguera, explores the teachers' salary structure in Chile and its related incentives. In Chile, changes in wage levels were accompanied by changes in the overall number, as well as the quality, of applicants to the teaching profession. Teachers experienced a 32 percent decline in real salaries in the 1980s as a result of government budget reductions. Over this same period, the number of students entering education programs dropped 43 percent. In the 1990s, both trends reversed. Between 1990 and 2002, real teachers' salaries increased 156 percent, and as a result teachers in Chile are now paid higher salaries than comparable workers in other occupations. At the same time, there was a 39 percent increase in the number of education students, and the average score for applicants to education programs increased 16 percent. This improvement in applicant quality did not take place across all degree programs, such as engineering, where the average entrance exam score remained more or less constant. Those patterns suggest that changes in salary level can affect individuals' choices to become a teacher.

---

8. Note that teachers' pensions and other nonsalary benefits are not dealt with in this discussion. Pensions are, however, widely believed to be quite high when compared with nonteachers' pensions, to be earned at an earlier age, and to be fiscally secure. High, early, and secure pensions may be a strong incentive for teachers to enter and remain in the field.

SNED

In 1996, Chile introduced the SNED (Sistema Nacional de Evaluación de Desempeño de los Establecimientos Educacionales, or National System of School Performance Assessment), which offers monetary bonuses to schools that show excellent performance in terms of student achievement. Teachers in winning schools receive what has typically amounted to one-half of one month's salary, or between 5 and 7 percent of a teacher's annual salary. Although impact evaluations of the SNED are difficult owing to the absence of a natural control group, this chapter provides some preliminary evidence that the incentive has had a cumulative positive effect on student performance for those schools facing relatively good chances of winning the award.

In Chapter 5, Nora Gordon and Emiliana Vegas evaluate the effect that a large reform of educational finance has had in Brazil on educational spending, teaching quality, and student outcomes. Brazil is a vast country characterized by large inequalities in educational spending and educational outcomes. Those inequalities exist between states and also between the different municipalities within each state. The Fundo de Manutenção e Desenvolvimento do Ensino Fundamental e de Valorização do Magistério (Fund for the Maintenance and Development of Basic Education and Teacher Appreciation, or FUNDEF) reform was implemented in 1998. FUNDEF is a national reform for finance equalization on behalf of primary education in which each state and municipal government in Brazil pools a percentage of educational funds at the state level. Those funds are then redistributed equally, on a per student basis, to each governmental education authority (state and municipal). Addressing a long-standing inequality in educational finance, this reform tends to increase per pupil educational funding in municipality-run schools and to decrease per pupil educational funding in state-run schools, particularly in the poor northern and northeastern regions of Brazil.

Among FUNDEF funds, 60 percent is earmarked specifically for teachers. Those funds are used to hire new teachers, to train underqualified teachers, and to increase teachers' salaries. Some evidence shows that the governments that experienced increases in mandated per pupil spending actually hired new teachers and decreased class sizes. Gordon and Vegas also document a sharp rise in teacher educational levels although they find that this rise was caused less by the FUNDEF reform and more by a legislative mandate enacted around the same time.

The FUNDEF reform and the changes it created in educational inputs have, in turn, generated changes in outcomes. More students are now attending school in the poorer states of Brazil as a result of the reform, specifically in the higher grades of basic education. Additionally, having teachers who have reached higher educational levels is related to lower levels of overaged students in the classroom. This finding suggests that having qualified teachers helps students stay on track in school, repeat less, drop out less, and perhaps also enter first grade on time. Furthermore, low-performing students suffer most from inequalities in per pupil spending. This result may indicate that finance equalization reforms that decrease the spending inequalities may also decrease the performance gap between high-performing and low-performing students and between white and nonwhite students. While the exact mechanism is not clear, giving teachers more competitive salaries, hiring more teachers, and ensuring that teachers have adequate educational levels appears to have particularly benefited low-performing and disadvantaged students in Brazil.

In Chapter 6, Miguel Urquiola and Emiliana Vegas analyze the teachers' salary system in Bolivia and, in particular, the effect of a teacher bonus to work in rural areas. As in many other countries, the rural teacher pay differential in Bolivia is intended to compensate teachers for the perceived hardship of living and working in a rural area. As a result of recent urbanization and demographic growth within cities, some designated rural schools have been incorporated into urban areas. In those cases, urban and rural teachers work in neighboring schools, sometimes even the same school, with indistinguishable groups of students. This chance occurrence creates a situation in which teaching quality can be compared between teachers who are classified as rural (and thus earn higher wages) and those classified as urban.

Urquiola and Vegas found no meaningful differences between the test scores and other educational outcomes of students of urban-classified and rural-classified teachers with the same background characteristics. This result suggests that the rural pay differential is not successful at attracting and retaining teachers who are more effective than average urban teachers. In further support of this finding, rural teachers nationally are twice as likely as urban teachers to lack full teacher preparation, and they are also more likely to abandon the profession.

In Chapter 7, Patrick J. McEwan and Lucrecia Santibáñez evaluate the effect on teaching quality and student outcomes of a teacher pay reform in Mexico. Mexico's Carrera Magisterial Program, which began in 1993, created a means by which teachers can move up consecutive levels of higher pay on the basis of year-long assessments of a series of factors, including their professional development and education, their years of experience, a peer review, and, most important, their students' performance. The purpose of the reform was to establish incentives for teachers to improve their qualifications and effectiveness in the classroom and to create a means by which teachers could receive promotions without being promoted out of the classroom and into administrative positions. The size of the bonuses offered by Carrera Magisterial are quite substantial, amounting to between 24.5 percent of teachers' base wage for the first promotion and 197 percent of base wage for the highest (fifth) promotion.

Despite the program's promise, McEwan and Santibáñez find no apparent effect of the Carrera Magisterial program on student performance as measured by a standardized exam. Teachers who face greater incentives because of the reform do not tend to have students with higher achievement. Test scores do not capture the spectrum of ways in which teaching and learning can improve. The fact (a) that Carrera Magisterial measures test scores specifically—thereby creating a strong incentive for teachers to focus on improving scores—and (b) that, nonetheless, test scores have not gone up under the reform suggests that it is unlikely that any major unmeasured improvements in Mexico's classrooms resulted from the reform.

The next three chapters explore the effect of school-based management reforms on teaching quality and student outcomes in three Central American countries: El Salvador, Honduras, and Nicaragua. Many people hypothesize that school-based management generates several incentives and conditions that can improve teaching quality and teaching. Those improvements include greater accountability to local stakeholders, direct communication between communities and schools concerning their needs and interests, and more flexible and meritocratic pay and advancement structures associated with closer-to-the-source evaluation and weaker teachers' unions.

Chapter 8, by Yasuyuki Sawada and Andrew Ragatz, analyzes the effect on teaching quality and student learning of the EDUCO program (Programa de Educación con Participación de la Comunidad, or Education with Community Participation Program) in El Salvador. They find that this school-based management reform has had important effects on management practices, teacher behavior, and student outcomes although not all of those changes are precisely the ones that were expected or desired. In terms of management practices, Sawada and Ragatz find that although a few important powers have been relocated to the school level, most notably the ability to hire and fire teachers, many other decisions appear to continue to be made primarily by central authorities. Next, they find that most of the local decisionmaking power has been given to parents as opposed to principals. They also find important behavioral differences between EDUCO and control schools, such as fewer school closings, less teacher absenteeism, more meetings between teachers and parents, and longer work hours for teachers. The changes, in turn, are related to higher achievement in Spanish in EDUCO schools.

Chapter 9, by Emanuela di Gropello and Jeffery H. Marshall, finds some effects of the Honduran PROHECO (Proyecto Hondureño de Educación Comunitaria, or Honduran Community Education Project) that are similar to those found in El Salvador. Like EDUCO, PROHECO is a school-based management reform for rural primary schools. As in reports from El Salvador, di Gropello and Marshall present evidence that teacher behavior and characteristics differ between PROHECO and control group schools. Specifically, they find that PROHECO teachers are less frequently absent because of union participation, although they are more frequently absent as a result of teacher professional development. They also find evidence that PROHECO teachers are paid less than are comparison teachers and have fewer years of experience. Similar to El Salvador, evidence shows that PROHECO teachers teach more hours in an average week than do comparison teachers and that they have smaller classes and assign more homework. The examples lend credence to the idea of greater efficiency and teacher effort in decentralized schools. Yet, school-based management in Honduras has not had much effect in some important areas where people expected it would. Namely, little evidence was found that teachers in community-managed schools differ from their colleagues in conventional schools in terms of their classroom processes, planning, or motivation.

Nevertheless, PROHECO students score higher on math, science, and Spanish exams than do students in similar non-PROHECO schools. The benefits of PROHECO are, in part, explained by the qualities and characteristics found to be different in PROHECO schools. Specifically, the more hours per week that a teacher works, the higher the student achievement in all three subjects. The frequency of homework is associated with higher achievement in Spanish and math. Finally, smaller classes and fewer school closings are related to higher student achievement in science.

Chapter 10 covers Caroline E. Parker's findings from her analysis of Nicaragua's Autonomía Escolar (School Autonomy) program. Her findings from the Nicaragua reform differ considerably from those of the other two Central American reforms. To a large degree, those differences may result from the major differences in reform design and objectives. Unlike PROHECO and EDUCO, Autonomía Escolar was aimed initially at urban secondary schools and, in particular, at schools with higher than average resources. In contrast to their peers in neighboring El Salvador and Honduras, parent associations and teachers in Nicaragua's autonomous schools report little decisionmaking power. A decade after the reform was first implemented, very few differences existed between autonomous and non-autonomous schools that were not present in those same schools before the reform. Student background continues to be one of the most important factors explaining differences in student achievement in Nicaragua, and there is no systematic effect of the reform on student learning. Although third-grade students in autonomous schools have higher average test scores in mathematics than students in traditional schools, by the sixth grade, students at autonomous schools score lower than students in traditional schools in both Spanish and mathematics tests. Furthermore, very little evidence exists in Nicaragua that the observed differences between autonomous and traditional schools are responsible for the differences in test scores.

In the final chapter of our volume, Luis Crouch explores how the political economy of reforms to teacher incentives affect their design, their implementation, and, ultimately, their effect. He focuses on the role of teachers'
unions as critical stakeholders in the education sector in Latin America.
Teachers' unions typically oppose teacher incentive mechanisms, particularly those that generate competition among teachers and those that link
pay to testing outcomes or other proxies for student learning or teaching
quality. When powerful teachers' unions oppose teacher incentive mechanisms, the unions can thwart effective reform implementation. Yet, in several cases, including Chile's SNED and Mexico's Carrera Magisterial
(discussed earlier), powerful unions not only have consented to teacher
incentive programs but also have collaborated in the design of the programs. Improving teaching and learning through effective incentives will
require this type of collaboration.

Improving Teaching Quality and Student Learning through Incentives

Many types of education reforms affect teaching quality and student learning. When we think about the structure of teacher incentives, we often
think of the level and structure of teacher compensation. Our findings support the intuitive notion that teaching quality is sensitive to the level and
structure of compensation. For example, Chile's more-than-doubling of
average teacher salaries in the past decade is associated with an increase
in the quality of entering students to teacher education programs. Similarly,
the increased and more equitable distribution of resources resulting from
FUNDEF in Brazil led to improvements in student outcomes. While the
Chilean school-based teacher bonus for student performance did not initially have a great impact on student performance, it is associated with
better student performance in its most recent available application. Moreover, average student achievement is increasing in schools that have had a
chance of winning the SNED bonus in each of the three applications, suggesting that the program is having some of the expected results.

Changes in other aspects of teacher contracts can also have a great
impact on teaching quality and student learning. Education reforms, even
those not specifically designed to affect teachers, can influence—and
sometimes have even greater effects than changes in compensation—the
characteristics of those who choose to enter and remain in teaching
and, importantly, their work in classrooms. For example, EDUCO and
PROHECO, two school-based management reforms that devolved decisionmaking authority to the school, were found to have had an important
impact on teacher performance and student learning. In particular, the
authority on the part of EDUCO school councils to hire and fire teachers

was found to be an important factor in EDUCO students' better outcomes as compared to traditional schools serving similar populations in El Salvador.

A key lesson from previous research and from the evaluations in this study is that teachers do not always respond to incentives in predictable ways. Although teachers generally respond to incentives, they do not always do so in ways we would expect or hope. Sometimes, programs that are specifically designed to reward teachers who adopt specific behaviors or achieve higher results fail to generate a behavioral response from teachers. Bolivia's bonus for teaching in rural areas is not resulting in higher quality rural teachers. Carrera Magisterial, Mexico's innovative teacher career system specifically designed to reward teachers with better performance, was found not to result in changes in teacher performance, and thus has not led to improved student outcomes. These cases highlight the importance of design and implementation of teacher incentive reforms.

The cases discussed in this volume point to three design flaws in teacher incentive reforms: (1) only a small proportion of teachers face greater incentives to improve learning in their classrooms (i.e., most teachers would either receive the award regardless of performance or have no chance at all of receiving it); (2) the size of the award may be so small that teachers feel it is not worth the extra effort; and (3) the award may not be sufficiently linked to teacher performance. First, even though Mexico's Carrera Magisterial and Chile's SNED are both nationwide programs involving most of the country's teachers, in each program application, a minority of teachers face any real likelihood of receiving a promotion in the case of Carrera Magisterial, or a bonus in the case of SNED. In other words, for the majority of teachers in a given application, there are no real incentives to improve performance. These findings point to the importance of crafting teacher incentives that affect a majority of, if not all, teachers. Only when the majority of teachers are susceptible to receiving the benefits of hard work and improved outcomes, will the resources invested in both designing and implementing the reform as well as in the incentive mechanism itself have the potential to result in improved outcomes in a majority of students.

It is important to distinguish between being susceptible to receive a reward and actually earning it. Although all teachers should be susceptible to earning the incentive reward, only a subset of them should receive it. For an incentive scheme to work effectively, it must recognize only the share of teachers who truly exhibit the desired performance and results. Weak links between desired performance and, for example, extra pay, tend to result in misallocation of rewards.

Second, the size of the reward matters for its impact on improving teaching quality and student learning. Often, a teacher's base salary accounts for a large share of her total compensation, and incentives for specific behaviors (e.g. working in rural schools, serving children with special needs) account for only a small proportion of total pay. In these cases, the compensation may be strongly linked to the desired outcome or behavior, but the reward size may be too small for teachers to be induced to adopt the desired behavior.

Third, incentives are most effective when there is a tight link between teacher performance and rewards. Faced with pressures from teacher unions to increase salaries for all teachers and with countervailing pressures to improve the efficiency of education spending and improve incentives for teacher performance, education policymakers run the risk of doling out numerous bonuses for different behaviors and characteristics (e.g. working in rural areas, attendance, time for preparing classes, etc.). A typical Peruvian teacher, for example, receives compensation for about 15 different "behaviors," though these are not monitored and awarded to all teachers. In Peru, as in many other countries, each bonus is small in size and accrues to most or all teachers, and thus together amount to increases in pay without any strong association with teacher performance or clear messages to teachers regarding specific behaviors.

Finally, the case studies in this volume suggest that school-based management reforms strengthen the accountability relationship between teachers (and schools) and communities. The Central American experiences show that these reforms can result in, among others, less teacher absenteeism, more teacher work hours, more homework assigned, and closer parent-teacher relationships. These are promising changes, especially in contexts of low educational quality where teacher absenteeism is high and schools are often not functioning at all.

An Agenda for Further Research on Teacher Incentives

Together, the studies contained in this volume affirm the centrality of teacher incentives in any education system. They challenge us to think carefully and critically about both the explicit and implicit incentives that affect who teaches and how they teach. It is our hope that the studies also provide insights into designing and implementing successful education reforms that will boost learning in a region that increasingly recognizes educational quality as a fundamental pillar of national development and competitiveness. Although we hope to have shed light on the important question of how to design effective teacher incentive reforms to improve teaching and learning, there are still many areas in need of further investigation.

First, few countries have experimented with performance-based schemes for teachers in the region, and thus we could only learn from the (very different) Chilean and Mexican experiences in this area. As more countries feel the pressure to improve educational quality under fiscal constraints, linking teacher incentives to student performance is likely to become more popular. More and more varied performance-based teacher incentive reforms will give us opportunities to better understand their impact on teaching quality and student outcomes.

Second, although education reforms are common in the region, it is rare to find cases where findings from sound evaluations inform reform design. Our hope is that this book will contribute to fill this void.

Third, important issues affecting who enters and remains in teaching were not addressed in this book, such as non-salary benefits including pensions, insurance, etc. These non-salary teacher expenditures are substantial in the majority of Latin American countries, and their impact on teaching quality is likely to be non-trivial. Future research should address their role in attracting, developing, and retaining effective teachers.

Finally, we hope that education policymakers incorporate plans to conduct impact evaluations in the process of reform design, so that it becomes common practice to learn from one's (and others') experiences. As mentioned in the Introduction, conducting impact evaluations of education programs is challenging given the impossibility of knowing what would have happened to those affected by the program in its absence. This evaluation problem plagues all social programs, and is particularly problematic when assignment of the program to participants is based on factors that could also affect the outcome of the program. Separating the effects on outcomes of variables that impact who (or what school) participates in a specific program from the program itself is known as the selection problem in the impact evaluation literature. For example, the team conducting the evaluation of Mexico's Carrera Magisterial program had to address the issue that program participation by teachers is voluntary, and thus teachers who choose to participate in Carrera Magisterial may be different from teachers who choose not to participate in ways that also affect their students' learning. These issues need to be taken into consideration when designing teacher incentive reforms and their impact evaluations.

References

Corcoran, S., W. Evans, and R. Schwab. 2004. "Changing Labor-Market Opportunities for Women and the Quality of Teachers, 1995–2000." *American Economic Review* 94(2): 230–35.

Cullen, J. B., and R. Reback. 2002. "Tinkering toward Accolades: School Gaming under a Performance Accountability System." University of Michigan, Ann Arbor. Processed.

Figlio, D. N., and L. Getzler. 2002. "Accountability, Ability, and Disability: Gaming the System." NBER Working Paper 9307. National Bureau of Economic Research, Cambridge, Mass.

Figlio, D. N., and J. Winicki. 2002. "Food for Thought: The Effects of School Accountability Plans on School Nutrition." NBER Working Paper 9319. National Bureau of Economic Research, Cambridge, Mass.

Glewwe, P., N. Ilias, and M. Kremer. 2003. "Teacher Incentives." NBER Working Paper 9671. National Bureau of Economic Research, Cambridge, Mass.

Hanushek, E. A., J. F. Kain, D. M. O'Brien, and S. G. Rivkin. 2005. "The Market for Teacher Quality." Stanford University, Stanford, Calif. Processed.

Hoxby, C. M., and A. Leigh. 2004. "Pulled Away or Pushed Out? Explaining the Decline of Teacher Aptitude in the United States." *American Economic Review* 94(2): 236–46.

Jacob, B. A., and S. D. Levitt. 2003. "Rotten Apples: An Investigation of the Prevalence and Predictors of Teacher Cheating." *Quarterly Journal of Economics* 118(3): 843–77.

Kane, T. J., and D. O. Staiger. 2001. "Improving School Accountability Measures." NBER Working Paper 8156. National Bureau of Economic Research, Cambridge, Mass.

Koretz, D. 2002. "Limitations in the Use of Achievement Tests as Measures of Educators' Productivity." *Journal of Human Resources* 37: 752–77.

Lavy, V. 2004. "Performance Pay and Teachers' Effort, Productivity, and Grading Ethics." NBER Working Paper 10622. National Bureau of Economic Research, Cambridge, Mass.

Liang, X. 1999. "Teacher Pay in 12 Latin American Countries: How Does Teacher Pay Compare to Other Professions, What Determines Teacher Pay, and Who Are the Teachers?" Latin America and the Caribbean Region Human Development Department Paper 49. World Bank, Washington, D.C.

Murnane, R. J., and D. K. Cohen. 1986. "Merit Pay and the Evaluation Problem: Why Most Merit Pay Plans Fail and a Few Survive." *Harvard Education Review* 56: 1–17.

Navarro, J. C., ed. 2002 *¿Quiénes son los maestros? Carreras e incentivos en América Latina.* Washington, D.C.: Inter-American Development Bank.

Navarro, J. C., and A. Verdisco. 2000. "Teacher Training in Latin America: Innovations and Trends." Sustainable Development Department, Technical Papers Series. Inter-American Development Bank, Washington, D.C.

Park, A., and E. Hannum. 2001. "Do Teachers Affect Learning in Developing Countries? Evidence from Matched Student–Teacher Data from China." Paper prepared for the conference on Rethinking Social Science Research on the Developing World in the 21st Century, Park City, Utah, June 7–11.

Prendergast, C. 1999. "The Provision of Incentives in Firms." *Journal of Economic Literature* 37 (March): 7–63.

Rivkin, S., E. Hanushek, and J. Kain. 1998. "Teachers, Schools, and Academic Achievement." NBER Working Paper 6691. National Bureau of Economic Research, Cambridge, Mass.

Rockoff, J. 2004. "The Impact of Individual Teachers on Student Achievement: Evidence from Panel Data." *American Economic Review* 94(2): 247–57.

Sanders, W., and J. Rivers. 1996. *Cumulative and Residual Effects of Teachers on Future Student Academic Achievement.* Knoxville: University of Tennessee Value-Added Research and Assessment Center. Available at http://www.heartland.org/pdf/21803.

Villegas-Reimers, E. 1998. "The Preparation of Teachers in Latin America: Challenges and Trends." Latin America and the Caribbean Region Human Development Department Paper 15. World Bank, Washington, D.C.

Wright, S. P., S. Horn, and W. Sanders. 1997. "Teacher and Classroom Context Effects of Student Achievement: Implications for Teacher Evaluation." *Journal of Personnel Evaluation in Education* 11: 57–67.

2
A Literature Review of Teacher Quality and Incentives
Theory and Evidence

Ilana Umansky
The World Bank

Incentives in general and teacher incentives in particular have been the subject of much academic and policy debate. It is clear that "Incentives do matter, for better or for worse" (Prendergast 1999). That is, incentives have direct implications on teachers' characteristics and behavior. However, it is much less clear how incentives work and under what conditions they create the types of changes desired (see, for example, Clotfelter and others 2004; Dee and Keys 2004; Eberts, Hollenbeck, and Stone 2002; Hanushek 2003; Jacob and Levitt 2002; Koretz 2002; Lavy 2002, 2003, 2004; Prendergast 1999). Similarly, it is intuitively clear that teaching quality affects student learning, but it is less clear what qualities make a good teacher or what precise behavior composes good teaching (see, for instance, Darling-Hammond 2000; Goldhaber and Anthony 2004; Goldhaber, Brewer, and Anderson 1999; Jacob and Levitt 2002; Rice 2003; Rivkin, Hanushek, and Kain 1998; Wright, Horn, and Sanders 1997). This chapter provides a review of the literature on incentives as they relate to teacher quality, characteristics, and behavior, as well as to student development and learning. The chapter presents the various arguments and findings on many of the types of incentives that teachers frequently face.

The chapter begins with a review of the Principal-Agent Theory, which is the economic rationale behind the provision of incentives by employers to employees. After presenting the theory, the chapter examines some research on the determinants of teacher quality. Next, it reviews literature on the efficacy of current educational spending. In particular, it looks at the incentives embedded in teacher pay level, relative pay, and salary

I wish to thank Emiliana Vegas for her ongoing suggestions, comments, and guidance on this paper. I also am grateful to Luis Crouch for his help and input for the section on teacher unions. Any remaining errors are entirely my own.

structure. Then, we examine the literature dealing with alternative compensation schemes, namely merit pay conditioned on either performance
or some other skill or behavior. Here the chapter examines how incentives
and disincentives affect teachers, their decisions to enter and remain in
the field, their characteristics, and their behavior. The chapter then looks
at teacher incentives generated by larger school management reforms,
specifically decentralization and demand-side financing. Last, before
concluding, it discusses the role and effect of the larger political economy, focusing on the role of teacher unions, on teacher quality, and on
incentive reforms.

Wherever possible this literature review draws on research conducted
in developing countries in general and Latin America in particular. Unfortunately, the preponderance of scholarship on teacher quality and incentives has focused on industrial countries. Some sections, therefore, report
findings coming largely from industrial nations, the United States in particular. We hope that the case studies included in this study will contribute
to the acute need for more research on this subject in less affluent nations.

Principal–Agent Theory: Description and Critiques

Principal–Agent Theory has been a dominant economic theory concerning
how principals, such as employers, design compensation structures to get
agents, such as employees, to work in the principals' interest (Ross 1973).
In education, the principal–agent relationship can take multiple forms in
the sense that teachers, as agents, can be considered as working on behalf
of multiple principals, including parents, school principals, or education
officials. Principal–Agent Theory rests on the assumption that the interests of principals and agents are frequently not aligned. Instead, employers want high employee productivity and efficiency while employees
want high compensation for little effort. Principal–Agent Theory states
that employers design schemes to motivate their employees to behave in
certain ways that employers believe will result in high productivity and
efficiency. Those schemes are often, but not exclusively, monetary incentives that reward or sanction specific behaviors (Prendergast 1999).

To what extent an agent will alter his or her behavior, theorists claim,
depends, in part, on the agent's degree of risk aversion, his or her assessment of the risk involved in the behavior, and the desirability of the
reward or aversion to the sanction (Baker 2002; Prendergast 1999). A
teacher offered a potentially large reward is more likely to put substantial
effort into changing his or her behavior than a teacher offered a small
reward. Likewise, a teacher offered a reward based on behavior that
requires little effort or risk is more likely to change his or her behavior than
a teacher offered a reward for behavior that requires substantial effort or
involves significant risk.

The success of incentive schemes depends on the employers' ability to accurately determine and evaluate the desired behavior of employees. Making this determination is one of the foremost challenges in designing incentive schemes. Principals use a variety of measures of agent output, effort, or input depending on the type of work, facility of measurement, and outcome goals. Measures can be quantitative, such as student test scores, or qualitative, such as in-class teacher evaluations (Murnane and Cohen 1986). The designs of teacher incentive schemes vary enormously.

- *Individual merit pay* rewards individual teachers with pay bonuses that are based on particular outcomes or behaviors, such as improvements in student test scores.
- *Group performance-based incentives* reward or sanction a group of teachers, frequently a school, on the basis of some measure(s) of performance.
- *Competitive incentives,* such as tournaments, put teachers or schools in competition with one another for a limited prize, such as job promotion or cash.
- *Automatic incentives* are incentives such as seniority pay or job security that teachers receive irrespective of performance measurements. Many incentives are not exclusively monetary; they may offer educational and training opportunities, increased decisionmaking authority, or other nonmonetary rewards or sanctions (Prendergast 1999).

As does any influential theory, Principal–Agent Theory has received much attention and critique over the past 30 years. First, some argue that the assumptions that underlie Principal–Agent Theory are faulty, specifically in that they fail to address agents' intrinsic motivation. Advocates of this critique argue that incentives, as they are designed when following Principal–Agent Theory, actually undermine worker productivity (Bénabou and Tirole 2000, 2003; Holmström and Milgrom 1991; Kohn 1993). Bénabou and Tirole (2003) assert that extrinsic incentives can damage agents' perception of their own capacity, as well as damage interest in the desired task or behavior. Kohn (1993) posits that rewards and punishments in the workplace undermine worker interest, discourage risk-taking, ignore the underlying reasons for suboptimal performance, and damage work relationships. In an influential paper, Murnane and Cohen (1986) argue that this critique is particularly applicable to the work of teachers. They assert that individual merit-pay plans harm the important multidimensional and cooperative aspects of teachers' work.

Second, others hypothesize that although the idea behind creating incentives for employees may be a good one, in practice identifying and measuring employees' work is too difficult, complex, or expensive to be able to create the appropriate incentives for the desired behavior. Weaknesses in measurement and evaluation make incentives particularly vulnerable to employee manipulation and 'gaming' (Heckman, Heinrich, and Smith 2002; Holmström and Milgrom 1991; Prendergast 1999). Holmström and Milgrom (1991) write: "Given a highly incomplete set of performance measures and a highly complex set of potential responses from the agent, how can the agent be motivated to act in the social interest?" Most employees have multiple tasks and responsibilities, many of which are difficult or expensive to measure. In many cases incentives that are meant to increase a desired behavior or outcome may result instead in unintended behavioral responses on the part of employees, such as a reallocation of effort, a change in use of resources, or other gaming of the incentive scheme to receive greater compensation.

Findings on manipulations of merit pay and undesired behavior responses by teachers are discussed at length in the section of this chapter on merit pay. They include behaviors such as cheating on exams (Jacob and Levitt 2002), increasing student caloric intake on the day of the exam (Figlio and Winicki 2002), offering out-of-class test preparation tutorials (Glewwe, Ilias, and Kremer 2003), and removing low-achieving students from the classroom (Murnane and Cohen 1986).

Those findings suggest that merely looking at changes in the measured output, such as improvements in student test scores, may not tell the whole story of the effect of incentive reforms. More important, changes in the measured output do not necessarily correlate with changes in the desired outcome. Rather, observed and measured output changes may mask unintended effects, such as damage to assets, reallocation of effort, or manipulation of measurement indicators.

Although some authors have theorized that broadening or changing how and what indicators are measured could overcome this problem, Prendergast (1999) argues that "dysfunctional behavioral responses" may be impossible to overcome. She reviews impact studies of responses to both objective and subjective measurement systems and concludes that objective measurements are often too rigid, making them vulnerable to efforts at gaming. Simultaneously, subjective measurements can damage working relationships and are subject to biases.

Holmström and Milgrom (1991) suggest that in fields where performance of any of the activities of workers is difficult to measure, fixed wages and salaries may themselves be the most optimal and appropriate incentive structure. They point out that the costs to quality teaching—which may be manifested, for example, in a reallocation of effort toward test-taking skills and away from creative and critical thinking skills, in damage to teachers' intrinsic motivation and collaborative efforts, or in increased cheating—may far outweigh any potential benefits, such as increased teacher effort or accountability. They suggest that this countervailing effect may explain why, despite the promise of the Principal–Agent Theory, most occupations do not use performance incentives.

The teaching profession is no exception. Murnane and Cohen (1986) report that although the 1960s and 1970s witnessed a surge of interest in teacher merit-pay reforms in the United States, by the 1980s more than 99 percent of teachers were back to being paid on the basis of uniform salary scales. In recent years, however, concern has revived regarding the implicit incentives in rigid salary structures, seniority pay, and high job security in the teaching profession (see section on Salary Scales). Those concerns have prompted renewed interest in and experimentation with alternative compensation structures such as merit pay and skill- or behavior-based pay (Ballou and Podgursky 1993; Conley, Muncey, and Gould 2002; Kerchner, Koppich, and Weeres 1998; Solomon 2004).

In summary, Principal–Agent Theory has begun to unearth the complex dynamics of how employers affect employees' work. On one hand, incentives clearly do affect agents' behavior. On the other hand, incentives frequently do not succeed in generating the specific behaviors desired by employers.

Teacher Quality and Its Determinants

A large body of literature investigates the role of teachers and the characteristics and behaviors of teachers that are most beneficial to student learning. Studies generally confirm common knowledge that teachers are extremely important in children's success or failure in schools. Yet studies on the determinants of teacher quality have not been able to agree on what specifically makes a teacher successful. The lack of any clear measurable variables that predict teacher quality makes it difficult and problematic to design pay structures and compensation schemes that are based on measurable indicators.

That good teachers are one of the pillars of student success is intuitively obvious but statistically difficult to prove. The easily observable variables logically linked to teacher quality, such as years of experience or educational level, are often not clearly associated with improved educational outcomes. Measuring the effect of individual teachers using techniques such as value-added modeling or matching requires largely unavailable detailed panel data. Several recent studies have used just such data and techniques to test the hypothesis of a teacher quality effect (Park and Hannum 2001; Rivkin, Hanushek, and Kain 1998; Rockoff 2004; Sanders and Rivers 1996; Wright, Horn, and Sanders 1997). All of the studies indicate both that a teacher effect exists and that the effect is potentially quite large.

Those studies take advantage of panel data in China and in New Jersey, Tennessee, and Texas in the United States. Their methods vary somewhat, as do their findings of the size of the teacher effect. Rivkin, Hanushek, and Kain (1998) find that at a minimum teachers account for 7.5 percent of the variation in student achievement. Sanders and Rivers (1996) conclude that teacher sequencing from grades 3–5 accounts for differences in student achievement of 50 percentile points. Wright, Horn, and Sanders (1997) find that teacher effects are the single largest factor affecting student academic gain in 20 of 30 analyses in Tennessee.

Sanders and Rivers (1996) study two metropolitan districts in Tennessee and find that teacher effects are not only large but also cumulative— observable 2 years later, regardless of the effectiveness of later teachers. They also find that on the scale of teacher effectiveness, low-performing students are the first to benefit from more-effective teachers. This last finding, however, has been methodologically questioned (see McCaffrey and others 2003).

Most of the empirical literature investigating the specific factors that affect teacher quality is limited to looking at the effect of measurable variables of teacher characteristics. Typically, studies look at variables such as years of schooling, years of experience, salary levels, and certification. Although most of this research has found that one or more variables tested are positively associated with student achievement, no common thread among the studies indicates that certain variables are undeniably linked to teacher quality (Hanushek 1986; Rice 2003; Rockoff 2004; Velez, Schiefelbein, and Valenzuela 1993).

Although the evidence is mixed, certain teacher attributes do tend to be more likely to emerge internationally as significant in education production functions. Those attributes include teacher experience, educational level, subject preparation, certification, time-on-task, and test scores (Hanushek 1986, 1995; Ingersoll 2003; Rice 2003; Rockoff 2004; Velez, Schiefelbein, and Valenzuela 1993).

Yet, Hanushek (1986) reviews 147 studies of the determinants of student achievement and finds that no teacher characteristics are consistently significant and unidirectional in explaining student performance. Although the quality of education production function studies varies significantly, Hanushek suggests that the major inconsistencies in findings indicate that teacher quality is not easily pinned down by observable characteristics. In a later piece, Hanushek (1995) reports on education production function studies in developing countries and finds again that results across studies are inconsistent.

Similarly, Velez, Schiefelbein, and Valenzuela (1993) in a review of education production function studies in Latin America find that observable teacher characteristics are only statistically significant about 50 percent of the time.

Studies that look at both teacher effect and teacher characteristics support the hypothesis that unobservable teacher characteristics, such as effort in the classroom, may have a greater effect on student achievement than the variables we can commonly observe. Goldhaber, Brewer and

Anderson's (1999) study of U.S. teachers finds that teacher quality explains only 8.4 percent of the variation in student achievement and that only 3 percent of this 8.4 percent is attributable to observable teacher characteristics. In their study in Texas, Rivkin, Hanushek, and Kain (1998) also find that observable characteristics represent very little of the variation in teacher quality. Their finding suggests that policies or reforms that target selecting teachers with certain characteristics or increasing a certain teacher input (that is, providing ongoing professional development) may not result in improvements in teaching quality.

Some researchers argue that large investments in improving teacher characteristics are not a cost-effective means of increasing student achievement. Jacob and Lefgren (2004), for example, look at the effect of in-service teacher education using regression discontinuity and find that it has no significant effect on elementary math and reading test scores in Chicago. But Angrist and Lavy's (1998) paper on in-service teacher education in Jerusalem came to the exact opposite conclusion—that in-service trainings are an effective and relatively inexpensive means of improving teacher practice. Those two studies are one example of the conflicting reports on what matters for good teaching. The different findings could result from methodological or data differences, from differences in the Chicago and Jerusalem settings, or from differences in the content or quality of the in-service trainings. (For informative discussions on teacher education and its evaluation, see Tatto 1997, 2002.)

Some evidence also shows that, even with additional resources, those employers hiring teachers may not be able to identify high-quality teachers in order to hire them. Hanushek and others (2004) use data from Texas to show that school districts with higher salaries and more attractive working conditions do not systematically hire teachers with better track records of improving student test scores.

Still others suggest that perhaps researchers are looking at the wrong teacher characteristics. In response to the difficulty in isolating specific teacher background characteristics that are associated with teacher quality and in recognizing the importance of classroom teacher practices, researchers have begun to investigate classroom practices as determinants of teacher quality. Those variables, such as one-on-one interactions with students, assignment of homework, and parent-teacher conferences, are costly to observe and difficult to measure accurately. Darling-Hammond (2000) reviews findings of U.S. production function research on classroom practices and reports that creative, flexible teacher practice that adapts to students and teaching context frequently will tend to result in higher student learning.

Ingersoll (2003) argues that whereas teacher educational level may not be a determinant of teacher quality, whether or not a teacher was educated in the same field that he or she subsequently teaches is critical to how well a teacher can teach. He finds that although most U.S. teachers have bachelor's degrees, many teach subject areas that they did not study. In the 1999/2000 school year, 38 percent of all 7th–12th graders were taught math by a teacher who did not major or minor in math or a math-related field. He warns that this situation has seriously detrimental implications.

Villegas-Reimers and Reimers (1996) report that largely because of the lack of clarity on what characteristics make a good teacher, education reforms in recent decades have tried to circumvent the work of teachers. They criticize this tendency while hypothesizing that the lack of coherent findings on teacher quality does not reflect the irrelevance of teacher attributes so much as it reflects the methodological and data limitations of the analyses. It also reflects the critical significance of the quality and context of teacher characteristics and practices. Methodologically, they highlight a frequent lack of variation, of confounded and unobservable variables, and of mediating conditions. Practically, they assert that unless education is designed to function without the central role of the teacher, the question should not be whether teachers affect learning but how to maximize their effect.

The debate on teacher quality aside, Latin America and many other parts of the world face a serious problem in education and teaching quality (Alvarez and Majmudar 2001; Eurydice 2004; Glewwe and Kremer forthcoming; Government of Chile 2003; Villegas-Reimers 1998; World Bank 2001). Teaching quality and student learning are low throughout the Latin American region (with Cuba as a notable exception). In regional and global comparative examinations, Latin American countries have nearly universal subpar achievement (OECD 2001; UNESCO 1998). Achievement gaps between rich and poor students are also at their worst in Latin American countries (OECD 2003). There is evidence that teacher quality may be declining because of increased employment opportunities for women outside of education, low salaries, and rigid pay structures (Hoxby and Leigh 2003). In the United States, for example, Lakdawalla (2001) demonstrates that between 1900 and 1950 the relative educational level of teachers compared to nonteachers declined approximately 3 years. Despite their internal challenges, many of the ministries and secretariats of education in Latin America are actively researching the barriers to high teaching quality in their countries and are developing policies to combat them (see, for example, Government of Chile 2003).

Current Educational Investment and Policies and Their Embedded Incentives

There is significant evidence that the current policies and structures governing investments in education are not producing results efficiently or effectively, especially in lower-income countries (Eberts and Stone 1984;

Glewwe 2002; Hanushek 2002; Lee and You 2000; Loeb and Reininger 2004; Pritchett and Filmer 1997). Hanushek (2002) and Eberts and Stone (1984) document how, despite relatively dramatic increases in educational investment, student achievement remains stagnant or low. Hanushek (2002) and Pritchett and Filmer (1997) suggest that the failure of financial resources to boost learning lies at least in part in the fact that educational investments have tended to be linked to educational inputs rather than to outputs or outcomes.

Pritchett and Filmer (1997) explore this subject in their discussion of relative investments in educational inputs. They argue that inputs directly or indirectly benefiting teachers, such as wage increases or smaller class sizes, are disproportionately favored in public education in many countries because of the lobbying power of teachers and teacher unions, despite the fact that alternative inputs such as textbook provision are frequently found to be more cost-effective in improving student learning (Fuller and Clark 1994; Hanushek 1995; Michaelowa 2002; Pritchett and Filmer 1997; Velez, Schiefelbein, and Valenzuela 1993). Pritchett and Filmer (1997) argue that political mechanisms, such as teachers' bargaining power in public education systems, have negatively affected educational investments.

Overinvestment in inputs favored by teacher unions appears not to increase teacher quality by increasing teacher satisfaction. Michaelowa (2002) finds that the primary determinants of teacher satisfaction—job security and small class sizes, for example—are not key determinants of student achievement in Sub-Saharan Africa. In fact, some determinants have opposing effects on the dependent variables. For example, teacher educational level, teacher control systems, and teacher incentive structures are positively related to student achievement but negatively related to teacher job satisfaction in her study. Interestingly, she finds that teacher satisfaction itself is positively and significantly related to student outcomes. Salary levels and small class size appear to be less beneficial than expected overall for both student achievement and teacher satisfaction, while simple school equipment such as textbooks has a positive effect on both students and teachers.

A recent study by Wils and O'Connor (2004) also questions an overly financial investment-based theory of educational improvement. Specifically, they argue that the most critical constraint to full primary enrollment is not insufficient investment in education but the shortage of medium to highly educated adults in the population of many low-income countries. Most Latin American countries may have significantly less of a shortage than other regions. However, the authors show that to attain universal primary enrollment more than 5 percent of all secondary education graduates in countries such as El Salvador, Guatemala, and Haiti would have to work as primary school teachers. Countries can compensate for their low levels of secondary graduates by employing a greater percentage of educated adults as teachers or by increasing class size.

The next three subsections review scholarship on the incentives embedded in the widespread current forms of teacher pay level, relative pay, and salary structure.

Teacher Pay Level and Working Conditions

Salary itself may be the most powerful and direct teacher incentive (Chapman, Snyder, and Burchfield 1993). It influences who goes into teaching, how long they stay, and how they perform their day-to-day work. There is a fair amount of disagreement among researchers, however, on the relative importance of salary level. Many researchers find that higher salaries can result in increased teacher retention (Guarino and others 2004; Hanushek, Kain, and Rivkin 2001; Murnane and others 1991).

Some researchers also find that higher salaries can attract more teachers of higher quality and can improve teacher effort and daily practice (Figlio 1997; Kingdon and Teal 2002; Loeb and Page 2000). In their view, higher teacher salaries could relieve serious problems in Latin America, where too few people go into teaching and those who do frequently are not the most promising candidates or end up working more than one job (Bennell 2004; Villegas-Reimers 1998). Others assert that salary levels themselves do not ensure higher quality teachers and that other factors such as the characteristics of students and school systems are often more important than salaries (Ballou and Podgursky 1997; Bennell 2004; Hanushek, Kain, and Rivkin 2001; Hoxby 1996).

Figlio (1997) conducts a cross-sectional analysis of the relationship between salaries and teacher quality in metropolitan areas in the United States. He finds that metropolitan areas with higher salaries and districts within metropolitan areas with higher salaries have a greater likelihood of recruiting a teacher who attended a selective university and who has subject-matter expertise. The findings support the hypothesis that salary levels have a sorting effect within the teaching profession, between teaching and other professions, or both.

Similarly, Kingdon and Teal (2002), using a relatively small data set of 30 public and private schools in India, find evidence that higher pay in private schools is associated with higher student achievement, controlling for student, teacher, and school observables. They hypothesize that the greater flexibility of private schools to reward teachers with higher pay and to threaten teachers with weaker job security increases teacher effort, which, in turn, increases student achievement.

But other researchers argue that pay level is not a sufficient incentive to attract and retain good teachers. Ballou and Podgursky (1997) find little evidence of improved teacher quality resulting from the across-the-board salary increases that took place in the United States in the 1980s. They hypothesize that the salary improvement's lack of effect on quality is caused by characteristics of the teacher labor market in which teachers have high job security and receive pay increments based on experience, independent of performance. Those qualities lead older teachers to remain in teaching, thus limiting positions for new teachers who might be attracted by the higher salaries (Murnane and others 1991). Ballou and Podgursky (1997) also argue that high salaries increase the overall number of applicants to teaching, making it more difficult for any single applicant to get a job. Because it is often difficult to predict who will be a good teacher, they argue that higher salaries may even decrease the overall quality of entering teachers.

Hanushek, Kain, and Rivkin (2001) also address the incentives created by pecuniary and nonpecuniary aspects of teaching. They find that although salaries do influence teacher retention and turnover, they are a less powerful predictor of labor market trends than other, nonmonetary, indicators. Teachers tend to leave their jobs less frequently in school districts with higher salaries in Texas. But the effect on teacher mobility of other characteristics, including a school's average academic performance and the percentages of African American and Latino students in a school, is greater than the effect of salary. Specifically, they find that districts with higher percentages of African American and Latino students and districts with lower average academic performance have much greater teacher turnover, especially among new teachers. They also find, however, that African American teachers tend to move to schools with more African American students rather than the reverse. The authors estimate that low-performing, high-minority districts would have to provide salary increases of between 20 and 50 percent to offset the high teacher attrition rates in those schools.

In a subsequent study, Hanushek and others (2004) find that even within an urban school district, schools with higher proportions of black and Latino students have significantly lower-quality teachers as defined by student test score improvement. This finding holds true even when controlling for teacher experience.

In the Latin American context, Vegas's (2002) study of school choice finds that only limited correspondence exists between those school sectors with the highest teacher salaries and those with characteristics we identify with quality teachers: high school grade point average, years of experience, and higher-education degree.

Overall, although analysts disagree as to the relative importance of salary levels as a useful tool for improving teacher quality, they agree that both wage levels and other work rules and conditions affect the work and decisions of prospective and active teachers. Loeb and Page (2000) find evidence of the importance of nonpecuniary job characteristics in their study, and the findings of Hanushek, Kain, and Rivkin (2001) indicate that salaries matter. Differences in the relative findings surely result, at least in part, from different methodologies, data sets and variables, and research focus.

Relative Salaries

In a recent paper Loeb and Page (2000) critique the hypothesis that salary is not a powerful incentive for teachers. They suggest that studies with those findings overlook two important factors: the relative wage of teachers as it relates to comparable workers, and nonpecuniary returns to teaching. Controlling for those factors in their state-level analysis of the United States, they find that higher salaries are related to lower student dropout rates and higher college enrollment rates.

Research has also examined how relative wages and rules concerning seniority, salary scale, and teacher autonomy affect teacher characteristics and behavior. In general, there is wide concurrence in the literature that the current rigid determinants of salary scale and work rules in much of the world have negative implications for who goes into teaching and the quality of the work those teachers perform (Ballou and Podgursky 2002; Delannoy and Sedlacek 2001; Morduchowicz 2002; Odden and Kelley 1997).

It is widely recognized that to attract the most promising and qualified candidates to teaching, teachers' salaries must be competitive with those of comparable occupations (López-Acevedo 2002; Odden and Kelley 1997; Psacharopoulos, Valenzuela, and Arends 1996; Temin 2002; Waterreus 2003). In many countries, that requirement is not met (Delannoy and Sedlacek 2001; Odden and Kelley 1997). Psacharopoulos, Valenzuela, and Arends (1996) find that whereas relative salaries of primary teachers vary extensively across the 12 Latin American countries in their study, those salaries have almost universally declined since 1979 relative to those of comparison occupations.

There is also evidence that the relative quality of teachers has declined as labor opportunities for women have widened. (Teachers in the United States have consistently been about three-quarters female from the 1960s through 2000.) Corcoran, Evans, and Schwab (2004) demonstrate that in the United States the average cognitive ability, as measured by standardized exams, of female teachers has fallen slightly over the past several decades. More pronounced has been the decline in top-achieving women who choose teaching as their profession. Interestingly, the authors find that the opposite is true for men; more top-achieving men choose teaching now than did so in the 1960s. Because of the high proportion of female teachers, however, this trend has not counterbalanced the decline in skilled teachers caused by changes in women's professional decisions.

In many countries, nonmonetary benefits of teachers' work such as high pensions, job stability, and fewer annual work hours may substantially offset uncompetitive salaries (Kimball, Heneman, and Kellor 2003; Liang 1999). Liang's (1999) review of teacher pay in 12 Latin American countries, for example, finds that when days and hours worked are factored into teachers' salaries, teachers earn as much as or more than workers in comparable fields. This finding is corroborated by other studies, such as López-Acevedo's (2004) analysis of teacher remuneration in Mexico.

Delannoy and Sedlacek (2001) look not only at starting salaries of teachers and comparable occupations but also at relative salary growth rates in Brazil. They find that although base salaries for teachers with low educational levels are similar or superior to those of other professions, salary growth for teachers with higher levels of education and experience is lower than in comparable occupations. The authors argue that this structure creates incentives for people with little experience and low educational levels to work as teachers while serving as a disincentive for individuals with high educational levels to enter teaching.

Similar undesired incentives have been documented in Mexico. López-Acevedo (2002) looks at profiles showing differences in earnings of teachers and other comparable groups. Like Delannoy and Sedlacek, she finds that although beginning teachers are paid significantly better than comparable occupations, the growth of earnings with greater experience is significantly less than that of workers in the public or private sector. Santibáñez (2002) concurs in her paper on teacher salary structure, also in Mexico. She finds that although hourly income is higher for teachers than those in comparable occupations—especially for women, total income is generally lower for teachers and there are fewer opportunities for advancement.

Salary Scales

Throughout Latin America and the United States, most teacher salary scales are rigidly determined by formulas involving seniority, years of experience, and educational level. Several studies have found that those determinants do not create the appropriate incentives for recruiting and retaining high-quality teachers or for improving student achievement (Ballou and Podgursky 2002; Coolahan and others 2004; Government of Chile 2003; Hanushek 1986; Hoxby 2002; Lankford, Loeb, and Wyckoff 2002; Morduchowicz 2002, Vegas 2000).

In Hanushek's (1986) review of international education production function studies, teacher education and experience are not consistently found to be associated with higher student achievement. Faced with this evidence, Hanushek and others have argued that even though teacher quality is important for student learning, basing salary growth on characteristics that do not systematically correspond with improved teaching creates problematic incentives that reward teachers for things other than their teaching.

Ballou and Podgursky (2002) support this argument. They make the same case concerning the prevalence of seniority-linked pay in the teaching profession in the United States. The United States spends an estimated US$24.4 billion—17 percent of instructional expenditures—on seniority pay each year. Ballou and Podgursky argue that despite this enormous investment, seniority pay is not an efficient response to the teacher labor market because there is no systematic evidence that teachers' skills increase progressively with experience. The Latin American Laboratory Study of the United Nations Educational, Scientific, and Cultural Organization, for example, found no significant relationship between teacher experience and student achievement (Casassus and others 2002). Ballou and Podgursky posit that seniority pay emerged not from an effort to promote high-quality teaching but rather from collective bargaining with teacher unions. They further warn that seniority pay may decrease teacher quality by reducing the number of positions and salary levels for new and talented teachers.

Hoxby (2002) also finds that the current determinants of salary scale—in this case, masters' degrees and teaching credentials—may not be good predictors of teacher quality and should not be heavily rewarded in teacher salary structures. In her study of the effect of school choice on teacher quality in the United States, she finds that greater school choice is associated with decreased demand for teachers with masters' degrees and teaching credentials. Hoxby hypothesizes that with school choice, schools become more responsive to parents' interests and that parents' interests fundamentally lie in quality education for their children. She suggests, therefore, that masters' degrees and teaching credentials may not be good predictors of quality teachers.

Rigid salary scales may also contribute to educational inequalities. Lankford, Loeb, and Wyckoff (2002) find that schools serving low-income, low-achieving, and nonwhite students in New York state tend to have less qualified teachers. They assert that salaries do not compensate for the more challenging settings and that, in some instances, beginning teachers serving low-income populations are paid less than their counterparts in more affluent areas. Similarly, Loeb and Reininger (2004) find that schools with low-income and low-performing students in the United States "systematically employ less experienced teachers with weak education background and academic skills."

Morduchowicz (2002) analyzes teacher remuneration in Latin America and argues that the current structure fails to "incentivize" appropriate or desired teacher characteristics and behavior. He discusses, for example, how promotions typically distance teachers from the classroom, and he criticizes the lack of linkages between pay and actual teacher practice.

López-Acevedo's (2004) study of teacher remuneration in Mexico came to a slightly different conclusion, however. She argues that the high relative hourly salary identified in Liang (1999)—combined with a steady increase in wages throughout a teacher's career, high job security, and good retirement income—has a positive benefit on the recruitment and retention of quality teachers. Vegas (2000), however, in her study of teachers in Brazil, argues that despite the relatively high hourly salaries of teachers in most areas of Brazil, low monthly and annual salaries relative to comparable workers in Brazil (because teachers generally work fewer hours and days than other workers) create a disincentive for quality teachers and teaching.

The next section of this study looks at evidence on the effect of alternative compensation schemes that attempt to create incentives by rewarding teachers who demonstrate promising behavior, outcomes, or skills.

Merit Pay

The critiques of the problematic incentives embedded in typical compensation systems for teachers lead some to conclude that incentives should be altered to reward particular teacher performance, skills, or behavior (Ballou 2001; Coolahan and others 2004; Hanushek 2003; Odden and Kelley 1997; Rockoff 2004; World Bank 2001). Rewards to good teachers could attract more promising candidates to the field, keep them teaching, increase teacher effort, and improve teaching (Lavy 2002, 2004; López-Acevedo 2002). Other theorists and analysts, however, critique those performance-based incentives. Those authors argue that (a) such incentives can damage teachers' intrinsic motivation and effort, and (b) they often elicit inappropriate teacher behavior and result in lower teaching quality and inferior student learning and development, especially in the long run (Clotfelter and others 2004; Dee and Keys 2004; Eberts, Hollenbeck, and Stone 2002; Glewwe, Ilias, and Kremer 2003; Jacob and Levitt 2002; Kohn 1993; Koretz 2002; Murnane and Cohen 1986). The main debates concerning performance-based pay are discussed next.

Performance-Based Pay Incentives

There is evidence that certain performance-based incentives positively affect student learning, particularly in the short term and in those curricular areas or indicators that the incentives target. By and large, however, studies find that merit-pay schemes cause unintended behavioral distortions and do not result in long-term or generalizable learning gains.

Lavy (2002) finds that a performance-based incentive positively affects student outcomes. This Israeli school-level group incentive offered monetary bonuses to the top one-third of participating schools on the basis of improvements in a variety of educational outcomes including test scores, credits taken, and matriculation exam completion. Lavy finds that the reform had a significantly positive effect on each of the measured outcomes at the end of the 2 years of the program. In addition, Lavy finds that the program effect was significantly larger for students from lower socioeconomic backgrounds and for students whose parents had lower levels of education. The results suggest that incentives can have positive effects, at least in the short term, and that they can target lower-performing children.

López-Acevedo's (2002) study of the Carrera Magisterial program in Mexico also finds a positive association between student achievement and enrollment in the horizontal promotion reform. This reform grants incremental pay increases to teachers on the basis of a series of factors, including a teacher exam and student achievement. (Other studies of Carrera Magisterial, including the one contained in this volume, however, have not found a positive program effect.)

Nonetheless, Lavy's and López-Acevedo's studies do not investigate several issues. The studies attempt to estimate effects of the teacher incentive reforms by examining their effect on student outcomes such as test scores. This method has been critiqued as "the black-box approach" because it does not identify what changes in behavior elicited the program effects and, therefore, cannot be used to judge whether those effects were the result of improvements in teaching and learning or were caused by distortions and manipulations. Furthermore, the studies do not examine the longer-term effects of the incentives.

Some recent studies have attempted to address those issues. In particular, three studies—Glewwe, Ilias, and Kremer (2003); Lavy (2003, 2004)— examine how incentive reforms affect or are correlated with teachers' pedagogical practices. Lavy (2003) investigates another teacher incentive reform in Israel, a rank-order tournament that offered bonuses to individual teachers on the basis of improvements in student matriculation exams in a set of schools. He finds that the reform led to a 3.3 percent increase in the matriculation rate. Lavy uses teacher surveys to examine teacher pedagogical behavior for participating and nonparticipating teachers. Although self-reporting of teaching methods is not ideal, his findings suggest that participating teachers were more likely to use small-group and individualized instruction, more likely to adapt instruction to students' abilities, and more likely to work more hours outside the regular classroom schedule, especially in the weeks leading up to the exam. Although the first two changes in behavior represent possible improvements in instructional methods, the last change—working more hours outside school hours— may represent test-taking tutorials offered by teachers for a fee to students.

Lavy's 2004 study of a similar individual-teacher incentive comes to similar conclusions, although again, it relies on teachers' reports rather than on classroom observations of teaching methods. Using regression-discontinuity and propensity-score matching techniques (to address the challenge of nonrandom assignment to the program), Lavy again finds that the reform was successful in improving high school matriculation rates. In this case, he finds that teachers who participated in the competitive incentive were more likely to report that they teach in small groups, use within-class ability tracking, give individualized instruction, and adapt their methods to student ability. As in Lavy's previous study (2003), teachers were also more likely to offer tutorials outside of regular class time in the weeks and months just before the exam.

Glewwe, Ilias, and Kremer's (2003) study of a performance-based incentive experiment in Kenya also investigates changes elicited in teacher practice and student outcomes. In this experiment, teachers were given a financial bonus if their students' performance in standardized test scores increased. As in Lavy (2003), Glewwe, Ilias, and Kremer investigate changes in specific teacher behaviors, particularly teacher absenteeism, homework assignment, pedagogy, and test preparation tutorials. They find no significant changes in how often teachers are absent, in the likelihood of homework being assigned, or in teaching styles or attitudes during the years of the reform compared with control schools. There is, however, a statistically significant positive difference in the amount of test-taking tutorials in the treatment schools.

The repeated findings of teachers' offering extended teaching hours in Kenya and Israel can be interpreted as a potential benefit and a potential hazard of teacher-incentive reforms. On one hand, the findings indicate greater teacher effort and more hours of schooling. On the other hand, the findings reflect a possible manipulation of the reform in which teachers, rather than improving their teaching, offer fee-based, private test-preparation classes after school. The special classes may further inequalities between more and less affluent students without improving education.

The randomized teacher incentive experiment analyzed by Glewwe, Ilias, and Kremer (2003) had several safeguards in place to prevent the possible adverse behavioral responses that were exposed in earlier research. The safeguards prevented schools from benefiting by changing their teaching force or removing weak students. Here, too, the authors find that the chosen outcome indicator—test scores—improves over the course of the reform compared with a control group of similar schools. Upon further examination, however, they find that the improvement lasted only the length of the incentive and was not generalizable to other tests, even of the same subject material. The short duration of the test score improvements and the inability to generalize to similar exams suggest that test tutorials were a method of "gaming" the incentive without improving teaching or learning.

A recent study by Clotfelter and others (2004) indicates that incentives, particularly accountability systems that both reward and sanction teachers on the basis of student performance, can negatively affect teacher quality in those schools that are most in need of excellent teachers. They studied a school accountability system in North Carolina that provided cash bonuses to schools that met growth targets for test scores. The study finds that teacher turnover was significantly higher in low-performing schools after the accountability system was implemented. Clotfelder and others also find that after implementation, low-performing schools did not increase their likelihood of hiring in-district transfers (that is, teachers with experience) or decrease their likelihood of hiring novice teachers relative to higher-performing schools. That is, there was no evident attempt to compensate low-performing schools for their loss of teachers after the accountability system began. Finally, they find mixed evidence as to the quality of the stock of teachers in low-performing schools. Although they do not find that the quality of the teachers declined after implementation, they do find evidence that relative to higher-performing schools the quality of teachers in low-performing schools may have declined. In conclusion, the authors warn that even very carefully designed teacher incentives, such as the one they studied, can end up harming the quality of education of the most-needy students.

The findings from Glewwe, Ilias, and Kremer (2003) and Clotfelter and others (2004) give credence to Holmström and Milgrom's (1991) criticisms of the application of Principal–Agent Theory to teachers. Those papers suggest that teachers' actual behavioral responses—charging students for after-school tutorials or transferring out of low-performing schools— are, in many cases, quite different from the behavioral responses that the incentives attempt to generate.

The evidence is also mixed regarding how accurately incentive schemes can effectively identify high-quality teachers for rewards. Dee and Keys (2004) investigate whether teachers rewarded by an incentive policy in Tennessee were actually more effective than those who did not apply for the rewards or who did not receive them. They find that whereas rewarded teachers have students with significantly higher math scores, the same is not true for reading. Furthermore, they find that although the incentive offers pecuniary and nonpecuniary benefits to teachers in a scaled ladder mechanism, the teachers who received awards and who had the strongest-performing students were actually those teachers on the lower rungs of the ladder rather than those at the top. The findings indicate that even this very carefully designed incentive that evaluates teachers in a number of areas and by different actors is only partially successful at identifying high-quality teachers.

As Murnane and Cohen (1986) reason, teachers support a broad range of forms of child development that includes but is not limited to social, personal, creative, physical, and intellectual development. Objective compensation systems promising bonuses or punishment based on unidimensional measurements encourage teachers to focus their attention on those indicators at the expense of other educational outcomes. The authors discuss two frequent distortions associated with merit pay: (a) teachers who teach only the material that is covered in the measured indicator, and (b) teachers who teach only to those students who they think will be most able to improve their results on the indicator (resulting in the exclusion of both low-performing and high-performing students).

Although test scores are increasingly used as the primary measure of educational outcomes, several researchers and theorists raise concerns about the validity and reliability of standardized assessments. Koretz (2002), for example, argues that using test scores to judge student learning and teacher performance tends to result in counterproductive behaviors, including the shifting of instructional resources, cheating, and coaching or "teaching to the test."

Test scores, he explains, measure only very limited areas of knowledge. They are samples of certain areas of learning that, in turn, comprise only certain areas of educational outcomes (for example, a history exam measures only a small sample of history knowledge, which, in turn, comprises only a fraction of all the knowledge and skills that are or can be taught in school). Those limitations leave tests vulnerable to both measurement error and corruption or inflation. Test score gains are frequently not generalizable, meaning they do not indicate that a real increase in learning has occurred. Koretz discusses numerous other problems inherent in teacher evaluation that is based on test scores. Accountability schemes such as teacher incentives, as well as familiarity, can inflate test scores. Moreover, test score gains are not necessarily attributable to a specific teacher's behavior; exogenous factors in students' lives heavily influence test scores. Also, because learning is largely cumulative, test score gains may result more from the behavior of previous teachers than from that of current teachers.

Kane and Staiger (2001) bring up a different criticism of testing as the basis of performance-based awards. Analyzing test score data from North Carolina, they argue that test scores cannot precisely measure long-term differences in school and student outcomes because of sampling variation caused by small sample sizes (class size or grade size) and because of one-time factors such as loud construction on the day of the test.

Supporting Koretz's (2002) and Kane and Staiger's (2001) critiques of standardized assessments, Jacob and Levitt (2002) find that the introduction of performance incentives is positively related to cheating in Chicago. Even more troubling, they find that among schools with high-stakes testing the incidence of cheating is highest in low-performing and high-poverty schools. Within schools, the incidence is highest with low-performing students.

Incentive reforms may not always have those adverse effects, however. In Lavy's (2004) study, he looks for evidence of manipulation of test scores and of potential negative spillover onto other subjects. He does not find any evidence of either of the potential negative effects of teacher incentive schemes—particularly those that reward bonuses to individuals rather than to schools. Although he does not measure cheating *per se*, Lavy compares the gap between national subject test scores and subject grades given by teachers in participating and nonparticipating schools to see whether there is evidence of teachers inflating subject grades because those grades contribute to teacher ranking for the bonus. He finds that participating teachers tend to grade their students *lower* than nonparticipating teachers for any given test score. Similarly, in terms of negative spillover into other subjects, Lavy finds no evidence of any negative effect of the incentive on history or biology attempted credits or exam scores. There is a possible indication of positive spillovers on attempted credits, as well as on test scores, for low-achieving students.

The diverse findings point to the important conclusion that education policies and reforms, such as performance-based pay, do not have homogenous effects across countries, schools, population groups, or time. Boozer (1999) suggests that, given the heterogeneity of program effects, a principal task of researchers is to see if there are systematic ways of accounting for the heterogeneity. In his analysis of merit pay reforms in South Carolina in the 1980s and 1990s, he suggests that merit pay may be more desirable in earlier grades than it is in higher grades. Finding preliminary evidence of test score gains attributable to the reforms in primary school grades but none in higher grades, he posits that there may be significant complementarity between basic skills (typically measured by standardized tests) and higher-order skills in the earlier grades, whereas in later grades basic and higher-order skills become substitutes.

A qualitative study of teachers' opinions about a performance-based pay incentive in a school district in North Carolina sheds light on another aspect of merit pay. Although teachers in Heneman's (1997) study generally feel positive about the merit-pay plan, they are insecure about their pedagogical ability to meet the required student achievement goals. They feel that they have sufficient resources at the school but that other teaching "enablers" are not in place. These enablers include team teaching and planning, curriculum alignment, best practices information, professional development activities, and parental support. This study indicates that merit-pay plans may need to ensure that teachers have the tools necessary to meet performance objectives. If accurate, this finding has important implications for Latin American schools, where even basic resources are often scarce or nonexistent.

Partly in reaction to the critiques, some people have advocated variations in the structure of merit pay. Most typically, the variations include subjective, rather than objective, performance evaluations and group awards that are distributed to an entire school rather than to individual teachers. Examples of a subjective performance assessment that is designed to replace or complement objective measures include classroom observations, interviews with teachers, and teacher portfolios (Porter, Youngs, and Odden 2001; Youngs, Odden, and Porter 2003). But those adaptations themselves have, in turn, received critique. Subjective evaluation incentives, which most frequently base merit pay on the evaluations of teachers by their supervisors, face the risk of demoralizing teachers because no clear standard or understanding exists of what behavior is necessary to obtain the merit pay or of why some receive it and others do not (Murnane and Cohen 1986). Prendergast (1999) also highlights that subjective performance evaluations are subject to the compression of ratings by evaluators in the form of leniency or "centrality bias," as well as by rent-seeking activities such as bribes.

Murnane and Cohen (1986) argue that individual compensation incentives are particularly detrimental in the education sector, where teachers and students alike benefit from cooperation and working together. Individual bonuses create incentives for teachers to compete rather than cooperate and can result in confusion, opportunistic behavior, and resentment. Murnane and Cohen suggest that group incentives that reward entire schools may avoid this problem by encouraging teachers to work together. Other theorists, however, have warned that group-level bonuses can create incentives for certain workers to take a "free ride" (Prendergast 1999).

The private education sector offers an interesting counterperspective on Murnane and Cohen's theory. Private schools typically have more-flexible pay structures and are more likely to use forms of performance-related pay. Ballou (2001) reports that in 1993 in the United States, 12 percent of public school districts had merit-pay plans, while 35 percent of nonsectarian private schools had those plans. He suggests that this finding may indicate that merit pay is not wholly inappropriate in the education sector but rather that political or technical difficulties may be impeding its success in public schools.

In conclusion, the findings concerning performance-based compensation incentives illuminate several challenges common to merit pay. First, they demonstrate that, as Bénabou and Tirole (2003) outlined, external incentives can have negative effects on long-term and internal motivation. Second, research indicates that although outcome measures, such as test scores, may improve, the actual educational improvements that the measure is supposed to proxy, such as increased learning and better teaching, often do not improve and may even decline. Third, the findings indicate that merit pay can promote perverse incentives in which agents change their behavior in negative ways to manipulate measurements and awards.

Skill-Based or Condition-Based Pay

Merit pay and group performance incentives are the most frequent, but not the only, types of compensation incentives. Odden and Kelley (1997) outline alternative incentive strategies that they argue avoid many of the dangers and difficulties associated with merit pay and group performance incentives. Specifically, they suggest competency-based pay and contingency pay (activity-based pay). Rather than select outcomes, those types of incentives reward teachers who expand and diversify teacher competencies in certain desired skills or who participate in certain desired activities. Odden and Kelley reason that those kinds of incentives, rather than jeopardizing intrinsic incentives, can expand intrinsic incentives by broadening teachers' skill sets, experiences, and capacity, factors that they believe will increase teacher interest and motivation.

Odden and Kelley suggest that competencies often can be fairly easily measured by using tests, evaluations, and certifications. Examples of types of competencies they discuss include classroom instructional competencies plus leadership and management competencies. Activities that they suggest may be worthy of rewarding include participating in professional development activities, participating in leadership positions, and initiating or conducting special projects. Although those types of incentives have a different measurement focus, they usually have the same overall goal as other incentives—to improve teacher quality and to enhance student learning. Substantially less research has been done on those types of reforms, but the research that exists indicates that many of the characteristic effects of performance-based incentives are present in behavior-, knowledge-, or skill-based incentives as well.

There is evidence that alternative compensation incentives also result in improvements in the specific indicator measured. Jacobson (1989) looks at the effect of an attendance incentive in one New York school district. This incentive provided a monetary bonus "share" to every teacher for every day fewer than 7 the teacher was absent in a school year. Comparing absences that year with absences the previous year in the same district using a paired sample t-test, Jacobson finds that absenteeism dropped significantly during the year of the incentive. The average total number of days absent dropped from 7.21 to 5.34, and the median dropped from 6.5 to 3.25 days. He also finds that the number of teachers with perfect attendance quadrupled in the year of the incentive. Although Jacobson finds the decrease in sick days was partially counterbalanced by an increase in the number of personal days taken by teachers, he concludes that targeted incentive reforms can contribute to reducing teacher absenteeism. He cautions that his research did not address whether the increase in teacher attendance outlasted the year of the reform or whether it affected student learning.

Evidence also exists that behavioral distortions emerge from alternative compensation reforms. Eberts, Hollenbeck, and Stone (2002) find significant evidence of distortions arising from a student retention–based reform in a Michigan school. That reform offered merit pay to teachers on the basis of student attendance on a random day in the last quarter of the school year. Attendance in the last quarter was used as a proxy for how many students had remained in school for the entire year. The authors compare educational outcomes at a school subject to the reform to those at a school with similar characteristics but no such reform. The authors find that the incentive succeeded in increasing student retention in the school undergoing the reform compared with the control school. But like Glewwe, Ilias, and Kremer (2003), they find that the specific measure that determined merit pay—attendance in the last quarter—was not sufficiently correlated or related to the actual behavioral changes that the reformers hoped to elicit. Grade point average, attendance, and passing rates all declined in the school undergoing the reform compared with in the control school. Eberts, Hollenbeck, and Stone dismiss the possibility that the negative changes are caused by the changes in class composition from increased retention of lower-performing students. Rather, the authors find evidence that the declines may be caused by changes in the rigor and depth of the curricula that teachers offered. Those changes in curricula, they gather from interviews with teachers and school officials, may have been an attempt to encourage more students to remain in school. If this finding is the case, the more fundamental goal of increasing student achievement may have been negatively affected by the merit-pay bonus.

School Organization

In later chapters in this volume, we will look at a range of reforms that affect teacher incentives. Some of those reforms, such as Mexico's Carrera Magisterial or Chile's Sistema Nacional de Evaluación de Desempeño de los Establecimientos Educacionales (National System of School Performance Assessment, or SNED) are clear examples of performance-based incentive programs. Others, such as Nicaragua's Autonomía Escolar (School Autonomy) decentralization reform or Brazil's school finance equalization reform, the Fundo de Manutenção e Desenvolvimento do Ensino Fundamental e de Valorização do Magistério (Fund for the Maintenance and Development of Basic Education and Teacher Appreciation, or FUNDEF), have also changed the incentives affecting teachers but are not purely teacher incentive reforms. These later reforms have not typically been analyzed in terms of the behavioral changes they have prompted. In the section that follows, we begin to look at those more atypical reforms affecting teacher incentives. We review the literature on school organization and management reforms, focusing particularly on findings regarding how those reforms affect teachers and why. The main focus in this section is on school organization and management broadly and on educational decentralization, school-based management, and demand-side financing particularly. As in previous sections, we are particularly interested in what types of changes in teacher quality the reforms are designed to promote and whether, in point of fact, they do so.

Decentralization

Decentralization reforms take many different forms, have many different goals, and focus on different areas, levels of educational responsibility, or both (McGinn and Welsh 1999). In any form, decentralization can create powerful changes that create incentives to improve or weaken teacher and teaching quality. Research evidence indicates that greater teacher or school accountability to local communities and teacher autonomy with supervision and support can improve teacher quality and student outcomes (Sawada 2003; Vegas 2002). At the same time, decentralization policies that place financial or managerial burdens on systems, schools, and communities that lack the capacity to handle the added responsibility can result in added stress and crises that may damage teacher morale and effort and, ultimately, may undermine student learning (Fuller and Rivarola 1998; Gunnarson and others 2004; McGinn and Welsh 1999).

Several studies have indicated that greater teacher and school accountability to local communities and parents can have a positive effect on teacher quality. Vegas's (2002) study of the Chilean voucher system provides evidence that certain management strategies in schools are associated with higher student performance when controlling for student socioeconomic background. She finds that for her sample of schools in the Santiago metropolitan area, student test scores are positively associated with local decisionmaking power (for example, when the main decisionmaker is a lead teacher or curricular guide) and stricter work rule enforcement. She also finds that greater teacher autonomy in implementing projects and designing teaching plans is associated with higher student outcomes when school decisionmaking power is close to the level of the teacher. Paralleling the work of Heneman (1997), this finding likely indicates that teachers are more able to improve their teaching through greater autonomy if they have significant support from supervisors. Vegas finds that the most powerful predictors of student achievement are school management characteristics rather than observable teacher characteristics. This finding suggests that school management reforms, such as decentralization, have the potential to create significant incentives affecting teacher quality.

Jimenez and Sawada (2003) and Sawada (2003) demonstrate that direct community management of schools can improve teacher effort and student achievement. Sawada (2003) finds that teachers in El Salvador's community-managed Educación con Participación de la Comunidad (Education with Community Participation, or EDUCO) schools show significantly higher levels of effort than teachers in centrally managed schools. Sawada hypothesizes that community control over the school budget allows community members to exert meaningful pressure on teachers and to design compensation systems that serve as an incentive for greater teacher effort. This local accountability, in turn, he argues, is the base for higher student academic outcomes in EDUCO schools as compared with traditional schools.

Nevertheless, other studies of decentralized school systems do not demonstrate such positive associations with teacher quality. Gunnarson and others (2004) look at school-based management in 12 countries across Latin America. They find that although a positive and significant association exists between school-based management and test scores, this relationship is reversed after controlling for endogeneity. This finding suggests that schools in which principals, staff members, or communities have the capacity and will to manage their schools will, in fact, benefit from decentralization. Where this condition is not met, however, students actually do worse in decentralized systems. The authors conclude that decentralization does not seem to work well when coming from a central mandate but rather only when emerging from local capacity and interest.

Evidence from the Nicaraguan decentralization reform, School Autonomy, leads to a similar conclusion. King and others (1996) find that teachers in autonomous schools report that they have less influence in school decisions than they had in traditional public schools. Although the authors do not investigate this phenomenon further, their study may hint that school autonomy can have a demoralizing effect on teachers. In contrast, teachers reported in surveys that they were more punctual and less frequently absent in autonomous schools than in traditional schools. If accurate, this finding could have a positive effect on student learning. It could also reflect inaccurate self-reporting caused by perceptions of less job security in autonomous schools. Such findings were preliminary as the reform had only been in effect a few years when the study was conducted. At the time, there was no empirical evidence on effects of the reform on student test scores.

Fuller and Rivarola (1998) also investigated the Nicaraguan decentralization reform. Their qualitative study of 12 autonomous schools indicates that teachers' financial difficulties associated with the reform may be causing out-of-class paid tutorials to increase and that teachers, who under the reform receive part of their salary from school fees charged to students, are having to spend considerable instructional time eliciting fees. This situation may be having a negative effect not only on the amount of instructional time but also on the relationship between teachers and students.

The results of studies of decentralized and community-managed schools demonstrate the diversity in decentralization reforms, as well as the powerful implications of seemingly small details of planning and implementation. Whereas in El Salvador local accountability to parents seems to be improving teacher practice, in Nicaragua evidence suggests that user fees are worsening classroom instructional time and morale. The broad range of results of those studies also surely reflects the different research questions of the authors, as well as the methodologies and data used. The next section looks at the incentives created by demand-side financing.

Demand-Side Financing

A current trend in school management reform is the introduction of demand-side financing, such as school choice or vouchers. There is emerging evidence that demand-side financing, in much the same way as decentralization, can create incentives that change teacher characteristics and student outcomes (Angrist and others 2002; Hoxby 2002; Hsieh and Urquiola 2003; McEwan 2001; Mizala and Romaguera 2000). Hoxby (2002) examines teacher attributes across the United States and finds that those attributes differ according to levels of school choice (Tiebout choice,[9] more private schools, and availability of charter schools). She hypothesizes that by relocating management and authority away from distant education officials and closer to principals and parents, schools become more accountable and, therefore, more effective. She argues that when parents can choose where to send their children, schools must compete to attract students. She finds that schools in systems with greater parental choice have higher demand for teacher effort and independence, math and science skills, and high-quality prior schooling. This competition results in schools paying more for those teachers' characteristics and hiring more teachers who exhibit those qualities.

But Hsieh and Urquiola (2003) argue that the Chilean school choice reform has not resulted in improved educational achievement. Rather, the primary effect of the reform has been one of student sorting as wealthier students migrate to private schools. In their study, student achievement does not improve in areas of greater school choice (more schools to choose from) compared to areas of less school choice. Repetition and age-by-grade distortion worsen comparatively. They reject Hoxby's hypothesis that greater parental choice results in schools competing for better teachers. Instead, they propose that parents may choose schools based not so much on teachers as on peer groups. Schools, therefore, compete for the best students rather than for the best teachers or best teaching, resulting in increased socioeconomic segregation.

---

9. *Tiebout choice* refers to parents choosing their place of residence in order to enroll their children in particular public schools.

Political Economy of Reform

The larger political, social, and economic contexts within countries have profound implications for education systems and their reform. The final section of this chapter examines literature that deals primarily with the role of teacher unions in the development, implementation, and effect of education reforms that affect teacher incentives. Because they are powerful organizations in Latin America, there is consensus that teacher unions affect educational inputs, outputs, and outcomes. In Latin America and beyond, however, there is debate over whether and in what ways those unions help or harm student learning (Loveless 2000; Murillo 2002).

A few studies have examined the relationship between teacher unionization and indicators of student achievement or teaching quality. Murillo and others (2002) investigate how teacher unions affect several "intermediate variables" that are thought to affect student achievement in their provincial-level analysis of Argentina. The analysis looks at the effect of teacher unions on lost days (from strikes), teacher tenure, class size, budget size and composition, and teacher satisfaction. They examine how those variables, in turn, explain variations in student test scores. The results are mixed, implying that unions can have both negative and positive effects on student learning, depending on the specific characteristics of the unions and on the characteristics of the environment surrounding the unions, such as political antagonism with provincial governments and per capita gross domestic product. They find, for example, that certain attributes of unions and their environment are associated with more strikes, and that strikes have a negative effect on student performance. They also find that higher union participation is negatively correlated with job satisfaction, while job satisfaction is positively correlated with student achievement. Job tenure, however, is a major goal of teacher unions and is positively correlated with student achievement according to their findings.

Hoxby (1996) finds that although teachers' unions have increased school inputs—primarily through higher teacher salaries and lower student-teacher ratios—their development is negatively associated with student learning. She shows that in the United States higher teacher salaries since 1980 in unionized schools are associated with higher student dropout rates.

Zegarra and Ravina (2003) adapt Hoxby's education production function for their analysis of the effect of unionization on the quality of teaching in Peru. Unlike Hoxby, they do not find evidence that the Peruvian teachers' union negatively affects student learning. Complementing their statistical analysis, they conducted classroom evaluations and student surveys. Those results suggest that unionized teachers have better classroom management skills and that unionized teachers use corporal punishment less frequently than nonunionized teachers. Finally, Zegarra and Ravina show that there is a positive correlation between access to infrastructure and to teacher unionization in multigrade (rural) schools.

Other studies have looked at how unionization affects resource allocation and wage structures in education. Pritchett and Filmer (1997) find that union bargaining power has shifted resources away from those inputs most frequently associated with increased learning and into inputs that teachers favor. Eberts and Stone (1984) find that unionized districts in the United States spend on average 15 percent more than nonunionized districts but do not exhibit significant differences overall in student achievement. Disaggregating students into low, middle, and high achievers, however, they find that unionized districts do better with middle achievers, whereas nonunionized districts do better with low and high achievers. The authors suggest that this result is caused by more differentiated instruction in nonunion districts.

Hoxby and Leigh (2003) find that in the United States much of the decline in teacher aptitude since 1960 is caused by unions' success at compressing teacher wages. Compressed wages means that two teachers in the same district with the same educational level and same years of experience are paid more or less the same wage irrespective of their effort, skill, or effectiveness. As discussed earlier, this system fails to reward good teaching, thereby pushing the high-aptitude teachers out of the field.

Indeed, in the past, teacher unions typically have tended to be against performance-based pay incentives or other incentives that make salary structures more flexible in response to differences in teacher behavior and attributes. Many of their stated reasons correspond to weaknesses in incentive schemes described earlier in this chapter (Ballou and Podgursky 1993). Other reasons also reflect unions' fear that performance pay could jeopardize unions' influential position in determining pay structures and could weaken teachers' sense of solidarity, as well as their need and support for unions.

Nevertheless, both unions and teachers are showing increased interest in innovative pay structures as a method of enhancing teaching and learning outcomes (Ballou and Podgursky 1993; Conley, Muncey, and Gould 2002; Kerchner, Koppich, and Weeres 1998; Solomon 2004). Working from a national survey in 1987–88 in the United States, Ballou and Podgursky (1993) find that 55 percent of teachers are in favor of merit pay, that teachers of low-performing students are not less inclined toward merit pay than other teachers, and that teachers who themselves are part of a merit-pay system are, in general, more supportive of merit pay than teachers who may have never been a part of such a reform. They also find that attitudes toward merit pay are much more positive among private school teachers than those of public schools.

Solomon (2004) and Murillo and Maceira (2002) suggest that the critical challenge ahead is not to convince unions to support merit pay but rather to bring unions and other doubtful stakeholders to the table to design effective and fair compensation schemes. Conley, Muncey, and Gould's (2002) paper exploring the role of the American Federation of Teachers in the design of alternative pay structures in three U.S. cities offers concrete examples of how unions can remain central actors in pay schemes that include performance or skill-based incentives.

This trend in which unions are increasingly less hostile toward and more engaged in bargaining complex pay structures parallels a larger trend in which teacher unions, whose roots are in industrial unionism, are taking on more qualities of professional organizations (Bascia 1998; Conley, Muncey, and Gould 2002). Raelin (1989), in his analysis of unionism in the United States, suggests that unionization of professions, including the teaching profession, most typically is a response to, rather than a cause of, declines in occupational professionalism. Bascia (1998) discusses the involvement of teacher unions in education reform in the United States and Canada. Until the 1980s, teacher unions focused primarily on "bread and butter" issues like salary scales and work rules. Since then, however, unions are increasingly involved in more "educational" decisions, such as those involving education reform, pedagogy, teacher professionalization, and curriculum. She argues that two main factors have contributed to this evolving shift. The first is an effort on the part of the unions to improve their public image and to gain credibility and leverage. The second is the result of the natural evolution of unions from more basic (though not unimportant) concerns such as working conditions to deeper involvement in more aspects of education policy.

Summary and Conclusions

This chapter has offered a review of both the theoretical and empirical literature on education plans and reforms that alter the incentives that teachers face. It has attempted to articulate the main policy debates concerning incentives, as well as to look at broader education reforms in light of the incentives they create for teachers. The incentives within current education policies and practices, as well as future reforms and innovations, fundamentally affect who teaches and how they teach. Whether such incentives are specifically structured reforms that are designed to increase student achievement or to attract more promising young teachers, or whether they are unforeseen consequences of community management or fiscal policies, their effects on teachers must be carefully taken into account. This literature review has revealed not only that incentives are present throughout the educational system and that they have enormous consequences on the teaching profession, but also that teachers' logical behavioral responses are often quite different from those that policymakers had hoped for and analysts had predicted.

The fundamental question that remains, therefore, is how and whether incentive structures can be designed to support improved teacher quality and student learning and development. Several factors have important implications for the success or failure of incentive structures. These factors include the indicators that are used to measure performance and their relationship to the precise outcomes desired, the ways those indicators are measured, the understanding of those schemes and the evaluation of their fairness by the teachers themselves and the unions that represent them, the encouragement by the schemes for cooperation or competition among teachers, and the distance between the teachers and the bodies evaluating their work. As experiential and analytic understanding of teacher incentives grows, there is hope that stakeholders can come together to plan and implement reforms that can truly improve both teaching and learning in Latin American schools.

Delannoy, F., and G. Sedlacek. 2001. *Brazil: Teachers Development and Incentives: A Strategic Framework.* Washington, D.C.: World Bank.

Eberts, R. W., and J. A. Stone. 1984. *Unions and Public Schools: The Effect of Collective Bargaining and American Education.* Lexington, Mass.: Lexington Books.

Eberts, R. W., K. Hollenbeck, and J. A. Stone. 2002. "Teacher Performance Incentives and Student Outcomes." *Journal of Human Resources* 37: 913–27.

Eurydice. 2004. *The Teaching Profession in Europe: Profiles, Trends, and Concerns; Report IV: Keeping Teaching Attractive for the 21st Century—General Lower Secondary Education.* Brussels.

Figlio, D. N. 1997. "Teacher Salaries and Teacher Quality." *Economics Letters* 55: 267–71.

Figlio, D. N., and J. Winicki. 2002. "Food for Thought: The Effects of School Accountability Plans on School Nutrition." NBER Working Paper 9319. National Bureau of Economic Research, Cambridge, Mass.

Fuller, B., and P. Clark 1994. "Raising School Effects While Ignoring Culture? Local Conditions and the Influence of Classroom Tools, Rules, and Pedagogy." *Review of Education Research* 64(1): 119–57.

Fuller, B. and M. Rivarola. 1998. "Nicaragua's Experiment to Decentralize Schools: Views of Parents, Teachers and Directors." Working Paper on Impact Evaluation of Education Reforms 5. World Bank, Washington, D.C.

Glewwe, P. 2002. "Schools and Skills in Developing Countries: Education Policies and Socioeconomic Outcomes." *Journal of Economic Literature* 40(2): 436–82.

Glewwe, P., and M. Kremer. Forthcoming. "Schools, Teachers, and Education Outcomes in Developing Countries." In E. Hanushek and F. Welch, eds., *Handbook on the Economics of Education.* Amsterdam: North-Holland.

Glewwe, P., N. Ilias, and M. Kremer. 2003. "Teacher Incentives." NBER Working Paper 9671. National Bureau of Economic Research, Cambridge, Mass.

Goldhaber, D., and E. Anthony. 2004. "Can Teacher Quality Be Effectively Assessed?" CRPE Working Paper. Center on Reinventing Public Education, University of Washington, Seattle.

Goldhaber, D., D. Brewer, and D. Anderson, 1999. "A Three-Way Error Components Analysis of Educational Productivity." *Education Economics* 7(3): 199–208.

Government of Chile. 2003. *Attracting, Developing, and Retaining Effective Teachers: OECD Activity, Country Background Report for Chile.* Santiago.

Guarino, C., L. Santibáñez, G. Daley, and D. Brewer. 2004. "A Review of the Research Literature on Teacher Recruitment and Retention." Technical Report 164-EDU. RAND, Los Angeles.

Gunnarson, V., P. Orazem, M. Sánchez, and A. Verdisco. 2004. "Does School Decentralization Raise Student Outcomes? Theory and Evidence on the Roles of School Autonomy and Community Participation." Department of Economics Working Paper 04005. Iowa State University, Ames.

Hanushek, E. A. 1986. "The Economics of Schooling: Production and Efficiency in Public Schools." *Journal of Economic Literature* 24(3): 1141–77.

———. 1995. "Interpreting Recent Research on Schooling in Developing Countries." *World Bank Research Observer* 10(2): 227–46.

———. 2002. "The Failure of Input-Based Schooling Policies." NBER Working Paper 9040. National Bureau of Economic Research, Cambridge, Mass.

———. 2003. "The Failure of Input-Based Schooling Policies." *Economic Journal* 113: F64–F98.

Hanushek, E. A., J. Kain, and S. Rivkin. 2001. "Why Public Schools Lose Teachers." NBER Working Paper 8599. National Bureau of Economic Research, Cambridge, Mass.

Hanushek, E. A., J. F. Kain, D. M. O'Brien, and S. G. Rivkin. 2004. "The Market for Teacher Quality." (preliminary version). Paper prepared for the American Economics Association meetings, Philadelphia, January 6–8, 2005.

Heckman, J., C. Heinrich, and J. Smith. 2002. "The Performance of Performance Standards." *Journal of Human Resources* 37: 778–811.

Heneman, H. 1997. "Assessment of the Motivational Reactions of Teachers to a School-Based Performance Award Program." Paper presented at the American Educational Research Association Annual Conference, Chicago, March 24–28.

Holmström, B., and P. Milgrom. 1991. "Multitask Principal–Agent Analyses: Incentive Contracts, Asset Ownership, and Job Design." *Journal of Law, Economics, and Organization* 7: 24–51.

Hoxby, C. M. 1996. "How Teachers' Unions Affect Education Production." *Quarterly Journal of Economics* 111(3): 671–718.

———. 2002. "Would School Choice Change the Teaching Profession?" *Journal of Human Resources* 37: 846–91.

Hoxby, C. M., and A. Leigh. 2003. "Pulled Away or Pushed Out? Explaining the Decline of Teacher Aptitude in the United States." Available at http://post.economics.harvard.edu/faculty/hoxby/papers/hoxbyleigh_pulledaway.pdf.

Hsieh, C.-T., and M. Urquiola. 2003. "When Schools Compete, How Do They Compete? An Assessment of Chile's Nationwide School Voucher Program." NBER Working Paper 10008. National Bureau of Economic Research, Cambridge, Mass.

Ingersoll, R. 2003. *Out-of-Field Teaching and the Limits of Teacher Policy.* Seattle, Wash.: Center for the Study of Teaching and Policy.

Jacob, B. A., and L. Lefgren. 2004. "The Impact of Teacher Training on Student Achievement: Quasi-Experimental Evidence from School Reform Efforts in Chicago." *Journal of Human Resources* 39(1): 50–79.

Jacob, B. A., and S. D. Levitt. 2002. "Rotten Apples: An Investigation of the Prevalence and Predictors of Teacher Cheating." NBER Working Paper 9413. National Bureau of Economic Research, Cambridge, Mass.

Jacobson, S. 1989. "The Effects of Pay Incentives on Teacher Absenteeism." *Journal of Human Resources* 24(2): 280–86.

Jimenez, E., and Y. Sawada. 2003. "Does Community Management Help Keep Kids in School? Evidence Using Panel Data from El Salvador's EDUCO Program." Discussion Paper CIRJE-F-236. Center for International Research on the Japanese Economy, Tokyo.

Kane, T. J., and D. O. Staiger. 2001. "Improving School Accountability Measures." NBER Working Paper 8156. National Bureau of Economic Research, Cambridge, Mass.

Kerchner, C. T., J. E. Koppich, and J. G. Weeres. 1998. *Taking Charge of Quality*. San Francisco: Jossey-Bass.

Kimball, S., H. Heneman, and E. Kellor. 2003. "Pensions for Teachers: Possible Changes and Implications." Consortium for Policy Research in Education Working Paper TC-03-09. University of Wisconsin, Madison.

King, E., L. Rawlings, B. Ozler, P. Callejas, N. Gordon, N. Mayorga de Caldera, W. López, R. López, Z. López, and Adolfo Huete. 1996. "Nicaragua's School Autonomy Reform: A First Look." Impact Evaluation of Education Reforms Working Paper 1. World Bank, Washington, D.C.

Kingdon, G., and F. Teal. 2002. "Does Performance-Related Pay for Teachers Improve Student Performance? Some Evidence from India." Working Paper 165. Center for the Study of African Economies, Oxford, U.K.

Kohn, A. 1993. *Punished by Rewards: The Trouble with Gold Stars, Incentive Plans, A's, Praise, and Other Bribes*. Boston: Houghton Mifflin.

Koretz, D. 2002. "Limitations in the Use of Achievement Tests as Measures of Educators' Productivity." *Journal of Human Resources* 37: 752–77.

Lakdawalla, D. 2001. "The Declining Quality of Teachers." NBER Working Paper 8263. National Bureau of Economic Research, Cambridge, Mass.

Lankford, H., S. Loeb, and J. Wyckoff. 2002. "Teacher Sorting and the Plight of Urban Schools: A Descriptive Analysis." *Education Evaluation and Policy Analysis* 24(1): 37–62.

Lavy, V. 2002. "Evaluating the Effect of Teachers' Group Performance Incentives on Pupil Achievement." *Journal of Political Economy* 110(6): 1286–317.

———. 2003. "Paying for Performance: The Effect of Teachers' Financial Incentives." Discussion Paper 3862. Center for Economic Policy Research, Washington, D.C.

———. 2004. "Performance Pay and Teachers' Effort, Productivity, and Grading Ethics." NBER Working Paper 10622. National Bureau of Economic Research, Cambridge, Mass.

Lee, J.-H., and K.-J. You. 2000. "The Political Economy of Linear Earnings Profile for Teachers in Korea." Korea Development Institute, Seoul. Processed.

Liang, X. 1999. "Teacher Pay in 12 Latin American Countries: How Does Teacher Pay Compare to Other Professions, What Determines Teacher Pay, and Who Are the Teachers?" Latin America and the Caribbean Region Human Development Department Paper 49. World Bank, Washington, D.C.

Loeb, S., and M. Page. 2000. "Examining the Link between Teacher Wages and Student Outcomes: The Importance of Alternative Labor Market Opportunities and Non-pecuniary Variation." *Review of Economics and Statistics* 82: 393–408.

Loeb, S., and M. Reininger. 2004. *Public Policy and Teacher Labor Markets.* East Lansing, Mich.: Education Policy Center at Michigan State University.

López-Acevedo, G. 2002. "Teachers' Incentives and Professional Development in Schools in Mexico." Policy Research Working Paper 2777. World Bank, Washington, D.C.

———. 2004. "Teachers' Salaries and Professional Profile in México." Policy Research Working Paper 3394. World Bank, Washington, D.C.

Loveless, T. 2000. *Conflicting Missions? Teachers Unions and Educational Reform.* Washington, D.C.: Brookings Institution.

McCaffrey, D., J. R. Lockwood, D. Koretz, and L. Hamilton. 2003. *Evaluating Value-Added Models for Teacher Accountability.* Santa Monica, Calif.: RAND.

McEwan, P. 2001. "The Effectiveness of Public, Catholic, and Non-religious Private Schools in Chile's Voucher System." *Education Economics* 9: 103–28.

McGinn, N., and T. Welsh. 1999. *Decentralization of Education: Why, When, What, and How?* Paris: United Nations Educational, Scientific, and Cultural Organization.

Michaelowa, K. 2002. "Teacher Job Satisfaction, Student Achievement, and the Cost of Primary Education in Francophone Sub-Saharan Africa." Hamburgisches Welt-Wirtschafts Archiv Discussion Paper 188. Hamburg Institute of International Economics, Hamburg, Germany.

Mizala, A., and P. Romaguera. 2000. "School Performance and Choice: The Chilean Experience." *Journal of Human Resources* 35(2): 392–417.

Morduchowicz, A. 2002. *Carreras, incentivos y estructura salariales, docentes.* Buenos Aires: Programa de Reforma Educativa en América Latina.

Murillo, M. V., ed. 2002. *Carreras magisteriales, desempeño educativo y sindicato de maestros en América Latina.* Buenos Aires: Facultad Latino-Americana de Ciencias Sociales.

Murillo, M. V., and D. Maceira. 2002. "Markets, Organizations, and Politics: Social Sector Reform and Labor in Latin America." Yale University, New Haven, Conn. Processed.

Murillo, M. V., M. Tommasi, L. Ronconi, and J. Sanguinetti. 2002. *The Economic Effects of Unions in Latin America: Teachers' Unions and Education in Argentina.* Washington, D.C.: Inter-American Development Bank.

Murnane, R. J., and D. K. Cohen. 1986. "Merit Pay and the Evaluation Problem: Why Most Merit Pay Plans Fail and a Few Survive." *Harvard Education Review* 56: 3–17.

Murnane, R. J., J. Singer, J. Willet, J. Kemple, and R. Olsen. 1991. *Who Will Teach? Policies That Matter.* Cambridge, Mass.: Harvard University Press.

Odden, A., and C. Kelley. 1997. *Paying Teachers for What They Know and Do.* Thousand Oaks, Calif.: Corwin Press.

OECD (Organisation for Economic Co-operation and Development). 2001. *Knowledge and Skills for Life: First Results from the OECD Programme for International Student Assessment (PISA) 2000.* Paris.

————. 2003. *Literacy Skills for the World of Tomorrow: Further Results from PISA 2000.* Paris.

Park, A., and E. Hannum. 2001. "Do Teachers Affect Learning in Developing Countries? Evidence from Matched Student–Teacher Data from China." Paper prepared for the conference on Rethinking Social Science Research on the Developing World in the 21st Century, Park City, Utah, June 7–11.

Porter, A., P. Youngs, and A. Odden. 2001. "Advances in Teacher Assessment and Their Uses." In V. Richardson, ed., *Handbook of Research on Teaching.* 4th edition. Washington, D.C.: American Education Research Association, 259–97.

Prendergast, C. 1999. "The Provision of Incentives in Firms." *Journal of Economic Literature* 37 (March): 7–63.

Pritchett, L., and D. Filmer. 1997. "What Education Production Functions Really Show: A Positive Theory of Education Spending." Policy Research Working Paper 1795. World Bank, Washington, D.C.

Psacharopoulos, G., J. Valenzuela, and M. Arends. 1996. "Teacher Salaries in Latin America: A Review." *Economics of Education Review* 15(4): 401–6.

Raelin, J. A. 1989. "Unionization and Deprofessionalization: Which Comes First?" *Journal of Organizational Behavior* 10(2): 101–15.

Rice, J. 2003. *Teacher Quality: Understanding the Effectiveness of Teacher Attributes.* Washington, D.C.: Economic Policy Institute.

Rivkin, S. G., E. A. Hanushek, and J. F. Kain. 1998. "Teachers, Schools, and Academic Achievement." NBER Working Paper 6691. National Bureau of Economic Research, Cambridge, Mass.

Rockoff, J. 2004. "The Impact of Individual Teachers on Student Achievement: Evidence from Panel Data." *American Economic Review* 94(2): 247–57.

Ross, S. 1973. "The Economic Theory of Agency: The Principal's Problem." *American Economic Review* 63(2): 134–39.

Sanders, W., and J. Rivers. 1996. *Cumulative and Residual Effects of Teachers on Future Student Academic Achievement.* Knoxville: University of Tennessee Value-Added Research and Assessment Center. Available at http://www.heartland.org/pdf/21803.

Santibáñez, L. 2002. "¿Están los maestros en México mal pagados? Estimado de los salarios relativos del magisterio." *Revista Latinoamericana de Estudios Educativos* 32(2): 9–41.

Sawada, Y. 2003. "Community Participation, Teacher Effort, and Educational Outcomes in a Developing Country." University of Tokyo Graduate School of Economics, Tokyo. Processed.

Solomon, L. 2004. "What's Fair about Performance Pay?" *Phi Delta Kappan* (January): 407–8.

Tatto, M. T. 1997. "Limits and Constraints to Effective Teacher Education." In W. Cummings and N. McGinn, eds., *International Handbook of Education and Development*. Oxford, U.K.: Pergamon.

———. 2002. "The Value and Feasibility of Evaluation Research on Teacher Development: Contrasting Experiences in Sri Lanka and Mexico." *International Journal of Educational Development* 22(6): 637–57.

Temin, P. 2002. "Teacher Quality and the Future of America." NBER Working Paper 8891. National Bureau of Economic Research, Cambridge, Mass.

UNESCO (United Nations Educational, Scientific, and Cultural Organization). 1998. *First International Comparative Study of Language, Mathematics, and Associated Factors in Third and Fourth Grades*. Santiago.

Vegas, E. 2000. "Teachers in Brazil: Who Are They and How Well Do They Fare in the Labor Market?" Harvard Graduate School of Education, Cambridge, Mass. Processed.

———. 2002. "School Choice, Student Performance, and Teacher and Student Characteristics: The Chilean Case." Washington, D.C.: World Bank.

Velez, E., E. Schiefelbein, and J. Valenzuela. 1993. "Factors Affecting Achievement in Primary Education." Human Capital Working Paper 12186. World Bank, Washington, D.C.

Villegas-Reimers, E. 1998. "The Preparation of Teachers in Latin America: Challenges and Trends." Latin America and the Caribbean Region Human Development Department Paper 15. World Bank, Washington, D.C.

Villegas-Reimers, E., and F. Reimers. 1996. "Where Are 60 Million Teachers? The Missing Voice in Educational Reforms around the World." *Prospects* 26(3): 469–92.

Waterreus, J. 2003. "Lessons in Teacher Pay: Studies on Incentives and the Labor Market for Teachers." Doctoral dissertation, University of Amsterdam, Netherlands. Processed.

Wils, A., and R. O'Connor. 2004. "Teachers Matter: Teachers Supply as a Constraint on the Global Education Agenda." Working Paper 04-01. Education Policy and Data Center, Washington, D.C.

World Bank. 2001. *Brazil Teachers Development and Incentives: A Strategic Framework*. Washington, D.C.

Wright, S. P., S. Horn, and W. Sanders. 1997. "Teacher and Classroom Context Effects of Student Achievement: Implications for Teacher Evaluation." *Journal of Personnel Evaluation in Education* 11: 57–67.

Youngs, P., A. Odden, and A. Porter. 2003. "State Policy Related to Teacher Licensure." *Educational Policy* 17(2): 217–36.

Zegarra, E., and R. Ravina. 2003. "Teacher Unionization and the Quality of Education in Peru: An Empirical Evaluation Using Survey Data." Research Network Working Paper R-474. Inter-American Development Bank, Washington, D.C.

3

Are Teachers Well Paid in Latin America and the Caribbean?
Relative Wage and Structure of Returns of Teachers

Werner Hernani-Limarino
University of Pennsylvania

Education is the output of a complex production process. Teachers' value added to this process is directly related to the person's overall quality. In turn, teachers' quality is determined by what kinds of people are attracted to the profession, what incentives they have to perform on the job, and whether high-ability teachers will stay. Whether teachers are well paid is, arguably, the most important determinant of recruitment, performance, and retention.

This chapter analyzes whether teachers in Latin America and the Caribbean are well paid. Although the general perception is that the teachers are underpaid, empirical research suggests that this may not be the case, at least in some countries. Psacharopoulos, Valenzuela, and Arends (1996) use 1989 household survey data from 12 Latin American countries to compare teachers' average wages with those of public and private sector employees above 15 years old, excluding agricultural workers. Their results show that teachers receive lower wages than do other employees in Argentina, Bolivia, Brazil, Peru, and Uruguay (21 percent lower on average), whereas teachers in Chile, Colombia, Costa Rica, Ecuador, Honduras, Panama, and Venezuela receive higher wages (31 percent higher on average). They also report conditional wage differentials for Chile, where they find positive but not statistically significant wage differentials between teachers and nonteachers.

Liang (1999) uses 1995 and 1996 household survey data from 12 Latin American countries to calculate conditional wage differentials between teachers and employees who are in the formal sector, who are more than

Readers may send comments to whl@sas.upenn.edu.

15 years old, and who work more than 20 hours in the week of reference. Her results show that, once the differences for observed characteristics are accounted for, teachers in Colombia, Costa Rica, El Salvador, Honduras, Panama, Uruguay, and Venezuela receive higher wages than those of formal sector employees. Teachers in Brazil and Ecuador receive lower wages. The coefficients for Bolivia, Chile, and Paraguay were not statistically significant and were not reported.

Vegas, Experton, and Pritchett (1998) use data from the 1994 household survey from Argentina and the National Census of Teachers from the same year to show that more than a third of the teachers receive wages lower than wages they would receive in other occupations. Piras and Savedoff (1998) use the 1993 household survey from Bolivia to show that the wages of teachers are at least as high as the wages they would have received if working in other sectors of the labor market. Urquiola and others (2000) use the 1997 household survey from Bolivia to show that whether teachers are well paid depends on the comparison group, even when differences in observable characteristics are accounted for. Conditional wage differentials are favorable to teachers when they are compared with all other workers or with workers who are not self-employed. However, the differentials are not favorable to teachers when they are compared with employees who have completed at least a secondary education or with employees in office or technical occupations.

Mizala and Romaguera (2004) use 1998 and 2000 household surveys from Chile to show that, once differences in observed characteristics are accounted for, the wages of teachers are at least as high as the wages they would have received if working in other sectors of the labor market. Mulcahy-Dunn and Arcia (1996) use household survey data from Ecuador to show that teachers' wages are similar to those of other professionals with similar observed characteristics. Carnoy and McEwan (1997) use 1990 household survey data from Honduras to show that primary teachers would have received a wage premium of 32 percent in urban areas and of 19 percent in rural areas.

Grupo de Economistas y Asociados (1998) shows that, once differences in observable characteristics are accounted for, primary teachers in the Federal District of Mexico receive higher wages than 89 percent of the workers who have 13 to 15 years of schooling. López-Acevedo and Salinas (2000) use data from the Encuesta Nacional de Empleo Urbano (National Urban Employment Survey, or ENEU) of Mexico to show that conditional wage differentials are favorable to teachers. Santibáñez (2002) uses the 1998 ENEU of Mexico to calculate conditional wage differentials between teachers and public and private employees who work in office, administrative, technical, or professional occupations; who are above 12 years old; and who have at least 10 years of schooling. Her results show that teachers in the public sector receive higher wages after differences in observable characteristics are accounted for.

This chapter contributes to the earlier studies. First, it completes the sample of Latin American countries and, in most cases, updates the year of the survey used in the analysis.[10] Second, it examines the robustness of conditional wage differentials when compared to the methods used and to the definition of the control group. A complete and updated sample might be useful to get a better picture of teachers' relative wage, given that teachers' average wages had increased significantly during the 1990s. The Economic Commission for Latin America and the Caribbean (ECLAC 1999) shows that, during this period, teachers' average wages have increased between 3 percent and 9 percent in Bolivia, Brazil, Chile, Costa Rica, Ecuador, Panama, Paraguay, and Uruguay. A robustness analysis might also be useful to determine whether we can rely on conditional wage differentials when studying whether teachers are well paid. As Urquiola and others (2000) note, the sensitivity of the sign and the magnitude of the teachers' wage differential shown next to alternative definitions of the comparison group may suggest important selection biases. At the least, important differences in unobserved characteristics appear that are not accounted for in conventional conditional wage differentials.

The structure of the chapter is as follows. The next section describes the methods used to determine whether teachers are well paid, as well as the data and the definition of teachers and comparison groups. The following section presents the results. The final section concludes the study.

How Can We Determine If Teachers Are Well Paid?

Recruitment, performance, and retention of teachers are directly related to their opportunity cost. In most papers, the definition of *opportunity cost* is restricted to the wage teachers would receive in an alternative occupation. However, it is important to note that this definition leaves out many other factors that may also affect the type of people who are attracted to the profession, the incentives they have to perform on the job, and the likelihood that high-ability teachers will stay.

Hours Worked and Nonmonetary Benefits

Wages are, arguably, the most important dimension of the labor contract, but they are not the only one. As noted in many of the public debates about teachers' salaries, many factors need to be considered to determine whether teachers are well paid. The stability of the job, the number of hours required at work, the flexibility of schedules, and all kinds of non-

---

10. My study excludes Guatemala from the analysis because the sample of teachers was too small in the Encuesta de Condiciones de Vida (National Survey of Living Conditions, or ENCOVI) and because there is not information about hours worked in the Encuesta de Ingresos y Gastos Familiares (National Survey on Family Income and Expenses, or ENIGFAM).

monetary benefits (such as vacations and in-kind payments) are also important dimensions of the labor contract.

Clearly, the sign and the magnitude of the teachers' relative wage will be sensitive to the inclusion or exclusion of those factors. For example, because teachers tend to work fewer hours than nonteachers (see figure 3.1), differences in monthly earnings will be less favorable to teachers than differences in hourly wages (see figure 3.2). Or as noted by Liang (1999), because teachers have longer vacations, the differences in vacation-adjusted wages will be less favorable to teachers than the differences in unadjusted ones.

A broader definition of the opportunity cost may provide more information about whether teachers are well paid and about the magnitudes of compensating wage differentials between teachers and other professions. However, it is important to note that the broader the definition of opportunity cost, the more information we require about nonwage dimen-

Figure 3.1. Unconditional Log Hourly Wage and Monthly Earnings Differential

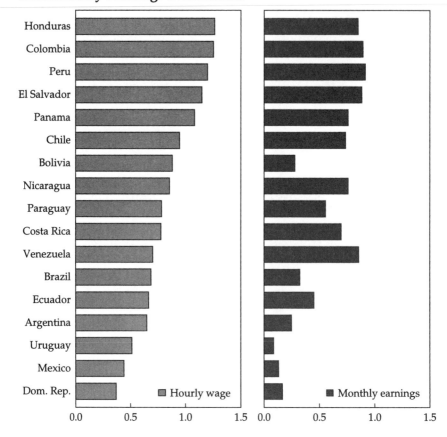

Figure 3.2. Hours Worked Per Week

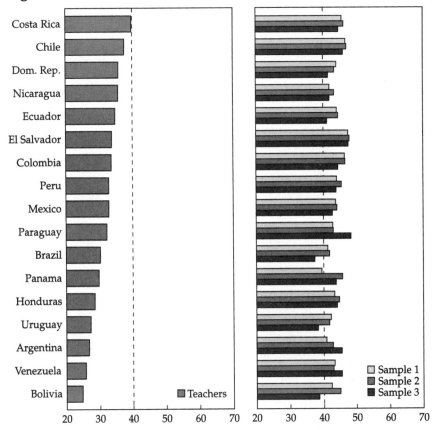

Note: Sample 1 includes all workers other than teachers who declared their labor earnings and hours worked. Sample 2 restricts sample 1 to those who have completed at least a secondary education. Sample 3 includes all workers other than teachers who are in office, technical, or professional occupations.

sions of the labor contract. For example, if we want to compare salaries adjusted by the length of vacations, we need to know not only the length of teachers' vacations but also the length of vacations for all members in the comparison group.

A broader definition of the opportunity cost may also complicate the analysis. For example, if we want to compare monthly earnings instead of wages, we should bear in mind that one part of the difference in earnings is due to differences in wages and another part is due to differences in labor supply. This chapter analyzes hourly wage differentials by taking labor supply as given and then excluding all types of nonmonetary benefits.

Wage Differentials

Once we restrict our definition of *teachers' opportunity cost* to the relative wage of teachers, the next step is to define how to estimate the wage that teachers would receive in an alternative occupation. In other words, how can we determine whether teachers are well paid?

Gross (Unadjusted) Wage Differentials

One alternative for determining the teachers' opportunity cost is to compare gross wages of teachers and of nonteachers. Let $\underline{W}_T$ and $\underline{W}_N$ be the average hourly wage of teachers and of nonteachers, respectively. The proportional (average) wage differential between teachers and nonteachers will be given by

(3.1) $$G_{TN} = \left(\underline{W}_T / \underline{W}_N\right) - 1$$

which is approximately equal to the (average) log wage differential:

(3.2) $$G_{TN} \approx \ln(G_{TN} + 1) = \ln\left(\underline{W}_T\right) - \ln\left(\underline{W}_N\right)$$

Note that this measure is sensitive to the definition of the comparison group. Gross wage differentials between teachers and nonteachers reflect not only differences in the structure of returns, but also differences in productive endowments. Therefore, to use gross wage differentials as measures of teachers' opportunity cost, one must restrict the definition of the comparison group to individuals with similar productive endowments.

Conditional (Adjusted) Wage Differentials

In a competitive labor market, wages are equal to the value of the marginal product of labor. In other words, wages are a function of the worker's productive endowments and the returns (the prices) of those endowments in the labor market. Therefore, gross wage differentials reflect not only differences in productive endowments, but also differences in the structure of returns. Let $\underline{W}_{T0}$ and $\underline{W}_{N0}$ be the average wages that teachers and nonteachers, respectively, would receive if both groups faced the same structure of returns to their productive endowments (that is, if there were no price differences between the education sector and the nonteachers' labor market). The productivity (average) wage differential—the part of the (average) gross wage differential that can be attributed to differences in endowments—will be given by

(3.3) $$Q_{TN} = \left(\underline{W}_{T0} / \underline{W}_{N0}\right) - 1$$

Therefore, the conditional (average) wage differential—the part that can be attributed to a different structure of returns—will be given by the difference between the gross and the productivity wage differentials:

(3.4) $$D_{TN} = [(\underline{W}_T/\underline{W}_N) - (\underline{W}_{T0}/\underline{W}_{N0})]/(\underline{W}_{T0}/\underline{W}_{N0})$$

Using equations 3.1, 3.3, and 3.4, one can decompose the gross wage differential as

(3.5) $$\ln(G_{TN} + 1) = \ln(Q_{TN} + 1) + \ln(D_{TN} + 1)$$

TEACHERS' WAGE PREMIUM. To estimate the conditional wage differential between teachers and nonteachers, one can assume that the relationship between wages, endowments, and prices takes this form:

(3.6) $$\ln(W) = T\delta + X\beta + \varepsilon$$

where X represents the productive endowments vector, β the market prices of those endowments, T a dummy variable for teachers, and δ the conditional (average) wage differential between teachers and nonteachers. To see equivalence more clearly, note that

(3.7) $$D_{TN} \approx \ln(D_{TN} + 1) = \ln(\underline{W}_T/\underline{W}_{T0}) - \ln(\underline{W}_N/\underline{W}_{N0}) = \delta$$

To obtain a consistent estimation of δ requires that

$$E[\varepsilon] = E[T\varepsilon] = E[X\varepsilon] = 0$$

In other words, the unobserved characteristics captured by the residual must be orthogonal to the decision to work as a teacher and to observed productive endowments. Otherwise, ordinary least squares (OLS) estimates of the conditional wage differential may be biased and inconsistent.

THE OAXACA DECOMPOSITION. An alternative method of estimating the conditional wage differential between teachers and nonteachers is to assume that the relationship between wages, endowments, and prices takes this form:

(3.8) $$\ln(W_i) = X_i\beta_i + \varepsilon_i$$

where $i = T, N$. Equation 3.8 assumes that teachers and nonteachers face a different structure of returns to their productive endowments. Using equation 3.8, one can decompose the (average) gross wage differential as follows:

(3.9) $$\ln(G_{TN} + 1) = \ln(Q_{TN} + 1) + \ln(D_{TN} + 1)$$
$$= (\underline{X}_T - \underline{X}_N)\beta_N + \underline{X}_T(\beta_T - \beta_N)$$

Equation 3.9 decomposes the gross wage differential in two components. The first term on the right-hand side captures the part that can be attributed to differences in the productive endowments—that is, an *endowment effect*. The second term on the right-hand side captures the part that can be attributed to differences in the structure of the returns of those endowments—that is, a *price effect*.

Whereas the price effect reveals the part of the wage differential that can be attributed to differences in the structure of returns between teachers and nonteachers, it does not reveal whether returns are higher in the education sector (that is, whether teachers are overpaid) or whether returns are lower in other sectors of the labor market (that is, whether nonteachers are underpaid). Conceptually, it is possible to further decompose the price effect to make the contribution of those two factors explicit.

Using equation 3.4, one can define a *favoritism effect* (δ_{T0}) as the difference between the (average) wage that teachers receive and the wage they would receive in a competitive labor market as follows:

(3.10)
$$\delta_{T0} = (W_T/W_{T0}) - 1$$

One can also define a *nondiscriminatory effect* as the difference between the (average) wage that non-teachers would receive in a competitive labor market and the wage they receive (δ_{0N}) as follows:

(3.11)
$$\delta_{0N} = (W_{N0}/W_N) - 1$$

Hence, the price effect can be decomposed further into

(3.12)
$$\ln(D_{TN} + 1) = \ln(W_T/W_{T0}) + \ln(W_{N0}/W_N)$$
$$= \ln(\delta_{T0} + 1) + \ln(\delta_{0N} + 1)$$

Replacing equation 3.12 into equation 3.9 results in

(3.13)
$$\ln(G_{TN} + 1) = \ln(Q_{TN} + 1) + \ln(\delta_{T0} + 1) + \ln(\delta_{0N} + 1)$$
$$= (\underline{X}_T - \underline{X}_N)\beta^* \underline{X}_T(\beta_T - \beta^*) + \underline{X}_N(\beta^* - \beta_N)$$

where β^* are the competitive prices (that is, the market prices that would prevail if both teachers and nonteachers faced the same structure of returns).[11]

Equation 3.13 identifies the three components of the (average) gross wage differential: (a) a *productivity effect*—that is, the wage differential that can be attributed to differences in productive endowments evaluated at market prices; (b) a *favoritism effect*—that is, the wage differential that can be attributed to a better structure of returns for teachers; and (c) a *nondiscriminatory effect*—that is, the part of the wage differential that can be attributed to worst structure of returns for nonteachers.

---

11. The market structure of returns is usually estimated using the pooled sample to estimate equation 3.8. See Oaxaca and Ransom (1994).

As before, a key assumption for consistent estimates of the structure of returns for teachers and nonteachers is that

(3.14) $$E[\varepsilon_i] = E[X_i\varepsilon_i] = 0$$

where $i = T, N$.

Accounting for Unobserved Heterogeneity

The presence of unobserved heterogeneity not only may bias the estimated structure of returns, but also may affect the magnitude and the sign of the teachers' wage differential. The methods described in the previous section are useful in calculating average wage differentials; however, averages are not informative of the situation at other parts of the distribution. The fact that average teachers are well paid does not imply that all teachers are well paid.

To see this point more clearly, note that among the factors picked up by the residual in equation 3.8, there will typically be, in addition to the usual purely random component (u), the unobserved productivity components (φ):

(3.15) $$\ln(W_i) = X_i\beta_i + \varphi_i + u_i$$

where $i = T, N$.

These unobserved productivity factors are important because they usually account for more than half of the variation in wages, as measured by the R squared coefficient. In the presence of unobserved heterogeneity, it is possible for the conditional wage differentials to be biased even when such heterogeneity is not related to the observed productive endowments. If wages are determined according to equation 3.15, then gross wage differentials will be given by

(3.16) $$\ln(G_{TN} + 1) = (X_T - X_N)\beta_N + X_T(\beta_T - \beta_N) + (\varphi_T - \varphi_N)$$

where the last term on the right-hand side stands for both the differences in unobserved productivity endowments and their prices. Note that, when using OLS methods to estimate the parameters, this unobserved heterogeneity effect is constrained to be zero at the average. However, at all other quantiles of the conditional wage distribution, this effect may be different from zero and may affect the magnitude and the sign of the teachers' wage differentials.

Although it is possible to compute the unobserved heterogeneity effect at different quantiles, it is not possible to distinguish the part that is due to differences in unobserved productivity endowments from the part that is due to differences in their returns. One alternative is to use quantile regressions to estimate a relationship that is between wages and observable endowments and that is conditional on the position of the individual in the conditional wage distribution (see Koenker and Bassett 1978). Thus,

$$(3.17) \qquad \ln(W_i) = X_i \beta_{\theta i} + \varepsilon_{\theta i}$$

where $i = T, N$. Because quantile regression constrains the residual of the θth quantile to be zero, so that $Q_\theta[\ln(W_i)] = X_i \beta_{\theta i}$, it allows us to compare teachers and nonteachers with the same level of unobserved productive endowments. For example, teachers who have unobserved characteristics and who situate their conditional wage expectation will compare themselves with nonteachers whose wage is also above their conditional wage expectation. In the same spirit of the Oaxaca decomposition, one can identify a productivity and a price effect by using the estimated coefficients of equation 3.17.

$$(3.18) \qquad Q_\theta[\ln(G_{TN} + 1)] = Q_\theta[\ln(Q_{TN} + 1)] + Q_\theta[\ln(D_{TN} + 1)]$$

$$= (X_T - X_N)\beta_{\theta N} + X_T(\beta_{\theta T} - \beta_{\theta N})$$

As this section illustrates, determining whether teachers are well paid is not straightforward. The analysis of wage differentials between teachers and nonteachers may be sensitive to the method used to calculate the wage between teachers and nonteachers. Another set of factors that may affect the results are (a) the source of the data, (b) the definition of teachers, and (c) the definition of the comparison group. As we see in the next three sections, all answers to the question of whether teachers are well paid depend on those three factors in a significant way.

The Data

Almost all papers that estimate teachers' relative wages rely on household surveys to obtain data on labor earnings, hours worked, and other sociodemographic characteristics. This chapter is not an exception. Table 3.1 describes the countries, years, and geographic coverage of the household surveys used for the analysis.

It is important to note that the teachers' relative wage and the structure of returns obtained from one type of household survey may be different from similar information obtained from other sources of information. For example, women's average wages are 12 percent higher than men's in the survey data, but they are only 1 percent higher in the payroll data. Wages of teachers living in rural areas are 8 percent lower than those of teachers living in urban areas in the survey data, whereas they are 16 percent higher in the payroll data. Finally, all observable characteristics included in the regression account for 20 percent of the variation

Table 3.1. Household Surveys

Country	Year	Executing agency	Survey name	Geographic coverage
Argentina	2000	INDEC	Encuesta Permanente de Hogares (EPH)	Urban
Bolivia	1997	INE	Encuesta Nacional de Empleo (ENE)	National
Brazil	2001	IBGE	Pesquisa Nacional por Amostra de Domicilios (PNAD)	National
Chile	2000	INE	Encuesta Nacional del Empleo (ENE)	Urban
Colombia	2000	DNP	Encuesta Continua de Hogares	National
Costa Rica	2000	DGEC	Encuesta Permanente de Hogares de Propositos Multiples (EHPM)	National
Dom. Rep.	1998	BCRD	Encuesta Nacional de Fuerza de Trabajo	National
Ecuador	2001	INEC	Encuesta Periodica de Empleo y Desempleo (EPED)	National
El Salvador	2001	DGEC	Encuesta de Hogares de Propositos Multiples (EHPM)	National
Honduras	2001	DGEC	Encuesta Permanente de Hogares de Propositos Multiples (EPHPM)	National
Mexico	2000	INEGI	Encuesta Nacional de Ingreso-Gasto de los Hogares (ENIGH)	National
Nicaragua	2001	INEC	Encuesta Nacional de Hogares sobre Medicion de Niveles de Vida (EMN)	National
Panama	2000	DEC	Encuesta de Hogares (EH)	National
Paraguay	2000	DGEEC	Encuesta Permanente de Hogares (EPH)	National
Peru	2000	CUANTO	Encuesta Nacional de Hogares sobre Medicion de Niveles de Vida (ENN)	National
Uruguay	1999	INE	Encuesta Continua de Hogares (ECH)	Urban
Venezuela	1998	OCEI	Encuesta de Hogares por Muestreo (EHM)	National

in teachers' wages in the survey data, but they account for 60 percent of the variation in the payroll data.

In addition, one should be extremely careful when making international comparisons using household survey data, especially when using income data. Household surveys usually differ in sample design among countries.

Table 3.1 shows that at least three different types of surveys were used in the analysis: employment surveys, Living Standards Measurement Surveys (LSMS), and income and expenditure surveys. There are also important differences in the definition of the variables, especially with respect to income, when the sources and periods of reference are very heterogeneous. Finally, there are obvious differences in the quality of household surveys.

The Definition of Teachers

Who is included in the definition of *teachers* may also affect the estimated relative wage. Some authors have found significant differences between the relative wages of primary teachers and those of compared to secondary teachers (see Psacharopoulos, Valenzuela, and Arends 1996). To define who are teachers, I used the declared occupation in the primary job. In most countries, I included in the definition of teachers those who were working in preschool, primary, or secondary education. In the cases of Argentina, Colombia, and Mexico, I also included those who were working in special, technical, or higher education. Table 3.2 describes the categories included in the definition of teachers for each country. Table 3.3 shows the size of the teacher sample for each country.

The Definition of the Comparison Group

Who is included in the comparison group may also affect the estimated relative wage. Conditional wage differentials account for differences only in observed productive endowments. They do not account for differences in all productive endowments. The definition of the comparison group is important because of the presence of unobserved heterogeneity. To test the sensitivity of the conditional wage differentials to the definition of the comparison group, I used three different samples of nonteachers. Table 3.4 describes them.

Are Teachers Well Paid?

In this section, we analyze how well teachers are paid relative to comparable workers. First, we explore wage differentials between these two groups of workers, and second, we evaluate differences in the salary structures of teachers and nonteachers.

Wage Differentials

Gross Wage Differentials
Figure 3.3 and table 3.5 present the gross wage differentials between teachers and different samples of nonteachers. The results show that the sign

Table 3.2. Occupational Codes Included in the Definition of Teachers

Country	Code	Description
Argentina	441	Trabajadores de la educación, de calificación profesional
	442	Trabajadores de la educación, de calificación técnica
	443	Trabajadores de la educación, de calificación operativa
	449	Trabajadores de la educación, de calificación ignorada
Bolivia	332	Profesores de enseñanza de ciclo medio
	333	Profesores de enseñanza de ciclo intermedio
	334	Profesores de enseñanza de ciclo basico
	335	Profesores de enseñanza pre-escolar
Brazil	213	Professor de ensino do segundo grau
	214	Professor de ensino do primeiro grau (de quinta a oitava serie)
	215	Professor de ensino do primeiro grau (de primeira a quarta serie)
	216	Professor de ensino do primeiro grau (sem especificação de serie)
	217	Professor de ensino pre-escolar
Chile	OF	Profesor de enseñanza media o secundaria
	OG	Profesor de enseñanza básica primaria
Colombia	13	Profesores de universidades y otros centros de educación superior
		Profesores de colegios, escuelas y demás centros de educación formal y no formal
Costa Rica	61	Profesores de enseñanza media, académica, técnica y comercial
	62	Maestros de enseñanza primaria
	63	Maestros de enseñanza preescolar
Dom. Rep.	232	Profesores de la enseñanza secundaria
	233	Maestros de nivel superior de la enseñanza primaria y preescolar
	332	Maestros de nivel meido de la enseñanza preescolar
	333	Maestros de nivel medio de la enseñanza especial
	334	Otros maestros e instructores de nivel medio
Ecuador	232	Profesores de la enseñanza secundaria
	233	Maestros de nivel superior de la enseñanza primaria y preescolar
	331	Maestros de nivel medio de la enseñanza primaria
	332	Maestros de nivel medio de la enseñanza preescolar

(Continued)

Table 3.2. Occupational Codes Included in the Definition of Teachers (*Continued*)

Country	Code	Description
El Salvador	232	Profesores de la enseñanza secundaria
	233	Maestros de nivel superior de la enseñanza primaria y preescolar
	331	Maestros de nivel medio de la enseñanza primaria
	332	Maestros de nivel medio de la enseñanza preescolar
Honduras	1228	Director o subdirector de Colegio, Escuela
	1231	Maestro de Colegio
	1249	Maestro de Escuela Primaria
	1250	Supervisores y similares Educación Primaria
	1273	Maestro de Enseñanza Preescolar
	1274	Supervisores y similares Educación Preescolar
Mexico	13	Trabajadores en la educación
Nicaragua	232	Profesores de la enseñanza secundaria
	233	Maestros de nivel superior de la enseñanza primaria y preescolar
	331	Maestros de nivel medio de la enseñanza primaria
	332	Maestros de nivel medio de la enseñanza preescolar
Panama	189–199	Profesores de Escuelas Secundarias y Vocacionales
	200–207	Profesores y Maestros de Enseñanza Primaria y Parvularia
Paraguay	360–370	Profesor de Escuelas Secundarias y Vocacionales
	380–387	Profesores y Maestros de Enseñanza Primaria y Parvularia
Peru	242	Profesores de educacion secundaria y basica
	243	Profesores y/o maestros de primaria
	244	Profesores de educacion inicial o pre-escolar
Uruguay	232	Profesores de la enseñanza secundaria
	233	Maestros titulados de la enseñanza primaria y preescolar
	331	Maestros no titulados de la enseñanza primaria
	332	Maestros no titulados de la enseñanza preescolar
Venezuela	5	Profesores y Maestros

of the unconditional wage differential depends on the definition of the comparison group. Note that when compared with all other workers in the labor market (sample 1), teachers receive higher average hourly wages in all countries analyzed. However, when teachers are compared with workers who have completed at least a secondary education (sample 2), the gross wage differential becomes favorable to nonteachers in Brazil, the Dominican Republic, and Nicaragua. When teachers are compared with

Table 3.3. Size of Teacher Sample

	Number of teachers	Percent of teachers (in employed pop.)
Argentina*	1,972	7.0
Bolivia	553	3.3
Brazil	4,719	2.8
Chile*	1,304	3.0
Colombia	2,138	3.8
Costa Rica	419	2.6
Dom. Rep.	346	4.1
Ecuador	578	2.2
El Salvador	349	2.7
Honduras	589	3.5
Mexico	198	1.2
Nicaragua	505	3.5
Panama	329	3.5
Paraguay	220	3.3
Peru	573	2.2
Uruguay*	783	3.3
Venezuela	1,355	4.8

Note: *Urban surveys.

Table 3.4. Alternative Definitions of Nonteachers

Comparison group	Categories included	Schooling levels included	Occupations included
Sample 1	All	All	All
Sample 2	All	At least complete secondary	All
Sample 3	All	All	Office; Technical/ Professional

Figure 3.3. Unconditional Log Wage Differential between Teachers and Different Samples of Nonteachers

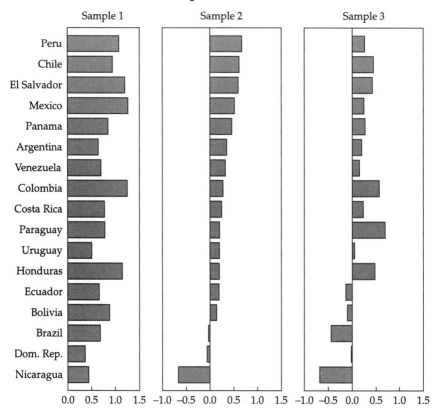

Note: Sample 1 includes all workers other than teachers who declared their labor earnings and hours worked. Sample 2 restricts sample 1 to those who have completed at least a secondary education. Sample 3 includes all workers other than teachers who are in office, technical, or professional occupations.

workers in office, technical, and professional occupations (sample 3), the gross wage differential also becomes favorable to nonteachers in Bolivia and Ecuador.

Notice that even for the countries where the sign of the gross wage differential is robust to the definition of the comparison group, the estimated magnitude is not. Teachers receive wages 93 percent higher than those of all other workers in the labor market (sample 1). However, the proportional gross wage differential decreases to 39 percent when teachers are compared with workers who have completed at least a secondary education (sample 2) and to 33 percent when teachers are compared with work-

Table 3.5. Unconditional Log Wage Differential between Teachers and Different Samples of Nonteachers: ln(GTN + 1)

Country	Sample 1	Sample 2	Sample 3
Argentina	0.65	0.35	0.20
Bolivia	0.88	0.14	−0.11
Brazil	0.69	−0.03	−0.44
Chile	0.95	0.62	0.44
Colombia	1.25	0.27	0.57
Costa Rica	0.77	0.24	0.23
Dom. Rep.	0.37	−0.06	−0.02
Ecuador	0.66	0.19	−0.14
El Salvador	1.20	0.59	0.42
Honduras	1.15	0.19	0.48
Mexico	1.26	0.52	0.24
Nicaragua	0.44	−0.66	−0.68
Panama	0.85	0.46	0.26
Paraguay	0.78	0.20	0.69
Peru	1.08	0.67	0.26
Uruguay	0.51	0.20	0.05
Venezuela	0.70	0.32	0.15

ers in office, technical, or professional occupations (sample 3). It is evident that the sign and magnitude of the estimated wage difference between teachers and nonteachers is affected by the choice of comparison group. Because significant differences in productive endowments exist between alternative definitions of nonteachers, gross wage differentials will tend to be higher when teachers are compared with workers with lower-productive endowments. Thus, gross wage differentials do not fully indicate whether teachers are well paid or not, although they may help us determine whether teachers' average wages are high or low relative to a specific group of workers. Recall that to determine whether teachers are well paid, one must compare their wages with those they would have received in other segments of the labor market. Can adjusted wage differentials help us answer this question?

Adjusted Wage Differentials: Teachers' Wage Premium

Figure 3.4 and table 3.6 present the adjusted wage differentials that are between teachers and different samples of nonteachers and were obtained from a regression of hourly wages on observed productive endowments (years of schooling and potential experience), socioeconomic factors (sex and place of residence), and a teachers' dummy. The results show that the sign and the magnitude of the conditional wage differential also depend on the definition of the comparison group.

In almost all countries (except Bolivia, Brazil, the Dominican Republic, and Nicaragua), the conditional wage differential is favorable to

Figure 3.4. Conditional Log Wage Differential between Teachers and Different Samples of Nonteachers: Estimated Coefficient for the Teachers' Dummy

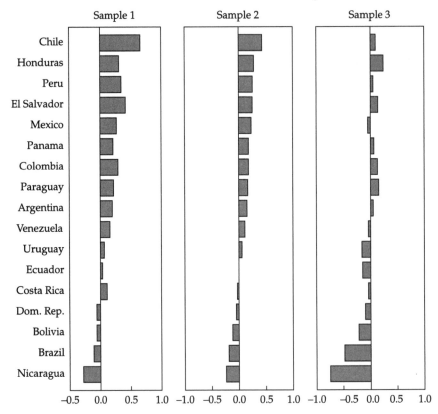

Note: Sample 1 includes all workers other than teachers who declared their labor earnings and hours worked. Sample 2 restricts sample 1 to those who have completed at least a secondary education. Sample 3 includes all workers other than teachers who are in office, technical, or professional occupations.

Table 3.6. Conditional Log Wage Differential between Teachers and Different Samples of Nonteachers: Estimated Price Effect from the Oaxaca Decomposition: E[ln(wT)\X] − E[ln(wN)\X]

Country	Sample 1	Sample 2	Sample 3
Argentina	0.21	0.16	0.05
Bolivia	−0.06	−0.12	−0.22
Brazil	−0.11	−0.19	−0.48
Chile	0.66	0.43	0.10
Colombia	0.30	0.18	0.13
Costa Rica	0.11	−0.03	−0.04
Dom. Rep.	−0.06	−0.05	−0.10
Ecuador	0.04	0.00	−0.15
El Salvador	0.42	0.26	0.14
Honduras	0.32	0.28	0.25
Mexico	0.28	0.23	−0.05
Nicaragua	−0.28	−0.24	−0.75
Panama	0.22	0.19	0.07
Paraguay	0.23	0.17	0.16
Peru	0.36	0.26	0.05
Uruguay	0.07	0.06	−0.16
Venezuela	0.16	0.11	−0.04

teachers when they are compared with all other workers in the labor market (sample 1). However, it becomes favorable to nonteachers in Costa Rica and both groups are equal in Ecuador when teachers are compared with workers who have completed at least a secondary education (sample 2). Moreover, it becomes favorable to nonteachers in Mexico, Uruguay, and Venezuela when teachers are compared with workers in office, technical, and professional occupations (sample 3). Thus, for 5 of the 17 countries analyzed, the answer to whether teachers are well paid depends on the definition of the comparison group, even when conditional wage differentials are used to control for differences in observable productive endowments.

For countries where the sign of the conditional wage differential is robust to the definition of the comparison group, the estimated magnitude is not. For Bolivia, Brazil, the Dominican Republic, and Nicaragua, the conditional wage differentials are favorable to nonteachers in all samples. However, on average, teachers earn 13 percent less when the comparison group includes all other workers in the labor market (sample 1). They earn 15 percent less when the comparison group includes workers who have completed at least a secondary education (sample 2) and 39 percent less when the comparison group includes workers in office, technical, or professional occupations (sample 3). For Argentina, Chile, Colombia, El Salvador, Honduras, Panama, Paraguay, and Peru conditional wage differentials are favorable to teachers in all samples. Nevertheless, on average, the estimated teachers' wage premium is 39 percent when the comparison group includes all other workers in the labor market (sample 1); 24 percent when it includes workers who have completed at least a secondary education (sample 2); and 12 percent when it includes workers in office, technical, or professional occupations (sample 3).

The fact that conditional wage differentials vary with the definition of the comparison group suggests that, even though we control for differences in observable productive endowments and socioeconomic characteristics, there are differences in unobserved characteristics between teachers and nonteachers that are related to the decision to work as a teacher and to other observed productive endowments.

Adjusted Wage Differentials: The Oaxaca Decomposition

The method described earlier allows us to decompose the gross wage differential into two components: (a) the part that can be attributed to differences in the productive endowments (that is, an *endowment effect*), and (b) the part that can be attributed to differences in the structure of returns of those endowments (that is, a *price effect*).

Figure 3.5 and table 3.7 present the part of the gross wage differential that can be attributed to differences in productive endowments. Notice that this measure accounts only for differences in observed productive endowments. The results show that, when teachers are compared to all other workers in the labor market (sample 1), they have better productive endowments in all countries, which account, on average, for 75 percent of the gross wage differential. When compared with workers who have completed at least a secondary education (sample 2), teachers have better productive endowments in 14 of the 17 countries (the Dominican Republic, Honduras, and Nicaragua are exceptions), which accounts for 50 percent of the gross wage differential. Finally, when compared with workers in office, technical, and professional occupations (sample 3), teachers have better productive endowments in 14 of the 17 countries (Brazil, Ecuador, and Nicaragua are exceptions), which accounts for 64 percent of the gross wage differential.

It is important to note that most of the productivity wage differential is due to differences in schooling levels. On average, teachers have between

Figure 3.5. Productivity Log Wage Differential between Teachers and Different Samples of Nonteachers: Estimated Endowment Effect from the Oaxaca Decomposition

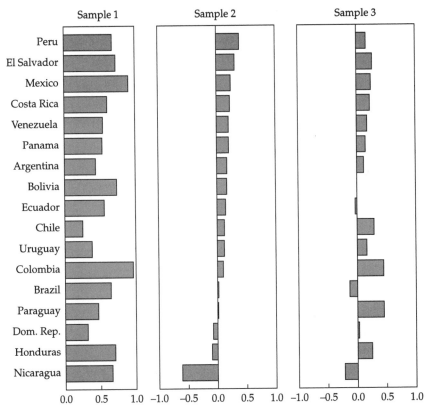

Note: Sample 1 includes all workers other than teachers who declared their labor earnings and hours worked. Sample 2 restricts sample 1 to those who have completed at least a secondary education. Sample 3 includes all workers other than teachers who are in office, technical, or professional occupations.

12 and 16 years of education, whereas all other workers in the labor market have between 5 and 10 years of education. Workers who have completed at least a secondary education have between 12 and 14 years of education, and workers in office, technical, and professional occupations have between 10 and 14 years of education.

Figure 3.6 and table 3.8 present the estimated conditional wage differential between teachers and different samples of nonteachers obtained from the Oaxaca decomposition (that is, the part of the gross wage differential that can be attributed to a different structure of returns). Notice that

Table 3.7. Conditional Log Wage Differential between Teachers and Different Samples of Nonteachers: Estimated Price Effect from the Oaxaca Decomposition: ln(DTN + 1)

Country	Sample 1	Sample 2	Sample 3
Argentina	0.21	0.18	0.08
Bolivia	0.14	−0.03	−0.11
Brazil	0.04	−0.05	−0.32
Chile	0.69	0.49	0.15
Colombia	0.29	0.17	0.12
Costa Rica	0.17	0.02	0.00
Dom. Rep.	0.05	0.02	−0.05
Ecuador	0.10	0.04	−0.11
El Salvador	0.47	0.28	0.15
Honduras	0.44	0.29	0.23
Mexico	0.35	0.27	0.00
Nicaragua	−0.23	−0.06	−0.46
Panama	0.32	0.26	0.12
Paraguay	0.32	0.19	0.24
Peru	0.40	0.28	0.09
Uruguay	0.13	0.08	−0.11
Venezuela	0.16	0.12	−0.03

this measure accounts only for differences in the returns to observed productive endowments.

The results show that the sign and the magnitude of the conditional wage differential depend on the definition of the comparison group. When teachers are compared with all other workers in the labor market (sample 1), the conditional wage differentials are favorable to teachers in all countries except Nicaragua. However, when teachers are compared with workers who have completed at least a secondary education (sample 2), conditional wage differentials become favorable to nonteachers in Brazil and Bolivia. When they are compared with workers in office, technical, and professional occupations (sample 3), the conditional wage differentials become zero or favorable to nonteachers in Costa Rica, the Dominican Republic, Ecuador, Uruguay, Venezuela, and Mexico. Therefore, for 8 of the 17 countries ana-

Figure 3.6. Conditional Log Wage Differential between Teachers and Different Samples of Nonteachers: Estimated Price Effect from the Oaxaca Decomposition

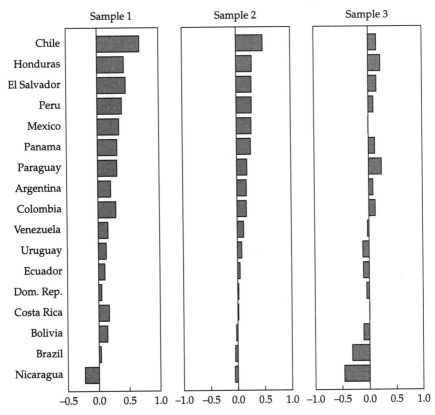

Note: Sample 1 includes all workers other than teachers who declared their labor earnings and hours worked. Sample 2 restricts sample 1 to those who have completed at least a secondary education. Sample 3 includes all workers other than teachers who are in office, technical, or professional occupations.

lyzed, the direction of the wage differential depends on the definition of the comparison group.

For the countries where the sign of the conditional wage differential does not change when the definition of the comparison group changes, the estimated magnitude is, however, affected by the definition of the comparison group. Although the conditional wage differential is favorable to nonteachers in all samples, in Nicaragua the magnitude of the differential varies with the comparison group. Teachers earn 23 percent less when the comparison group includes all other workers in the labor market (sample 1),

Table 3.8. Productivity Log Wage Differential between Teachers and Different Samples of Nonteachers: Estimated Endowment Effect from the Oaxaca Decomposition: ln(QTN + 1)

Country	Sample 1	Sample 2	Sample 3
Argentina	0.44	0.17	0.12
Bolivia	0.74	0.17	0.00
Brazil	0.65	0.02	−0.13
Chile	0.26	0.12	0.29
Colombia	0.96	0.10	0.45
Costa Rica	0.61	0.23	0.23
Dom. Rep.	0.32	−0.08	0.03
Ecuador	0.56	0.14	−0.03
El Salvador	0.73	0.31	0.27
Honduras	0.71	−0.10	0.25
Mexico	0.91	0.24	0.24
Nicaragua	0.67	−0.61	−0.22
Panama	0.53	0.20	0.15
Paraguay	0.47	0.02	0.46
Peru	0.68	0.39	0.16
Uruguay	0.38	0.12	0.17
Venezuela	0.54	0.21	0.18

6 percent less when the comparison group includes workers who have completed at least a secondary education (sample 2), and 46 percent less when the comparison group includes workers in office, technical, or professional occupations (sample 3). Conversely, although in Argentina, Chile, Colombia, El Salvador, Honduras, Panama, Paraguay, and Peru conditional wage differentials are favorable to teachers in all samples, the magnitude of the differential also varies with the comparison group. On average, after the differences in productive endowments are accounted for, teachers earn 39 percent more when the comparison group includes all other workers in the labor market (sample 1); 27 percent more when the comparison group includes workers who have completed at least a secondary education (sample 2); and 13 percent when the comparison group includes workers in office, technical, or professional occupations (sample 3).

Again, the fact that conditional wage differentials vary with the definition of the comparison group suggests that—even though one controls for differences in observable productive endowments and socioeconomic characteristics—there are differences in unobserved heterogeneity between teachers and nonteachers that are related to both the wages and the decision to work as a teacher.

In summary, when I combine my two estimates of the conditional wage differential, the results suggest that—after the differences in observed productive endowments are accounted for—teachers receive higher wages than nonteachers in Argentina, Chile, Colombia, El Salvador, Honduras, Panama, Paraguay, and Peru. They receive lower wages in Nicaragua. However, the sensitivity of the magnitudes of the conditional wage differentials to the alternative definitions of the comparison group also suggests that teachers are not a random sample of the population. Thus the estimates may be biased because of the presence of unobserved heterogeneity. In the cases of Bolivia, Brazil, Costa Rica, the Dominican Republic, Ecuador, Mexico, Uruguay, and Venezuela, it is not possible to determine whether teachers receive higher or lower wages without choosing a particular comparison group and method.

Differences in the Structure of Returns

The Oaxaca decomposition allows one not only to decompose the gross wage differential into an endowment and a price effect, but also to identify which returns explain most of the conditional wage differential: schooling, potential experience, women's wage premium, rural residence wage premium, or initial wage.

Returns to Schooling

Figure 3.7 shows how much the difference in the returns to schooling contributes to the conditional wage differential between teachers and different samples of nonteachers. In almost all countries, teachers' returns for an additional year of schooling are lower. When teachers are compared with all other workers in the labor market (sample 1), only Venezuela is an exception. When they are compared with workers who have completed at least a secondary education (sample 2), only Chile is an exception. When they are compared with workers in office, technical, or professional occupations (sample 3), only Venezuela is an exception. An additional year of schooling increases the wages of teachers by 5 percent on average, whereas it increases the wages of nonteachers by 8 percent to 14 percent, depending on the sample used.

It is important to note that, in most Latin American countries, significant differences exist in the character and quality of teachers' education compared with other types of higher education. Therefore, it may be inappropriate to

Figure 3.7. Contribution of the Difference in the Return to Schooling to the Conditional Log Wage Differential

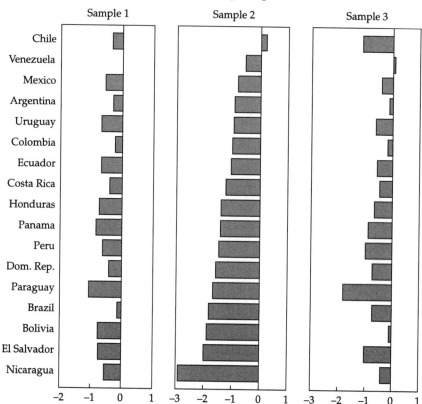

Note: Sample 1 includes all workers other than teachers who declared their labor earnings and hours worked. Sample 2 restricts sample 1 to those who have completed at least a secondary education. Sample 3 includes all workers other than teachers who are in office, technical, or professional occupations.

conclude that teachers would receive better returns for their education in other sectors of the labor market.

Potential Experience
Figure 3.8 shows how much the difference in returns to 5 years of potential experience contributes to the conditional wage differential between teachers and different samples of nonteachers. The results reveal that, in the cases of El Salvador, Honduras, Nicaragua, Paraguay, and Peru, teachers' expected wage growth after 5 years is higher compared with that of all other workers in the labor market (sample 1); with that of workers who

Figure 3.8. Contribution of the Difference in the Returns to Potential Experience to the Conditional Log Wage Differential

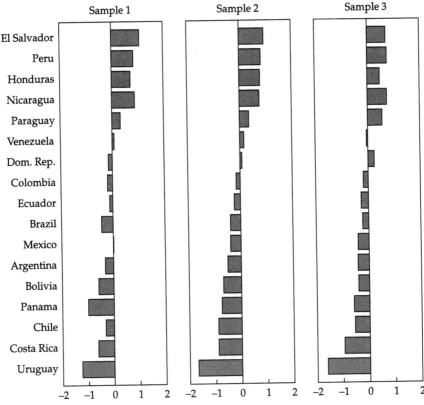

Note: Sample 1 includes all workers other than teachers who declared their labor earnings and hours worked. Sample 2 restricts sample 1 to those who have completed at least a secondary education. Sample 3 includes all workers other than teachers who are in office, technical, or professional occupations.

have completed at least a secondary education (sample 2); and with that of workers in office, technical, and professional occupations (sample 3). In the case of the Dominican Republic, Mexico, and Venezuela, the contribution of the difference in returns to potential experience depends on the definition of the comparison group.

Conversely, in the cases of Argentina, Bolivia, Brazil, Chile, Colombia, Costa Rica, Ecuador, Panama, and Uruguay, teachers' expected wage growth after 5 years is lower compared with that of all other workers in the labor market (sample 1); with that of workers who have completed at least a secondary education (sample 2); and with that of workers in office, technical, and professional occupations (sample 3).

One would expect a steeper wage–age profile for teachers given that, in most Latin American countries, job experience is the most important determinant for promotions. However, note that, although age may be a good proxy of the years of job experience, the correlation between age and job experience may differ between teachers and nonteachers. For example, because teachers include a greater percentage of women, and because women tend to spend longer periods out of the labor force, potential experience may be a better proxy of job experience in the comparison groups.

Sex Discrimination

Figure 3.9 shows how much the difference in women's wage premiums contributes to the conditional wage differential between teachers and different samples of nonteachers. For most countries (excluding Honduras and Nicaragua), the difference in women's wage premiums contributes positively to the conditional wage differential. This fact suggests that the education sector does not discriminate against women, or at least that, if it does, the discrimination is lower compared with that in other sectors of the labor market. However, we must note that the contribution of women's wage premiums to the conditional wage differential is second order compared with the contribution of the returns to education or potential experience.

In the teacher sample, the estimated women's wage premiums are negative and significant in Argentina, Brazil, Chile, Colombia, Ecuador, Honduras, Mexico, and Nicaragua (from −0.07 to −0.31). The Dominican Republic, Paraguay, Peru, and Uruguay exhibit estimates that are also negative but not statistically significant (from −0.07 to −0.16). Costa Rica, El Salvador, Panama, and Venezuela exhibit positive but not statistically significant estimates (from 0 to 0.04). Bolivia is the only country where the estimates were positive and statistically significant (0.13). Conversely, consistent with the presence of discrimination against women in the labor market, the estimated women's wage premiums are negative and statistically significant in all nonteacher samples and countries.

Although it is possible that there is discrimination against women in the education labor market, it is also possible that the dummy for women is correlated with other unobservable characteristics, particularly in the case of teachers. As noted earlier, because a greater percentage of women are teachers, and because women tend to spend longer periods out of the labor force, it may be the case that the dummy for women is capturing differences associated with the levels of job experience (and not captured by the age) instead of discrimination.

Rural Residence

Figure 3.10 shows how much the difference in rural residence wage premiums contributes to the conditional wage differential between teachers

Figure 3.9. Contribution of the Difference in Women's Wage Premiums to the Conditional Log Wage Differential

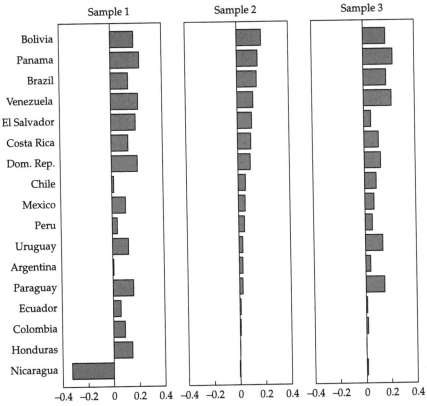

Note: Sample 1 includes all workers other than teachers who declared their labor earnings and hours worked. Sample 2 restricts sample 1 to those who have completed at least a secondary education. Sample 3 includes all workers other than teachers who are in office, technical, or professional occupations.

and different samples of nonteachers. In 10 of the 13 countries analyzed, the difference in rural residence wage premiums contributes positively to the wage differential. This fact suggests that the education sector does not discriminate against rural areas. At least, if it does, the discrimination is lower compared with that in other sectors of the labor market. However, as in the case of women's wage premiums, the contribution of rural residence wage premiums is of a second order when compared with the contribution of the returns to education or potential experience.

In the teacher sample, the estimated rural residence wage premiums are positive but not statistically significant for Colombia, the Dominican Republic, and Mexico (from 0.02 to 0.04). Costa Rica, Honduras, Nicaragua,

Figure 3.10. Contribution of the Difference in Rural Residence Wage Premium to the Conditional Log Wage Differential

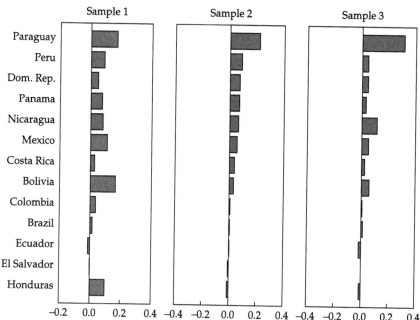

Note: Sample 1 includes all workers other than teachers who declared their labor earnings and hours worked. Sample 2 restricts sample 1 to those who have completed at least a secondary education. Sample 3 includes all workers other than teachers who are in office, technical, or professional occupations.

Panama, Paraguay, and Peru exhibit negative but not statistically significant estimates, whereas Bolivia, Brazil, Ecuador, and El Salvador exhibit negative and statistically significant estimates (from –0.08 to –0.25). However, all countries exhibit negative rural residence wage premiums in the nonteacher samples, which are statistically significant in almost all cases.

Note that the negative estimates for rural wage premiums in the teacher sample cannot be related to the presence of wage discrimination against teachers who work in rural areas. Most schools in rural areas in Latin America and the Caribbean are public, and in the public sector, there is generally no differentiation between urban and rural areas with respect to wages. If such differentiation does exist, wages are higher in rural areas. Therefore, it is possible that the rural dummy is also correlated with other unobservable characteristics. For example, the negative estimates of rural wage premiums may be related to the lower levels of qualification of teachers in rural areas that are not captured by the years of schooling or potential experience.

Initial Wage

Figure 3.11 shows how much the difference in the initial wage (the baseline wage that a person receives independent of his or her level of schooling, potential experience, sex, or area of residence) contributes to the wage differential between teachers and different samples of nonteachers. The estimates show that teachers' initial wages compensate for the lower returns to education (and, in some cases, the lower returns to potential experience) that they receive relative to those received by other sectors of the labor market. In all countries (excluding El Salvador, Nicaragua, and Venezuela), teachers' initial wages are 88 percent higher than those of all other workers in the labor market (sample 1); 162 percent higher than

Figure 3.11. Contribution of the Difference in Initial Wage to the Conditional Log Wage Differential

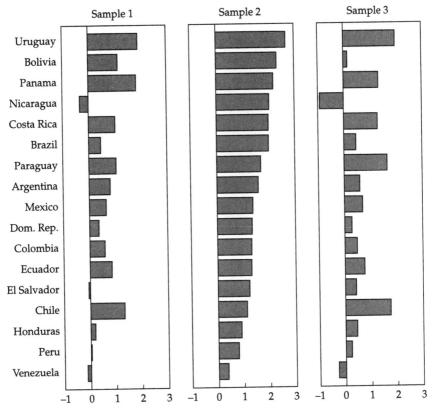

Note: Sample 1 includes all workers other than teachers who declared their labor earnings and hours worked. Sample 2 restricts sample 1 to those who have completed at least a secondary education. Sample 3 includes all workers other than teachers who are in office, technical, or professional occupations.

those of workers who have completed at least a secondary education (sample 2); and 86 percent higher than workers in office, technical, or professional occupations (sample 3).

The fact that teachers' hourly wages are independent of their levels of schooling, years of potential experience, sex, area of residence, and distribution of observed productive endowments explains why teachers' wage distributions are much more compressed. The coefficient of variation for the wage distribution is 58 percent for the teacher sample; 99 percent for all other workers of the labor market (sample 1); 91 percent for those workers who have completed at least a secondary education (sample 2); and 85 percent for those workers in office, technical, and professional occupations (sample 3).

Although higher initial wages and lower returns are important in explaining why we observe less inequality in teachers' wage distribution, the distribution of productive endowments is also more homogenous for the teacher sample. For example, the standard deviation of years of schooling levels is around 2.3 years for the teacher sample; 4.5 years for all other workers in the labor market (sample 1); 2.1 for all other workers who have completed at least a secondary education (sample 2); and 3.5 years for workers in office, technical, and professional occupations (sample 3).

Note that the variation in observed productive endowments accounts for only a small proportion of the total variation in teachers' wages. The R^2 coefficients of the estimated wage regressions for teachers are between 5 percent and 37 percent, and they are around 18 percent on average. This result suggests that unobserved heterogeneity plays an important role in the analysis of the teachers' relative wages.

Unobserved Heterogeneity and Wage Differentials

To compare people with similar levels of unobserved heterogeneity, I used Least Absolute Deviation (LAD) estimates to calculate conditional wage differentials for different quantiles of the conditional wage distribution. Figure 3.12 and table 3.9 present the estimates. Following Juhn, Murphy, and Pierce (1993), I interpreted the position in the conditional distribution of the logarithm of the wage as a measure of unobserved ability.

The estimates suggest that the answer to the question of whether teachers are well paid or not depends on the teachers' positions in the conditional wage distribution. After differences in productive endowments are accounted for, wage differentials tend to be positive and higher for low-ability teachers (teachers in the lower parts of the conditional wage distribution), whereas wage differentials tend to be zero or negative for high-ability teachers (teachers in the upper part of the conditional wage distribution).

Figure 3.12. Conditional Log Wage Differential between Teachers and Nonteachers by Quantile of the Conditional Wage Distribution

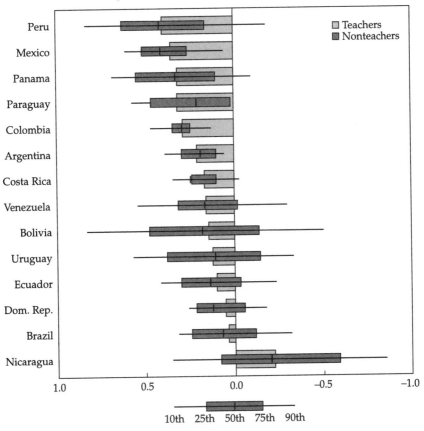

On average, after differences in productive endowments are accounted for, teachers in the 10th percentile of the conditional wage distribution receive wages 60 percent higher than their counterparts in the same percentile, teachers in the 25th percentile receive wages 43 percent higher, and teachers in the 50th percentile receive wages 24 percent higher (except in Nicaragua, where teachers' wages are 20 percent lower). At the other side of the conditional wage distribution, teachers in the 75th percentile receive wages at least as high as nonteachers (slightly higher in Argentina, Chile, Colombia, Costa Rica, El Salvador, Honduras, Mexico, Panama, Paraguay, and Peru and lower in Bolivia, Brazil, the Dominican Republic, Ecuador, Uruguay, and Venezuela). Teachers in the 90th percentile receive wages 14 percent lower (except in Argentina, Colombia, El Salvador, Honduras, Mexico, and Paraguay).

Table 3.9. Conditional Log Wage Differential between Teachers and Sample 1 of Nonteachers by Quantile

Country	10th	25th	50th	75th	90th	Mean
Argentina	0.40	0.30	0.19	0.10	0.06	0.21
Bolivia	0.84	0.48	0.18	−0.14	−0.50	0.14
Brazil	0.33	0.25	0.07	−0.11	−0.31	0.04
Chile	1.19	0.82	0.43	0.14	−0.12	0.69
Colombia	0.47	0.35	0.29	0.24	0.13	0.29
Costa Rica	0.35	0.24	0.25	0.10	−0.02	0.17
Dom. Rep.	0.27	0.23	0.13	−0.05	−0.18	0.05
Ecuador	0.42	0.31	0.14	−0.03	−0.23	0.10
El Salvador	0.92	0.68	0.51	0.31	0.08	0.47
Honduras	0.86	0.67	0.43	0.25	0.03	0.44
Mexico	0.61	0.52	0.41	0.26	0.06	0.35
Nicaragua	0.36	0.09	−0.20	−0.59	−0.86	−0.23
Panama	0.69	0.56	0.33	0.10	−0.09	0.32
Paraguay	0.58	0.47	0.21	0.02	0.37	0.32
Peru	0.84	0.63	0.42	0.16	−0.18	0.40
Uruguay	0.58	0.38	0.11	−0.15	−0.33	0.13
Venezuela	0.55	0.32	0.17	−0.02	−0.30	0.16

Conclusions

Teachers' value added to the education production process is directly related to their overall quality. Teachers' quality is, in turn, determined by what type of people are attracted to the profession, what incentives they have to perform on the job, and whether highly productive teachers will stay. Recruitment, performance, and retention are directly related to teachers' opportunity cost (that is, the wage teachers would receive in an alternative occupation).

It is important to note that although age is (arguably) the most important factor that affects recruitment, performance, and retention, it is not the only one. The stability of the job, the number of hours required at work, the flexibility of the schedule, and all kinds of nonmonetary benefits (vacations, in-kind payments, and so forth) are also important dimensions of the labor contract. Therefore, the positive or negative sign and the magnitude of the teachers' relative wage may be affected by the inclusion or exclusion of those factors. For example, because teachers tend to work fewer hours and have longer periods of vacation, earnings differentials that account for those factors will be higher than hourly wage differentials. This chapter analyzes wage differentials by taking labor supply as given and excluding all kinds of nonmonetary benefits.

The estimates of teachers' relative wages rely on data from recent household surveys. When using household surveys, one should bear in mind that teachers' relative wages and the structure of returns obtained from alternative sources of information may be different from those described in this chapter. One should also be cautious when making international comparisons, because household surveys usually have important differences in the sample design, the definition of some variables (particularly income), and the quality.

The data reveal that not only the direction, but also the magnitude of the unconditional and conditional wage differential depends on the definition of the comparison group. The fact that unconditional wage differentials vary with the definition of the comparison group is obvious, because significant differences exist in productive endowments between teachers and alternative definitions of nonteachers. Therefore, unconditional wage differentials tend to be higher when teachers are compared with workers who have lower productive endowments. Differences in observed productive endowments account for 75 percent of the gross wage differential when teachers are compared to all other workers in the labor market (sample 1); for 50 percent when they are compared with workers with at least a secondary education (sample 2); and for 64 percent when they are compared to workers in office, technical, and professional occupations (sample 3).

However, the fact that conditional wage differentials are also sensitive to the definition of the comparison group suggests that—even though one controls for differences in observable productive endowments and socioeconomic characteristics—differences in unobserved characteristics are related to wages and the decision to work as a teacher. The sign and magnitude of the adjusted or conditional wage differential also depend on the definition of the comparison group. This result suggests that even though differences in observable productive endowments and socioeconomic characteristics are accounted for, differences in unobserved heterogeneity exists between teachers and nonteachers and are related to both wages and the decision to work as a teacher. When one combines the two alternative estimates of the conditional wage differential, the results suggest that teachers receive higher wages than nonteachers in Argentina, Chile,

Colombia, El Salvador, Honduras, Panama, Paraguay, and Peru; they receive lower wages in Nicaragua. In the cases of Bolivia, Brazil, Costa Rica, the Dominican Republic, Ecuador, Mexico, Uruguay, and Venezuela, it is not possible to determine whether teachers receive higher or lower wages without choosing a particular comparison group and method.

About the structure of returns, the data reveal that, in most Latin American countries, the difference in initial wages compensates for the lower return to education (and, in some cases, the lower return to potential experience) that teachers receive. Being a woman and living in a rural area also contribute positively to the conditional wage differential. This result suggests that the education sector does not discriminate against women or those in rural areas. If it does, the discrimination is lower compared with that found in other sectors of the labor market. However, one must note that the contribution of these factors to the conditional wage differential is of a second order when compared with the contribution of the returns to education or potential experience.

Note that, when analyzing teachers' relative structure of returns, one should be cautious about the presence of unobserved heterogeneity. It may be the case that the estimated coefficients are biased because of correlation between productive endowments and unobserved characteristics, particularly in the case of teachers. For example, because a higher percentage of women work as teachers and because women tend to spend longer periods out of the labor force, the lower returns to potential experience and the negative wage premiums estimated for female teachers may be capturing differences in the levels of job experience and not necessarily the flatter wage–age profiles or sex discrimination in the education sector. It may also be the case that the negative estimates for rural wage premiums for teachers are capturing the lower levels of qualification of teachers in the rural area and not necessarily the wage discrimination against teachers in those areas.

To compare people with similar levels of unobserved heterogeneity, I used Least Absolute Deviation (LAD) estimates to calculate conditional wage differentials for different quantiles of the conditional wage distribution, and I interpreted the position in the conditional distribution of the logarithm of the wage as a measure of unobserved ability. The estimates suggest that the answer to the question of whether teachers are well paid depends on the teachers' position in the conditional wage distribution. After differences in productive endowments are accounted for, wage differentials tend to be positive and higher for low-ability teachers, and they are zero or negative for high-ability teachers. On average, after differences in productive endowments are accounted for, teachers in the 10th percentile of the conditional wage distribution receive wages 60 percent higher than their counterparts in the same percentile, teachers in the 25th percentile receive wages 43 percent higher, and teachers in the 50th percentile receive wages 24 percent higher (except in Nicaragua, where teachers' wages are 20 percent lower). At the other side of the conditional wage distribution, teachers in the 75th percentile receive wages at least as high as nonteachers (slightly higher in Argentina, Chile, Colombia, Costa Rica, El Salvador, Honduras, Mexico, Panama, Paraguay, and Peru and lower in Bolivia, Brazil, the Dominican Republic, Ecuador, Uruguay, and Venezuela). Finally, teachers in the 90th percentile receive wages 14 percent lower (except in Argentina, Colombia, El Salvador, Honduras, Mexico, and Paraguay).

References

Carnoy, M., and P. McEwan. 1997. "La educación y el mercado laboral en Honduras." Report for the Secretaría de Educación–ASED Project. Stanford University, Stanford, Calif. Processed.

ECLAC (Economic Commission for Latin America and the Caribbean). 1999. *Panorama social de América Latina 1998*. Santiago.

Grupo de Economistas y Asociados. 1998. "Análisis de las percepciones monetarias de los maestros de educación primaria." Mexico City. Processed.

Juhn, C., Murphy, K. M., and Pierce, B. 1993. "Wage Inequality and the Rise in Returns to Skill." *Journal of Political Economy* 101: 410–42.

Koenker, R., and G. Bassett. 1978. "Regression Quantiles." *Econometrica* 46: 33–50.

Liang, X. 1999. "Teacher Pay in 12 Latin American Countries: How Does Teacher Pay Compare to Other Professions, What Determines Teacher Pay, and Who Are the Teachers?" Latin America and the Caribbean Region Human Development Department Paper 49. World Bank, Washington, D.C.

López-Acevedo, G., and A. Salinas. 2000. "Teachers' Salaries and Professional Profile in Mexico." Latin America and the Caribbean Region, World Bank, Washington, D.C. Processed.

Mizala, A., and P. Romaguera. 2004. "Teachers' Salary Structure and Incentives in Chile." World Bank, Washington D.C. Processed.

Mulcahy-Dunn, A., and G. Arcia. 1996. "Teachers' Salaries and Living Standards in Ecuador." Center for International Development, Research Triangle Institute, Research Triangle Park, N.C.

Oaxaca, R., and M. Ransom. 1994. "On Wage Discrimination and the Decomposition of Wage Differentials." *Journal of Econometrics* 16(1): 5–21.

Piras, C., and W. Savedoff. 1998. "How Much Do Teachers Earn?" IDB Working Paper 375. Inter-American Development Bank, Washington, D.C.

Psacharopoulos, G., J. Valenzuela, and M. Arends. 1996. "Teacher Salaries in Latin America: A Review." *Economics of Education Review* 15(4): 401–6.

Santibáñez, L. 2002. "¿Están los maestros en México mal pagados? Estimado de los salarios relativos del magisterio." *Revista Latinoamericana de Estudios Educativos* 32(2): 9–41.

Urquiola, M., W. Jiménez, W. Hernani, and M. L. Talavera. 2000. "Los maestros en Bolivia: Impacto, incentivos y desempeño." Maestrías para el Desarrollo Universidad Católica Boliviana, La Paz.

Vegas, E., W. Experton, and L. Pritchett. 1998. "Teachers in Argentina: Under-(Over) Worked? Under- (Over) Paid?" World Bank, Washington, D.C. Processed.

4
Teachers' Salary Structure and Incentives in Chile

Alejandra Mizala and Pilar Romaguera
Center for Applied Economics, Department of Industrial Engineering,
University of Chile

The purpose of this chapter is to analyze the level, trends, and structure of teachers' salaries in Chile and to compare the salaries with those of other workers who have similar characteristics. Analyzing what is going on with teachers' salaries is interesting because, in many countries—and Chile is no exception—teachers' salaries are often perceived to be low and less than those of other professionals. If this perception were the case, it would have three possible effects on the efficiency of the educational process.

First, lower salaries would affect the effort and the quality of teachers' work. Second, low salaries would negatively affect the quality of education students and, therefore, the pool of future teachers. Third, it would be hard to keep good teachers in the profession, because they would seek better income elsewhere. Those effects would produce significant inefficiencies in the educational process and negative effects in students' learning.

A question that arises is why debate occurs more about teachers' salaries than about salaries of other kinds of workers. In particular, many studies ask whether teachers are underpaid. We think the explanation lies in the fact that, in education, the quality of teaching cannot be observed directly and, therefore, teachers' productivity cannot be directly measured either. This fact affects how teachers' salaries are determined and structured.

One way of dealing with this issue is to introduce incentive systems that motivate teachers to give the best quality service they can. This approach requires study not only of the level and structure of teachers' salaries but also of the incentives embedded within teachers' salary structure.

This chapter is organized in the following manner. The first section briefly summarizes the main characteristics of Chilean teachers. The second

We acknowledge the support of the World Bank. We are grateful for valuable comments from Emiliana Vegas and the participants at the World Bank workshop on Teacher Quality and Incentives in Latin America. We also thank Marcelo Henríquez for collaborating with us.

analyzes the institutional context of the teachers' labor market. The third analyzes trends in salaries from 1990 on. In the fourth section, we analyze how salaries affect the behavior of those applying to study teaching. The fifth section provides an econometric analysis of teachers' salaries, which makes it possible to compare them with those of other similar workers. In the sixth section, we study the incentives implicit in the current salary structure for teachers. The seventh section describes the National System of Performance Assessment (Sistema Nacional de Evaluación de Desempeño de los Establecimientos Educacionales, SNED) and offers a preliminary assessment of the effect of the SNED on student's outcomes. We examine the SNED for two reasons. Until recently, it was the sole monetary incentive associated with evaluating teachers' performance. Similarly, it is the sole incentive that evaluates teachers' performance according to students' results on standardized tests. The eighth section presents the opinions of teachers and principals about performance evaluation and monetary incentive payments associated with such evaluations, and the ninth section summarizes the conclusions.

Who Are Chile's Teachers?

Figures from the Ministry of Education (MINEDUC) for 2001 indicate a total of 146,918 teachers were in the country. Of those, 55 percent work in municipal (public) schools, 31 percent work in subsidized private schools, and the rest work in fee-paying private schools. Within this total group, 86 percent of teachers work in urban schools. In terms of educational levels, 59 percent work in primary education, 27 percent work in secondary education, 8 percent work in preschool education, 4 percent work in special education, and 1.6 percent work in adult education. In terms of responsibilities, 85.5 percent are classroom teachers, 6.5 percent are principals, 2.9 percent are principals of rural schools with fewer than three teachers, and 3.5 percent are technical–pedagogical personnel.[12]

Education is dominated by women, with 70 percent of teachers being women. Most are concentrated in preschool and primary education. In secondary education, the distribution of men and women is more even. Despite the high percentage of women teachers, 51 percent of principals are men; figures are similar for the leadership of the national teachers' association (Colegio de Profesores).

With respect to education and experience, the vast majority of teachers (90 percent) have a university degree. One-third (33 percent) have fewer than 10 years of experience, 25 percent have 10 to 19 years of experience, 27 percent have from 20 to 29 years of experience, and 15 percent have 30 years of experience or more.

---

12. The rest consist of unclassified others.

As with most countries, teachers work fewer hours than the average Chilean worker. Just 22 percent of teachers work 44 hours a week (this amount is the maximum number of hours of work allowed with the same employer in the subsidized system) whereas the work week defined by the Chilean Labor Code currently amounts to 48 hours per week and will fall to 44 hours in 2005. Of the remaining teachers, 35 percent work from 31 to 43 hours, 29 percent work 30 hours, and 15 percent work fewer than 30 hours. Just 10 percent work more than 44 hours a week, which is consistent with the fact that just 13 percent of teachers work in more than one school.

How Teachers' Salaries Are Determined

Chile has three types of schools: municipal (public) schools, subsidized private schools, and fee-paying private schools.[13] Therefore, the Chilean school system has three types of employment contracts. The first type consists of those corresponding to the municipal sector, governed by the Teachers' Statute (Estatuto Docente) established in 1991.[14] The second type includes those in the subsidized private sector, governed by the Labor Code, which covers all private sector workers, but for which certain rules in the Teachers' Statute are binding. Among the rules are minimum salaries, length of the working day, legal holiday periods, and termination. Finally, the third type of contracts is those in the fee-paying private sector, also governed by the Labor Code, but for which the rules in the Teacher Statute are not binding.[15]

In the case of municipal schools in Chile, the Teachers' Statute establishes a common salary structure that is based on the Basic National Wage (Remuneración Básica Mínima Nacional, or RBMN) per teaching hour. This basic wage is increased by a series of allowances, many of which are linked to the RBMN. Those allowances reflect years of experience, responsibility, training, and work in difficult conditions, among other things.

---

13. Municipal schools are financed through a per student subsidy that is provided by the state and run by municipalities (local governments); they serve some 56 percent of enrollment. Subsidized private schools are financed by the per student subsidy that is provided by the state but are owned and operated by the private sector; they account for 34 percent of enrollment. Fee-paying private schools operate on the basis of fees paid by parents and represent approximately 10 percent of enrollment. For more information about the Chilean education system, see Mizala and Romaguera (2000b).

14. In the early 1980s, the Chilean education system was decentralized, with public schools becoming dependent on municipal governments. Teachers thus ceased to be public employees and came under the private Labor Code. With the return of democratic rule, a special statute was created that defined new labor conditions for teachers.

15. See Mizala and others (2002) for a detailed analysis of the different types of teachers' contracts in Chile.

In the municipal sector, control over contracts and salaries is, nonetheless, centralized in the Ministry of Education. Likewise, centralized collective bargaining is not established by law but is a consequence of the creation of a national scale that standardizes teachers' pay. In practice, wage negotiations have the characteristics of a bilateral monopoly (González 1998).

In the private sector, teachers enjoy collective bargaining rights according to private sector regulations, although parties may agree to function under the rules governing the municipal sector.

As a result of the Teachers' Statute of 1991, the number of students whom schools managed to retain in their classrooms ceased to affect teachers' job security. For this reason, Law 19410 of 1995 attempted to restore some flexibility to the system. This legislation abolished lifetime employment, making it possible to adjust staffing, to transfer teachers between schools in the same municipality, to rationalize resources, and even to merge schools. In addition, the law introduced periodic competitions for management posts in municipal schools, which is important because school principals can exert leadership that has a significant effect on a school's results.

In addition, the wage agreement that ended the dispute between the teachers' union and the Ministry of Education in 1994 established a bonus payment that was unrelated to teachers' years of service but was inversely proportional to excess staffing levels in the school or municipality. This legislation also set up the SNED, which awards an excellence bonus to the best schools in each region of the country.[16] Also, in 2000, a parallel teaching excellence bonus (*Asignación de Excelencia Pedagógica*) was added for those teaching the first 4 years of primary education. This bonus consists of a voluntary, individual evaluation that is associated with a money award. To receive this award, teachers must successfully pass knowledge-based examinations, present their curricula, and submit a sample recording of a class they have taught.

The shift toward more flexibility has been difficult because the teachers' association has embraced the Teachers' Statute as an historic aspiration that protects teachers from job insecurity and arbitrary actions by administrators.[17] However, in recent years and independent of the teachers' association stance, signs of a change have been evident in teachers' attitude toward greater acceptance of elements such as evaluation and payment for performance (see last section of this chapter). This change is important because, for good management of human and financial resources, it is necessary to design more flexible labor regulations that make managerial efficiency possible and that encourage the improvements required for educational quality.

---

16. See Mizala and Romaguera (2002) for further details on the SNED.
17. For more details, see Belleï (2001).

Table 4.1. Monthly Real Salaries of Full-Time (44 Hours) Teachers (average Chilean pesos, 2001)

Years	Municipal sector		Private subsidized sector
	Average salary[a]	Starting salary[b]	Starting salary[b]
1990	258,242	142,591	73,337
1991	276,574	172,166	160,026
1992	323,311	191,293	184,123
1993	363,540	202,458	187,950
1994	413,452	234,933	210,122
1995	454,991	259,263	253,888
1996	488,420	284,977	283,746
1997	533,762	312,885	311,272
1998	561,318	340,970	340,721
1999	589,431	363,942	363,942
2000	615,368	385,331	385,331
2001	631,813	390,354	390,354
2002[c]	660,161	389,422	389,422

Note: All figures in the table are calculated on the national zone average.

a. The average salary includes RBMN plus benefits (10 two-year periods of experience plus allowances for responsibility, upgrading, performance, difficult conditions), Professional Improvement Unit (UMP), proportional bonuses, total handicap, excellence bonuses, and additional salaries.

b. The starting salary includes RBMN, UMP base; the proportional bonus includes complementary allowances.

c. Estimates, assumptions: Consumer price index 2002 = 3.0 percent; public wage cost of living adjustment in 2002 = 3.0 percent.

Source: Ministry of Education, Chile.

Changes in Teachers' Salaries

Figures from the Ministry of Education reveal that, between 1990 and 2002, teachers' average salaries rose 156 percent. Meanwhile, the entry-level salary rose 173 percent in the municipal sector and 431 percent in the subsidized sector during the same period[18] (see table 4.1). Unfortunately, except for the starting salary established in the Teachers' Statute, there is

---

18. The strong rise in the starting salary in the subsidized private sector reflects the fact that it was very low in 1990.

Table 4.2. Comparison of Teachers' Salaries with the Average Wage and Professionals' Salaries (average Chilean pesos, 2001)

Years	Average wage	Professional salaries	Teachers' salaries	Teachers' salaries relative to average wage	Teachers' salaries relative to professional salaries
1993	201,083	441,903	363,540	1.81	0.82
1994	215,567	490,243	413,452	1.92	0.84
1995	226,338	517,801	454,991	2.01	0.88
1996	234,106	545,510	488,420	2.09	0.90
1997	240,084	580,160	533,762	2.22	0.92
1998	242,987	612,452	561,318	2.31	0.92
1999	245,797	645,324	589,431	2.40	0.91
2000	248,612	652,428	615,368	2.48	0.94
2001	249,479	663,804	631,813	2.53	0.95
2002	252,394	688,529	660,161	2.62	0.96
Rate of change from 1993 to 2002 (percent)	25.52	55.81	81.59		

Source: National Institute of Statistics (INE) and Ministry of Education, Chile.

no information on the salaries paid in the private sector because they are the result of decentralized bargaining at each school.

An important point to note is that, between 1981 and 1990, teachers' monthly real salaries declined 32 percent because of budgetary reductions throughout the economy. Therefore, part of the increase during the 1990s was to make up for this decline. Nonetheless, by 1997, teachers' monthly real salaries were already 23 percent higher than their 1981 peak.[19]

If we examine table 4.1, the question arises about how teachers' salaries compare with others in the economy. For this purpose, table 4.2 shows the changes in the general wage index, professional salaries, and teachers' salaries for the period 1993–2002.[20] The rate of change in teachers' salaries (81.5 percent) went far beyond that of the general wage index (25.5 percent) and that of professionals (55.8 percent).

---

19. No time series information is available on teachers' average salaries before 1990, so it is difficult to make time comparisons of teachers' salaries before then.

20. The series starts only in 1993 because, that year, the National Statistics Bureau calculated a new wage index with a substantially different methodology from the previous one, so it would not be suitable to compare series.

Table 4.3. Comparison of Teachers' Starting Salary with the National Minimum Wage (Chilean pesos of each year)

Year	National minimum wage	Municipal teachers' starting salary	Municipal teachers' starting salary relative to minimum wage	Rate of annual change (percent) National minimum wage	Municipal teachers' starting salary
1993	42,917	126,039	2.94		
1994	49,588	163,024	3.29	15.54	29.34
1995	56,088	194,703	3.47	13.11	19.43
1996	62,750	229,793	3.66	11.88	18.02
1997	68,942	267,825	3.88	9.87	16.55
1998	76,708	306,794	4.00	11.26	14.55
1999	86,333	338,409	3.92	12.55	10.30
2000	96,042	372,057	3.87	11.25	9.94
2001	103,208	390,344	3.78	7.46	4.92
2002	111,420	401,087	3.60	7.96	2.75

Source: National Institute of Statistics (INE) and Ministry of Education, Chile.

In 1993, teachers earned 1.8 times the income of an average worker within the economy whereas, by 2001, teachers were averaging 2.6 times that income. It is important to compare teachers' earnings with those of other workers in the economy. If we compare teachers with professionals, which is the occupational group whose salaries rose the most in this period (see Cowan and others 2002), we see that teachers' salaries went from 82 percent of professionals' salaries in 1993 to 96 percent in 2001. In other words, in 2001, teachers on average earned practically the same as professionals.[21]

Table 4.3 compares the evolution of starting salaries for teachers in the municipal sector[22] with the minimum wage within the economy. Teachers' starting salary in 2002 was about 3.6 times the general minimum wage. Until 1998, teachers' starting salary grew more than the minimum wage every year. Only as the country's growth slowed (in 1999) because of the effect of

---

21. At this point, we compared only the evolution of teachers' salaries vis à vis other occupational groups. In a later section of the chapter, we analyzed teachers' salaries compared with those of workers with similar characteristics.

22. From 1998 on, teachers' minimum wage became the same for both the municipal and the private subsidized sector.

the Asian crisis did teachers' starting salary decrease to less than the general minimum wage.

Comparing teachers' salaries in Chile with those of Organisation for Economic Co-operation and Development (OECD) and developing countries such as Chile provides a helpful context. Table 4.4 provides information for 2001 on starting salaries and for teachers with 15 years' experience in primary and secondary education in U.S. dollars comparable for purchasing power parity (PPP). The ratio between salaries and per capita gross domestic product (GDP) in each country is provided for the purpose of comparison. When compared with the OECD mean, a selection of OECD countries, and some developing countries, Chile pays relatively similar salaries in relation to its per capita GDP.

The rise in teachers' salaries documented in table 4.1 explains a significant part of the increase in the Ministry of Education's expenditures during the period 1990–2001 (see table 4.5). This increase is confirmed by noting that total MINEDUC spending tripled between 1990 and 2001 and that the corresponding expenditure on the per student voucher that the ministry pays to schools also tripled, maintaining a share of about 64 percent of total expenditure of the ministry during the decade.

The information available indicates that a significant part of the resources transferred by means of vouchers goes to pay teachers' wages in the municipal system.[23] A study by González, Mizala, and Romaguera (2001) estimates that, on average at the municipal level, spending on remuneration absorbs about 85 percent of voucher income, with a standard deviation of 14 percent.

Thus, one can conclude that the rise in teachers' salaries does to a large degree explain the significant rise in MINEDUC spending for the period studied.

Effect of Salary Trends on Individuals
Applying to Study Education

Despite a significant rise in teachers' salaries in the past 13 years, teachers continue to say that their salaries are lower than those of other professionals. This perception of low salaries is worrisome because it directly affects the quality of students entering education programs. All things being equal, the best students would prefer other fields.

In fact, from 1980 to 1994, the number of students training for the education field fell by about 43 percent (Ormeño 1996). Many reasons could explain this behavior, one being the plunge in teachers' salaries, which occurred as monthly real salaries declined 32 percent in real terms during

---

23. No information is available on what percentage of the subsidy received by private subsidized schools goes to salaries.

Table 4.4. International Comparisons of Teachers' Salaries, 2001 (equivalent U.S. dollars converted using purchasing power parities)

Country	Primary education				Lower secondary education				Upper secondary education			
	Starting salary[a]	Salary after 15 years[a]	Salary at top of scale[a]	Ratio of 15-year salary to GDP[b]	Starting salary[a]	Salary after 15 years[a]	Salary at top of scale[a]	Ratio of 15-year salary to GDP[b]	Starting salary[a]	Salary after 15 years[a]	Salary at top of scale[a]	Ratio of 15-year salary to GDP[b]
OECD countries:												
Australia	27,980	39,715	39,715	1.45	28,025	39,668	39,668	1.44	28,024	39,668	39,668	1.44
Czech Republic	10,704	13,941	18,429	0.97	10,704	13,941	18,429	0.97	12,200	15,520	21,045	1.08
France	21,702	29,193	43,073	1.14	24,016	31,507	45,501	1.23	24,016	31,507	45,501	1.23
Germany	38,412	46,459	49,839	1.75	39,853	49,053	51,210	1.84	43,100	5,839	55,210	1.99
Italy	23,537	28,483	34,339	1.07	25,400	31,072	37,798	1.17	25,400	31,959	39,561	1.20
Korea, Rep. of	25,177	42,845	68,581	2.69	25,045	42,713	68,449	2.69	25,045	42,713	68,449	2.69
Mexico	11,703	15,455	25,565	1.69	14,993	19,588	32,240	2.14	—	—	—	—
New Zealand	17,544	33,941	33,941	1.61	17,544	33,941	33,941	1.61	17,544	33,941	33,941	1.61
Portugal	19,585	28,974	52,199	1.56	19,585	28,974	52,199	1.56	19,585	28,974	52,199	1.56
Spain	26,875	31,357	39,123	1.50	30,228	35,215	43,790	1.68	31,345	36,500	45,345	1.74
United Kingdom	23,297	36,864	36,864	1.46	23,297	36,864	36,864	1.46	23,297	36,864	36,864	1.46
United States	28,681	41,595	50,636	1.19	28,693	41,595	49,728	1.19	28,806	41,708	49,862	1.19
OECD mean	21,982	30,047	36,455	1.31	23,283	31,954	38,787	1.34	24,350	34,250	41,344	1.43

(Continued)

Table 4.4. International Comparisons of Teachers' Salaries, 2001 (equivalent U.S. dollars converted using purchasing power parities) (Continued)

Country	Primary education				Lower secondary education				Upper secondary education			
	Starting salary[a]	Salary after 15 years[a]	Salary at top of scale[a]	Ratio of 15-year salary to GDP[b]	Starting salary[a]	Salary after 15 years[a]	Salary at top of scale[a]	Ratio of 15-year salary to GDP[b]	Starting salary[a]	Salary after 15 years[a]	Salary at top of scale[a]	Ratio of 15-year salary to GDP[b]
Non-OECD countries:												
Argentina	8,181	11,362	13,568	0.92	10,617	15,249	18,454	1.23	10,617	15,249	18,454	1.23
Brazil	7,922	10,695	11,628	1.45	14,900	17,263	18,800	2.35	16,701	17,777	20,326	2.42
Chile	11,631	12,902	17,310	1.37	11,631	12,902	17,310	1.37	11,631	13,487	18,107	1.43
Peru[c]	5,597	5,597	5,597	1.22	5,536	5,536	5,536	1.20	5,536	5,536	5,536	1.20
Philippines	10,777	11,896	12,811	3.06	10,777	11,896	12,811	3.06	10,777	11,896	12,811	3.06
Uruguay[d]	5,734	6,872	8,295	0.76	5,734	6,872	8,295	0.76	6,240	7,378	8,801	0.82

Note: — = not available.
a. With minimum training.
b. Ratio of salary after 15 years of experience to GDP per capita.
c. Year of reference 2000.
d. Salaries for a position of 20 hours per week. Most teachers hold two positions.
Source: OECD (2003).

Table 4.5. Total Expenditures of the Ministry of Education, 1990–2001, in Millions of 2001 Chilean pesos (and percentages)

Year	Total expenditures	Total operational expenditures	Current transfers								Total capital expenditures[e]
			Total	Vouchers	Higher education expenses	Learning resources[a]	Programs[b]	Scholarships[c] and categorical aid	Research[d] and development	Other transfers	
1990	556,474	53,349	502,783	355,070	88,645	589	1,448	45,531	9,465	2,035	341
(%)	(100)	(9.6)	(90.4)	(63.8)	(15.9)	(0.1)	(0.3)	(8.2)	(1.7)	(0.4)	(0.1)
1991	605,500	57,547	547,606	364,449	103,181	1,587	4,853	58,850	11,643	3,043	347
(%)	(100)	(9.5)	(90.4)	(60.2)	(17.0)	(0.3)	(0.8)	(9.7)	(1.9)	(0.5)	(0.1)
1992	685,751	66,194	612,973	403,986	109,519	2,406	2,056	74,217	10,931	9,859	6,584
(%)	(100)	(9.7)	(89.4)	(58.9)	(16.0)	(0.4)	(0.3)	(10.8)	(1.6)	(1.4)	(1.0)
1993	766,272	77,326	685,955	442,076	115,399	4,841	2,718	80,371	21,878	18,673	2,991
(%)	(100)	(10.1)	(89.5)	(57.7)	(15.1)	(0.6)	(0.4)	(10.5)	(2.9)	(2.4)	(0.4)
1994	831,749	76,310	755,405	501,751	120,108	2,747	4,328	82,935	25,416	18,121	33
(%)	(100)	(9.2)	(90.8)	(60.3)	(14.4)	(0.3)	(0.5)	(10.0)	(3.1)	(2.2)	(0.0)
1995	959,779	73,395	886,406	607,521	134,545	3,651	4,946	84,013	22,371	29,359	–22
(%)	(100)	(7.6)	(92.4)	(63.3)	(14.0)	(0.4)	(0.5)	(8.8)	(2.3)	(3.1)	(0.0)
1996	1,088,436	85,417	989,349	685,526	137,655	9,598	4,322	92,773	22,171	37,304	13,670
(%)	(100)	(7.8)	(90.9)	(63.0)	(12.6)	(0.9)	(0.4)	(8.5)	(2.0)	(3.4)	(1.3)
1997	1,221,888	91,870	1,100,674	777,612	142,758	8,882	6,580	90,635	23,265	50,942	19,343
(%)	(100)	(7.6)	(90.8)	(64.2)	(11.8)	(0.7)	(0.5)	(7.5)	(1.9)	(4.2)	(1.6)

(Continued)

Table 4.5. Total Expenditures of the Ministry of Education, 1990–2001, in Millions of 2001 Chilean pesos (and percentages) (Continued)

Year	Total expenditures	Total operational expenditures	Current transfers								Total capital expenditures[e]
			Total	Vouchers	Higher education expenses	Learning resources[a]	Programs[b]	Scholarships[c] and categorical aid	Research[d] and development	Other transfers	
1998	1,335,315	106,363	1,206,914	836,220	157,648	11,793	9,832	97,002	24,662	69,757	22,038
(%)	(100)	(8.0)	(90.4)	(62.6)	(11.8)	(0.9)	(0.7)	(7.3)	(1.8)	(5.2)	(1.7)
1999	1,453,084	102,231	1,311,213	905,325	162,899	14,799	11,078	106,771	31,067	79,273	39,640
(%)	(100)	(7.0)	(90.2)	(62.3)	(11.2)	(1.0)	(0.8)	(7.3)	(2.1)	(5.5)	(2.7)
2000	1,570,038	97,614	1,386,094	988,769	164,912	20,377	9,295	112,945	26,173	63,623	86,330
(%)	(100)	(6.2)	(88.3)	(63.0)	(10.5)	(1.3)	(0.6)	(7.2)	(1.7)	(4.1)	(5.5)
2001	1,687,861	105,500	1,495,466	1,080,992	171,262	16,333	14,969	119,168	29,051	63,690	86,894
(%)	(100)	(6.3)	(88.6)	(64.0)	(10.1)	(1.0)	(0.9)	(7.1)	(1.7)	(3.8)	(5.1)

Note: MECE = Program for the Improvement of the Quality of Education; JUNAEB = National School Support and Scholarship Board; CONICYT = National Scientific and Technological Research Commission.

a. The category includes textbooks, pedagogical resources, learning guides, classroom libraries, computers, and software. It does not include the expenses of specific programs.

b. Programs considered: Intercultural Bilingual Education; Drug Addiction and Alcoholism; Preschool Education; PEBM Workers, P900; Know Your Child; Elementary School MECE; Adult Education; Anticipation High School; Elementary Rural School.

c. Scholarships considered: Indigenous Scholarships; Outstanding Students in Pedagogy, Secondary Education Scholarships and Categorical Aid, JUNAEB Scholarships, Higher Education Scholarships.

d. Research here corresponds to research funds managed by CONICYT

e. The category corresponds to capital contributions to the following: Full day school, High school for all, Higher Education infrastructure, and Financial investment.

Source: Ministry of Education, Chile.

the 1980s. This plunge occurred because of budgetary reductions explained by the downturn in Chilean economy.

However, the information available suggests that this downward trend of students training to become teachers turned around in 1997, with registration in education programs rising along with average entry scores. This turnaround could partly reflect extensive publicity from the Ministry of Education for education reforms, the scholarship policy it implemented for outstanding pedagogy students, and higher teachers' salaries. Moreover, the ministry has implemented special programs to reinforce the teaching profession. Unfortunately, no information is available that could allow us to isolate the effect that each of those policies has had on the number and quality of teacher education students.

The number of education students rose 39 percent, from 19,995 in 1997 to 27,817 in 2001. Table 4.6 shows a simultaneous improvement in applicant quality, which is measured using scores on national university entrance examinations (the PAA, or Prueba de Aptitud Académica). This increase in average scores is not a generalized phenomenon. In fact, the PAA is a national test with a mean score of 500 and a standard deviation of 100. At the school of engineering during the same period, the change of the score of the first student selected fluctuated between 1.1 percent and 0.03 percent, and the score of the last student selected fluctuated between 1.2 percent and −1.2 percent. The increase in the quantity and quality of education students is important because it points to the successful accomplishment of education reforms that require creating a pool of competent, highly trained teachers.

Analysis of Relative Teacher Pay

The information presented gives a general picture of trends in teachers' salaries and differences in remuneration between teachers and other people. However, it does not enable us to draw any definite conclusion about

Table 4.6. Average Score for Admission to Teaching Programs

Admission year	Average score (PAA)	Change (percent)
1998	536.50	
2000	590.93	10.1
2001	604.80	2.3
2002	616.65	2.0
2003	624.29	1.2

Source: OECD (2004), based on the Department of Measurement of Educational Results, University of Chile.

teachers' pay compared to that of other workers. To be able to answer the question of whether teachers are overpaid or underpaid, we need to compare individuals with similar characteristics in terms of both human capital and the jobs they perform.

It is, therefore, worthwhile to explore in more depth the differences between teachers' salaries and those of workers with similar characteristics.[24]

This analysis is based on data from the 1998 and 2000 Encuesta Nacional de Caracterización Socioeconómica (National Socioeconomic Characterization Survey, or CASEN).[25] The CASEN provides information on personal characteristics and individuals' occupations. Table 4.7 gives information on the income, human capital characteristics, and employment of teachers and nonteachers.[26]

One first important element to point out is that the hourly wage obtained from the 1998 CASEN is very similar to the one teachers declared in a survey conducted by the authors of this study in Greater Santiago between November 1998 and January 1999.[27] The hourly income from their main job was 1,849 pesos, according to the 1998 CASEN, and 1,805 pesos, according to the authors' survey, both expressed in 1998 Chilean pesos (Ch pesos). The exchange rate stood at 460.3 pesos per U.S. dollar in 1998 and 539.5 pesos per U.S. dollar in 2000.

The comparative analysis between teachers and other nonagricultural workers shows that hourly earnings from the main occupation are higher for teachers than for other occupational groups. The same is true for total earnings from the main job and earnings from all sources of labor income (see table 4.7).

---

24. In recent years, several studies have examined the issue of teachers' salaries in Latin America; appendix 4.B summarizes the main findings. The results are mixed, indicating that no robust empirical evidence has proven that teachers receive lower salaries than a comparative group receives. Nonetheless, not all the studies control for workers' characteristics. Many of the studies consist of a relatively aggregate comparison of salaries between teachers and other groups. Similarly, studies based on econometric analyses, except for those of Piras and Savedoff (1998) and López-Acevedo and Salinas (2000), assume that returns are similar for teachers and other workers.

Other studies also address this issue for non–Latin American countries. For instance, Komenan and Grootaert (1990) study differences in pay for teachers and nonteachers in the Côte d'Ivoire, and Zymelman and DeStephano (1989) study teaching salaries in Sub-Saharan African countries. In the case of the United States, this issue was analyzed by Ballou and Podgursky (1997), Flyer and Rosen (1996), and Lankford and Wyckoff (1997), among others.

25. The analysis using the 1998 CASEN survey was published in Mizala and Romaguera (2000a).

26. In 1998, 1,791 people employed as teachers in either elementary or secondary schools were identified according to their job and profession. The comparison group consists of 58,006 people who were over the age of 15 years and who reported receiving income from work in either the public or private sector, excluding agricultural workers. In 2000, 2,394 people employed as teachers were identified; the comparison group comprised 51,917 people.

27. For more details about the survey, see Mizala and others (2002).

Table 4.7. Means and Standard Deviations of Selected Variables in a Comparison of Teachers and Nonteachers, 1998 and 2000

Variables	1998 Mean and standard deviation		2000 Mean and standard deviation	
	Teacher	*Nonteacher*	*Teacher*	*Nonteacher*
Hourly earnings in main job	1,849	1,242	1,962	1,256
(Chilean pesos)	(1,465)	(3,151)	(1,504)	(2.292)
Average hours worked	156	197	157	194
per month[a]	(50)	(100)	(70)	(88)
Income from main job	263	213	277	215
(thousand Chilean pesos)	(183)	(541)	(164)	(351)
Age	40	38	41	39
	(10)	(12)	(11)	(13)
Years of schooling	15.7	9.6	15.3	10.0
	(2.2)	(3.8)	(2.5)	(3.9)
Percentage having a	78	10	76	12
professional degree	(41)	(29)	(43)	(32)
Years of potential experience	18.6	21.9	19	23
(age—education—6 years)	(10.3)	(13.8)	(11)	(14)
Men (percent)	30	69	31	64
	(46)	(46)	(46)	(48)
Number of observations	1,791	58,006	2,394	51,917

Notes: The exchange rate was 460.3 pesos per U.S. dollar in 1998 and 539.5 pesos per U.S. dollar in 2000. We use hourly earnings because teachers are paid by the hour, and they work fewer hours than other workers.
a. Teachers declare they work 21 days per month; nonteachers declare they work 23 days per month.
Source: Authors' calculations are based on the 1998 and 2000 CASEN household surveys.

On average, teachers have more years of schooling than do other workers and less potential experience. A high percentage hold a professional degree or diploma of some kind. Table 4.7 also reflects the well-known fact that a high proportion of teachers are women.

The six items shown in figures 4.1 and 4.2 show the distribution of hourly income from teachers' main job compared to distribution by other workers for 1998 and 2000, respectively. The figures also show a comparison between teachers and more educated workers (13 or more years of education and 17 or more years of education). The distribution of hourly income from the main job held by workers with 17 or more years of education is to the right of teachers' distribution. This, however, is not the case

Figure 4.1a. Hourly Income Distribution of Teachers and All Nonteachers, 1998

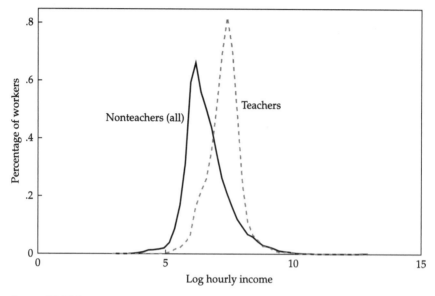

Source: CASEN 1998.

Figure 4.1b. Hourly Income Distribution of Teachers and Nonteachers with 13 or More Years of Schooling, 1998

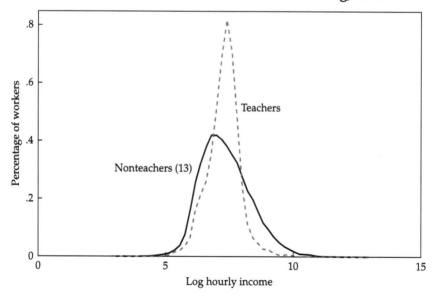

Source: CASEN 1998.

Figure 4.1c. Hourly Income Distribution of Teachers and Nonteachers with 17 or More Years of Schooling, 1998

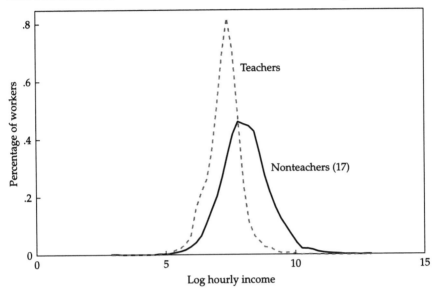

Source: CASEN 1998.

Figure 4.2a. Hourly Income Distribution of Teachers and All Nonteachers, 2000

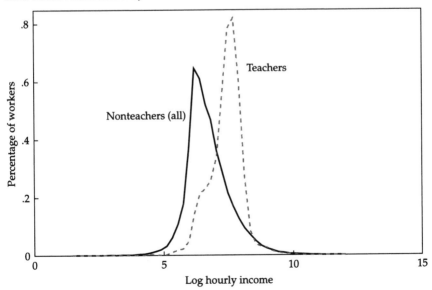

Source: CASEN 2000.

Figure 4.2b. Hourly Income Distribution of Teachers and Nonteachers with 13 or More Years of Schooling, 2000

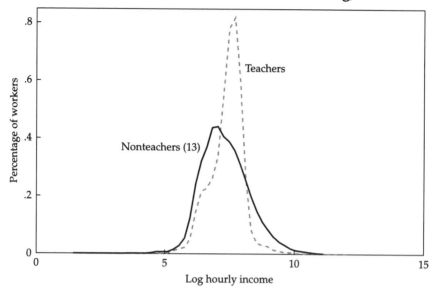

Source: CASEN 2000.

Figure 4.2c. Hourly Income Distribution of Teachers and Nonteachers with 17 or More Years of Schooling, 2000

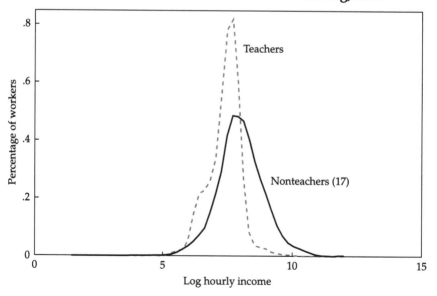

Source: CASEN 2000.

when we compare teachers with workers with 13 or more years of education who on average have the same years of schooling as teachers have.[28]

To compare the earnings of different workers, we estimated a Mincer (1974) type earnings equation for the complete sample of people who reported receiving income in the 1998 and 2000 CASEN, distinguishing between teachers and other workers.

The estimated equation is

$$(4.1) \qquad Ln(W/hr)_i = \beta + \beta_N N X_i + \beta_T TX_i + v_i$$

where $Ln(W/hr)$ is the logarithm of hourly earnings from primary employment, X is a vector of personal and job characteristics of individual i, T represents teachers, and N represents nonteachers (comparison group). T and N are dummy variables used to distinguish teachers from nonteachers. $T = 1$ if the individual is a teacher; $N = 1$ if the individual is a nonteacher.

The reason for estimating a full interaction earnings equation is to explore whether the return on human capital, mainly education and experience, varies between teachers and nonteachers. We also estimate a single model in which the coefficients are assumed to be the same for teachers and nonteachers. In this case, the dummy variable for being a teacher would capture overpayment or underpayment to the teaching profession.

The dependent variable is the logarithm of hourly earnings from primary employment. We use hourly earnings (a) because, as mentioned, teachers work fewer hours than other workers and (b) because, in Chile, teachers are paid by the hour. It can be argued that teachers probably do not declare in the survey the amount of hours they work at home preparing lectures or correcting exams. However, in this study, we have not corrected for the larger number of vacation days that teachers enjoy. They have 8 weeks of vacation per year, whereas other workers have 3 weeks. Therefore, if there is a bias, it tends to overestimate the number of hours that teachers work.

Tables 4.8 and 4.9 give the results obtained from estimating equation 4.1 with data for 1998 and 2000. These tables indicate whether or not the estimated coefficients for the two groups are statistically different. The results are similar for both years.

Considerable differences are apparent between the earnings profiles of the two groups. The constant term is higher for teachers than for other workers. However, the return on schooling is less for teachers, as is the return on holding a professional degree, which means that the earnings profile for teachers starts above the profile for nonteachers but is flatter.

Also, unlike that of other workers, teachers' pay does not vary according to gender. Similarly, men's and women's rate of return on experience

---

28. Workers with 13 or more years of education are people with postsecondary—but not necessarily university—education.

Table 4.8. Determinants of Labor Income, Teachers Compared with Nonteachers, 1998 (dependent variable: logarithm of hourly earnings from primary employment)

Variable	Teacher		Nonteacher	
	Coefficient	t-test	Coefficient	t-test
Constant[a]	6.704	38.75**	5.227	258.57**
Years of schooling[a]	0.024	2.09*	0.095	88.15**
Potential experience[a]	−0.003	−0.55	0.013	11.10**
Potential experience squared[a]	0.0003	2.35*	−0.00004	−1.79
With professional qualification (degree)[a]	0.277	4.87**	0.469	48.67**
Male × potential experience[a]	−0.008	−0.79	0.006	3.95**
Male × potential experience squared[a]	0.0003	1.47	−0.0001	−4.16**
Single person	−0.073	−1.95*	−0.102	−14.37**
Male[a]	0.088	0.93	0.110	7.14**
Urban[a]	−0.002	−0.02	0.153	16.49**
Owner	0.758	4.79**	1.176	86.16**
Self-employed[a]	1.125	13.67**	0.567	80.62**
Domestic service, living out	—	—	−0.139	−10.02**
Unpaid family member	—	—	0.159	0.41
Armed forces	—	—	0.166	6.57**
Region 1[a]	−0.088	−0.94	−0.167	−9.72**
Region 2[a]	0.125	1.30	0.015	0.91
Region 3[a]	−0.031	−0.29	−0.168	−7.82**
Region 4[a]	−0.150	−1.92	−0.207	−14.09**
Region 5[a]	−0.099	−2.10*	−0.192	−20.91**
Region 6	−0.188	−2.49*	−0.177	−13.77**
Region 7[a]	−0.099	−1.55	−0.233	−19.05**
Region 8[a]	−0.066	−1.54	−0.264	−28.99**
Region 9[a]	−0.122	−2.04*	−0.278	−20.93**
Region 10[a]	−0.039	0.67	−0.332	−28.47**

(Continued)

Table 4.8. Determinants of Labor Income, Teachers Compared with Nonteachers, 1998 (dependent variable: logarithm of hourly earnings from primary employment) (*Continued*)

Variable	Teacher		Nonteacher	
	Coefficient	t-test	Coefficient	t-test
Region 11[a]	0.226	1.31	−0.038	−1.11
Region 12[a]	0.133	0.95	0.082	3.15**
Adjusted R^2	0.49			
F	1,130.0**			
N	59,791			

Notes: This regression considers all nonagricultural workers who are age 15 years and older. Reference dummy variables: 13th Region (Santiago Metropolitan Region); employees.
* = statistically significant at 5 percent; ** = statistically significant at 1 percent.
a. Difference between coefficients significant at 1 percent.
Source: 1998 CASEN household survey.

Table 4.9. Factors Determining Labor Income, Teachers Compared with Nonteachers, 2000 (dependent variable: logarithm of hourly earnings from primary employment)

Variable	Teacher		Nonteacher	
	Coefficient	t-test	Coefficient	t-test
Constant	6.237	56.37**	5.458	228.83**
Years of schooling[a]	0.055	7.79**	0.091	77.47**
Potential experience[a]	0.007	1.61	0.010	8.86**
Potential experience squared[a]	0.000	1.55	−0.000	−2.06*
With professional qualification (degree)[a]	0.327	8.66**	0.462	47.28**
Male × potential experience[a]	0.002	0.30	0.010	7.03**
Male × potential experience[a] squared	0.000	−0.34	0.000	−6.20**
Single person	−0.045	−1.67	−0.113	−14.37**
Male[a]	0.115	1.47	0.074	4.43**
Urban[a]	−0.075	−1.48	0.068	4.96**
Owner	0.142	0.78	1.083	74.52**

(*Continued*)

Table 4.9. Factors Determining Labor Income, Teachers Compared with Nonteachers, 2000 (dependent variable: logarithm of hourly earnings from primary employment) (*Continued*)

Variable	Teacher		Nonteacher	
	Coefficient	*t-test*	*Coefficient*	*t-test*
Self-employed[a]	1.058	17.45**	0.401	51.97**
Domestic service, living out	—	—	−0.116	−8.37**
Armed forces	—	—	0.118	5.11**
Region 1[a]	−0.080	−1.06	−0.220	−12.42**
Region 2[a]	−0.059	−0.87	0.158	9.28**
Region 3[a]	−0.331	−4.58**	−0.135	−5.78**
Region 4[a]	−0.252	−4.24**	−0.197	−11.08**
Region 5[a]	−0.164	−4.35**	−0.204	−20.42**
Region 6[a]	−0.280	−5.59**	−0.188	−12.56**
Region 7[a]	−0.075	−1.68	−0.237	−16.21**
Region 8[a]	−0.195	−5.81**	−0.271	−26.83**
Region 9[a]	−0.103	−2.10*	−0.242	−15.92**
Region 10[a]	−0.103	−2.34*	−0.243	−17.82**
Region 11	0.194	1.27	−0.029	−0.74
Region 12[a]	0.239	2.59*	0.113	3.96**
Adjusted R^2	0.311		0.431	
F	47,920		1,575.370	
N	2,394		51,917	

Notes: This regression considers all nonagricultural workers who are age 15 years and older. Reference dummy variables: 13th Region (Santiago Metropolitan Region); employees.
* = statistically significant at 5 percent; ** = statistically significant at 1 percent.
a. Difference between coefficients significant at 1 percent.
Source: 2000 CASEN household survey.

does not vary. In the case of nonteachers, men have a higher rate of return on experience and a greater depreciation of their human capital over time than women do.

A similar phenomenon can be observed with respect to geographical location. The pay of teachers does not vary according to whether they work in urban or rural areas or in other administrative regions within the country.[29] This improved degree of earning equality by gender and location among teachers reflects how teachers' pay is calculated, especially for those working in the municipal school sector, as set out in the Teachers' Statute.

An interesting point to note is that—when we run a single equation in which the returns are assumed to be the same for both groups—we obtain a dummy variable for being a teacher that is equal to 0.028 (for 1998), which is statistically significant at a 10 percent level, and another variable equal to 0.044 (for 2000), which is statistically significant at a 5 percent level. The results imply that, on average, teachers earn salaries similar to workers with the same characteristics, although this difference is slightly more positive for 2000.

However, if we allow the returns to be different for teachers and non-teachers, the analysis shows that the earnings profile for teachers is different from the earnings of other workers. Although gender and region have statistically significant effects on the earnings of nonteachers, those factors do not affect teachers' pay. In addition, although the return on years of schooling and on having a professional degree is statistically significant, it is less so for teachers than for nonteachers. However, the constant term is higher for teachers, so the earnings profile for teachers starts above the profile for nonteachers but is flatter.[30]

To better understand the results obtained from estimating equation 4.1, we first broke down earning differentials between teachers and nonteachers. Second, we simulated earnings that were predicted by the estimated model, distinguishing between men and women.

Breakdown of Earning Differentials between Teachers and Nonteachers

The exercise to break down earning differentials enabled us to determine the extent to which earning differentials reflect differences in individual characteristics and the returns on those characteristics. For this purpose, we applied the Oaxaca (1973) decomposition formula. This formula can be written as

$$(4.2) \qquad Ln(W_T/hr) - Ln(W_N/hr) = \beta_N(X_T - X_N) + (\beta_T - \beta_N)X_T$$

---

29. The country is divided into 13 administrative regions. Santiago, the capital city, is in the Metropolitan Region.

30. These results do not change when the income equation takes into account only teachers (937) and nonteachers (2,696) with 17 or more years of schooling. The constant term remains higher for teachers than for other workers, but the return on years of schooling is not statistically significant for teachers. Only the variable of having a professional degree significantly affects teachers' hourly income.

In other words, the difference predicted by the regression model in the log of hourly earnings between teachers and nonteachers can be broken down in two parts. One part is explained by the differences in individual characteristics between the two groups (years of schooling, experience, and so forth) weighted by the coefficients estimated for nonteachers in the income equation. The other part is explained by the differences in rates of return on each of those characteristics between teachers and other workers.

Equation 4.2 can be broken down still further. The first term on the right-hand side can be separated into (a) factors relating to personal characteristics (P) such as employee, self-employed, or owner and (b) characteristics of the job (J) such as geographic location (that is, urban or rural). The results from carrying out this exercise are shown in equation 4.3:

$$(4.3) \qquad Ln(W_T/hr) - Ln(W_N/hr) = \beta_N^p(X_T^p - X_N^p)$$
$$+ \beta_N^J(X_T^J - X_N^J) + (\beta_T - \beta_N)X_T$$

The results show that the difference in the log of main-job hourly earnings between teachers and nonteachers favors teachers in both years (0.70 for 1998 and 0.54 for 2000). This finding is explained by differences in the personal characteristics of teachers such as years of schooling, holding a professional title, and so forth (0.81 for 1998 and 0.64 for 2000). Moreover, characteristics that can be attributed to the job rather than to the teachers themselves (mainly occupational category) reduce this differential (–0.14).

The final term in the equation shows the fraction of the earnings differential between teachers and nonteachers that are attributed to differences in returns on personal characteristics. The result obtained (+0.03 in 1998 and +0.04 in 2000) indicates that teachers receive a little bit more in return for their personal characteristics than nonteachers do.

This result occurs despite the fact that the return on education and experience for teachers is lower than for other workers. Several elements combine to explain this situation. First is the fact that teachers start with higher salaries than other workers with similar characteristics.[31] Second, salaries are similar for male and females teachers; this fact does not occur for salaries of other men and women in the labor market. In most occupations, women receive lower yields than men for their human capital. Third, unlike other workers, teachers do not earn less because they are single or work outside the Metropolitan Region. All those elements tend to offset the differences between teachers and nonteachers when it comes to their returns on education and experience.

---

31. This element is reflected in the constant term of the estimated model (see tables 4.7 and 4.8).

Earning Differentials between
Teachers and Nonteachers

The above results show that researchers must pay attention to differences between men and women when we compare salaries of teachers and non-teachers. In this section, we explore the issue in more detail.

Figure 4.3 presents the differences obtained from the estimated equation 4.1 in the log of main-job hourly earnings between teachers and non-teachers in 1998, for different levels of schooling and potential experience. Figure 4.3a presents the case of women and figure 4.3b that of men. The estimates for 2000 is similar, although a small improvement occurs for male teachers.[32]

Female teachers with up to 16 years of schooling earn more than female nonteachers for any level of experience. Only female teachers with more than 17 years of schooling (with graduate studies) earn less than non-teachers. Of female teachers, 64.9 percent receive higher salaries than non-teachers do.

For male teachers, the situation is different. Only male teachers with 13 years of schooling or less earn more than male nonteachers for any level of experience. With 14 or 15 years of schooling, they earn more than non-teachers only at the beginning of their working lives and then again after many years of experience. Male teachers with 16 or more years of schooling earn less than nonteachers, given their education and experience. Only 21.8 percent of male teachers receive higher salaries than nonteachers.

The differences found between men and women reflect the fact that, in contrast with what happens in the rest of the Chilean labor market, no wage discrimination occurs against women in the teaching profession.[33]

Incentives Embedded within Teachers' Salary Structure

The previous section shows that the basic issue with respect to teachers' salaries in Chile is not their average level but the fact that salaries are exceptionally uniform from one teacher to another. Our analysis reveals that this characteristic occurs because the returns on education and experience are low, comparably speaking, for teachers.

---

32. The figures start at 8 years of education because some teachers are trained at normal schools with that level of education (see appendix 4.F).

33. This lack of discrimination can be better explained by the regulated pay scales intended to ensure teachers' pay equity than by the fact that the teaching profession is a female-dominated occupation. Verdugo and Schneider (1994) examined earning differentials between male and female teachers in the United States and found that the latter appear to experience wage discrimination. The cost associated with being a woman is approximately 5 percent of the average annual salary.

Figure 4.3a. Salary Differentials between Female Teachers and Nonteachers, 1998

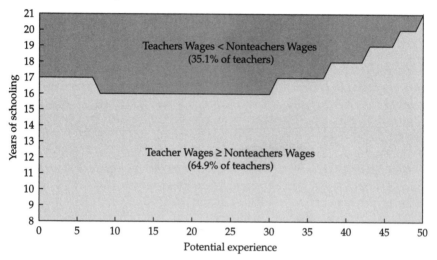

Source: Authorsí calculations.

Figure 4.3b. Salary Differentials between Male Teachers and Nonteachers, 1998

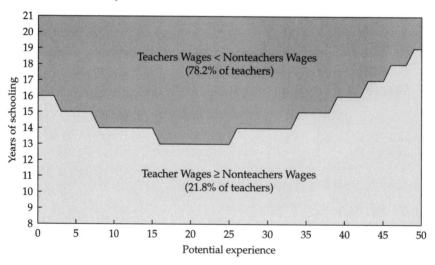

Source: Authors' calculations.

Permitting a more flexible salary structure in which part of salaries depends on teachers' performance could decompress the salary structure for teachers, allowing the government to pay better salaries to those who perform better. Since 1996, Chile has had a mechanism, the SNED, which makes it possible to adjust the salaries of teachers to their performance in the country's publicly financed schools. This mechanism is a collective incentive open to all schools receiving government funding (that is, municipal and subsidized private schools).

The amount of money that teachers receive under the SNED, however, is the lowest of all the monetary incentives to which they can aspire. In figure 4.4, we compare the average increase received by a teacher at a school with a SNED award (23,000 Chilean pesos per month) with other available incentives. In each case, we compare the maximum amounts of the allowances.

An interesting point to note is that, since 2002, two incentives have been provided to reward individual excellence among teachers: (a) an individual allowance for teaching excellence and (b) an allowance for the teachers' tutor program. In the case of the former, teachers must voluntarily participate in having their files evaluated and must take a test of their knowledge. Teachers obtaining the reward receive double the SNED award, that is, 46,000 pesos per month.[34] Moreover, if the teacher is willing to participate in peer training, then he or she may receive an additional 50,000 pesos per month.

Despite the recent appearance of those collective and individual performance incentives, the most important incentive offered to teachers is seniority: a teacher with 30 years of service receives an additional 275,000 pesos per month. The second most significant incentive is the pursuit of further professional training, in which case teachers' monthly income may increase by 110,000 pesos. If teachers work in difficult conditions, for example, in geographic isolation or with poor students, marginal students, or both, then they receive an additional 80,000 pesos per month. Finally, if teachers leave the classroom to assume management or technical positions, their monthly income rises 55,000 pesos.

Table 4.10 demonstrates the importance of different wage incentives to the average teacher working in the municipal sector. The table presents the relative importance of the different kinds of bonuses in 2003. In each case, except for the basic national wage, the allowance has been calculated as the total amount of money allocated to the municipal sector for this purpose, divided by the total number of municipal teachers.[35] The first noteworthy element here is the complex salary structure.

---

34. See appendix 4.A for more details on the amounts paid for this purpose—in particular, pedagogical excellence allowance and variable allowance for individual performance.

Figure 4.4. Allowances and Monetary Incentives for Teachers, 2002/03 (Thousands of Chilean pesos)

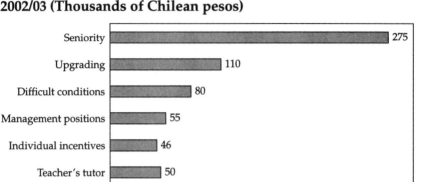

Note: In each case, the maximum amount of the allowance is considered.
Source: Cox (2003).

Table 4.10. Breakdown of the Wage of an Average Municipal Sector Teacher, 2003

Concept	Percentage
Basic National Wage (RBMN)	42.5
Experience allowance (20 years)	28.4
Responsibility allowance	1.7
Difficult conditions allowance	3.4
Training allowance	5.3
Regional complement	5.5
Additional salary	1.7
Law 19200 taxable bonus	2.5
Professional Improvement Unit (UMP)	2.4
Complementary UMP	0.6
Proportional bonus	5.1
Excellence bonus (SNED)	0.9
Total	100.0

Source: Ministry of Education, Chile.

One can conclude that—despite the inclusion of performance incentives—traditional incentives continue to be extremely important to Chilean teachers' salaries. Seniority is the main way of increasing income, which ultimately means that loyalty rather than actual job performance is rewarded in the teaching profession. Undoubtedly, this situation has limited the SNED's ability to effectively change teachers' behavior.

Nonetheless, some significant changes have occurred recently, and those changes have boosted the importance of variable, performance-linked salaries. Specifically, in 2003 during the last round of collective bargaining between the teachers' association and the Ministry of Education, both parties agreed that salary increases would be variable and assigned through the SNED, an agreement that became Law 19933 and came into effect on February 12, 2004. In the next section, we describe this system in more detail, along with the changes that will take place in coming years. This system also established a new individual incentive for rewarding those with distinguished or competent skills under individual evaluation processes currently under way. (In contrast to the teaching excellence bonus, this evaluation is compulsory.) Notwithstanding, the only evaluation under way that links teachers' salaries to students' performance is the SNED.

Effect of the SNED on Schools' Academic Achievement: A Preliminary Evaluation

In this section,[36] we first describe the SNED and then estimate its effect on schools' academic achievement after the first four applications. This study is preliminary, so the results presented here are still of an exploratory nature.

The SNED rewards teachers for their performance and seeks to improve their motivation. The schools that perform with excellence are chosen every 2 years and receive an excellence bonus as an incentive. The bonus is defined on a per student basis, so the amount each school receives depends on the number of students in attendance. Schools representing up to 25 percent of each region's enrollment receive awards. One requirement is that 90 percent of the amounts assigned must go directly to the school's teachers, in proportion to their hours of employment; each school decides the

---

35. For instance, in the case of the SNED, approximately 27 percent of municipal teachers receive the award, but the figure (0.9 percent) in table 4.10 assumes that the total amount of excellence bonus allocated to municipal teachers is divided by the total number of municipal teachers.

36. This section is based on Mizala, Romaguera, and Henríquez (2004). More details on the SNED can be found in Mizala and Romaguera (2002).

Table 4.11. SNED: Beneficiaries and Resources

	1996/97	1998/99	2000/01	2002/03
Schools receiving awards	2,274	1,832	1,699	1,863
Percentage of schools receiving awards	—	20.2	18.4	19.7
Teachers receiving awards	30,600	31,400	32,600	34,400
Percentage of teachers receiving awards	—	27.3	27.7	27.7
Excellence subsidy per teacher (annual in 2001 US$)	345.2	364.4	428.3	439.4
Total SNED budget (in thousands of 2001 US$)	10,563	11,442	13,963	15,115

Note: The average exchange rate in 2001 was 634.9 Chilean pesos per U.S. dollar.
Source: Ministry of Education, Chile.

distribution of the remaining 10 percent. The SNED has been applied four times since 1996.[37]

On average, 20 percent of the schools and approximately 27 percent of the teachers received awards in different applications of the SNED. Those figures varied for each year (see table 4.11).[38] The subsidy for excellence that teachers received during 2002/03 was 279,000 Chilean pesos per year (US$439.40),[39] slightly more than the 219,000 pesos they obtained in 1996 when the system began. This figure currently amounts to 87 percent of the monthly starting salary for teachers and a little more than an additional half salary per year for a teacher working 36.3 hours per week. The SNED's excellence award implies a salary increase that ranges from 7.2 percent per year among those receiving the teachers' starting salary to 4.7 percent for those earning an average salary for 36.3 hours per week. As already mentioned, the additional income involved in the award is relatively low, which could seriously limit the effect of this policy on teachers' behavior.

The changes covered by the law that was recently approved by Congress significantly increase the excellence subsidy paid per student and, therefore, the average annual amount that teachers at prize-winning schools will receive. Table 4.12 shows that the amount of the per student excellence award will rise 91 percent between 2004 and 2006, which means that teach-

37. In March 2004, the results from the fifth application SNED were published.
38. For the total number of SNED applications, 50.9 percent of schools have never received the award; 27.7 percent have won once, 13.7 percent twice, 5.8 percent three times, and just 1.8 percent every time the SNED has been applied.
39. This amount is paid quarterly during a period of 2 years.

Table 4.12. Trends in SNED Award Amounts (2001 U.S. dollars)

Years	1996/97	1998/99	2000/01	2002/03	January 2004	January 2005	January 2006
Per student excellence subsidy	1.27	1.39	1.60	1.63	1.79	2.77	3.42
Average annual amount for award-winning teachers	345.20	364.40	428.30	439.40	512.80[a]	827.00[a]	—

Note: The average exchange rate in 2001 was 634.9 Chilean pesos per U.S. dollar.
a. Based on the number of teachers who will receive the SNED award during 2004/05.
— = not available.
Source: Ministry of Education, Chile.

ers working in a SNED prize-winning school will receive about double what they are receiving today.

At the same time, the law establishes that more schools and teachers will receive awards because the share of regional enrollment covered by awards will rise from 25 percent to 35 percent in 2006. Schools ranking in the upper 25 percent of regional enrollment will receive 100 percent of the excellence subsidy, while those in the next 10 percent will receive 60 percent of the excellence subsidy.

The Effect of the SNED on Schools' Academic Achievement

We had to deal with several methodological challenges before we could evaluate the SNED's effect. In the first place, by definition, all Chilean schools receiving state funding participate in the SNED, with no need to compete formally, so no schools are available for a comparison group. Because of this situation, the only feasible design to evaluate the SNED's effect in schools is a reflexive comparison.[40]

Second, we had to deal with a problem of endogeneity. We are trying to evaluate the SNED's effect on schools' academic achievement, but the school's performance on students' standardized tests is precisely one of the main variables considered (with a weight of 65 percent—factors "Effectiveness" and "Improvement") to calculate the SNED index, which ranks schools and selects those to receive awards.

---

40. In a reflexive comparison, the counterfactual state is given by the pre-program participation of participants (prefactual scenario). See Duflo (2002), Grossman (1994), Heckman and Smith (1995), Ravallion (2001), and Regalia (1999).

At the international level, some studies have estimated the effect of accountability systems that are associated with incentive payments. Among them are Ladd (1999), Lavy (2002a, 2002b), and Henry and Rubinstein (2002). In Chile's case, virtually no studies have evaluated the SNED's effect on educational achievement. One exception is Contreras and others (2003), which analyzes the effect of the 1998/99 SNED application on schools' educational achievement, measured by the results obtained on the 2000 Sistema de Medición de la Calidad de la Educación (Education Quality Measurement System, or SIMCE) test. Using ordinary least square (OLS) estimates and the matching propensity score method, they found that the SNED increased SIMCE scores by an amount that fluctuates from 4 to 18 points. However, Contreras and others (2003) did not correct for the problem of endogeneity when estimating the SNED's effect on schools' academic output, so their results might be biased.

The problem of endogeneity is common when evaluating programs, and the literature reveals different attempts to resolve it. The most widely used solution is the use of instrumental variables, which would mean, in the case of the SNED, finding a variable highly correlated to winning the SNED award but not highly correlated with the school's ability to obtain high scores on the SIMCE test. Finding the right instrumental variable is not easy, and the use of variables that do not totally satisfy the requirements leads to biases greater than those already existing.[41]

An alternative strategy for dealing with the problem of endogeneity is to estimate a model with fixed effects for each school, which makes it possible to model its heterogeneity. Schools' fixed effects can vary or not over time. In this case, we consider only schools' fixed effects that do not change over time. Therefore, there may still be biases caused by changes that are not controlled by the fixed effects.

In this study, we apply a general fixed-effect model that makes it possible for the (SNED) policy effects and biases to vary over time. Traditional fixed-effect models, which assume coefficients that are constant over time and that assume a bias caused by the also-constant, nonrandom selection of schools, can be nested in this more general model.

In the case of the SNED, one could assume that the treatment effects are the same every year because the methodology that has been applied (at least in the past three applications) and even the resources that have been allocated have not changed significantly. In other words, the same pro-

---

41. In the case of the SNED, it is natural to think of the other SNED index factors as instrumental variables. This strategy works only if one seeks to evaluate the effect of the SNED of one period on achievements of the next period. However, when one considers an analysis of several periods, it becomes difficult to use the other SNED indicators because they are all relative to each application and are not comparable (in value) from one period to another.

gram has been applied every 2 years since 1996. However, schools' awareness of the SNED, its reception, and its level of acceptance may eventually change over time, and that change would make it possible for a different effect to occur for each period.

The traditional, fixed-effect model assumes a constant bias because of the nonrandom selection of schools, a selection that is based on fixed characteristics. This constant bias tends to be true in the SNED's case because schools that perform well tend to always receive rewards, just as other schools that have never received awards will probably not receive them in the future. Moreover, criteria for awards have remained stable over time. Therefore, it would seem that the assumption holds true in the SNED's case. Nonetheless, as in the previous case, it might be interesting to consider a model that relaxes this restriction, assuming instead that the criteria for allocating the awards change between applications. The advantage of using this kind of "relaxed" model is that the different SNED applications can be considered in a single regression, thereby producing more precise and robust estimates than other methods such as the difference-in-difference method.

The Model

We consider the following type of model for the production function[42] as we evaluate the SNED's effect on schools' educational achievement (effectiveness measured by SIMCE scores):

$$(4.4) \qquad E_{st} = \alpha'_t X_{st} + \beta'_t \, SNED_{s,t-1} + \gamma'_t C_s + \varepsilon_{st}$$

In this model, E_{st} represents effectiveness of school s over time t, X_{st} represents characteristics of school s over time t, $SNED_{s,t-1}$ represents the SNED award (dummy variable) of school s over time $t - 1$, C_s represents unobservable fixed characteristics of school s, and F_s represents observable fixed characteristics of school s.

This model assumes that the unobserved fixed effect (C_s) of school s does not correlate with the error term (ε_{st}), although it may correlate with other characteristics of the school, whether fixed (F_s) or variable (X_{st}). Our main interest is in the relationship between unobservable characteristics (C_s) and the SNED selection variable ($SNED_{st}$). Note that the model considers the effect of the SNED award from the previous period because, when the next period starts, the granting of the award has been completed.

---

42. Jakubson (1991) uses this model to estimate unions' effects on salaries. Meanwhile, Tokman (2002) uses a similar model to analyze the effects of the P900 program on schools' educational performance.

If we assume that C_s can be correlated with the $SNED_{st}$ variable, we can model the SNED's effect on unobservable school characteristics as follows:

(4.5) $$C_s = \lambda_1\, SNED_{s0} + \lambda_2\, SNED_{s1} + \lambda_3\, SNED_{s2}$$

$$+\, \xi_{st} = \lambda' SNED_s + \xi_{st}$$

where t, as 0, 1, 2, refers to the 1996/97, 1998/99, and 2000/01 SNED application periods. Note that the coefficients λ_j may vary with the period, thus incorporating the possibility that schools' unobservable characteristics affect the award differently in each period, thereby incorporating a bias in estimated effects that may vary over time.

Substituting the expression for C_s from equation 4.5 in equation 4.4, we get the following specification:

(4.6) $$E_{st} = \alpha_t'\, X_{st} + \beta_t'\, SNED_{s,t-1}$$

$$+\, \gamma_t' \lambda_s'\, SNED_s + \delta_t F_s + (\gamma \xi + \varepsilon_{st})$$

in which γ and λ together determine the bias.

Equation 4.6 is a restricted version of the following more general model:

(4.7) $$E_s = \Phi X_s + \Pi SNED_s + e_s$$

where

$$E_s = \begin{bmatrix} E_{s1} \\ E_{s2} \\ E_{s3} \end{bmatrix}, X_s = \begin{bmatrix} F_s & X_{s1} \\ F_s & X_{s2} \\ F_s & X_{s3} \end{bmatrix}, SNED_s = \begin{bmatrix} SNED_{s0} \\ SNED_{s1} \\ SNED_{s2} \end{bmatrix} \text{ and } e_s = \begin{bmatrix} e_{s1} \\ e_{s2} \\ e_{s3} \end{bmatrix}.$$

Depending on our assumptions, we find different specifications of matrix II and, therefore, different specifications of equation 4.7. Consider two possibilities in particular. First, if we consider that the SNED effect, the effect of unobservable characteristics, and the effect of biases change over time, then the coefficients β_j, γ_j, and λ_j are different for each period, yielding the following specification for Π, which corresponds to equation 4.3:

(4.8) $$\tilde{\Pi} = \begin{bmatrix} \beta_1 + \gamma_1\lambda_1 & \gamma_1\lambda_2 & \gamma_1\lambda_3 \\ \gamma_2\lambda_1 & \beta_2 + \gamma_2\lambda_2 & \gamma_2\lambda_3 \\ \gamma_3\lambda_1 & \gamma_3\lambda_2 & \beta_3 + \gamma_3\lambda_3 \end{bmatrix}$$

Second, if we consider that the SNED effect (β_j) is the same for each period, but that the effect of unobservable characteristics and biases changes over time, then the coefficients γ_j and λ_j are different for each period, yielding the following specification for Π:

$$(4.9) \qquad \tilde{\Pi} = \begin{bmatrix} \beta + \gamma_1\lambda_1 & \gamma_1\lambda_2 & \gamma_1\lambda_3 \\ \gamma_2\lambda_1 & \beta + \gamma_2\lambda_2 & \gamma_2\lambda_3 \\ \gamma_3\lambda_1 & \gamma_3\lambda_2 & \beta + \gamma_3\lambda_3 \end{bmatrix}$$

To evaluate the admissibility of those different restrictions, we can use minimum distance estimators (Chamberlain 1982, 1990) and can estimate parameters using generalized least squares with (nonlinear) restrictions.

As mentioned, the models estimated use effectiveness as a dependent variable. This variable is defined as a valid average[43] of each school's score on the SIMCE tests closest to the year being considered.[44] The explanatory variable is whether or not the school won a SNED award. The control variables are school characteristics such as socioeconomic level, which is measured using an index that combines parental income, household income, and the Junta Nacional de Auxilio Escolar y Becas (National School Support and Scholarship Board, or JUNAEB) vulnerability index; size, which is measured by enrollment; full or partial school day (*jornada escolar completa*); participation in other programs such as the P900; educational level (primary or secondary); location (urban or rural); students' gender; region where the school is located; type (municipal or private subsidized); and effectiveness in previous years (we used 1996 as our base year).[45]

The variables are available for each school in a panel-type data set where the observations correspond to schools that have participated in all SNED applications since 1998 and have taken the SIMCE tests, so those schools have data for the effectiveness variable.

One important issue to consider is that the SNED may not be an incentive for all schools, although the system does allow for some turnover in

---

43. A *valid average* is defined as the average of scores for the tests to which the school must submit, depending on the school type.

44. It is important to note that the effectiveness variable included in the SNED index for time t and the effectiveness variable used in the model (E_{st}) are not the same, although one of the tests is included in both indicators in each period.

45. Finally, given the possibility that "noise" in the results of standardized tests may limit using the tests in school rankings and in accountability systems (Chay, McEwan, and Urquiola 2003; Kane and Staiger 2002), we analyze to what degree the effectiveness variable may present more variability in smaller schools. However, the effectiveness variable is similar in every decile of school size (see appendix 4.H). This similarity may reflect the fact that the effectiveness variable includes language and mathematics tests given to different grades (4th, 8th, and 10th) in different years.

the schools receiving awards. On the one hand, a few schools enjoy such excellent academic results that they win the SNED award every time it is applied. For those schools, it is possible that the SNED acts more as a prize, a kind of recognition, than an incentive.[46] On the other hand, approximately half of the schools have never won a SNED award, and it is likely they will never win one because they are constantly ranked in the lower part of their homogeneous group. For those schools, the SNED may not motivate a change in behavior that leads to some improvement in results because people in those schools think they will never win.[47]

Because of this dynamic, the model is estimated for a subset of schools that, in the different SNED applications, come close to the cutoff value for receiving an award according to the SNED index. Those schools have some likelihood of receiving the prize and compete against one another. For them, the SNED may be a stronger incentive to improve performance. The selection criterion used was to consider those schools that, in some SNED application, have held a place in the ranking of their homogeneous group within a range defined as the SNED index cutoff value plus or minus one-third of a standard deviation of the SNED index of their group. This selection approach yields a panel-type data set with 1,610 schools.

The estimates presented next consider the effect of SNED applications from 1996/97 through 2000/01. The 2002/03 application is not included because those data should be reflected in tests conducted after 2002, information that is not yet available. Consequently, the SNED effect on effectiveness over time t corresponds to that which would result from winning an award over time $t - 1$.

Table 4.13 presents the results from estimating the unrestricted equation 4.7. Given that there are statistically significant elements outside the diagonal, the data validate the specification of equation 4.6.

We then estimated models with restrictions, starting with those that include nonlinear restrictions among the coefficients and allowing different values for β, λ, and γ (see equation 4.8 in matrix Π). This estimation leads to the conclusion that only the 2000/01 SNED had a positive rela-

---

46. As carried out by the authors, an exploratory qualitative study among all schools in the low socioeconomic segment in Metropolitan Santiago—schools that have always obtained the SNED award—reveals that, in fact, for those schools, the SNED represents a recognition of their efforts and work rather than an incentive to improve their SIMCE test results. This study included two schools from the middle socioeconomic level that have always obtained the SNED award, and results were similar for them.

47. The SNED compares and ranks schools within homogeneous groups, calculated as a function of their location, level of education that is offered, and students' socioeconomic characteristics. Schools compete to win the prize only within their homogenous groups. Despite a change in the methodology used to build homogeneous groups between the first and second SNED application, the classification within a homogeneous group remained relatively stable. In the 2002/03 version of the SNED, 109 homogeneous groups were constructed.

Table 4.13. SNED's Effect on Effectiveness (unrestricted generalized least squares)

Year	Effectiveness 1998		Effectiveness 2000		Effectiveness 2002	
	Coefficient	Standard error	Coefficient	Standard error	Coefficient	Standard error
1996/97 SNED	−0.468	0.536	0.710	0.607	0.913	0.685
1998/99 SNED	−1.734***	0.542	−0.994	0.613	−0.939	0.692
2000/01 SNED	8.899***	0.490	2.756***	0.555	3.270***	0.625

Note: *** = statistically significant at 1 percent.

tionship to effectiveness, with the effect of the other two applications being nil (see table 4.14, upper section).

The bias caused by the presence of unobserved schools' fixed characteristics is significant for some periods. The correlation between the selection of SNED award-winning schools and unobserved school characteristics has not indicated a clear pattern. This correlation is positive for the latest SNED (2000/01), negative for the 1998/99 SNED, and insignificant for the first SNED.[48] Meanwhile, the effect of schools' unobserved characteristics on effectiveness is positive for the second SNED application and not significant for the third (see table 4.14).[49]

The results reported in the lower part of table 4.14 assumes that the SNED's relationship to effectiveness is independent of the year in which it was implemented (equation 4.9 in matrix Π). In this case, we obtain a positive and significant coefficient, so there is a joint positive effect of the three SNED applications being considered. This finding means that the SNED has a combined positive effect on those schools' educational achievement.

Similarly, the assumption of constancy over time is rejected for the effects of unobserved characteristics on effectiveness and for the correlation between those unobserved characteristics and the SNED award. The validity of the traditional fixed-effect model is also rejected.

This estimation is a first attempt to assess the effect of the SNED on schools' academic performance. More research is required to obtain consistent and robust results. In particular, future research needs to consider several elements. First, the methodology for measuring the effect of this kind of policy must be improved so it can deal with the problems implicit

---

48. A positive and significant λ coefficient means that the SNED tends to select schools that perform better than the others, after controlling for the observed characteristics.

49. A positive and significant γ means that schools' unobserved characteristics tend to increase their effectiveness.

Table 4.14. SNED Relationship to Effectiveness ($N = 1{,}610$ schools)

		β_1	β_2	β_3	λ_1	λ_2	λ_3	γ_2	γ_3
Nonlinear restrictions on coefficients	Coefficient	0.0727	0.2652	2.5883	−0.8189	−1.6101	8.9477	0.2753	0.0106
	Standard error	1.9328	0.5576	3.0571	1.9525	0.5221	0.4763	0.0586	0.3377
	Significance			*		***	***	***	
	χ^2 (1)	7.56							
Constant SNED coefficient: Single impact of the program	Coefficient	0.7576			−1.3708	−1.7387	8.7119	0.2235	0.0752
	Standard error	0.5260			0.7293	0.5149	0.4758	0.0582	0.0900
	Significance	**			**	***	***	***	
	χ^2 (3)	14.14							

Note: * = statistically significant at 10 percent; ** = statistically significant at 5 percent; *** = statistically significant at 1 percent.

in the lack of a control group and endogeneity. Second, data from the most recent SNED application must be included because obtaining reliable results requires lengthy time series, particularly given that the SNED was not at first widely publicized among schools. Third, key evaluations will be those that measure the SNED's effects after the amounts allocated rise in 2005 and again in 2006, when SNED coverage will increase to 35 percent of each region's enrollment. This increment will be important because today, as mentioned, the SNED offers only a modest monetary incentive to which teachers can aspire.

Evaluating Performance and Incentives: Teachers' and Principals' Perceptions

Despite the fact that, when compared with other monetary incentives to date, the SNED is not notably significant, it has affected teachers' attitudes. In fact, teachers seem more open today to performance evaluations and the associated incentive payments. This apparent openness explains to a large degree why the teachers' association agreed to increase the variable portion of performance-linked salaries. Likewise, the experience with the SNED likely helped in reaching the agreement in 2000 in which individual performance evaluations were accepted as a criterion for teaching careers.

Several surveys of teachers reveal this change in teachers' traditional resistance to evaluation systems. A first survey was done of a random sample of Greater Santiago teachers to find out what they thought of the education system, and it included some questions about the SNED.[50] In terms of their acceptance of performance evaluations and awards, responses were positive. There was a high degree of consensus:

- Among teachers, 74.7 percent agreed or strongly agreed with the statement that the Ministry of Education should apply a performance evaluating mechanism to subsidized private and public schools.
- Also among teachers, 87.6 percent agreed or strongly agreed with the statement that it is important to recognize schools that perform better than others.

The sample group showed less agreement, although still more than half, with statements about the effect of the excellence award on the quality of education and, therefore, on the link between salaries and evaluation:

---

50. Field work took place from November 26, 1998, to January 6, 1999, using surveyors. A random sample of 400 teachers in Greater Santiago was selected in two stages: (a) randomly selecting 50 award-winning schools and 50 schools that had never received the SNED award (42 municipal schools and 58 subsidized private schools) and (b) selecting four teachers per school at random. Of the selected sample of 400 teachers, 355 were actually interviewed (at 48 award-winning schools and at 50 with no award). See Mizala and others (2002).

- Among teachers, 55.6 percent agreed or strongly agreed with the statement that the excellence award for performance contributes to improving the quality of education.
- Also among teachers, 58.3 percent agreed or strongly agreed with the statement that the rise in teachers' salaries should be linked to an evaluation of each person's teaching.

Similarly, national surveys done by the Centro de Investigación y Desarrollo de la Educación (Center for Educational Research and Development, or CIDE) confirm the idea that teachers have greater acceptance of performance evaluations. In the first survey (CIDE 2000), conducted in 1999 with 1,053 teachers, 78.6 percent of teachers strongly agreed with an individual evaluation of teaching performance. In the second survey, conducted in 2000 with 1,060 teachers, 70.3 percent said they strongly agreed with individual evaluation of teaching performance. If replies are broken down by type of school, the data reveal that 62 percent of teachers in municipal schools; 76.7 percent of teachers in private subsidized schools; and 84.8 percent of teachers in private, fee-paying schools agree with individual performance evaluations (Mella and Ostoic 2001). In the fourth survey (CIDE 2003), of 1,154 teachers, 64 percent of those surveyed indicated that they agreed with implementing a teaching performance evaluation system that included incentives and sanctions. Again, the strongest agreement was among teachers in private, fee-paying schools (75 percent), followed by teachers in private subsidized schools (63 percent), and finally by teachers in municipal schools (58 percent).

Moreover, a voluntary survey of principals of private subsidized and municipal schools in Chile, with responses from 3,338 out of 9,684 schools, found significant support for performance evaluations and performance-related monetary incentive payments.[51] Moreover, most principals indicated that it is very useful to their work as principals to have a monetary reward that is for teachers and is associated with school performance.

Figures 4.5, 4.6, and 4.7 present the results of the survey of principals, differencing according to the number of times the school has obtained the SNED award. Note that the answers tend to be more positive the more times the school has received the reward. Nonetheless, even principals of schools that have never won the SNED show considerable acceptance of performance evaluations and payment of monetary incentives. Among

---

51. Although this survey design with voluntary participation implies self-selection of those responding, no bias is apparent after comparing characteristics of schools that participated with the characteristics of the total group of schools. Characteristics compared were the region where the school is located, type (public or private), and level of education (primary or secondary, adults, preschool, and so forth). Although the respondents' sample is slightly skewed in favor of schools that have received an award, this deviation is not worrisome (see appendix 4.J). More details can be found in Mizala and Romaguera (2004).

Figure 4.5. Responses of Principals: "I Agree or Strongly Agree with MINEDUC Regularly Evaluating Schools Receiving State Subsidies"

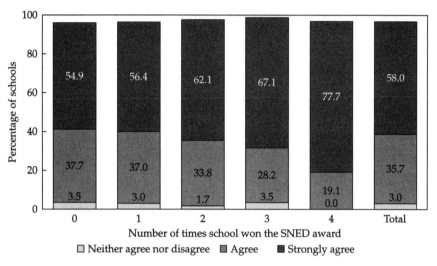

Note: Other response options were "Strongly disagree" and "Disagree."
Source: Ministry of Education, Chile, 2003.

Figure 4.6. Responses of Principals: "I Agree or Strongly Agree That MINEDUC Should Provide Resources for Regularly Rewarding the Best Performing Schools"

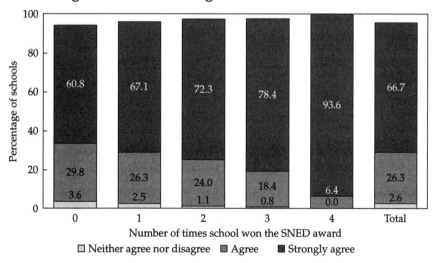

Note: Other response options were "Strongly disagree" and "Disagree."
Source: Ministry of Education, Chile, 2003.

Figure 4.7. Responses of Principals: "It Is 'Very Useful,' 'Somewhat Useful,' 'Useful' to Principal's Work That There Is a Monetary Award to Teachers, Associated with School Performance, Financed and Designed to MINEDUC Standards"

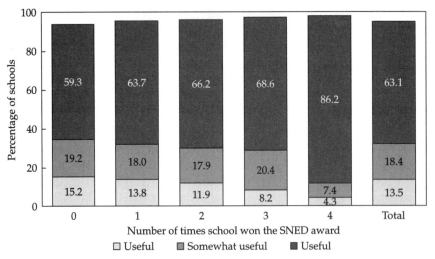

Note: Other response options were "Not useful at all" and "Not very useful."
Source: Ministry of Education, Chile, 2003.

principals, 78.5 percent consider this policy rather useful or very useful to their work (see figure 4.7).

Conclusions

In this chapter, we have tried to look at teachers' salaries in Chile and the incentives available to teachers from different perspectives. We have analyzed the evolution and structure of teachers' salaries, along with differentials that may exist when salaries are compared with those of other professionals with similar characteristics.

An important point to emphasize is that most of the information available refers to salaries paid in the municipal sector. No data are available on the private sector because those salaries are negotiated at the individual school level. The only information on the private sector is the starting salary, plus some allowances that are valid for teachers in both public and private sectors.

This analysis makes it possible to conclude that—early in the 1990s—with the return of democracy, teachers' salaries rose significantly in real terms, over and above the average wage of the economy and more than the average salary for professionals. This conclusion is also apparent in the starting salary for teachers, which has risen by more than the minimum wage within the economy. This rise in salaries may be one reason behind the turnaround in the number of students going into training for the education field and the turnaround in their scores because both have risen significantly since 1998.

Given that comparing teachers' and other workers' salaries may not be appropriate because of the differences in human capital involved, we also carried out an econometric analysis that allowed us to compare similar workers. This analysis showed that, on average, teachers' earnings are similar to those of nonteachers with the same characteristics. However, the earnings profile for teachers is different from that of other workers because of how teachers' salaries are calculated, especially for those in municipal schools. The return on schooling and on having a professional degree, though statistically significant, is lower for teachers than for other workers. The same is true with the return on experience.

Moreover, the income profile for teachers starts at a higher point than for other similar workers, but is flatter. Thus, teachers with less education and experience earn more than they would in other sectors, whereas teachers with more education and experience earn less than similar workers in other occupations.

This salary structure suggests that teaching probably attracts people with a preference for job stability and discourages the entry of people willing to take more risks. In this sense, even more educated teachers would not necessarily be underpaid but, rather, could be accepting a compensatory differential in exchange for job stability and security.

Similarly, we analyzed the incentives embedded in the salary structure for teachers. We found that, despite the recent appearance of collective and individual performance incentives, the main incentive to teachers continues to be seniority and professional training. The SNED is the oldest of the performance evaluations that are linked to monetary incentives and the only one that uses students' academic achievement as the basic criterion. This incentive currently accounts for a small percentage of teachers' average monthly salary.

Preliminary estimates reveal that the SNED has had a positive effect on educational achievement in those schools that have been involved in its different applications and are close to (higher or lower than) the cutoff point between SNED award winners and losers. For this group of schools, it can be concluded that, on the one hand, the effect of an individual SNED (2000/01 being the most recent one considered) is significant. On the other hand, there is a cumulative effect from the different SNED applications on schools' academic achievement.

Also, the SNED has had an effect on teachers' attitudes. In fact, teachers today are more open to performance evaluation and the payment of monetary incentives linked to it. Principals consider evaluations and monetary incentives useful in carrying out their work.

This change in attitude explains to a large degree why the teachers' union recently accepted a proposal to boost the variable part of salaries linked to performance. The experience with the SNED made it easier to reach agreement in 2000 about including voluntary accreditation of classroom skills, which is associated with a payment (pedagogical excellence allowance). Similarly, in the recent round of collective bargaining in 2003, parties agreed to create an allowance to reward (a) those who qualified as distinguished or competent in their compulsory individual performance evaluation and (b) those who demonstrated their disciplinary and pedagogical knowledge in a written test. The parties also agreed that part of wage increases will be variable and will be allocated through the SNED. This agreement means that, from now until 2006, the monthly amount received by teachers working at a SNED-winning school will double. At the same time, the percentage of school enrollment receiving an award will rise from 25 percent to 35 percent, which means that more teachers and schools will receive this monetary incentive. It will be interesting to assess the SNED's effect on schools' academic performance after these changes have been implemented.

Such changes are very important because they represent significant progress toward a more flexible salary structure in which part of salaries depends on teachers' performance. This change would decompress teachers' salary structure, allowing the government to pay better salaries to those who perform better. This wage policy would also encourage better candidates to enter and remain in the teaching profession.

References

Ballou, D., and M. Podgursky. 1997. *Teacher Pay and Teacher Quality.* Kalamazoo, Mich.: W. E. Upjohn Institute for Employment Research.

Belleï, C. 2001. "El talón de Aquiles de la reforma. Análisis sociológico de la política de los 90 hacia los docentes en Chile." In S. Martinic and M. Pardo, eds., *Economía política de las reformas educativas en América Latina.* Centro de Investigación y Desarrollo de la Educación–Programa de Promoción de la Reforma Educativa en América Latina, Santiago.

Chamberlain G. 1982. "Multivariate Regression Models for Panel Data." *Journal of Economics* 18: 5–46.

———. 1990. "Panel Data." In Z. Griliches and M. Intriligator, eds., *Handbook of Econometrics* (vol. 2). Amsterdam: Elsevier/North-Holland.

Chay, K. Y., P. J. McEwan, and M. Urquiola. 2003. "The Central Role of Noise in Evaluating Interventions That Use Test Scores to Rank Schools." NBER Working Paper 10118. National Bureau of Economic Research, Cambridge, Mass.

CIDE (Centro de Investigación y Desarrollo de la Educación). 2000. "Encuesta nacional a los actores del sistema educativo 1999." Centro de Investigación y Desarrollo de la Educación. Santiago. Processed.

———. 2003. "IV encuesta nacional a los actores del sistema educativo: Medición 2003." Centro de Investigación y Desarrollo de la Educación, Santiago. Processed.

Contreras D., L. Flores, F. Lobato, and V. Macías. 2003. "Monetary Incentives for Teachers and School Performance: Evidence for Chile." University of Chile, Department of Economics, Santiago. Processed.

Cowan, K., A. Micco, A. Mizala, C. Pages, and P. Romaguera. 2002. "Un diagnóstico del desempleo en Chile." Inter-American Development Bank, Washington, D.C. Processed.

Cox, C. 2003. "Las políticas educacionales de Chile en las últimas dos décadas del siglo XX." In C. Cox, ed., *Políticas educacionales en el cambio de siglo.* Santiago: Editorial Universitaria.

Duflo, E. 2002. "Empirical Methods." Handout of courses MIT 14.771 and Harvard 2390b. Department of Economics, Massachusetts Institute of Technology, Boston. Processed.

ECLAC (Economic Commission for Latin America and the Caribbean). 1999. *Panorama social de América Latina 1998*. Santiago.

Flyer, F., and S. Rosen. 1996. "Some Economies of Precollege Teaching." In W. Becker and W. Baumol, eds., *Assessing Educational Practices: The Contribution of Economics*. Cambridge, Mass.: MIT Press.

González, P. 1998. *Financiamiento de la educación en Chile*. Santiago: Programa de Promoción de la Reforma Educativa–United Nations Educational, Scientific, and Cultural Organization.

González, P., A. Mizala, and P. Romaguera. 2001. "Recursos diferenciados para la educación subvencionada en Chile." Centro de Economía Aplicada, Departamento de Ingeniería Industrial, University of Chile, Santiago.

Grossman, J. B. 1994. "Evaluating Social Policies: Principles and U.S. Experience." *World Bank Research Observer* 9(2): 159–80.

Heckman, J., and J. Smith. 1995. "Assessing the Case for Social Experiments." *Journal of Economic Perspectives* 9(2): 85–110.

Henry, G., and R. Rubinstein. 2002. "Paying for Grades: Impact of Merit-Based Financial Aid on Educational Quality." *Journal of Policy Analysis and Management* 21(1): 93–109.

Jakubson, G. 1991. "Estimation and Testing of the Union Wage Effect Using Panel Data." *Review of Economic Studies* 58(5): 971–91.

Kane, T. J., and D. O. Staiger. 2002. "The Promises and Pitfalls of Imprecise School Accountability Measures." *Journal of Economic Perspectives* 16(4): 91–114.

Komenan, A. G., and C. Grootaert. 1990. "Pay Differences between Teachers and Other Occupations: Some Empirical Evidence from Côte d'Ivoire." *Economics of Education Review* 9(3): 209–17.

Ladd, H. 1999. "The Dallas School Accountability and Incentive Program: An Evaluation of Its Impacts on Student Outcomes." *Economics of Education Review* 18(1): 1–16.

Lankford, H., and J. Wyckoff. 1997. "The Changing Structure of Teacher Compensation, 1970–94." *Economics of Education Review* 16(4): 371–84.

Lavy, V. 2002a. "Evaluating the Effect of Teachers' Group Performance Incentives on Pupil Achievement." *Journal of Political Economy* 110(6): 1286–317.

————. 2002b. "Paying for Performance: The Effect of Teachers' Financial Incentives on Students' Scholastic Outcomes." Hebrew University of Jerusalem, Department of Economics, Jerusalem. Processed.

Liang, X. 1999. "Teacher Pay in 12 Latin American Countries: How Does Teacher Pay Compare to Other Professions, What Determines Teacher Pay, and Who Are the Teachers?" Latin America and the Caribbean Region Human Development Department Paper 49. World Bank, Washington, D.C.

López-Acevedo, G., and A. Salinas. 2000. "Teachers' Salaries and Professional Profile in Mexico." Latin America and the Caribbean Region, World Bank, Washington, D.C. Processed.

Mella, O., and D. Ostoic. 2001. "II encuesta nacional a los actores del sistema educativo 2000." Centro de Investigación y Desarrollo de la Educación, Santiago. Processed.

Mincer, J. 1974. *Schooling, Experience, and Earnings.* New York: Columbia University Press.

Mizala, A., and P. Romaguera. 2000a. "Remuneraciones al pizarrón." *Perspectivas en Política, Economía y Gestión* 4(1): 65–88.

————. 2000b. "School Performance and Choice: The Chilean Experience." *Journal of Human Resources* 35(2): 392–417.

————. 2002. "Evaluación del desempeño e incentivos en la educación Chilena." *Cuadernos de Economía* 39(118): 353–94.

————. 2004. "Encuesta acerca del SNED a directores de establecimientos subvencionados." Ministerio de Educación de Chile, Santiago. Processed.

Mizala, A., P. Romaguera, and M. Henríquez. 2004. "El SNED y el logro educativo de los establecimientos educacionales en Chile." Centro de Economía Aplicada, Departamento de Ingeniería Industrial, University of Chile, Santiago. Processed.

Mizala, A., P. González, P. Romaguera, and A. Guzmán. 2002. "Chile: La recuperación de la profesión docente es possible." In J. C. Navarro, ed., ¿Quiénes son los maestros? Carreras e incentivos docentes en América Latina. Washington, D.C.: Inter-American Development Bank.

Mulcahy-Dunn, A., and G. Arcia. 1996. "Teachers' Salaries and Living Standards in Ecuador." Center for International Development, Research Triangle Institute, Research Triangle Park, N.C. Processed.

Oaxaca, R. 1973. "Male-Female Wage Differentials in Urban Labor Markets." International Economic Review 14(3): 693–709.

Ormeño, A. 1996. "Evolución de la formación de profesores en Chile: Análisis por región, dependencia y nivel del sistema educacional." Working Paper. Corporación de Promoción Universitaria, Santiago.

Piras, C., and W. Savedoff. 1998. "How Much Do Teachers Earn?" IDB Working Paper 375. Inter-American Development Bank, Washington, D.C.

Psacharopoulos, G. 1987. "Are Teachers Overpaid? Some Evidence from Brazil." Teaching and Teacher Education 3: 315–18.

Psacharopoulos, G., J. Valenzuela, and M. Arends. 1996. "Teacher Salaries in Latin America: A Review." Economics of Education Review 15(4): 401–6.

Ravallion, M. 2001. "The Mystery of the Vanishing Benefits: An Introduction to Impact Evaluation." World Bank Economic Review 15(1): 115–40.

Regalia, F. 1999. "Impact Evaluation Methods for Social Programs." Poverty and Inequality Technical Note 2. Inter-American Development Bank, Washington, D.C.

Tokman, A. 2002. "Evaluation of the P900 Program: A Targeted Education Program for Underperforming Schools." Working Paper 170. Banco Central de Chile, Santiago.

Vegas, E., W. Experton, and L. Pritchett. 1998. "Teachers in Argentina: Under- (Over-) worked? Under- (Over-) paid?" World Bank, Washington, D.C. Processed.

Verdugo, R., and J. Schneider. 1994. "Gender Inequality in Female-Dominated Occupation: The Earnings of Male and Female Teachers." Economics of Education Review 13(3): 251–64.

Zymelman, M., and J. DeStephano. 1989. "Primary School Teachers' Salaries in Sub-Saharan Africa." Discussion Paper 45. World Bank, Washington, D.C.

5

Educational Finance Equalization, Spending, Teacher Quality, and Student Outcomes
The Case of Brazil's FUNDEF

Nora Gordon
University of California at San Diego

and Emiliana Vegas
World Bank

Improving access to and quality of basic education for all children is a primary concern of policymakers throughout the world. Expanding access to basic education is still needed in many developing countries, and doing so while raising the quality of schooling has proved to be a challenge. Just which policy reforms are most effective at expanding access and improving school quality is still an open question. The reform of the Fundo de Manutenção e Desenvolvimento do Ensino Fundamental e de Valorização do Magistério (known as the Fund for the Maintenance and Development of Basic Education and Teacher Appreciation, or FUNDEF) is an educational finance reform to improve access to and quality of basic education for all Brazilian children. The recent experience of FUNDEF can provide useful evidence with respect to the effect that strategies to equalize educational finance have on access, quality, and equity of schooling.

The federal government of Brazil implemented FUNDEF in 1998. Its main objective was to promote greater equity in educational opportunities among states and across the municipalities within states by guaranteeing a minimum per pupil expenditure in primary schools throughout the country and by partially equalizing per pupil funding within states. Before 1998, education in Brazil was financed by a mandated share of subnational governments' revenue (both own source and revenue sharing), without considering the variation in enrollment or costs, which led to widespread inequalities in per pupil financing among municipalities not only within states but also across states (Soares 1998).[52]

FUNDEF consists of funds for each state. State and municipal governments contribute a proportion of their tax revenues to that fund; those revenues are then redistributed to the state and municipal governments in each state on the basis of the number of students enrolled in their respective basic education systems. The per capita nature of the funding mechanism is a central part of the reform and introduces incentives for schools to enroll more students. The federal government supplements the per pupil allocation in states where FUNDEF revenues per student are below a yearly established spending floor. The law requires that at least 60 percent of the additional funds provided by FUNDEF be allocated to teacher wages.

Previous research on FUNDEF has found that, after 3 years of carrying out the reform, its use was associated with substantial increases in enrollment in municipal basic education systems, especially in the poorest regions of the north and northeast sections of Brazil (World Bank 2002). Studies have also documented positive trends in repetition, dropout, and age-by-grade distortion that correspond to the reform's fulfillment and have predicted a reduction in inequality in educational expenditures among states (Abrahão de Castro 1998; World Bank 2002).

This paper continues the investigation of the FUNDEF reform on enrollment, school spending, and age-by-grade distortion and makes two new contributions. First, in estimating the effect of the FUNDEF revenue on school spending, inputs, and student outcomes, we allow for the possibility that local revenue streams will respond directly to the new FUNDEF grants. Second, we use state-level data from student achievement tests to more directly evaluate the effect of the reform on the achievement gap. We next discuss the relevance of those two innovations.

Research on educational finance reforms in the United States has found that it is important to explore the extent to which previously allocated revenues for education are redirected to other areas as a result of the reform (Hoxby 2001). For example, Gordon (2004) found that districts in the United States that receive federal funds under the Title I program tend to redirect own-source revenues that had previously been targeted for education. Those findings suggest that, in evaluating the effect of educational finance reforms, one must take into account the possibility that reforms may crowd out other sources of financing.

---

52. Brazil consists of 26 states (and the federal district), and within those states are more than 5,000 municipalities. Unlike many countries, however, municipalities are largely independent of the states in which they are located. State and municipal governments run separate and parallel education systems throughout the country.

The choice of student achievement scores as a dependent variable is an intuitive one; this reform—and most education reforms—are motivated primarily by a desire to improve student achievement rather than to prescribe particular levels or mixes of educational inputs. Because achievement data are available at the state but not the municipal level, we examine the effect that within-state equalization of inputs have on the state's distribution of student achievement. Research in the United States has presented mixed evidence about the merits of such reforms and about whether the educational finance equalization really reduces inequality in student test scores. For example, while Card and Payne (2002) find evidence that equalization of educational expenditures across U.S. school districts led to less dispersion in student test scores on the SAT among children of diverse socioeconomic backgrounds, Clark (2003) finds no evidence that the equalization of educational expenditures resulting from the Kentucky Education Reform Act led to a narrowing of the gap in test scores between rich and poor districts.

In this paper, we explore further how FUNDEF affected educational expenditures by municipal and state governments. We examine the effect of the reform on enrollment levels within states.

Next, we focus on the effects of the reform on aspects related to teachers—their credentials and the numbers of students per class—and on how those variants translate into student outcomes. Further, we evaluate the extent to which the reduction in spending inequality among states led to a decrease in inequality in student test scores. Unlike previous work that has evaluated the effect of FUNDEF, we explore the extent to which the reform crowded out other tax revenues that had been designated for educational expenditures.

From this research, three findings become clear. First, we find that FUNDEF-induced spending increases raised enrollment modestly in the higher grades of basic education (grades 5–8) in states most affected by the reform (those that would fall below the minimum per pupil revenue level without federal intervention through FUNDEF).

Second, we find that changes in educational spending that were induced by the reform were used to reduce class size and did not significantly affect the share of teachers with credentials higher than primary education. Although we find important increases in the share of qualified primary teachers, this increase was more the result of accompanying legislation mandating that teachers be qualified than the result of the changes in educational finance that were induced by FUNDEF. The reduction in class size and the increase in the share of qualified teachers in primary grades are, in turn, associated with reducing the student age-by-grade distortion.

Third, we find that state-level inequality in per pupil spending is associated with a wider distribution of student achievement, with lower

↑ Teachers qualifications
↓ Class size
↓ gap student achiev,

achievement at the bottom of the distribution and higher achievement at the median and above. To the extent that FUNDEF or other reforms help equalize per pupil spending within states, one may observe a narrowing of the gap between high- and low-achieving students.

In the next section of this presentation, we list relevant background information on Brazil and FUNDEF, highlighting characteristics that the reform was designed to affect. In the third section, we describe the data used in our analyses, and the fourth section discusses our empirical strategy. The fifth section presents our findings on the effect of FUNDEF on educational expenditures, teacher training, class size, and student outcomes. In the final section, we draw conclusions from our results and discuss policy implications.

Background on Brazil's Education System and FUNDEF

Brazil's education system historically has been characterized by high levels of inequality and overall low levels of achievement. The recent reform efforts were designed to address both of these conditions.

Main Features of the Brazilian Education System

In the mid-1990s, education in Brazil was characterized by enormous inequality in terms of finance, access, and quality. In part, this inequality was the result of a highly decentralized governance structure in which, historically, 26 state governments and more than 5,000 municipal governments independently had administered basic education systems. Basic education (Ensino Fundamental, or EF) in Brazil comprises two levels: EF1 and EF2. EF1 includes grades 1–4 and is stipulated to include children aged 7–10; EF2 includes grades 5–8 and, notionally, children aged 11–14. Because of late entry and particularly high repetition and dropout rates, however, many children enrolled in school are attending grades for which they are overaged, which thus results in high age-by-grade distortion rates in some regions.[53]

As shown in table 5.1, before FUNDEF, the relatively wealthy regions in the South (S), Southeast (SE), and Central West (CW) had mean per pupil expenditures that were almost twice the figures for the poor regions in the North (N) and Northeast (NE). Similarly, gross and net enrollment rates in primary education varied greatly among regions; for example,

---

53. Age-by-grade distortion is the average difference between students' actual ages and the age appropriate for their level of education. For example, the average age for EF1 would be 8.5 if all students entered at age 7 and progressed one grade per year. If the actual average age for EF1 were 10, then the age-by-grade distortion for EF1 would be 1.5 years.

Table 5.1. Mean Per Pupil Spending and Enrollment Rates by Region

Region	Mean per pupil expenditure, 1996	Gross enrollment rate, 1994	Net enrollment rate, 1994
N	742	106.9	81.5
NE	565	104.5	77.3
S	1,146	111.8	93.8
SE	1,045	113.0	94.4
CW	991	122.7	92.0

Sources: INEP Web site (http://www.inep.gov.br/) and STN Web site (http://www.stn.fazenda.gov.br/).

the poor NE region had a net enrollment rate of only 77.3 while the SE region had a net enrollment rate of 94.4 in 1994.[54]

Table 5.2 shows great disparities in teacher qualifications by region, especially among municipal systems. While only about 66 percent of grade 1–4 teachers in municipal schools of the N and NE regions in 1996 had completed more than primary education, the figures in the S and SE regions were 93 percent and 95 percent, respectively.

Assessment results of Brazilian students have been mixed in international assessments. In student assessments of mathematics and language in 13 Latin American countries by the First International Comparative Study of the Latin American Laboratory for Assessment of Quality in Education (Casassus and others 2002), Brazilian students performed slightly above the average in math and language. But in the 2002 Programme for International Student Assessment (PISA), which assessed 15-year-old students on reading, mathematics, and scientific literacy from 43 countries, Brazilian students were the worst performers in mathematics. Students from only 4 countries (Albania, Indonesia, Peru, and the former Yugoslav Republic of Macedonia,) performed worse in reading than Brazilian 15-year-olds.

Educational Finance in Brazil before and after FUNDEF

In the mid-1990s, the Brazilian government launched a wide-ranging education reform to decrease inequalities in access and finance, as well as to

---

54. Late school entry and grade repetition can make gross enrollment rates exceed 100 percent because those rates are the ratio of all enrolled students in an education grade or level in relation to the age-appropriate population. The net enrollment ratio includes in the numerator only those students who are of the appropriate age and who are enrolled in school. In the denominator is the population in the relevant age group.

Table 5.2. Share of Teachers in Grades 1–4
with Credentials Higher Than Primary Education, 1996

Region	State	Municipal	Both state and municipal
N	0.87	0.66	0.83
NE	0.96	0.66	0.82
S	0.98	0.93	0.96
SE	0.99	0.95	0.98
CW	0.97	0.83	0.93
All regions	0.97	0.80	0.92

Source: INEP Web site (http://www.inep.gov.br/).

improve the quality of education. FUNDEF was at the center of the program. The Lei de Diretrizes e Bases da Educação Nacional (Law of Guidelines and Foundations of Education, or LDB), approved in 1996, laid the foundations for the reform by assigning to the federal government the lead role in national policy and in guaranteeing equity and quality of education (World Bank 2002). The LDB enabled Brazilian officials to revise national curriculum standards and to establish minimum standards for teacher education. The law mandated that state and municipal governments share the responsibility of providing primary education (grades 1–8), that municipal governments assume responsibility over providing preschool education, and that state governments take authority over providing secondary education.

Before FUNDEF, 25 percent of all state- and municipal-level taxes and transfers were mandated to be spent on education. As a result, access and quality of education varied enormously not only by region, as shown above, but also across systems (municipal- or state-level) within any given state. As mentioned in the introduction, the main feature of FUNDEF is the creation of a state fund to which state and municipal governments contribute a proportion of their tax and transfer revenues. Those revenues are then redistributed to the state and municipal governments in each state on the basis of the number of students enrolled in their respective basic education systems. Thus, the reform addresses spending inequalities within the state. The federal government supplements the allocation in states where FUNDEF revenues per student are below a yearly established spending floor, thereby promoting adequacy across all states. Imbedded in the reform is a requirement that at least 60 percent of the additional funds provided by FUNDEF must be allocated to teachers. Table 5.3 summarizes the sources and distribution mechanisms of FUNDEF.

Table 5.3. Sources and Distribution Mechanisms of FUNDEF Funds, by Government Level

	Sources of funding	*Ways of distributing funds*
Federal government	• Salário-educação[a] • 18 percent of federal tax revenues (excluding the Social Security budget) • Others	• Provide complementary funding to states that do not reach the minimum per pupil expenditure average.
States and federal district	• At least 15 percent of ICMS owed to states or Federal District[b] • At least 15 percent of FPE[c] • At least 15 percent of FPEX[d]	• Distribute between states and municipalities proportional to the number of students enrolled in each system. • Appropriate at least 60 percent of FUNDEF funds to pay for salaries of active teachers in basic education. (During the first 5 years, some of this funding can be used for professional development of untrained teachers.)
Municipalities	• At least 15 percent of ICMS owed to municipalities • At least 15 percent of FPM[c]	

a. *Salário-educação* is a proportion of income tax earmarked for education. Specifically, it is 2.5 percent of wages in the formal sector, but companies have the choice of spending this amount on the education of their own employees. If they do not have in-company education programs, as most do not, then they pay the tax to the federal government, which then transfers two-thirds to the government of the state in which it was collected. The remaining one-third that stays with the federal government is used as a potential source of government contributions.
b. *Imposto sobre operações relativas a circulação de mercadorias e sobre prestações de serviços de transporte interestadual e intermunicipal e de comunicação* (ICMS) is the tax on goods and services (similar to value added tax).
c. Fundo de Participação dos Estados (FPE) and Fundo de Participação dos Municípios (FPM) are the transfers to states and municipalities, respectively, from the federal government.
d. Fundo de Exportação (FPEX) is a compensation given to states for losing ICMS on exports originating in each state. Because of political negotiations, it is driven by a complex formula that involves, among other things, compensation for taxes that would not be collected (tax breaks given by states to attract industries), instead of just calculating the total value added of exports.
Sources: Abrahão de Castro (n.d.); Soares (1998).

Not all previously earmarked tax and transfer revenues for education are included in FUNDEF. Instead, states and municipalities are
required by law to spend on education an additional 10 percent of the
FUNDEF sources of funding and 25 percent of revenue sources not tapped
by FUNDEF. The FUNDEF legislation stipulated that the program would
have a 10-year duration; thus, it will end in the year 2007 unless it is
extended (World Bank 2002). Most analysts believe that the program will
be extended, both in time and in scope. One of President Luiz Inacio Lula
da Silva's main education objectives is to develop Fundo de Manutenção
e Desenvolvimento do Ensino Básico (Fund for the Maintenance and the
Development of Basic Education, or FUNDEB)—the extension of the
FUNDEF to secondary schools.

Aside from the equalization of educational resources, one of the key
differences between FUNDEF and the previous mechanism for educational
finance is that resources are now available to municipal and state education
secretariats on a timely basis in their respective accounts with the Banco
do Brasil. In general, accrual into the account ranges from 10 to 30 days,
depending on the revenue source, and no intermediaries are involved in
the distribution of FUNDEF resources, thus enabling a more efficient and
timely flow of resources for education (World Bank 2002).

Data

For the 1996–2002 period, we used a panel data set that includes education
indicators and financial data on the FUNDEF reform for all municipalities
and states in Brazil. We used data on public municipal and state schools
only. Because the reform began in 1998, we have data for two pre-program
years and five post-program years. Our data came from several sources
and are publicly available. We describe our data below and present means of
the key variables used in our analyses, by level of basic education (EF1 and
EF2) for (a) the years 1996 (pre-reform) and (b) 2000 and 2002, which represent 2 and 4 years after reform implementation, respectively.

Education Indicators

The education data used in our analyses came primarily from the Instituto
Nacional de Estudos e Pesquisas Educacionais (National Institute for Education Statistics and Research, or INEP). INEP collects a school census
annually, which is our primary data source. We used the survey for years
1996–2002, which is filled out at the school level. We aggregated the information to the government-type level. School census data include information on student enrollment, numbers of teachers, teachers' educational
attainment, and student age-by-grade distortion for each year. Because of

potential errors in reporting enrollment data in the census, we used INEP's own calculations of enrollment and enrollment rates. All INEP data are publicly available on its Web site.

Substantial changes took place in key education indicators during the 1996–2002 period. In addition, great regional variability exists in those changes. First, although the number of students enrolled in EF1 declined slightly, likely because of demographic factors, impressive increases occurred in enrollment in EF2. On average, enrollment in EF2 increased by about 19 percent in the 1997–2002 period. This increase is shown in figures 5.1 and 5.2. As can be seen in figure 5.2, the average enrollment increase was generated by enormous increases in enrollment in the NE and N regions—61 percent and 32 percent, respectively, during 1997–2002. Thus, the poorest regions appear to have benefited the most from FUNDEF in terms of the ability to incorporate children—particularly relatively older children—into the education system.

Second, net enrollment rates increased while gross enrollment rates decreased in all regions during 1994–2000, the most recent years for which data are available (see figures 5.3 and 5.4). However, those trends, which suggest internal efficiency improvements, appear to be reversing toward the end of the period.

Third, a large increase also occurred in the number of teachers in EF2, especially in the poorest regions of the N and NE (see table 5.4). In fact, the number of teachers in EF2 increased at a faster rate during 1997–2002 than did the number of students—by an average of 29 percent for Brazil

Figure 5.1. Evolution of Enrollment in Basic Education, by Level and Region, 1996–2002: EF1 (grades 1–4)

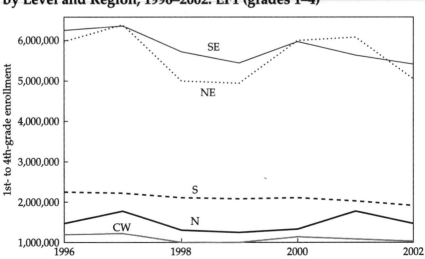

Figure 5.2. Evolution of Enrollment in Basic Education, by Level and Region, 1996–2002: EF2 (grades 5–8)

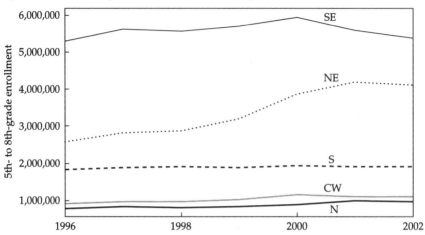

as a whole and by 61 percent and 48 percent in the NE and N regions, respectively.

Fourth, the average pupil-to-teacher ratio in Brazil declined in both EF1 and EF2 by 7.4 percent and 8.5 percent, respectively, especially after 1998 (see table 5.5). The regions with the greatest decreases were those already with relatively small class sizes in 1996: S, SE, and CW. Although the poorest regions of the N and NE also experienced declines in class size, their

Figure 5.3. Gross Primary Enrollment Rates by Region, 1994–2000 (percent)

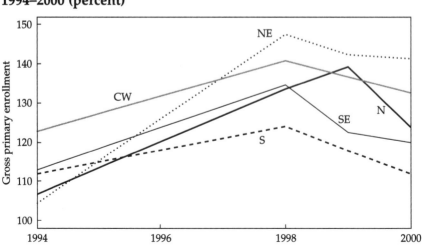

Figure 5.4. Net Primary Enrollment Rates by Region, 1994–2000 (percent)

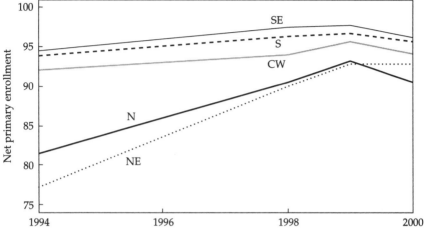

average pupil-to-teacher ratios in basic education in 2002 were the highest in the country and, in some cases, were as high as the 1996 values of the more industrial regions.

Fifth, as shown in figure 5.5, the poorest regions of the N and NE made great strides to catch up with the more industrial regions of the S, SE, and CW in terms of the percentage of teachers for grades 1–4 (EF1) who had completed credentials of higher than primary education. By 2002, almost all teachers in Brazil had acquired the minimum required training.

Table 5.4. Number of Teachers by Level, Region, and Year

	EF1				EF2			
Region	1997	2000	2002	1997–2002 change (percent)	1997	2000	2002	1997–2002 change (percent)
N	67,678	72,463	72,090	6.52	32,202	41,684	47,795	48.42
NE	250,184	262,443	245,511	−1.87	116,315	158,923	187,660	61.34
SE	225,779	226,882	234,357	3.80	226,576	262,693	264,404	16.70
S	105,146	102,018	101,124	−3.83	99,877	107,002	114,427	14.57
CW	44,950	48,334	47,699	6.12	41,287	52,241	53,343	29.20
Total	693,737	712,140	700,781	1.02	516,257	622,543	667,629	29.32

Table 5.5. Mean Pupil-to-Teacher Ratio by Level, Region, and Year

	EF1				EF2			
Region	1996	2000	2002	1996–2002 change (percent)	1996	2000	2002	1996–2002 change (percent)
N	31.2	31.0	30.0	−3.8	26.1	28.0	24.4	−6.5
NE	30.0	29.5	28.5	−5.0	24.7	27.7	26.7	8.1
S	22.8	22.2	21.8	−4.4	17.8	16.9	16.0	−10.1
SE	31.3	29.6	28.2	−9.9	26.9	22.3	20.8	−22.7
CW	30.3	26.4	25.4	−16.2	23.1	22.5	21.8	−5.6
All regions	29.6	28.4	27.4	−7.4	24.6	23.8	22.5	−8.5

Finally, the average years of age-by-grade distortion declined in EF1 and increased in EF2 (see table 5.6). This shift could reflect a possible reform effect in which more age-appropriate children began to enroll in the first year of the primary level, thus decreasing late entry into first grade. In addition, more older children may have returned to the higher grades of basic education after abandoning school, thus increasing age-by-grade distortion in EF2. This shift may reflect changes in demographic patterns. The trend

Figure 5.5. Percentage of Qualified Teachers by Region, 1996–2002

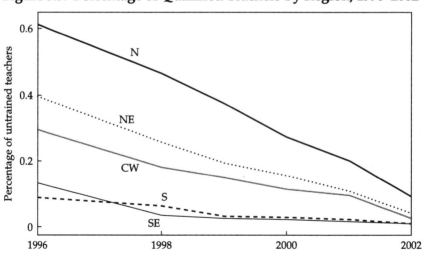

Table 5.6. Age-by-Grade Distortion by Region, Level, and Year (mean and standard deviation)

	EF1				EF2			
Region	1996	2000	2002	1996–2002 change (percent)	1996	2000	2002	1996–2002 change (percent)
N	2.46	2.14	1.86	−24.4	1.99	2.95	2.72	36.7
	(0.47)	(0.70)	(0.71)		(0.23)	(0.67)	(0.84)	
NE	2.86	2.87	2.36	−17.5	2.21	3.66	3.35	51.6
	(0.61)	(0.95)	(0.99)		(0.27)	(0.64)	(0.66)	
S	0.83	0.70	0.62	−25.3	1.12	1.4	1.24	10.7
	(0.21)	(0.31)	(0.32)		(0.25)	(0.33)	(0.40)	
SE	1.16	0.98	0.84	−27.6	1.42	1.74	1.48	4.2
	(0.28)	(0.49)	(0.48)		(0.17)	(0.61)	(0.64)	
CW	1.73	1.50	1.38	−20.2	1.79	2.71	2.35	31.3
	(0.40)	(0.44)	(0.48)		(0.24)	(0.49)	(0.48)	
Total	1.77	1.68	1.43	−19.2	1.68	2.51	2.25	33.9
	(0.92)	(1.11)	(1.00)		(0.46)	(1.09)	(1.08)	

Note: Standard deviations are in parentheses.

toward lower fertility rates means that new cohorts of children are smaller in number as time goes by and that the demographic pressure in lower primary is easing up at the same time as the "bulge" is entering upper primary and secondary levels. We will explore these dynamics further in the discussions that follow.

Financial Data

Our primary resource for financial data in 1996–2002 was the Brazilian Secretariat of the National Treasury (Secretaria do Tesouro Nacional, or STN). The STN Web site offers information on annual state and municipal revenue from a number of federal transfers. Those transfers include the State Participation Fund (Fundo de Participação dos Estados, or FPE); the Municipal Participation Fund (Fundo de Participação dos Municípios, or FPM); and various transfers that go to both states and municipalities, including the tax on financial operations (imposto sobre operações financeiras, or IOF), the tax on industrialized products relative to exports (imposto sobre produtos industrializados, or IPI-exp), the tax on rural territorial property (imposto sobre a propiedade territorial rural, or ITR), and various components of the Complementary Law 87 (LC 87/96).[55]

STN also gives information on FUNDEF revenue to each municipality and state as well as on state and municipal spending. We used the Education and Culture spending to calculate per pupil expenditure. In only one year (2002) and for only the states was information available separately for Education and Culture expenditure. In that year, state spending on culture was on average 2.2 percent of Education and Culture spending (ranging from 0.06 percent to 7.25 percent).

Table 5.7 reports the FUNDEF state allocations from 1998 through 2002 and the minimum spending floor mandated each year. The table shows that FUNDEF may be more effective in addressing within-state inequality in educational spending than inequality across states. Substantial inequalities in per pupil FUNDEF revenue exist along historical lines of regional economic and social inequalities in the country. The NE states of Brazil, specifically, tended to have smaller per pupil FUNDEF allocations than wealthier and more industrial states.

Table 5.8 shows the mean per pupil spending in constant values, by region and year. The means provide evidence of the great inequality in per pupil spending across regions in Brazil while the large standard deviations reveal within-region inequality. The table also indicates that educational expenditures in all regions increased in the 1996–2002 period, especially in the SE, N, and NE. Given that the N and NE regions are the two poorest of the country, the substantial increase in real per pupil spending in those regions suggests that the reform is having much of the desired effect. However, because the reform establishes only a minimum spending per pupil, wealthy areas such as the SE region have been able to increase spending at a faster rate than less advantaged areas.

Table 5.9 reports mean net FUNDEF allocations in per pupil terms and mean per pupil expenditures by year (a) for the top and bottom 20 percent of municipalities in terms of FUNDEF net allocations in 1998 and (b) for the full sample. The figures suggest that FUNDEF losers were, for the most part, mature systems with high per pupil expenditures. Thus, in losing resources, they were unable to reduce educational expenditures. FUNDEF winners were able to substantially increase their per pupil expenditures in 1998–2002, which suggests that the reform led to a crowd-in of

---

55. The only tax that contributes to FUNDEF but is not available from STN is the state tax on the circulation of goods and the tendering of interstate and intermunicipal transportation and communication services (imposto sobre operações relativas à circulação de mercadorias e sobre serviços de transporte interestadual e intermunicipal e de comunicação, ainda que as operações se iniciem no exterior, or ICMS). The revenue generated from this state tax was available on the Web site of the Central Bank. The data are available by state and year from 1996 to 2002. One-fourth of the revenue generated from the ICMS tax is distributed by each state to its municipalities. We used those data in our calculations of FUNDEF and of revenue earmarked for education.

Table 5.7. Annual FUNDEF Per Pupil Allocations in Current Reais by Region, State, and Year (regional means)

Region and state	1998	1999	2000	2001	2002
North	529	553	639	762	935
Acre	607	636	750	890	1,087
Amapá	690	709	813	1,040	1,211
Amazonas	425	422	506	592	669
Pará	309	329	340	377	432
Rondônia	388	428	539	563	711
Roraima	901	927	1,037	1,232	1,551
Tocantins	383	422	490	643	887
Northeast	325	340	379	428	515
Alagoas	336	317	360	402	468
Bahia	303	330	341	377	442
Ceará	312	330	354	393	468
Maranhão	290	329	342	362	435
Paraíba	325	320	354	432	505
Pernambuco	314	318	370	432	514
Piaui	306	326	338	376	443
Rio Grande do Norte	346	378	453	475	633
Sergipe	395	413	498	605	727
Southeast	523	587	673	778	879
Espirito Santo	463	542	622	750	815
Minas Gerais	354	390	466	560	642
Rio de Janeiro	619	635	687	776	868
São Paulo	657	780	915	1,027	1,189
South	485	542	651	752	893
Paraná	418	480	598	688	821
Rio Grande do Sul	561	606	718	829	966
Santa Catarina	477	540	638	740	891
Central West	296	358	407	452	562
Federal District	49	54	69	89	110
Goias	346	381	459	543	677
Mato Grosso	421	513	563	541	738
Mato Grosso do Sul	366	483	535	635	722
Legislated minimum allocation	315	315	333/349.65*	363/381.15*	418/438.90*

Note: For 2000–2002, different minimum amounts of per pupil allocations of state FUNDEF were established for the first series (grades 1–4) and second series (grades 5–8) of basic education. The two numbers correspond to those two levels, respectively.

Table 5.8. Mean Per Pupil Spending, by Region and Year
(in constant 1995 *reais*)

Region	1996	2000	2002	1996–2002 change (percent)
N	614	777	880	43.4
	(275)	(278)	(370)	
NE	466	562	673	44.4
	(218)	(256)	(411)	
S	978	1,226	1,277	30.6
	(391)	(382)	(357)	
SE	890	1,354	1,513	70.0
	(498)	(720)	(501)	
CW	844	1,005	1,055	25.0
	(450)	(518)	(466)	
All regions	751	1,010	1,120	49.1
	(450)	(626)	(572)	

Note: To convert current per pupil spending into constant values, we used the gross domestic product deflator in constant national currency from the IMF's *International Financial Statistics* (2004). The *real*-to-U.S. dollar exchange rate devaluated substantially during this period. In 1996, the exchange rate was approximately 1:1; by 2002, it was 2.92:1 (IMF 2004).

educational expenditures. We will further address this question in our regression analyses.

Student Achievement Data

The Sistema Nacional de Avaliação da Educação Básica (National System for Basic Education Evaluation, or SAEB) is a national educational assessment system administered approximately every 2 years beginning in 1995. It contains standardized exams in math and Portuguese, as well as questionnaires to students, teachers, and school directors. In 2003, it was administered to 300,000 students and 17,000 teachers.

With respect to our study, one limitation of SAEB is that—although the assessment is conducted in all 26 states (and the Federal District) of Brazil—the data cannot be disaggregated at the municipal level. Instead, the test results are representative only for state, municipal, and private schools at the state level.

Tables 5.10 and 5.11 present means, standard deviations, and the Gini inequality coefficient[56] of SAEB language and mathematics test scores

56. The Gini inequality coefficient (or concentration ratio) expresses the overall inequality present in a distribution. It has a theoretical range from 0 (perfect equality) to 1 (perfect inequality).

Table 5.9. Mean Net FUNDEF Per Pupil Allocation and Mean Per Pupil Expenditures, 1998–2002 (in *reais*)

Year	Full sample	Top 20 percent of municipalities by net FUNDEF per pupil in 1998	Bottom 20 percent of municipalities by net FUNDEF per pupil in 1998
Mean net FUNDEF per pupil:			
1998	−76.73901	242.0814	−704.9258
1999	−80.96458	254.6308	−666.4001
2000	−33.41097	280.7323	−640.7048
2001	−12.48755	313.1553	−667.6835
2002	28.05855	388.3044	−635.4375
Average 1998–2002	−34.51019	288.6141	−665.3754
Mean per pupil expenditure:			
1996	1,295.196	525.0750	2,621.689
1998	1,528.070	679.7418	3,118.298
1999	1,646.889	772.7175	3,028.961
2000	1,737.586	894.8524	3,274.638
2001	1,834.941	1,001.1100	3,504.272
2002	1,791.767	1,057.6790	3,153.661
Average 1996–2002	1,718.390	869.5564	3,209.397

Table 5.10. Means, Standard Deviations, and Gini Coefficients for SAEB Language Scores in 1995, 2001

Region	1995		2001	
	Mean	Gini	Mean	Gini
N	174.90 (42.54)	0.14	164.57 (46.28)	0.16
NE	181.26 (45.35)	0.14	161.85 (47.92)	0.17
SE	197.71 (46.37)	0.13	187.92 (52.62)	0.16
S	197.11 (45.81)	0.13	188.98 (48.39)	0.15
CW	193.92 (43.20)	0.13	175.19 (51.29)	0.17
National	187.17 (45.72)	0.14	171.71 (50.27)	0.17

Note: Standard deviations are in parentheses.

Table 5.11. Means, Standard Deviations, and Gini Coefficients for SAEB Mathematics Scores in 1995, 2001

Region	1995		2001	
	Mean	*Gini*	*Mean*	*Gini*
N	176.24	0.10	172.63	0.14
	(31.96)		(42.72)	
NE	182.28	0.12	172.90	0.15
	(38.20)		(45.50)	
SE	199.92	0.12	200.28	0.15
	(42.14)		(51.71)	
S	193.91	0.11	201.53	0.13
	(38.94)		(46.09)	
CW	193.54	0.11	187.56	0.15
	(39.06)		(49.65)	
National	187.85	0.12	182.85	0.15
	(39.18)		(48.37)	

Note: Standard deviations are in parentheses.

by region for 1995 (pre-FUNDEF) and 2001 (post-FUNDEF). As expected, students in the N and NE regions have lower average test scores than do students in the wealthier regions of the country. Overall, the Gini coefficients are small in relative terms, indicating that the variation in student test scores among and between regions is not substantial. Surprisingly, given the equalization objectives of the reform, there appears to have been a slight increase in test score inequality in all regions during 1995–2001.

Empirical Strategy

We used various strategies to address our set of research questions. We grouped our empirical strategies by the nature of our three main research objectives: (a) assessing the effect of FUNDEF-induced spending on state-level enrollment, (b) evaluating system-level mean effects of FUNDEF-induced spending on educational inputs and outcomes, and (c) evaluating the distributional effects of FUNDEF-induced resources on student achievement.

Although the FUNDEF reform was a major force underlying shifts in the allocation of educational resources beginning in 1998, as discussed earlier, it took place at a time of much education reform in Brazil. Thus, the discussion of pre- and post-reform effects does not solely explain the effect of the reform. For example, as FUNDEF overhauled the educational finance in Brazil, the government mandated that teachers must have at least a secondary education degree, thus eliminating the existence of *leigos* teachers—teachers who had completed only primary school. The combination of increased resources for some municipalities and of this mandate is associated with a sharp increase in some states and municipalities in their share of teachers with higher than primary education credentials in the late 1990s, as shown earlier. The policy evaluation problem is complicated by the fact that the two mandates were implemented nationally and at the same time. Any uniform effect of the teacher education mandate will be captured with the year fixed effects. However, if the effect of that mandate varies with FUNDEF-induced spending (for example, if systems with higher spending can more easily eliminate untrained teachers), then our ordinary least squares (OLS), instrumental variable (IV), and reduced-form regression frameworks will attribute that varying effect—along with the direct effects of spending—to FUNDEF.

Assessing the Effect of FUNDEF-Induced Spending on State-Level Enrollment

One of the explicit goals of FUNDEF is to increase enrollment throughout Brazil by guaranteeing the availability of the minimum level of resources needed to meet the legal mandate of mandatory schooling in grades 1–8 in all municipal and state systems. Although narrowing the enrollment rate gap was not explicitly a goal of FUNDEF, it is a fundamental concern not only for education policymakers throughout the world but also for the international donor community in the context of the Millennium Development Goals.[57]

As shown in table 5.1, enrollment rates varied considerably within Brazil before the FUNDEF reform. The net enrollment rate, which is the percentage of age-appropriate children enrolled in fundamental education, ranged from 77.3 percent in the NE region to 94.4 percent in the SE region in 1994. This difference reflects both wide regional disparities and an overall enrollment rate that is far from universal (the countrywide fundamental education enrollment rate is 87.5 percent).

Figures 5.1 and 5.2 show that the timing of the FUNDEF reform coincided with both increased average enrollment and decreased inequality in enrollment rates across regions. Enrollment rates are influenced by a number of factors beyond the school finance environment, however, so we cannot interpret those trends as indicative of a causal relationship. Figure 5.1 shows that enrollment increased in the early 1990s and in the mid- and late-1990s, which cannot be explained by FUNDEF (Duryea, Lam, and Levinson 2003). Duryea, Lam, and Levinson point out the intuitive and empirically

---

57. In September 2000, members of the United Nations unanimously adopted the Millennium Declaration, which establishes eight Millennium Development Goals to be achieved by 2015, including universal primary education.

observed tradeoff between child labor and schooling, and they describe declining child labor in the 1990s (including declines before the introduction of FUNDEF). Lam and Marteleto (2002) analyze the decision to enroll students in school at the individual level, and they find that increasing levels of parental education, decreasing family size, and decreasing cohort size all contributed to increasing enrollment rates in the 1990s.

To avoid conflating the effects of the reform with these other contributors to enrollment growth, we focused on how the amount of spending attributable to the FUNDEF reform affects enrollment. Because the reform also has been associated with shifts from state schools to municipal schools, we conducted our analysis at the state rather than system level. (Note that shifts from municipal schools to state schools within a state will show up as no change in state-level enrollment, so state-level totals will more accurately reflect changes in the number of children enrolled in any public school.) Our approach is quite similar to the empirical strategies already described, with the main difference being that the data are aggregated up to the state level. We estimated the following specifications:

$$(5.1) \qquad Enrollment_{s,y} = \alpha_s + \beta_y + y^* Ed\ Exp_{s,y} + \varepsilon_{s,y}$$

$$(5.2) \qquad Enrollment_{s,y} = \alpha_s + \beta_y + y^* Ed\ Exp_{s,y}$$
$$+ \delta^* Ed\ Exp_{s,y}^{*} BOUND_s + \varepsilon_{s,y}$$

We calculated results separately for enrollment in levels EF1 and EF2 (grades 1–4 and grades 5–8, respectively). $Ed\ Exp_{s,y}$ is aggregate spending on fundamental education (total, not per pupil spending) in state s in year y. The parameters α_s and β_y control for state and year fixed effects. In the specification from equation 5.2, we allow the effect of spending on enrollment to differ according to whether or not a state was bound by the federal revenue floor instituted by FUNDEF. Those states (7 of the 27 total) were the only ones to receive positive net transfers from the federal government as a result of the program. We first estimated equation 5.1 using OLS. Then, to isolate spending changes that are within a state and are attributable to the reform, we used the same instrumental variable approach as described earlier, in which mandated spending under the current policy regime serves as an instrumental variable for actual spending.

Evaluating System-Level Mean Effects of FUNDEF-Induced Spending on Educational Inputs and Outcomes

We investigated the effect of the FUNDEF reform on educational inputs and outcomes first in an OLS regression, then with IV and reduced form approaches that use the funding formula to isolate changes in inputs that are attributed to the reform and not to any unobserved changes in demographic composition or preferences. Because the different regions of the country are so heterogeneous, we chose to present all our results not only by region but also for the nation as a whole.

First, we analyzed the effect of educational expenditures on inputs and outputs using OLS. We estimated the following model:

(5.3) $Outcome_{j,y} = \alpha_j + \beta_y + y^*Ed\ Exp_{j,y} + \varepsilon_{j,y}$

In this model, *Outcome* is, alternatively, educational inputs (teacher qualifications and class size) or outputs (age-by-grade distortion). *Ed Exp* is total educational expenditure in each system (municipal or state), and we analyzed separately the aggregate and per pupil figure. Subscript *j* denotes the jurisdiction, which is either a municipality or state, and subscript *y* denotes the year. We estimated equation 5.3 using system-level (municipality or state) and year fixed effects, with and without controlling for enrollment levels. The system-level fixed effects allow us to control for unobserved, system-level tax bases or preferences for educational spending that could affect outcomes and educational spending if those unobserved variables are constant over time. In this model, the main coefficient of interest is that of *Ed Exp*.

Because of the system and year fixed effects, the OLS results were estimated from changes in educational spending within a municipal or state system and, therefore, do not attribute to the reform (a) any time trends that are uniform across all systems or (b) any correlations between FUNDEF amounts and any municipal or state characteristics that are constant over time. The effects of the FUNDEF reform varied widely across systems, so sufficient variation exists to identify the OLS estimates. Those estimates, however, may capture changes in educational spending at the system level that are attributed to factors beyond the reform such as changes in the demographic composition of a municipality or changes in preferences for educational spending. This effect is problematic if those factors influence the outcomes of interest and the levels of educational spending.

As we addressed this possibility, our second empirical approach was to isolate the changes in educational spending that are attributed to the FUNDEF reform. We examined levels of educational spending and inputs with quantities predicted by the amount of aid that systems received from FUNDEF. If unobservables such as preferences for education or system tax bases were, for example, to push down (or up) educational spending within a system, then the IV estimates of the effect of the reform would be higher (or lower) than the OLS estimates.

Next, we presented reduced-form estimates of the reform's mean effect on the relevant outcome with system-level fixed effects, so that, over time, the variation in outside revenue from FUNDEF—rather than the variation in spending or input levels—within each municipal or state system identifies changes in other variables. The simplest way to think of the distinction between the IV and the reduced-form approaches is that the IV approach uses policy-induced, exogenous variation to identify the effect of spending on student outcomes whereas the reduced-form approach identifies the effect of the revenue from the policy itself on outcomes. We estimated the following model:

(5.4) $Outcome_{j,y} = \alpha_j + \beta_y + y^* Mandated_{j,y} + \varepsilon_{j,y}$

In this model, *Outcome* and all subscripts are defined as before. *Mandated* is the total revenue mandated to be spent on basic education, which varies depending on whether the year is before or after realization of FUNDEF. Before 1998, *Mandated* equaled 25 percent of all contributing taxes and transfers. In 1998 and after, it equaled 10 percent of the taxes and transfers that contribute to the FUNDEF account, 25 percent of the noncontributing taxes and transfers, and payments from FUNDEF. Also note that actual payments to municipal and state systems from FUNDEF vary with enrollment or, more specifically, with a school system's share of total current enrollment in that state. Estimating the effect of the reform on enrollment, however, is of independent interest to our study. We, therefore, estimated the effect of the *Mandated* variable on inputs and outputs by holding the enrollment share of each school system (within its state) constant over time at its level before the realization of the reform. As before, we estimated equation 5.4 using system-level (municipality or state) fixed effects, with and without controlling for enrollment levels. We also estimated per pupil variations of that equation in which educational spending and revenue mandated for education are both in per pupil terms. In this model, the main coefficient of interest is that of *Mandated*.

In addition to exploring the effects of spending on inputs to and outputs from the education production function, we also directly examined the production function itself. We did this by analyzing the effect of inputs (again, class size and teacher training) on student outcomes. The setup was the same as in the previous analyses: (a) variables are year and system fixed effects, (b) OLS looks at direct effects of inputs, and (c) the IV approach uses mandated spending as an instrument for actual inputs.

Evaluating the Distributional Effects of FUNDEF-Induced Resources on Student Achievement

Because our student achievement data are representative only at the state and not at the municipal level, we explored the effect of the distributional changes in resources on student achievement, asking whether more equalized spending and inputs help to close the gap in student outcomes. Thus, we evaluated the effect of the reform on students at the 25th, 50th, and 75th percentiles of the achievement distribution. We fit the following models using quantile regression analysis:

(5.5) $$Score_{i,s,y} = \beta_0 + \beta_1 PPE_{s,y} + \varepsilon_{s,y}$$

(5.4) $$Outcome_{j,y} = \alpha_j + \beta_y + y^* Mandated_{j,y} + \varepsilon_{j,y}$$

where $Score_{i,s}$ is the math or language score of student i in state s in year y, $PPE_{s,y}$ is per pupil spending on fundamental education in state s in year y, and $Ineq\_Ed\ Exp_{s,y}$ is the 75:25 inequality ratio in aggregate spending on basic education among the municipalities in state s in year y. In these models, we included state and year fixed effects.

Findings

We found that changes in spending induced by the reform are associated with reduced class size and do not significantly affect the share of teachers with credentials higher than primary education. Those inputs are, in turn, associated with negligible reductions in the student age-by-grade distortion rate. We found small positive effects on enrollment and mixed findings on the distributional effect on student achievement.

Before presenting our results, we must note the first-stage results in tables 5.12, 5.13, and 5.14, which show that applying the formula that determines FUNDEF revenue to states and municipalities will provide a strong predictor of what those jurisdictions ultimately spend on schooling.

Table 5.12. Stage 1: Effect of Mandated Educational Spending on Actual Educational Spending

	Educational expenditures (total)	Educational expenditures per pupil	Educational expenditures per pupil	Educational expenditures per pupil
Mandated spending	1.020 (0.004)	1.027 (0.005)		
Mandated spending per pupil			1.020 (0.009)	1.016 (0.009)
Enrollment		−1.030 (0.272)		−0.000 (0.000)
Number of observations	22,879	22,879	17,957	17,957
R^2	0.77	0.77	0.52	0.53

Note: Standard errors are in parentheses.

Table 5.13. Stage 1: Effect of Mandated Educational Spending on Actual Per Pupil Educational Spending, by Geographic Region

	N	NE	S	SE	CW
Mandated spending per pupil	1.134	1.065	1.046	1.138	0.799
	(0.057)	(0.022)	(0.019)	(0.014)	(0.038)
Enrollment (students)	−0.000	−0.000	−0.001	−0.000	−0.001
	(0.000)	(0.000)	(0.000)	(0.000)	(0.000)
Number of observations	1,253	7,022	6,000	6,690	1,914
R^2	0.63	0.59	0.51	0.70	0.43

Note: Standard errors are in parentheses.

Tables 5.12, 5.13, and 5.14 show results from estimating equation 5.4 with actual educational spending, either total spending or per pupil spending, as the dependent variable as opposed to other inputs or outcomes.

For ease of interpretation, we prefer the per pupil specification of inputs on outcomes, so our preferred specifications in table 5.12 are in columns 3 and 4. The inclusion of enrollment as a control does not affect the strength with which formula-driven, mandated spending predicts actual spending (compare columns 3 and 4). The coefficient on mandated spending (in column 3) is 1.02, which is highly statistically significant with a standard error of 0.009. The R^2 for the specification is 0.52. Table 5.13 shows that this predictive power holds across all regions of the country, and table 5.14 shows that it is also robust across all post-reform years for which we have data.

The fact that mandated spending per pupil predicts actual spending per pupil with such strong t statistics is important for the validity of the instrumental variables and reduced-form estimations that follow. That mandated spending predicts actual spending with coefficients so close to

Table 5.14. Stage 1: With Year-Specific Predictors

	1998	1999	2000	2001	2002
Mandated spending per pupil	0.984	1.005	0.962	0.979	1.012
	(0.016)	(0.015)	(0.015)	(0.016)	(0.016)
Enrollment	−0.001	−0.000	−0.000	−0.000	−0.000
	(0.000)	(0.000)	(0.000)	(0.000)	(0.000)
Number of observations	6,091	6,121	6,649	6,730	6,294
R^2	0.62	0.64	0.60	0.63	0.65

Note: Standard errors are in parentheses.

one is informative independently. States and municipalities can devote some additional revenue beyond that mandated for educational spending. A coefficient less than 1 (for example, 0.8) would suggest that jurisdictions reduced their voluntary educational revenue efforts by 20 percent of an increase in mandated spending per pupil, whereas a coefficient greater than 1 (for example, 1.5) would suggest that jurisdictions increased their voluntary educational revenue efforts by 50 percent of an increase in mandated spending per pupil. Our results suggest quite small and statistically insignificant crowd-out, with a point estimate of under 2 percent in 1998, the first year of implementation. For each year that follows, the coefficients are statistically insignificantly different from 1, suggesting that the reform led to the planned increase in educational expenditures. That those coefficients are so close to 1 also explains why the OLS estimates are so similar to the IV estimates: FUNDEF allocations by the state, rather than unobserved changes in preferences or local responses to the reform, were largely responsible for changes in spending at the local level over this period.

Effects of FUNDEF-Induced Spending on State-Level Enrollment

Table 5.15 presents OLS and IV results for the state-level analysis of the effect that FUNDEF-induced spending has on enrollment levels (estimated from equation 5.1). FUNDEF appears to be driving the bulk of the variation over time within jurisdictions (here, within states), so the OLS and IV estimates are quite similar. We have aggregated the data used in our estimates from all the municipalities and the state system for each year. The number of municipal systems reporting varies by year. This variation may reflect not only changes in school system organization such as consolidation but also missing data. Missing data are not a problem in the municipal-level analyses, which contain municipal fixed effects. In the

Table 5.15. State-Level Effects of Spending on Enrollment, by Level

	EF1 (grades 1–4)		EF2 (grades 5–8)	
	OLS	IV	OLS	IV
Educational spending	−0.004	−0.005	−0.002	−0.001
	(0.001)	(0.001)	(0.001)	(0.001)
Educational spending × bound by FUNDEF floor	0.007	0.004	0.022	0.025
	(0.004)	(0.004)	(0.002)	(0.003)
State-year observations	162	162	162	162
State observations	27	27	27	27

Note: Standard errors are in parentheses.

aggregated case, the state observation will not be missing, even if there are missing components. More municipalities reported in 1996 than in later years. If this decrease is driven by systematically lower reporting rates after the reform, then the results will be biased toward finding declines in enrollment. Another impetus for the aggregation is that an effect of the reform appears to have been that municipal systems now focus on providing basic education (grades 1–8), while state education systems are increasingly focusing on post-basic education. By aggregating to the state level, therefore, we are evaluating the effect of the reform on actual changes in enrollment and not on transfers between municipal systems or flows of students from state systems to municipal, or vice versa.

Table 5.15 describes the type of result for EF1 that could be attributed to decreases in reporting rates by municipal systems: The OLS and IV estimates both report statistically significant but economically negligible effects of spending on enrollment. Because our financial data are in hundreds of reais, the −0.005 coefficient on spending for EF1 enrollment in the IV specification means that a R$100,000 increase in spending, statewide, would reduce EF1 enrollment by five students. For EF1 enrollment, there is no differential effect for whether or not a state is bound by the federal floor of educational revenue per pupil (the coefficient on educational spending × bound by floor is insignificant).

The results for EF2 enrollment, however, present a different picture. For states that are not bound by the FUNDEF floor, the effect of FUNDEF-induced spending on enrollment is statistically insignificant for the IV specification. For states that are bound by the floor, however, enrollment increases with spending. To interpret the 0.025 coefficient, we should consider the mean total spending increase of about R$190 million from 1996 to 1998 among states bound by the floor. An increase of this kind predicts an increase in EF2 enrollment to slightly fewer than 5,000 students. Mean EF2 enrollment for those states was 353,935 in 1996 and 386,672 in 1998. The predicted increase is, therefore, less than 2 percent of base enrollment and accounts for 15 percent of the total observed increase in EF2 enrollments from 1996 to 1998. Although this effect is not huge, the data do indicate that spending was more positively associated with enrollment gains in grades 5–8 in the states that benefited the most from the reform. (Those states also had the lowest initial enrollment rates, but analyzing the interaction between spending and pre-FUNDEF enrollment rates, not shown, yields statistically insignificant responses.)

System-Level Mean Effects of FUNDEF-Induced Spending on Educational Inputs and Outcomes

In the paragraphs that follow, we evaluate the effect of FUNDEF on educational inputs and outcomes. In particular, we focus on how systems responded to the changed levels of resources available for education resulting from FUNDEF in decisions about class sizes and teacher qualifications. In addition, we explore the effect of the reform on student outcomes, specifically age-by-grade distortion rates and the distribution of student achievement.

Effects of FUNDEF-Induced Spending on Inputs

How did school systems spend the money they received from FUNDEF? Conversely, for those systems losing money, how did they cut back? We focused on two key variables: the teacher-to-pupil ratio and the share of teachers with credentials of only primary education.[58] We analyzed both variables at the EF1 and EF2 levels separately. We presented estimates from the OLS, IV, and reduced-form specifications of spending on class size in table 5.16 and on the share of teachers with credentials higher than primary education in table 5.17.

Table 5.16 shows that increasing mandated spending has a statistically significant and negative effect on class size at both the EF1 and EF2 levels. If we interpret the coefficients, the IV point estimate of −0.184 for EF1 class size implies that an increase of R$1,000 in mandated spending per pupil is associated with a reduction in class size of 1.84 students. (Recall that mean spending per pupil, in all levels combined, increased from about R$750 to a little more than R$1,100 from 1996 to 2000.) For EF2, an increase of R$1,000 in mandated spending per pupil would lead to a predicted decrease in class size by 2.1 students.

The findings on teacher training generally are not statistically significant, and the point estimates are not economically significant. From the comparison of means, we know that the share of teachers with more education background was rising over this period, especially in EF1 and in the N and

Table 5.16. Effects of Educational Spending Per Pupil on Class Size, by Level

	EF1 (grades 1–4)			EF2 (grades 5–8)		
	OLS	IV	Reduced form	OLS	IV	Reduced form
Spending per pupil	−0.127 (0.004)	−0.184 (0.007)		−0.166 (0.031)	−0.208 (0.044)	
Mandated expenditures per pupil			−0.185 (0.007)			−0.218 (0.047)
Number of observations	23,460	17,954	18,002	16,445	12,873	12,903
R^2	0.14		0.14	0.01		0.02

Note: Standard errors are in parentheses.

Table 5.17. Effects of Educational Spending Per Pupil on Share of Teachers with Credentials Higher Than Primary Education, by Level

	EF1 (grades 1–4)			EF2 (grades 5–8)		
	OLS	IV	Reduced form	OLS	IV	Reduced form
Spending per pupil	0.0001 (0.0002)	0.0018 (0.0003)		–0.0002 (0.0001)	–0.0000 (0.0003)	
Mandated expenditures per pupil			0.0018 (0.0003)			–0.0000 (0.0003)
Number of observations	23,516	17,954	18,002	16,482	12,873	12,903
R^2	0.32		0.34	0.02		0.02

Note: Standard errors are in parentheses.

NE regions where the proportion of untrained teachers was highest. This trend is likely to be a direct result of the new requirement that teachers have secondary degrees. The IV estimates for EF1 in table 5.17 show us that an additional R$1,000 of spending per pupil increased the share of EF1 teachers with credentials higher than primary education by 1.8 percentage points. The increase in the share of teachers with credentials higher than primary education far exceeded this estimate: Teachers without secondary degrees were nearly completely eliminated over this period in all areas of Brazil, so the mandate was likely influential beyond the scope of the FUNDEF revenue received by a jurisdiction.

Effects of FUNDEF-Induced Spending and Inputs on Student Outcomes

We have seen that the revenue redistributed by the FUNDEF system corresponds with changes in educational inputs and, in particular, to changes in class size. At the same time, teacher qualification rates changed, but this was independent of the FUNDEF redistribution. In this section of the chapter, we initially show how, first, spending and, then, class size and teacher qualification rates correlate with student outcomes. We used the average number of years of age above the norm for a specific grade (known as age-by-grade distortion) as our outcome variable. Age-by-grade distortion usually reflects not only late school entry but also repetition and periodic school dropout and reentry. All three (late entry, dropout, reentry) have been identified as major obstacles in education in Brazil, as well as in the South

---

58. We were unable to analyze how FUNDEF allocation is associated with teacher salaries because we could not find any municipal-level data on teacher salaries.

American and Central American regions. Next, we explore how reducing the inequality of educational spending that results from FUNDEF can affect inequality in student achievement among and within states.

Table 5.18 presents results for spending effects on age-by-grade distortion. It shows nearly identical results for the OLS and reduced-form specifications of the effect of spending on age-by-grade distortion. That is, whether the independent variable of interest is actual or mandated, spending per pupil makes little difference. The key finding is that, although educational spending is statistically related to age-by-grade distortion, thus reducing the average number of years of age above the norm (delay) is quite costly. Increasing actual or per pupil spending by R$1,000 reduces delay in EF1 by only 0.05 of one year and, in EF2, by only about 0.01 of one year. This dynamic is likely a result, in part, of simultaneous changes in the demographic composition of enrolled students. If the reform increases enrollment, then the marginal student who attends would likely be less prepared for school than before, so expected delays should be greater. As before, the IV estimates are quite similar to the OLS and reduced-form estimates.

The results of table 5.18 relate spending levels to student outcomes and prompt the question of whether some municipalities and states were able to direct their educational spending more effectively than others. In table 5.19, we estimate a rough education production function in which class size and teacher training determine age-by-grade distortion. In the IV regressions, we used mandated spending as an instrument for class size and percentage of qualified teachers.

The OLS estimates suggest that larger classes have a statistically significant, but economically insignificant, association with greater delay in EF1 but not EF2 and that teacher training contributes to positive student outcomes

Table 5.18. Effects of Educational Spending Per Pupil on Age-by-Grade Distortion, by Level

	EF1 (grades 1–4)			EF2 (grades 5–8)		
	OLS	IV	Reduced form	OLS	IV	Reduced form
Spending per pupil	−0.003 (0.001)	−0.005 (0.001)		−0.009 (0.001)	−0.001 (0.002)	
Mandated expenditures per pupil			−0.005 (0.001)			−0.001 (0.002)
Number of observations	23,463	17,954	18,002	14,409	11,359	11,388
R^2	0.14		0.15	0.38		0.40

Note: Standard errors are in parentheses.

Table 5.19. Effects of Education Inputs
on Age-by-Grade Distortion, by Level

	EF1 (grades 1–4)		EF2 (grades 5–8)	
	OLS	IV	OLS	IV
Class size	0.002	0.023	0.000	0.005
	(0.001)	(0.005)	(0.000)	(0.013)
Share of teachers with	−0.488	−0.551	−0.049	−0.107
at least primary education	(0.025)	(0.031)	(0.064)	(0.079)
Observations	23,516	18,002	14,388	11,343
R^2	0.16		0.38	

Note: Standard errors are in parentheses.

in EF1 but not in EF2. A 10 percent increase in the share of teachers with credentials higher than primary education corresponds to a statistically significant 0.05-year decline in average delay in EF1 and to a 0.005-year decline in
EF2. The weaker result for EF2 reflects the small variation in the share of
EF2 teachers with credentials higher than primary education both before and
after the teacher education mandate. An increase of one student per teacher
is associated with a 0.002-year increased delay in EF1, but there is no effect for
EF2. The IV estimates are a bit stronger than the OLS estimates for EF2 and
are quite similar for EF1. Interpreting the welfare effects of the estimates
would require valuing the negative effects of age-by-grade distortion and
then comparing them with local costs of class-size reduction.

Distributional Effects of FUNDEF-
Induced Resources on Student Achievement

Because the SAEB standardized test scores are not representative at the
municipal level but they are at the state level, our evaluation of the effect
of FUNDEF on student achievement necessarily focused on FUNDEF's
effect on the distribution of achievement among and within states. Ideally,
we would have wished to analyze how the FUNDEF-induced, student-
specific change in resources affected achievement. We analyzed the effect
of the reform on the distribution of student achievement in math and language among states. We used quantile regression analysis to assess the
differential effect of the reform at various levels of the achievement distribution. We conducted the same analyses for math and language, and the
results do not differ substantively. For ease of presentation herein, we
include only the math achievement results.

Table 5.20 presents the effect of changes in mean actual per pupil spending across states on the distribution of achievement among states. Our
analyses included the effect of mean actual per pupil spending on the 25th,

Table 5.20. Estimated Effect of Changes in State-Level Mean Per Pupil Spending on Mathematics Student Achievement by Percentile

	$q(0.25)$	$q(0.50)$	$q(0.75)$
Actual mean per pupil spending	−0.001	−0.001	−0.001
	(4.66e−11)	(4.90e−17)	(2.68e−11)
Pseudo R^2	0.787	0.784	0.797
Number of observations	78	78	78

Notes: Standard errors are in parentheses. All models include year and state dummies.

50th, and 75th percentiles of the mathematics achievement distribution. The results in the table show that the effect of state-level, actual average, per pupil spending on student achievement does not differ by percentiles of the achievement distribution and that the effect is economically insignificant. To interpret the coefficients, we must recall that the mean mathematics score for Brazil fell from 188 (standard deviation 39) in 1995 to 183 (standard deviation 48) in 2002 and that mean spending per pupil in Brazil rose R\$369, from R\$751 in 1996 to R\$1,120 in 2002. Applying the coefficient at the median—the $q(0.50)$ column—suggests that the mean R\$369 increase in per pupil spending is associated with a 0.00369-point (or less than one-thousandth of a standard deviation) decline in math achievement for the typical student. Though precisely estimated, this effect clearly is not behaviorally or economically significant.

Table 5.21 presents the results from an analysis of the effect that changes in actual spending inequality among states had on the distribution of achievement. We use the ratio of the 75th to the 25th percentiles in mean actual per pupil expenditures as our measure of spending inequality. This ratio was equal to 1.51 for all of Brazil in 1996 and equal to 2.35 in 2002 (weighting school systems by their current enrollments).

The results in table 5.21 suggest that inequality in actual per pupil spending is associated with lower scores for students in the bottom per-

Table 5.21. Estimated Effect of Changes in State-Level Inequality in Per Pupil Spending on Mathematics Student Achievement by Percentile

	$q(0.25)$	$q(0.50)$	$q(0.75)$
Actual per pupil expenditure inequality 75/25	−1.213	0.843	1.135
	(6.31e−09)	(1.25e−14)	(5.58e−15)
Pseudo R^2	0.786	0.784	0.8
Number of observations	78	78	78

Notes: Standard errors in parentheses. All models include year and state dummies.

centiles of the achievement distribution and is associated with positive effects for students at the top. For example, the second panel of the table shows that an increase of 1 in the state-level ratio of per pupil expenditures of the 75th to the 25th percentile is associated with a reduction of about 1.2 points in student achievement of the students in the 25th percentile. In contrast, the same increase in this state-level inequality ratio is associated with an increase of about 1.1 points in mean student achievement of students in the 75th percentile. The direction of those effects is not surprising given that schools with higher socioeconomic status students tend to spend more and to have higher achievement levels. The unexpected result is, rather, that the magnitude of the relationship is so small.

Conclusions and Policy Implications

We find that the revenue flows from FUNDEF translated fully into educational spending, suggesting that municipal and state governments used the new funds as supplemental, thus not as substitutes, for their own revenue. From a policy perspective, this finding alone is important. Unlike many educational finance reforms, FUNDEF succeeded in its goal of ensuring that the resources allocated to education by the reform were indeed used as intended.

We find that some part of the new influxes of revenue through the FUNDEF system were used to reduce class size and that the federal legislation mandating that teachers have at least a secondary education degree was successful. The improvements in both teacher education and class size are negatively correlated with age-by-grade distortion, but we note that the magnitude of those correlations is quite small, particularly given their costs.

Although assessing the effect and cost-effectiveness of the class size reduction on student achievement is beyond the scope of this paper, it is not clear that reductions in average class sizes would result in improvements in student achievement in Brazil. First, compared with other middle-income countries, Brazil already has relatively small average class sizes. Second, the literature on the effect of class size on student achievement in the United States has shown, at best, inconclusive evidence that class size reductions are associated with improvements in student learning.[59] Moreover, given the current average class size in Brazil, pursuing further reductions in class size is probably not warranted from a fiscal standpoint.

---

59. Measuring the effect of class size on student achievement is made difficult because the preponderance of variations in class size results from choices made by parents, schools, or policymakers. As a result, most of the observed variation in class size is correlated with other determinants of student achievement, which leads to biased estimates of the effect of class size (Hoxby 2000). For reviews of the evidence on class size, see Betts (1995), Card and Krueger (1996), and Hanushek (1996, 1986). Hoxby (2000) uses natural population variation to identify the effect of class size on student achievement and finds that reductions in class size have no effect on achievement.

Furthermore, though the per capita–based funding system makes it difficult to draw causal inference from the relationship between spending and enrollment, the timing of the FUNDEF system has coincided with significant increases in enrollment for grades 5–8. Our analyses indicate that FUNDEF had the greatest effect on increasing enrollment in municipalities that were spending below the reform-mandated minimum per pupil. Thus, a policy implication is that educational finance reforms that include required minimum spending floors can have a positive effect on improving access to education.

Our analyses of the effect of the reform on student achievement provide some evidence that the reduction in spending inequality resulting from FUNDEF may have positive effects on nonwhites and students at the bottom of the achievement distribution. Consistent with most research on the relationship between spending and student outcomes, the relationship that we found between mean spending and student achievement is quite weak throughout the distribution of achievement. However, this finding may simply reflect insufficient variation in mean spending within states over time. The development of a restricted-access version of the SAEB achievement data with more specific geographic identifiers would greatly aid in research efforts such as this study and others.

References

Abrahão de Castro, J. 1998. "O fundo de manutenção e desenvolvimiento do ensino e valorização do magisterio e seu impacto no financiamento do ensino fundamental." Texto para Discussão 604. Instituto de Pesquisa Económica Aplicada, Brasília.

————. n.d. "Financiamento da educação no Brasil." Instituto de Pesquisa Económica Aplicada, Brasília. Processed.

Betts, J. 1995. "Is There a Link between School Inputs and Earnings? Fresh Scrutiny of an Old Literature." In G. Burtless, ed., *Does Money Matter? The Link between Schools, Student Achievement, and Adult Success*. Washington, D.C.: Brookings Institution.

Card, D., and A. B. Krueger. 1996. "Labor Market Effects of School Quality: Theory and Evidence." In G. Burtless, ed., *Does Money Matter? The Link between Schools, Student Achievement, and Adult Success*. Washington, D.C.: Brookings Institution.

Card, D., and A. A. Payne. 2002. "School Finance Reform, the Distribution of School Spending, and the Distribution of Student Test Scores." *Journal of Public Economics* 83: 49–82.

Casassus, J., S. Cusato, J. E. Froemel, and J. C. Palafox. 2002. *First International Comparative Study of Language, Mathematics, and Associated Factors for Students in the Third and Fourth Years of Primary School: Second Report*. Santiago: United Nations Educational, Scientific, and Cultural Organization.

Clark, M. A. 2003. "Education Reform, Redistribution, and Student Achievement: Evidence from the Kentucky Education Reform Act." Mathematica Policy Research, Princeton, N.J. Processed.

Duryea, S., D. Lam, and D. Levinson. 2003. "Effects of Economic Shocks on Children's Employment and Schooling in Brazil." PSC Research Report 03-541. Population Studies Center at the Institute for Social Research, University of Michigan, Ann Arbor.

Gordon, N. 2004. "Do Federal Grants Boost School Spending? Evidence from Title I." *Journal of Public Economics* 88(9–10): 1771–92.

Hanushek, E. A. 1986. "The Economics of Schooling: Production and Efficiency in Public Schools." *Journal of Economic Literature* 24(3): 1141–77.

———. 1996. "Measuring Investment in Education." *Journal of Economic Perspectives* 10: 9–30.

Hoxby, C. M. 2000. "The Effects of Class Size on Student Achievement: New Evidence from Natural Population Variation." *Quarterly Journal of Economics* 115(4): 1239–85.

———. 2001. "All School Finance Equalizations Are Not Created Equal." *Quarterly Journal of Economics* 116(4): 1189–231.

International Monetary Fund. 2004. *International Financial Statistics.* Electronic database. Washington, D.C.

Lam, D., and L. Marteleto. 2002. "Small Families and Large Cohorts: The Impact of the Demographic Transition on Schooling in Brazil." PSC Research Report 02-519. Population Studies Center at the Institute for Social Research, University of Michigan, Ann Arbor.

Soares, S. 1998. "The Financing of Education in Brazil: With Special Reference to the North, Northeast, and Center-West Regions." Latin American and the Caribbean Social and Human Development Paper Series 17. Latin America and the Caribbean Regional Office, World Bank, Washington, D.C.

World Bank. 2002. *Brazil Municipal Education: Resources, Incentives, and Results.* Vols. I and II. Washington, D.C.

6

Arbitrary Variation in Teacher Salaries:
An Analysis of Teacher Pay in Bolivia

Miguel Urquiola
Columbia University

Emiliana Vegas
World Bank

Understanding teacher compensation is important in developing countries, where teacher pay accounts for most educational expenditures. Although teacher compensation schemes have been criticized by economists, largely because of their perceived rigidity, only a limited set of studies seem to consider their details. Most research on teacher compensation has focused on how well teachers are paid relative to comparable individuals in other occupations.[60] One exception is Morduchowicz (2002), which reviews the salary structures of several Latin American countries and describes the most common determinants of teacher pay.

This study differs from the previous literature in that we are less concerned with how well teachers are paid and more interested in exactly what is remunerated in a specific salary structure—that of Bolivia. As in Morduchowicz (2002), we focus on understanding the incentives embedded in teacher pay. We not only provide a description of its structure, but also

For useful comments and suggestions, we thank Daniel Cotlear, Patrick McEwan, Orlando Murillo, John Newman, Carolina Sanchez-Páramo, Maria Luisa Talavera, Eric Verhoogen, and Till Von Wachter. We are grateful to the Bolivian Ministry of Education for providing data, and to Rafael Joffré at Geosystems for coordinating the collection of the geo-coded school data. Miguel Urquiola can be contacted at msu2101@columbia.edu. Emiliana Vegas can be contacted at evegas@worldbank.org.

60. See for instance Ballou and Podgursky (1997); Lankford and Wyckoff (1997); Liang (1999); Mizala and Romaguera (2001); Piras and Savedoff (1998); Podgursky (2000); and Vegas, Pritchett, and Experton (1999).

decompose teacher pay to assess the extent to which it rewards traits such as training and experience. In doing so, we find some arbitrary variation in teacher pay by location, and we exploit it to better understand the effect of teacher pay incentives on teacher quality and student performance.

More specifically, this chapter carries out four tasks. We first provide a detailed description of Bolivia's teacher compensation scheme as we point out that it essentially rewards three characteristics in teachers: their training, their location of work (urban or rural), and their experience or seniority. Further, it does so in a relatively mechanistic fashion: a regression of salaries on dummy variables characterizing teachers along those dimensions produces an R-squared statistic in excess of 0.9.

Second, we present a simple decomposition to calculate the extent to which those three components are emphasized. It allows one to address questions, such as "Does the pay scale implicitly place more emphasis on training or on seniority than on location of work?" Such information is relevant, for instance, because the Bolivian government has implemented special bonus payments to address a perceived shortage of certified teachers in the rural area. To evaluate such policies, one must understand the incentives that encourage teachers to work in rural areas and that already exist in the pay scale.

Third, we analyze the movement of teachers through the salary structure, particularly in light of recent changes to the regulations that govern salaries. This exercise reveals some contradictions in the compensation policy, as well as significant budgetary implications.

A fourth set of analyses is necessary because the Bolivian Ministry of Education makes a distinction between urban and rural schools. In practice, the growth of cities has meant that some rural schools have been absorbed into an urban area. The Ministry, however, has not stripped those schools of their rural status, which generates arbitrary variation in teacher salaries. Two teachers who have similar training and who work the same number of hours in nearby schools may have different salaries simply because one school is classified as urban and the other as rural. We find that this variation is associated with teachers' labor supply behavior, but we find no evidence that it affects student performance.

Our findings are, of course, specific to Bolivia. Nonetheless, the exercises we present may provide a useful template for analyzing teacher compensation in other developing countries with relatively centralized and rigid compensation schemes.

The chapter is organized as follows. The following section describes the data. Then, we detail the structure of teacher compensation. Next, we decompose teacher pay to identify the extent to which certain teacher traits are actually remunerated. The next section analyzes the flow of teachers through the salary structure and assesses budgetary implications. Then, we analyze the effect of arbitrary variation in teacher salaries on the labor supply of teachers and on student outcomes. Finally, we present some conclusions.

Data

To consider such issues, we have assembled the following data, all of which we are able to match to the school, the teacher level, or both for approximately the year 2002:

- Payroll information on the universe of teachers for March 2002. This information comes from the actual payroll database used by the Ministry of Education. It includes the amount paid to each teacher, as well as his or her essential training and experience characteristics, hours worked, and schools worked in.
- Administrative data on schools' physical characteristics and on their performance in a school-level incentive scheme. This information comes from the ministry's Educational Information System (Sistema de Información Educacional, or SIE) tabulations for 2002.
- Third-grade language and math test scores for a sample of schools for 1999. These data are from Bolivia's Educational Quality Measurement System (Sistema de Medición de la Calidad Educativa, or SIMECAL).
- Geographic Information System (GIS) information on the universe of schools in one city, Santa Cruz. We collected these data specifically for this project.

Teacher Pay in Bolivia

Bolivia's national pay scale for teachers is fairly rigid. Compensation is largely determined by three characteristics: formal credentials of preservice training, location of work, and years of experience. First, to calculate base salaries, divide teachers into four groups according to their training:

- *Interim* teachers (*interinos*) are those who have not completed formal training and have fewer than 9 years of experience in public schools. Particularly in rural areas, they may not even have graduated from high school.
- *Experience-certified* teachers (*titulares por antigüedad*) are in a category that is composed of individuals who are not trained but to whom the state accords a special status in view of experience—a minimum of 9 years of work in public schools.
- *All but degree (ABD)* teachers (*egresados*) have completed their formal preservice training but are missing some requirement for certification. Frequently, the (nontrivial) missing prerequisite is the completion of 2 years of service in rural or provincial areas.
- *Certified* teachers (*normalistas*) are those who have graduated from teacher training and who have completed 2 years of service in a rural or provincial school.

Table 6.1. Base Salaries by Geographic Region and Training Status

	Location of work		
Training status	Urban	Provincial	Rural
Interim	100	110	120
Experience-certified	110	121	131
ABD	121	134	145
Certified	133	146	160

Note: Salaries are given as a percentage of the amount paid to an urban interim teacher.

As this discussion suggests, the Ministry of Education assigns each public school to one of three geographical areas: urban, provincial, and rural. Urban schools are those in the major cities, typically department capitals (of which the country has nine). Rural schools are in sparsely populated areas, while provincial ones are typically in towns linked to a larger urban center by a major road. As we discuss below, those distinctions are not hard and fast.

Training and location of work determine base salaries. The salaries (see table 6.1) are standardized relative to those of an urban interim instructor. This lowest-paid teacher, as of early 2002, received a monthly base salary of about US$65.

As these data illustrate, the more trained teachers are, the more they are paid; the farther away they work from an urban area, the more they are paid. The highest-paid teacher (in terms of base salaries only) makes 60 percent more than an urban interim instructor.

The pay scale, furthermore, makes a distinction between a teacher and an "item," or teaching position. Until 2001, the standard, or full-time-equivalent, position required that a teacher work for 72 hours per month.[61] In practice, this measurement refers to pedagogic hours, which are defined as 45 minutes of teaching time and 15 minutes of preparation. Teachers who have 72-hour positions, therefore, need to spend only about 4 hours daily in school, which allows them to hold more than one position, although in practice most teachers do work 72 hours. The base salaries in table 6.1 refer to the 72-hour benchmark item.

To arrive at total compensation, we see that a key additional factor is each teacher's position in the scheme known as the *Escalafón Docente*. This system, originally instituted in the 1950s, creates a scale based primarily on seniority. The possible classifications and the salary increases *over the base salary* that these classifications accord are listed in table 6.2.

---

61. In late 2002, this standard was extended to 96 hours.

Table 6.2. Seniority-Based Pay Increases: Escalafón

Category	Percentage increase
Without category	0
Interim	10
Fifth	30
Fourth	45
Third	60
Second	75
First	100
Zero	125
Merit	150

In the worst-case scenario, a teacher can be "without category," in which case he or she makes only a base salary. This status is transitional, usually for teachers straightening out their paper work. The next category entails a 10 percent increase over the base salary and is labeled "interim," which is not to be confused with the training category of the same name. Indeed, it is possible for relatively trained teachers (such as an ABD) to be in this category; likewise, interim (by training) teachers can attain higher seniority categories.

When the Escalafón was first instituted, the transition between categories was purely a matter of years of experience, with 4 years required for each transition.[62] The Educational Reform Law (1994) introduced an exam that must be passed to switch to a higher category, and teachers have the option of taking the exam every 4 years. The pass rate seems to be high, but, in practice, not all teachers who are eligible will take the exam.

Combining the three described criteria yields a comprehensive relative salary structure, as summarized in table 6.3. As these data indicate, the additions to the lowest salary (shown in bold) range from 10 to 300 percent. To again benchmark these numbers to an absolute amount, we see that the highest-paid teacher (by the criteria considered thus far) received a monthly salary of about US$260 in early 2002. Again, those amounts refer to individuals in full-time-equivalent positions; in practice, some teachers earn more by working more than one position.[63]

---

62. An exception is the first one, which requires 5 years.

63. Although table 6.3 includes an entry for each possible cell, in practice teachers with certain types of training cannot attain certain seniority categories, an issue we will return to later in this chapter.

Table 6.3. Salary Structure

Area of work and training category	Without category		Seniority category							
		Interim	5	4	3	2	1	0	Merit
Urban										
Interim	100	110	130	145	160	175	200	225	250
Experience-certified	110	121	143	160	176	193	220	248	275
ABD	121	133	157	175	194	212	242	272	303
Certified	133	146	173	193	213	233	266	300	333
Provincial										
Interim	110	121	143	160	176	193	220	248	275
Experience-certified	121	133	157	175	194	212	242	272	303
ABD	134	147	174	194	214	235	268	302	335
Certified	146	161	190	212	234	256	292	329	365
Rural										
Interim	120	132	156	174	192	210	240	270	300
Experience-certified	131	144	170	190	210	229	262	295	328
ABD	145	160	189	210	232	254	290	326	363
Certified	160	176	208	232	256	280	320	360	400

Note: Salaries are given as a percentage of the amount paid to an urban interim teacher.
Source: Tables 6.1 and 6.2.

What Does the Pay Scale Reward?

Although teachers receive other payments, those salaries implicit in table 6.3 account for more than 85 percent of all of the Ministry of Education's expenditures on teachers. Further, a regression of payroll salaries (amounts of teachers' actual paychecks) on dummy variables for all the categories in tables 6.1 and 6.2, as well as hours worked, produces an R-squared statistic close to 0.9. Thus, the state rewards essentially three traits in teachers: their training, their location of work, and their experience.

Obtaining a More Precise Decomposition

One might want to know how the expenditure is divided among all these components. For example, is the government implicitly rewarding location of work more than training? In this section, we address this issue in a simple way. Specifically, we split the salary associated with every possible combination of training, area of work, and seniority (each cell in table 6.3) into four components: (a) a base payment (in some sense) made simply to put an adult in each classroom, (b) a payment for training, (c) a reward for location of work, and (d) a payment for experience. We can then add up the components to calculate how much the state spends on each of those traits.

Figure 6.1 illustrates the idea behind this exercise. In it, we focus only on urban areas and, therefore, consider only payments for training and experience (recall that the urban area is the benchmark; teachers receive greater pay for working outside of it). The figure shows how urban teachers' salaries evolve with experience for each of the four training categories (that is, it essentially graphs the first panel of table 6.3). As one moves to the right, the steps reflect seniority increases. This graph implicitly assumes, therefore, that teachers move between the Escalafón categories purely on the basis of experience. It abstracts from the exams in place since 1994 and from any other factors that may impede their progress (some of which we discuss later in the chapter). For this reason, the following calculations should be seen as providing an approximation rather than a fully precise accounting.

To see the spirit of the decomposition, consider the highest-paid teacher in this figure: the certified instructor who earns 332.50. What portion of this payment is attributable to training and what portion to seniority? One can divide the 332.50 into three components as follows:

- A base salary of 100 (the payment to an interim instructor without seniority), which is the minimum any teacher receives regardless of his or her characteristics.
- An additional 150 payment for seniority. This calculation reflects the difference between 100 and 250, where the latter is the payment made to an interim teacher who is also in the highest experience category. Thus, this payment is made for a teacher's experience, regardless of his or her training.
- Finally, 82.50 is a reward this teacher receives for training. This figure comes from the difference between 332.50 and 250, which is the amount paid to a teacher who is certified, that is, the amount paid over and above the salary of an interim instructor who has just as many years of experience.[64]

---

64. This calculation might overstate the payment to training and underestimate the payment for seniority somewhat. With experience, interim teachers should eventually become certified by experience, although, as we discuss later, this certification does not always happen. In other words, one might expect the two bottom lines in figure 6.1 to merge, but in practice this does not always happen. Thus, we carry out calculations as if it never did. Again, because of the necessity for such simplifying assumptions, our results should be interpreted as an approximation.

**Figure 6.1. Salary Progression for Urban Teachers
of All Training Levels**

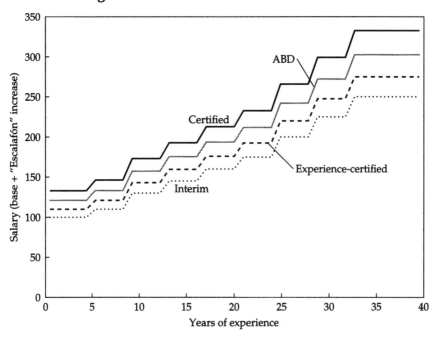

We carried out a similar calculation for every cell in table 6.3 (for now under the unrealistic assumption that there is an equal number of teachers in each cell). Then we aggregated the payments across cells.[65]

Table 6.4 presents the results of the decomposition for the data in table 6.3. If this were the case, almost half the total wage bill would go to the base payment (equal to the salary of an urban interim teacher). Of the

---

65. Mechanically, the easiest way of making these calculations is to regress the log of salaries on dummies for each of the training, seniority, and location of work categories, where the excluded categories are those corresponding to the teacher with the lowest base pay (urban, interim, and no seniority). Not surprisingly, the R-squared statistic on this hypothetical decomposition is close to 1. The exponents of the coefficients (in column 2) indicate the percentage increase over the base salary that accrues to teachers with the associated characteristics. For instance, one can see that those for seniority essentially correspond to table 6.2. To obtain the decomposition in table 6.4, we see that the increments implicit in column 2 are then multiplied by the number of teachers who receive them. For example, the increments attributed to provincial and rural status accrue to 36 (each) of the 108 cells in table 6.3. Similarly, the increments attributed to the highest seniority accrue to only 12. We then add all these increments to obtain the decomposition in table 6.4. The results of this exercise are, of course, close to those one obtains doing a manual calculation such as that illustrated using figure 6.1.

Table 6.4. A Hypothetical Decomposition of the Teacher Wage Bill

Percentage	Category
52.1	Base payment
5.2	Location of work
8.3	Training (preservice)
34.4	Seniority (experience component of the Escalafón)
100.0	Total

remaining half, the majority (about 31 percent) are payments for experience, followed by payments for training (13 percent) and for location of work (9 percent).

Factoring in Other Payments

To further flesh out table 6.4, one must consider other payments that teachers receive. The key additions fall into two categories: bonuses (*bonos*) and incentive payments. In the first case, two mutually exclusive payments accrue to some teachers according to their location of work: the Zone and Frontier bonuses. Each of those is equal to 20 percent of the teacher's base salary. In the first case (Zone), the payment goes to teachers who work in schools classified as being in inaccessible areas. In the second (Frontier), the payment is for instructors in schools within 50 kilometers of international borders.

Another class of bonus payments, unlike those first two, consists of fixed amounts paid to all qualifying teachers regardless of their base salaries. The first two of those are the Pro-book bonus and the Economic bonus, which in 2002 were equal to one monthly minimum wage and 726 bolivianos (Bs.) (about US$100), respectively.

In addition, there is the Attendance bonus, earned by teachers who work at least 200 days per year. In practice, almost all instructors receive it. Until March 2002, this payment consisted of a lump sum of Bs. 303 per year (about US$42). As a result of negotiations that ended a 3-week-long strike, that amount was doubled. None of those amounts enter teachers' base pay; therefore, they do not lead to seniority-related pay increases.

Additionally, at the time of our analysis the Ministry of Education had three broadly understood incentive schemes targeted at teachers:

- A payment for teachers who work in and remain in poor, rural regions, called the IPR (Incentivo a la Permanencia en el Area Rural Pobre).
- A payment for teachers who work in bilingual instruction programs, called the IMB (Incentivo a la Modalidad Bilingue).

- A payment for teachers who engage in certified training, test-taking activities, or both, called the IAD (Incentivo a la Actualización Docente).

Table 6.5 presents a decomposition that considers all payments. Additionally, those results are now weighted to reflect the actual number of teachers in each cell of table 6.3.

Each of the categories in table 6.4 is now broken down into its components. Base payments cover not only the payments made to an interim teacher in the lowest seniority category, but also the Economic and Pro-book bonuses. Those flat amounts are paid regardless of teachers' characteristics or behavior. Furthermore, the location of work category now includes not only the rewards implicit in the Escalafón, but also those that arise from the Zone, Frontier, and IPR bonuses. Finally, we add an entry for other behaviors: payments made for traits not rewarded implicitly or explicitly in the base salary, or Escalafón, calculations.

Despite being purely descriptive, those analyses have several implications. For instance, they reveal that the Ministry of Education spends about half of its salary budget in what are essentially lump-sum payments to teachers, payments that leave no latitude for rewarding training, experience, or location of work, let alone effort or other behaviors.

Table 6.5. A Decomposition of the Teacher Wage Bill

Percentage		Category
47.0		**Base payments**
	40.0	Payments to an urban interim teacher without category
	4.3	Economic bonus
	2.5	Pro-book bonus
12.5		**Location of work**
	7.7	Rewards to geography implicit in the Escalafón
	1.7	Zone bonus
	2.0	Frontier bonus
	1.1	IPR (bonus for rural area work)
15.2		**Training (preservice)**
21.9		**Seniority (experience component of the Escalafón)**
3.4		**Other behaviors**
	1.0	Administrative bonus
	0.3	IMB (bonus for bilingual education)
	2.0	IAD (bonus for in-service training)
100.0	100.0	Total

Additionally, the payments for location of work do not loom large; they account for only about 13 percent of all salary expenditures. Furthermore, the IPR bonus for work in rural areas, which was implemented 2 years ago (and recently abolished), is unlikely to have influenced teachers' location choices very much. Rather, it introduced a marginal change on the overall compensation pattern. That change accounts for about 1 percent of overall compensation and only one-tenth of the overall payments for location of work. Those results also suggest that it might be possible to keep the total wage bill constant and yet reduce the base payment while allocating greater rewards to encourage teachers to work in rural locations.

Determining whether the allocations in table 6.5 are high or low, or what effects changing them would have, is beyond the scope of this chapter. Nonetheless, policymakers should find such decompositions useful.

The Flow of Teachers through the Salary Structure

Understanding the movement of teachers through the salary structure is useful in assessing the structure's budgetary implications. For this analysis, we use the payroll data and limit our analysis to teachers in standard 72-hour-per-month positions. This restriction simplifies the analysis, and our sample still accounts for 78 percent of all teaching positions (the remainder of our analyses refer to about 83,000 positions).

Table 6.6 shows the distribution of those teachers by area of work and training status. Looking at training status, we see that roughly half the teachers (48 percent) are fully certified. As discussed, ABD teachers often have as much formal preparation as certified instructors, and if we count them as such, the "trained" share exceeds 75 percent. The remainder is made up of interim and experience-certified instructors.

Table 6.6. Distribution of Teachers by Geographic Region and Training Status

Training status	Location of work			
	Urban	Provincial	Rural	Totals
Interim	3,144 (3.8)	3,080 (3.7)	9,095 (10.9)	15,319 (18.4)
Experience-certified	1,840 (2.2)	1,031 (1.2)	1,370 (1.6)	4,241 (5.0)
ABD	5,515 (6.6)	6,863 (8.2)	11,902 (14.2)	24,280 (29.0)
Certified	19,930 (23.9)	6,037 (7.2)	13,749 (16.5)	39,716 (47.5)
Totals	30,429 (36.4)	17,011 (20.4)	36,116 (43.2)	83,556 (100.0)

Note: Absolute numbers of department capital are in each category, followed by percentage shares in parentheses.

The data also show a significant variation in the prevalence of trained instructors across areas: 16 percent of urban teachers lack formal training, whereas in the provincial and rural areas, 24 and 29 percent, respectively, are in a similar situation. Table 6.6 also shows that about 4 percent of all teachers earn the lowest base salary, while 17 percent earn the highest.

Now consider the distribution according to training and seniority category, as presented in table 6.7. More than half of the teachers are in the bottom three experience categories, largely in the interim and fifth category of the Escalafón. This situation is important to keep in mind—it highlights that despite the significant returns to experience implicit in the pay structure, more than half of all public school teachers receive relatively small seniority-related payments. This "bunching up" of teachers at the bottom of the Escalafón has important implications to which we return later.

Note also that there are no teachers in a number of training-experience combinations (shaded in gray). For instance, the first column shows that the highest seniority category that interim teachers reach is the fifth one.[66] As the untrained teachers enter the profession, they go into the interim category in the Escalafón, and receive a 10 percent increase over the base salary (see table 6.2). After 5 years, they can transition into the fifth category and receive a 30 percent increase.[67] After those 9 years of service, interim teachers can become experience-certified. This transition is visible in table 6.7, where the number of experience-certified teachers jumps from 30 to 1,472 between the fifth and the fourth categories, while the number of interim teachers drops from 2,708 to essentially zero.[68]

These numbers are also consistent with the presence of high attrition among the interim teachers. Although the numbers are not sufficient to prove this impression, they are in line with anecdotal evidence suggesting that eventually many interim teachers find other forms of employment, and very few make it (as experience-certified instructors) into the upper reaches of the Escalafón. This attrition rate may partially reflect that for the first 9 years of their careers, those individuals dwell in the lowest-paying parts of the scale.

There are also shaded cells in the column for ABD teachers. In particular, ABD instructors do not progress past the fifth Escalafón category; indeed, being a certified teacher is a requirement for attaining the fourth category. This evidence suggests that to the extent some teachers have difficulties in fulfilling all the certification requirements, a significant number of them get "stuck" in the fifth category—almost one of every four teachers (not just the ABDs) is in this cell.

The existence of this bottleneck is a key characteristic of the teacher compensation system. Although we do not have direct evidence, the prob-

---

66. The lone position in the fourth category may reflect a coding error.
67. At this point they come to be known as *interinos inscritos al Escalafón*.
68. There is one position in the fourth category—again, this might be a coding error.

Table 6.7. Distribution of Teachers by Training and Experience (Escalafón category)

Seniority category	Training category				
	Interim	Experience-certified	ABD	Certified	Total
Without category	357 (0.4)	72 (0.1)	544 (0.7)	607 (0.7)	1,580 (1.9)
Interim	12,253 (14.7)	117 (0.1)	4,476 (5.4)	0 (0.0)	16,846 (20.2)
Fifth	2,708 (3.2)	30 (0.0)	19,258 (23.1)	3,223 (3.9)	25,219 (30.2)
Fourth	1 (0.0)	1,472 (1.8)	2 (0.0)	5,399 (6.5)	6,874 (8.3)
Third	0 (0.0)	748 (0.9)	0 (0.0)	5,447 (6.5)	6,195 (7.4)
Second	0 (0.0)	764 (0.9)	0 (0.0)	7,648 (9.2)	8,412 (10.1)
First	0 (0.0)	453 (0.5)	0 (0.0)	5,192 (6.2)	5,645 (6.7)
Zero	0 (0.0)	373 (0.5)	0 (0.0)	5,532 (6.6)	5,905 (7.1)
Merit	0 (0.0)	212 (0.3)	0 (0.0)	6,668 (8.0)	6,880 (8.3)
Total	15,319 (18.3)	4,241 (5.1)	24,280 (29.2)	39,716 (47.5)	83,556 (100.2)

Note: Absolute numbers are in each category, followed by percentage shares in parentheses.

lem seems to arise because many teachers fail to fulfill the 2 years of provincial or rural service that are required for full certification. Perhaps the absence of such service is caused by an unwillingness to incur the costs of moving to a rural area or, in some cases, to serve in faraway towns.

This bottleneck has probably had significant consequences. On one hand, it probably resulted in financial savings for the ministry and thus helps to account for the relatively small payments allocated to seniority observed in table 6.5 (compared with table 6.4). On the other hand, it might have resulted in attrition among ABD teachers, who, after losing hope of fulfilling the provincial service requirements, realized that their earning potential in the teaching profession was in some sense capped. This bottleneck also led to some potential contradictions in the ministry's human resources policies. For example, the ministry puts a priority on increasing the number of trained teachers, but the bottleneck, in fact, implies that some experience-certified teachers, who have no formal training, earn more than fully trained ABD instructors.

In a major change to the operation of the labor market for teachers, a recent ruling, RM 432,[69] has effectively eliminated the provincial service

---

69. Resolución Ministerial 432; November 16, 2001.

requirement to become a certified teacher. Because of regular bureaucratic delays and the number of years it takes to move between Escalafón categories, the effects of RM 432 are only starting to be observed, and the ruling's complete consequences will be evident only after several years.

What effects will it ultimately have? RM 432 is likely to eliminate some contradictions in the ministry's compensation policies, as well as to introduce others. At a purely financial level, RM 432 will allow large numbers of ABD teachers to become fully certified, which in a few years might place significant pressure on the ministry's budget (this potential outcome does not seem to have been carefully analyzed).

At the same time, RM 432 removes what was perhaps the strongest incentive that teachers had for working in the rural area. To the extent that the ministry is seeking to increase the presence of trained teachers in the rural area through initiatives like the IPR bonus, these initiatives seem to be contradictory. More specifically, RM 432 seems to remove one of the most powerful (and largely unexploited) policy levers that the ministry had, because it could have used the eligibility of certain provincial schools to direct teachers to relatively poor rural areas (as it tried to do with the IPR). For instance, the ministry could have reclassified schools or announced that 1 year of provincial service in particularly poor rural schools would be equivalent to 2 in others. Importantly, such measures could have been implemented without modifying any part of the Escalafón, with respect to which the teacher unions seem to favor the status quo. Those initiatives might well have been more powerful than incentive payments like the IPR.

Arbitrary Variation in Teacher Salaries

As noted, one source of variation in teacher salaries is the classification of schools into urban and rural areas, and the concomitant higher compensation given to instructors in the latter. A final set of exercises arises because, in practice, the growth of cities has meant that some rural schools have been absorbed into an urban setting. One might expect such institutions to be reclassified, but given the pay scale, that reclassification would amount to lowering the instructors' salaries. Apparently fearing union opposition, the Ministry of Education has rarely stripped those schools of their rural status. As a result, two teachers with similar training and experience, working in physically very proximate schools, can now earn significantly different salaries.

Urban Rural Schools

The prevalence of this phenomenon is described in table 6.8 for the three main districts in the country: La Paz/El Alto, Cochabamba, and Santa

Table 6.8. Types of Schools in the Three Largest Cities

City	Rural (1)	Mixed (2)	Urban (3)	Total (4)	N (5)
La Paz/El Alto	7.3	0.5	92.2	100.0	642
Cochabamba	5.3	0.7	94.0	100.0	283
Santa Cruz	14.2	6.4	79.4	100.0	681
Total	9.9	3.1	87.0	100.0	1,606

Note: Column numbers are in parentheses.

Cruz.[70] We determine whether a school is urban or rural by using payroll data. That is, we inspect how a school's teachers are classified and paid. Column 1 describes schools that we will label rural: they contain rural teachers exclusively. They exist in all three cities, but they are particularly prevalent (14 percent of the total) in Santa Cruz—the urban area that has grown the fastest in the past decades.

Column 2 describes the prevalence of mixed schools, a term we use to refer to schools that contain both urban and rural teachers. In theory, mixed schools should not be observed because the school is classified as rural, not the teacher. They reflect an irregularity with which successive administrations have been unable or unwilling to deal. Again, they are much more prevalent in Santa Cruz, where more than 20 percent of schools are either rural or mixed.

Table 6.9 presents related information at the teacher level. As expected, the largest concentration of rural teachers is found in Santa Cruz.[71] In every city, the average salary is higher among rural instructors. Figure 6.2 describes the actual distribution of salaries in the three cities. The variation is greatest in Cochabamba and smallest in Santa Cruz. This distribution reflects the fact that in Cochabamba, rural teachers tend to be more trained and experienced. In Santa Cruz, rural and urban instructors are much more similar; hence their salary differences are not as great.

Table 6.10 presents some basic results about the association between rural and urban pay differentials and about teachers' labor supply within the profession.[72] In panel A, we present results from ordinary least squares regressions of total hours worked in a rural status. Column 1 reports results from the simplest bivariate specification, suggesting that rural teachers

---

70. La Paz and El Alto are legally separate jurisdictions, but we combine them because they are adjacent and essentially form only one urban center. Those districts may not exactly coincide with their respective cities, an issue we return to later.

71. Matters are actually slightly more complicated because there are also provincial teachers in these districts. As it turns out, however, very few teachers (less than 0.2 percent) have that classification. For simplicity, we include them in the rural category.

72. Observations are, of course, now aggregated (from positions) to the teacher level.

Table 6.9. Descriptive Statistics on Teachers

City	Santa Cruz			Cochabamba			La Paz		
	Urban	Rural	Total	Urban	Rural	Total	Urban	Rural	Total
Number of teachers	7,629	1,541	9,170	5,910	356	6,266	14,935	412	15,347
Percentage of teachers	83.2	16.8	100.0	94.3	5.7	100.0	97.3	2.7	100.0
Mean salary (US$)	193.1	255.6	203.6	218.5	313.8	223.9	204.2	266.2	205.9
Training status (percentage by category)									
Interim	18.0	13.2	17.2	8.7	2.8	8.4	9.8	7.5	9.7
Experience-certified	6.5	6.9	6.6	5.5	1.7	5.3	6.8	0.7	6.6
ABD	25.9	24.7	25.7	15.7	14.3	15.7	17.6	20.9	17.7
Certified	49.5	55.3	50.5	70.1	81.2	70.7	65.9	70.9	66.0
Seniority status (percentage by category)									
No category	6.9	2.1	6.1	11.7	1.7	11.1	11.9	1.9	11.6
Interim	17.0	15.4	16.8	6.5	2.8	6.3	7.6	9.0	7.6
Fifth	26.5	23.8	26.1	18.2	15.4	18.0	21.3	23.8	21.5
Fourth	8.8	7.0	8.5	7.1	3.4	6.8	8.3	5.8	8.2
Third	6.9	6.6	6.9	7.5	5.9	7.4	10.2	7.0	10.1
Second	10.1	10.8	10.2	12.3	14.9	12.5	14.3	17.0	14.4
First	7.2	7.9	7.3	9.7	4.8	9.4	9.6	11.7	9.6
Zero	9.3	9.9	9.4	12.5	13.8	12.6	8.8	11.2	8.8
Merit	7.4	16.5	8.9	14.5	37.4	15.8	8.0	12.6	8.1

work about 7 hours less than urban ones—an effect equivalent to about one-third of a standard deviation in hours worked. Columns 2 and 3 show that controlling for training and seniority results in a slight decline in the marginal effect of rural status, which remains highly significant. Finally, columns 4–6 report estimates (for the last specification) for the three cities separately. They again suggest that rural teachers work fewer hours than others.

In panel B, we analyze the effect of rural status on whether teachers hold more than one position. The results again suggest a labor supply

Figure 6.2. Distributions of Relative Salaries
for Urban and Rural Teachers

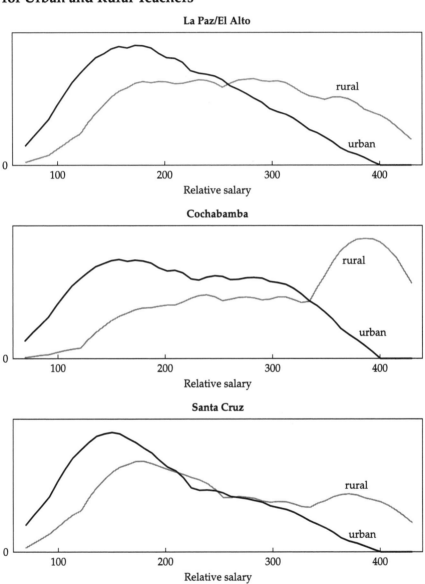

La Paz/El Alto

rural

urban

0   100   200   300   400

Relative salary

Cochabamba

rural

urban

0   100   200   300   400

Relative salary

Santa Cruz

rural

urban

0   100   200   300   400

Relative salary

Table 6.10. Hours Worked and the Probability of Holding a Second Teaching Job

	All cities			La Paz/El Alto	Cochabamba	Santa Cruz
	(1)	(2)	(3)	(4)	(5)	(6)
Panel A. Dependent variable = Total hours worked						
Rural status	-7.2***	-7.3***	-4.2***	-6.9***	-6.0***	-3.7***
	(0.5)	(0.5)	(0.4)	(0.8)	(0.9)	(0.6)
	[-0.35]	[-0.36]	[-0.21]	[-0.34]	[-0.30]	[-0.18]
Controls: Teacher and school characteristics	No	Yes	Yes	Yes	Yes	Yes
Dummies for experience categories	No	No	Yes	Yes	Yes	Yes
N	24,973	24,973	24,973	12,230	4,719	8,024
R^2	0.010	0.018	0.342	0.411	0.401	0.220
Panel B. Dependent variable = Dummy for holding more than one job (linear probability)						
Rural status	-0.16***	-0.16***	-0.09***	-0.10***	-0.16***	-0.06***
	(0.01)	(0.01)	(0.01)	(0.02)	(0.02)	(0.01)
Dummies for training categories	No	Yes	Yes	Yes	Yes	Yes
Dummies for experience categories	No	No	Yes	Yes	Yes	Yes
N	24,973	24,973	24,973	12,230	4,719	8,024
R^2	0.013	0.015	0.408	0.470	0.357	0.302

Note: Column numbers are in parentheses in the column heads. *** indicates significance at the 1 percent level. Huber-white standard errors are in parentheses. Brackets contain the proportion of a standard deviation change in the dependent variable.

effect: having rural status is associated with a reduction of about 15 percent in the probability that the teacher has a second teaching position. This conclusion is robust to the addition of training and experience controls, and to the estimation within cities.[73]

There are several things to note when interpreting the results. First, although it seems clear that rural teachers work less, we are unable to ascertain the mechanism behind this finding. In a conventional interpretation, one might think that having rural status and, hence, enjoying higher earnings would induce substitution and income effects on labor supply, and that the latter would dominate. In some sense, this assumption might not be shocking, given that, as elsewhere, a significant proportion of Bolivian teachers seem to be mothers and secondary earners who express a preference for spending part of the day at home (Urquiola and others 2000).

Such an inference, however, requires an assumption that the individuals who select into rural schools are not systematically different from those in urban institutions, so that any differences in the hours or the number of positions they work might plausibly be caused by variations in their pay. This assumption is strong, given that into the mid-1990s the route into the two types of schools was somewhat different. Specifically, in the past, urban and rural teachers were trained in different institutions and belonged to different unions.

Furthermore, to the extent that attaining rural status might require "gaming the system" (for example, the existence of mixed schools when they should not occur), then teachers who attain such positions might be different from others in unobserved ways. Another concern arises if it is administratively harder for rural teachers to increase either their hours or the number of positions they teach in, because, presumably, there is higher demand for those higher-paying posts. Finally, we note that our results originate in administrative data that capture only teachers' labor supply *within the profession*. The data do not tell us whether rural teachers might be engaging any more or less in outside activities, such as driving a cab.

Urban and Rural Pay Differentials and Achievement

A related question is whether rural teachers, perhaps because they are paid more, exert more effort and thus produce better outcomes. Again, using the urban and rural pay differences to address this issue requires significant assumptions. First, urban and rural teachers in these cities ideally should be similar except for their rural or urban status. In some of the following analyses, we focus on Santa Cruz; although the variation in teacher

---

73. Logit regression results, which we omit, yield qualitatively similar conclusions.

pay is more limited there than in the other two cities (figure 6.2), its urban and rural teachers appear to be more similar.

Second, similar students should attend each type of institution. One possible complication is that parents might seek out the rural schools with the knowledge that instructors there are better paid. This outcome seems unlikely because the majority of parents are not aware of teacher pay differences, for a variety of reasons. They would have to know the details of the way teacher pay is calculated, which is unlikely (in discussions we held, even ministry officials were surprised by the number of rural teachers in Santa Cruz). Moreover, the unions do not seem to call attention to this situation. Finally, the extra expenditure is directed purely at salaries—these schools receive exactly the same infrastructure and other allocations as the rest, so at least physically they cannot be singled out. Indeed, most ministry officials do not know whether a particular teacher is classified as urban or rural unless they examine the payroll data carefully.

Nonetheless, other mechanisms could generate differences in the characteristics of students each type of school serves. To get a sense of whether this factor is a concern, at least among observable student characteristics, table 6.11 presents socioeconomic characteristics of a sample of students broken down by whether they are in urban schools or in rural

Table 6.11. Student Characteristics in Urban and Rural Schools[a]

City	All schools (1)	Urban (2)	Rural or mixed (3)	Difference between (2) and (3)
Panel A. All schools				
Percentage male	49.50	49.90	47.40	2.5
Percentage who work	43.90	44.40	41.70	2.7
Age	8.97	8.95	9.08	−0.1
Percentage with Spanish as first language	74.30	73.90	76.50	−2.6
Panel B. Santa Cruz				
Percentage male	49.40	50.40	47.80	2.6
Percentage who work	35.90	36.50	35.00	1.5
Age	9.09	9.06	9.14	−0.1
Percentage with Spanish as first language	82.80	82.30	83.60	−1.3

Note: Column numbers are in parentheses.
a. Numbers indicate the difference is significant at the 5 percent level.

and mixed schools. These variables are drawn from a student questionnaire administered to students along with the standardized examinations. They include the student's gender, age, whether she or he works outside of school, and whether Spanish is his or her native language. As the table shows, for none of these variables is the difference across types of schools statistically significant.

Table 6.12 presents results on whether student outcomes vary across these two sectors. Panels A and B refer to language and math test scores

Table 6.12. Hours Worked by Teachers and Probability of Holding a Second Job

	All cities		Santa Cruz	
	(1)	(2)	(3)	(4)
Panel A. Average third-grade language score				
Rural status	−0.10	−0.11	0.03	0.08
	(0.12)	(0.12)	(0.18)	(0.19)
	[−0.10]	[−0.11]	[0.03]	[0.08]
Controls: Teacher and school characteristics	No	Yes	No	Yes
N	698	698	225	225
R^2	0.001	0.009	0.000	0.021
Panel B. Average third-grade math score				
Rural status	0.06	0.09	0.15	0.27
	(0.12)	(0.12)	(0.20)	(0.21)
	[0.12]	[0.12]	[0.20]	[0.21]
Controls: Teacher and school characteristics	No	Yes	No	Yes
N	698	698	225	225
R^2	0.000	0.005	0.002	0.041
Panel C. Repetition rate				
Rural status	−0.006**	−0.004	−0.000	−0.000
	(0.003)	(0.003)	(0.004)	(0.004)
	[−0.13]	[0.09]	[−0.00]	[−0.00]
Controls: Teacher and school characteristics	No	Yes	No	Yes
N	1,220	1,220	477	477
R^2	0.003	0.043	0.000	0.007

(Continued)

Table 6.12. Hours Worked by Teachers and Probability of Holding a Second Job (*Continued*)

	All cities		Santa Cruz	
	(1)	(2)	(3)	(4)
Panel D. Pass rate				
Rural status	0.014***	0.00***	0.010**	0.009**
	(0.004)	(0.004)	(0.005)	(0.00)
	[0.28]	[0.24]	[0.20]	[0.18]
Controls: Teacher and school characteristics	No	Yes	No	Yes
N	1,187	1,187	467	467
R^2	0.010	0.044	0.010	0.024
Panel E. Dropout rate				
Rural status	0.009***	0.006***	0.004	0.003
	(0.001)	(0.001)	(0.001)	(0.001)
	[0.56]	[0.38]	[0.25]	[0.19]
Controls: Teacher and school characteristics	No	Yes	No	Yes
N	975	975	412	412
R^2	0.055	0.340	0.018	0.276

Note: Column numbers are in parentheses in the column heads. **, *** indicate significance at the 5 and 1 percent level, respectively. Huber-white standard errors are in parentheses. Brackets contain the proportion of a standard deviation change in the dependent variable.

and contain no significant evidence that scores are significantly different between rural and urban schools. Columns 1 and 2 present pooled results for schools in all three cities, and columns 3 and 4 refer to Santa Cruz only.

The results in panels C–E draw on administrative data to examine to what extent repetition, pass, or dropout rates differ across the two types of schools. We find some contradictory evidence. Rural schools appear to have lower repetition and higher pass rates, but also higher dropout rates—although those results are not always significant. The bottom line is that, given the strong assumptions required and the weak results, we cannot draw substantial conclusions from our regressions.

In an attempt to identify better comparison groups for this analysis, we collected GIS information on the location of all schools in Santa Cruz. Figure 6.3 presents those data; the dots represent urban schools, and the triangles stand for rural institutions. We carried out analyses by using

Figure 6.3. GIS Data for Santa Cruz Schools

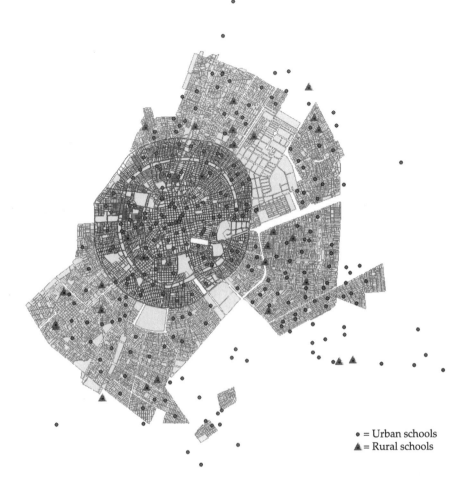

• = Urban schools
▲ = Rural schools

comparison groups for each rural school and by selecting the urban schools closest to that school (for example, within a certain radius). The logic behind this method is that, to the extent schools serve neighborhood households, the surrounding schools might provide better comparison groups. We again do not find consistent evidence of performance differences for urban and rural schools using this classification criterion.

In short, we find no systematic differences in achievement between urban and rural schools. Although this result may be because our empirical strategies do not successfully identify those differences, it leaves open the possibility that the extra expenditure in this area is not really buying better outcomes.

Conclusions

In many developing countries, the teacher wage bill accounts for the vast majority of recurrent educational expenditures. Additionally, teacher pay scales are frequently fairly rigid and have features that governments find politically very costly to change. In such contexts, it is important to understand well the details of the pay scheme. What is the state implicitly paying for and obtaining? What implicit and explicit incentives does the pay scale contain?

In this chapter, we have addressed such questions for Bolivia. We have provided a detailed characterization of teacher compensation and of the teacher traits—training, location of work, and experience—that the salary structure seems to reward. Additionally, we analyzed the flow of teachers through the pay scale, highlighting budgetary implications and potential contradictions in the ministry's human resources policy. Finally, we attempted to determine whether the arbitrary variation in teacher salaries that the pay scale generates in some cities has any effect on teachers or student outcomes (as measured by standardized test scores). Although our findings indicate that the rural and urban teacher pay differential is associated with a variation in the labor supply for teachers, we do not find any systematic relation with student achievement.

All of our conclusions are, of course, specific to Bolivia. Nonetheless, the exercises we present may provide a useful template for analyses in other developing countries that also have fairly centralized and rigid teacher compensation schemes.

References

Ballou, D., and M. Podgursky. 1997. *Teacher Pay and Teacher Quality.* Kalamazoo, Mich.: W. E. Upjohn Institute for Employment Research.

Lankford, H., and J. Wycoff. 1997. "The Changing Structure of Teacher Compensation, 1970–94." *Economics of Education Review* 16(4): 371–84.

Liang, X. 1999. "Teacher Pay in 12 Latin American Countries: How Does Teacher Pay Compare to Other Professions, What Determines Teacher Pay, and Who Are the Teachers?" Latin America and the Caribbean Region Human Development Department Paper 49. World Bank, Washington, D.C.

Mizala, A., and P. Romaguera. 2001. "Are Teachers Underpaid? Evidence from Chile." Center for Applied Economics, Department of Industrial Engineering, University of Chile, Santiago. Processed.

Morduchowicz, A. 2002. *Carreras, incentivos y estructura salariales, docentes.* Buenos Aires: Programa de Reforma Educativa en América Latina.

Piras, C., and W. Savedoff. 1998. "How Much Do Teachers Earn?" IDB Working Paper 375. Inter-American Development Bank, Washington, D.C.

Podgursky, M. 2000. "The Relative Pay and Contractual Work Hours of New York City Teachers." Department of Economics, University of Missouri–Columbia. Processed.

Urquiola, M., W. Jiménez, M. L. Talavera, and W. Hernany. 2000. *Los maestros en Bolivia: Impacto, incentivos y desempeño.* La Paz: Sierpe.

Vegas, E., L. Pritchett, and W. Experton. 1999. "Attracting and Retaining Qualified Teachers in Argentina: Impact of the Level and Structure of Compensation." Latin America and the Caribbean Region Human Development Department Paper 38. World Bank, Department of Human Development, Latin America and the Caribbean Regional Office, Washington, D.C.

7
Teacher and Principal Incentives in Mexico

Patrick J. McEwan
Wellesley College

and Lucrecia Santibáñez
RAND Corporation

Across the world, teacher pay is overwhelmingly determined by teachers' levels of education and years of experience. There is mounting concern that rigid compensation structures weaken teachers' incentives to exert effort and to improve student performance. In the United States and elsewhere, such concerns have led to the use of monetary performance incentives, often based on the level or growth of students' test scores. Nonetheless, pay for performance is relatively rare, and existing plans are often small scale and short lived.[74]

In contrast, since 1993, Mexican public school teachers and principals have been eligible for large financial awards that are based on students' test scores, among other factors. Under the Carrera Magisterial program,[75] personnel voluntarily participate in a year-long assessment process that awards 100 points for education, experience, students' test scores, and other factors. In recent years, personnel scoring above a nationally specified cut-off score (70) have a sharply higher probability of receiving an award. The awards are substantial, and they persist for the teacher's entire career.

We would like to thank Felipe Martínez Rizo and Alfredo González V. from Instituto Nacional para la Evaluación Educativa (INEE) for supplying data and replying to many inquiries. Victor Sastré from Carrera Magisterial was also very helpful in answering our questions. The research received financial support from the World Bank, Wellesley College, and RAND. Those individuals and institutions are not responsible for any errors or interpretations. Patrick J. McEwan can be contacted at pmcewan@wellesley.edu. Lucrecia Santibáñez can be contacted at lucrecia@rand.org.

74. Only nine U.S. states have laws that encourage such policies (*Education Week* 2004). On the short-lived nature of early merit pay plans, see Murnane and Cohen (1986). For recent reviews, see Glewwe, Ilias, and Kremer (2003) and Lavy (2002).

75. Carrera Magisterial roughly translates into English as Teachers' Career Ladder.

This chapter examines whether the incentives provided by Carrera Magisterial have induced teachers and principals to improve students' test scores.[76] One avenue by which improvements could have occurred was increased effort, although the recent literature on accountability has emphasized that a variety of gaming behaviors could also produce improvements in test scores.[77] In either case, the essential challenge is to compare a group of personnel who are receiving incentives—or rather, their students' outcomes—to a reasonable counterfactual.[78] At first glance, there is no obvious counterfactual against which to gauge the program's effects on students' test scores. The Mexican data were collected for the administrative purpose of allocating rewards. As such, they include observations on only those teachers and principals who are putatively considered to receive incentives and who participated in the assessment process (our first group).

This chapter argues that many teachers and principals within the Carrera Magisterial program (our second group) faced weak incentives and that these educators provide useful counterfactuals. Among teachers, for example, 80 points are determined by background characteristics (such as education and experience) and by a teacher's test score. Those points are determined before the students' tests, which account for the remaining 20 points, are administered. A significant number of teachers obtained so few points from their background characteristics that even perfectly scoring students would not place them above the cutoff. Other teachers scored above the cutoff even without the additional points from students' test scores. Both groups of teachers had little incentive to exert much effort to raise their students' test scores.

---

76. Because the Carrera Magisterial reform is so far reaching, it resembles an across-the-board wage increase for personnel. Thus, a substantial effect might be that the quality of entering cohorts of teachers has increased in the past decade. In the United States, Figlio (2002) examines whether higher teacher salaries attracted high-quality new teachers.

77. We will remain agnostic about the exact mechanisms by which such an improvement might occur. One possibility is that teachers exert greater effort in the classroom over the course of the school year. Others are that cheating occurs (see Jacob and Levitt 2003); that low-achieving students are excluded from high-stakes testing (see, for example, Cullen and Reback 2002; Figlio and Getzler 2002); that students receive coaching on test-taking (see, for example, Glewwe, Ilias, and Kremer 2003); or even that schools increase students' caloric intake on the day of the test (see Figlio and Winicki forthcoming). For a recent overview of this literature, see Hanushek and Raymond (2002).

78. A small body of literature has applied experimental and quasi-experimental approaches. In a recent evaluation of a pilot teacher incentive scheme in Kenya, incentives were allocated to 50 schools, which were randomly selected from a group of 100 (Glewwe, Ilias, and Kremer 2003). Lavy (2002) examined a small-scale program in Israel that provided incentives to teachers in 62 secondary schools. He used a regression-discontinuity approach to compare student outcomes in the 62 schools to those of schools that just missed treatment because of eligibility rules.

A third group of teachers face a stronger incentive to improve student test scores, because they are close to—but not assured of—receiving an award.[79] We argue that the nonlinear structure of the awards introduces a discontinuity in the relationship between a teacher's initial point score (excluding points from students' test scores) and his or her classroom test score. Our initial focus is on testing for existence of such as a discontinuity, which could be plausibly attributed to a program-induced improvement in test scores.

As an additional empirical strategy, we note that many teachers' probabilities of being promoted—even when conditional on scoring above the national cutoff—are not the same across Mexico's 32 states. (Each state is responsible for allocating promotions.) In some states, teachers scoring above the cutoff have lower promotion probabilities. We argue that such teachers perceive the expected value of the monetary award to be lower. Hence, they face relatively weaker incentives than teachers working in states with a higher probability. We use teachers in lower-probability states as a counterfactual for other teachers in a difference-in-differences framework.

In addition to analyzing incentives for teachers, we consider those for principals.[80] Principals are subject to the same annual evaluations as teachers, but instead of the students' test score, they receive a school performance score, which reflects the student performance score for participating teachers, as well as teachers' test scores. We use empirical strategies similar to the ones previously described for teachers to analyze whether the incentives offered by Carrera Magisterial to school principals had any effect on school performance.

---

79. A related phenomenon has been noted in other pay-for-performance systems in which awards are a nonlinear function of a performance measure, such as fixed sales quotas (for a review, see Prendergast 1999). Prendergast (1999, p. 26) notes that "an agent who is close to winning the prize will have greater incentive . . . than one who has either exceeded the quota or is unlikely to reach that quota." Courty and Marschke (2004) provide recent evidence of such incentives—and the gaming response of participants—in the national Job Training Partnership Act program, in which bonuses received by local job training centers were a nonlinear function of their graduation rates.

80. Research on school effectiveness has shown that school principals play a key role in improving schools. For example, see Zigarelli's (1996) review on school effectiveness. It cites the leadership and involvement of principals as one of the three constructs that define school effectiveness. Other researchers who argue that principals play a key role in school effectiveness are Bossert and others (1982), Eberts and Stone (1988), and Hallinger and Murphy (1986). However, incentive programs for school principals are extremely rare. In Mexico, school principals are unionized and are subject to uniform salary schedules in the same way that teachers are. In the United States and other countries, principals in larger or otherwise more difficult schools receive higher salaries (Gates and others 2003). However, school principals in Mexico who work in very large urban schools will receive almost the same compensation as those in very small, suburban schools. Mexican principals, therefore, have very little incentive to perform outside their assigned duties under this uniform structure.

The empirical analysis for teachers and principals, relying on both counterfactuals, does not provide strong, robust evidence that personnel improve their outcomes when they face stronger incentives. The discussion explores several possible reasons for this finding. The next section provides institutional background on the Carrera Magisterial program.

The Carrera Magisterial Program

Carrera Magisterial was instituted in January 1993 as one component of a large education reform known as the National Agreement for the Modernization of Basic Education.[81] Before the reform, teacher and school administrator pay was determined by levels of education and years of experience. Since the reform, teachers and principals are eligible for substantial and permanent wage increases if they perform well in a year-long assessment process that emphasizes many factors, including students' test scores or school performance. Teachers and principals consent to the assessment process in October, near the beginning of the school year. The process is voluntary, but the vast majority of Mexico's eligible teachers and principals have participated.[82] Personnel are evaluated in six areas and are awarded points in each. These areas are (a) education degrees; (b) years of experience; (c) professional development, including federal and state in-service training courses; (d) peer review; (e) teacher (or principal) knowledge, which is based on a test score; and (f) student performance, which is based on students' test scores.

Table 7.1 describes the points that are currently awarded for each factor, summing to 100 points.[83] The assessment process places substantial weight on individuals' formal education and experience, awarding up to 25 points for those two areas. Another 17 points is awarded for participation in short training courses offered by the federal or state governments, and 28 points

---

81. Besides Carrera Magisterial, the reform instituted a massive administrative decentralization of Mexico's public schools from the nation to its 32 states, as well as revised curricula and textbooks. For details, see Presidency of the Republic of Mexico (1992). The Carrera Magisterial program is jointly managed by the Ministry of Education (Secretaría de Educación Pública, or SEP) and the teachers' union, Sindicato Nacional de Trabajadores de la Educación (National Education Workers' Union, or SNTE).

82. To be eligible, teachers must belong to the SNTE and must meet a minimum seniority requirement that varies by education degree. In addition, both teachers and principals must hold specific kinds of contracts with SEP (such as a permanent teaching position, or plaza, which is roughly analogous to a tenured position in the United States, or a contract position that can be renewed indefinitely, which is called interinato ilimitado).

83. The program has experienced a number of administrative modifications during the past 10 years, including the weighting of the factors. We will argue that the program's features before its ninth year (the 1999/2000 academic year) complicate our efforts to credibly identify its effect. Hence, the following discussion and empirical analysis will focus on the later years of the program.

Table 7.1. Evaluation Scheme for Carrera Magisterial

Factor	Teachers' maximum points	Principals' maximum points
Education	10	10
Experience	15	15
Supervisor evaluation	10	10
Federal in-service training courses	12	12
State in-service training courses	5	5
Professional knowledge:		
Teacher test score	28	
Principal test score		28
Performance:		
Classroom test scores	20	
School average scores		20
Total	100	100

Source: National Coordinating Committee of Carrera Magisterial.

are awarded for a teacher (or principal) knowledge test that is administered in early March (SEP n.d.). Also, 10 points are awarded for supervisor review, in which principals rate teachers' performance and inspectors rate principals' performance. This element has little variation, because most teachers and principals receive very high ratings. Finally, the unadjusted mean test score of a teacher's students is worth 20 points.[84] The students' tests are administered at the end of the school year, in mid-June (SEP n.d.). Principals receive 20 points that are based on school performance, which is a composite of the teacher-specific scores of the participating teachers in the principal's school. These 20 points are made up of up to 10 points for the average of teachers' knowledge scores in the school and up to 10 points for the average of students' test scores in the school.

There are five levels of promotion in Carrera Magisterial, denoted A, B, C, D, and E. Each level represents a successively larger wage bonus. The levels must be pursued sequentially, beginning with level A.[85] Once promoted to a given level, individuals cannot be demoted, and their

---

84. Some teachers are given a small bonus in this factor (up to 4 points) as an ad hoc compensation for working with students with disabilities or for having students place in the top positions in various regional and national competitions.

85. In the initial years of the program, some teachers skipped level A and were promoted automatically to levels B and upward. This possibility was eliminated in the eighth year of the program.

wage bonus remains constant throughout their careers. They must wait for a specified number of years before they can attempt promotion to higher levels.[86] The wage bonuses for participants are substantial, consisting of a percentage of the base wage (determined from a standard wage schedule that emphasizes education and experience). In recent years, level A teachers receive 24.5 percent of their base wage, whereas level E teachers receive 197 percent (Ortiz Jiménez 2003). The bonuses are large when compared with those available under teacher incentive plans in other countries, particularly given that they are not simply one-time payments.[87]

Promotion opportunities are determined by each participant's final point score, which is calculated by the national office of Carrera Magisterial. The final point totals are distributed through an electronic spreadsheet to each of Mexico's 32 state-level offices, where the final selection is conducted. In the early years of the program, states were given much leeway in determining the cutoff score above which teachers and principals were promoted. Hence, the cutoffs apparently varied by state and, from year to year, within states. Since the program's ninth year (the 1999/2000 school year), each state has been constrained by a well-publicized national cutoff score (Ortiz Jiménez 2003).[88] No individual scoring below 70 points is eligible for promotion to levels A–E. Our evidence suggests that states overwhelmingly complied with this rule. Individuals scoring above 70 comprise the eligible pool of participants in each state, although not all of those scoring above the cutoff are actually awarded promotion. We will explore the possible determinants of promotion among high-scoring teachers in later sections.

Since 1992, the program has promoted a large number of Mexican teachers and principals (see tables 7.2 and 7.3). Close to 600,000 preschool,

---

86. Participants in levels A and B must wait 3 years before they are eligible for a promotion to the next level. If they work in specified poor areas, they must wait only 2 years. Those in levels C and D must wait 4 years before being eligible for a promotion. That timeframe is lowered to 2 years for individuals working in poor areas. Teachers and principals can participate in the assessment process each year while they are waiting to become eligible and can choose the highest score to use for their promotion.

87. For example, Glewwe, Ilias, and Kremer (2003) note that incentive plans in the United States typically offer one-time payments of 10 to 40 percent of the monthly wage. Israel has offered payments of 60 to 300 percent of the monthly wage, but they were still only one-time payments (Lavy 2002).

88. Up until the program's eighth-year, there appeared to be few rigid rules governing each state's approach to allocating the awards. Each state was provided a yearly budget that constrained the number of promotions that could be awarded. Once the number of promotions was determined, most states apparently relied heavily on the final point score to allocate rewards. However, it is not clear whether states adhered to a deterministic cutoff (that is, all teachers scoring above a given point value would receive a promotion).

Table 7.2. Teacher Promotions in Carrera Magisterial

Program year	School year	Promotions to level A (in that year)	Promotions to level A (cumulative)	Total teachers	Percentage of teachers promoted (cumulative/total)
1 and 2	1991/92 and 1992/93	315,773	315,773	764,796	41
3	1993/94	87,743	403,516	785,023	51
4	1994/95	58,391	461,907	812,358	57
5	1995/96	40,066	501,973	831,573	60
6	1996/97	32,033	534,006	858,054	62
7	1997/98	26,518	560,524	869,632	64
8	1998/99	10,468	570,992	888,126	64
9	1999/2000	9,210	580,202	896,917	65
10	2000/01	8,964	589,166	910,919	65
11	2001/02	6,808	595,974	921,588	65

Notes: The total for teachers includes preschool, primary, and secondary teachers in public schools. Carrera Magisterial promotion figures are for the teacher program category only (*primera vertiente*). Promotions refer to a teacher entering level A of the program for the first time.
Source: Secretaría de Educación Pública (http://www.sep.gob.mx) and Ortiz Jiménez (2003).

primary, and secondary teachers and about 85,000 principals have been promoted to level A, although fewer promotions have been awarded in recent years because the pool of eligible participants is declining.[89]

Data

In each year since the program's inception, the national office of Carrera Magisterial has collected data used in the assessment process described above. This chapter uses data from recent years (years 9–11) of the program. We do so principally because the program began relying on a sharp, national assignment cutoff in year 9. The sample of teachers is limited to primary teachers in grades 3–6, because teachers in grades 1–2 did not participate in the student assessment. The sample of principals is

---

89. Over half of the promotions occurred in the first 2 years of the program. It should be noted that these initial promotions occurred automatically—a diplomatic way of saying that the assessment process was not fully functional until the third year; thus, all applicants were promoted. As a result, the first 2 years of the program amounted to an across-the-board wage increase for many teachers and principals.

Table 7.3. Principal Promotions in Carrera Magisterial

Program year	School year	Promotions to level A (in that year)	Promotions to level A (cumulative)	Total principals	Percentage of principals promoted (cumulative/total)
1 and 2	1991/92 and 1992/93	52,565	52,565	76,724	69
3	1993/94	14,606	67,171	78,544	86
4	1994/95	5,479	72,650	82,671	88
5	1995/96	3,333	75,983	85,360	89
6	1996/97	2,105	78,088	86,270	91
7	1997/98	2,017	80,105	87,864	91
8	1998/99	553	80,658	89,161	90
9	1999/2000	520	81,178	88,457	92
10	2000/01	2,224	83,402	89,107	94
11	2001/02	1,420	84,822	89,307	95

Notes: The number of total primary school principals in the system is estimated from SEP (2003). It is estimated by taking the total number of public and private primary schools and multiplying by 90 percent (the assumed proportion of public primary schools). The calculation assumes that there is one principal per school; hence, the number of schools represents the number of principals. Carrera Magisterial promotion figures are for the principal program category only (segunda vertiente). Promotions refer to principals entering level A of the program for the first time. Principals who were later promoted into levels B–E would still be included in the cumulative level A figure. In years 1–7, some principals were promoted directly to levels B and higher; this provision was later eliminated. Figures for year 11 are estimated.
Source: SEP (2003); Carrera Magisterial (Estadística Básica Etapas 3–10 available at http://www.sep.gob.mx); and Ortiz Jiménez (2003).

limited to primary school principals. Finally, in both cases, the sample includes only participants seeking promotion to level A.

Table 7.4 reports descriptive statistics on the teacher sample. The sample contained 76,567 teacher observations in 27,213 schools.[90] The variables include the same ones used to construct each teacher's final score (see table 7.1). Note that a relatively small percentage of the sample (3 percent) received a final score above 70; we will corroborate that a majority of those teachers were the same ones promoted to level A. The data include a small number of other variables that we will use as controls, including the teacher's gender, the grade level of instruction, and the session of instruction. (Most Mexican primary classes are taught in a morning

---

90. Mexican teachers can hold positions in more than one school. In a given year, therefore, some teachers are observed more than once. The same is true for school principals.

Table 7.4. Descriptive Statistics for Teachers

Variable	Mean	Minimum	Maximum	Description
Education	7.94 (2.24)	0	15	Points awarded for educational degrees
Experience	5.31 (2.65)	0	10	Points awarded for years of experience
Peer review	9.17 (1.06)	0	10	Points awarded for peer review by teacher colleagues
Federal training	1.19 (2.85)	0	12	Points awarded for participation in federal-level training courses
State training	3.01 (2.39)	0	5	Points awarded for participation in state-level training courses
Teacher test	15.18 (3.89)	0	28	Points awarded for teacher knowledge test
Disability	0.04 (0.36)	0	4	Additional points awarded to teachers whose students have disabilities
Initial points	41.84	5	75.45	Sum of the 7 previous variables
Initial points < 50	0.85	0	1	
Initial points 50–70	0.15	0	1	
Initial points ≥ 70	< 0.01	0	1	
Test score	10.77 (2.78)	0.25	20	Points awarded for mean score of students in classroom
Final points	52.61 (8.71)	16.81	88.84	Sum of initial points and test score
Final points ≥ 70	0.03	0	1	
Promoted	0.03	0	1	Promoted to level A
Attempts	3.23 (2.26)	1	10	Number of attempts at promotion to level A, including current attempt
Male	0.48	0	1	
Grade 3	0.28	0	1	
Grade 4	0.26	0	1	

(Continued)

Table 7.4. Descriptive Statistics for Teachers (*Continued*)

Variable	Mean	Minimum	Maximum	Description
Grade 5	0.23	0	1	
Grade 6	0.22	0	1	
Morning	0.75	0	1	Teacher works in school's morning session
Afternoon	0.24	0	1	Teacher works in school's afternoon session
Evening	< 0.01	0	1	Teacher works in school's evening session
Year 9	0.34	0	1	9th year of Carrera Magisterial (1999/2000 school year)
Year 10	0.28	0	1	10th year of Carrera Magisterial (2000/01 school year)
Year 11	0.37	0	1	11th year of Carrera Magisterial (2001/02 school year)
Number of teachers	76,567			
Number of schools	27,213			

Note: Standard deviations are in parentheses for nondummy variables.
Source: Carrera Magisterial databases and authors' calculations.

session, although some occur in the afternoon and evening.) Table 7.5 includes similar descriptive statistics on 5,055 principals in 5,051 schools.[91]

Allocation of Promotions

We first ask whether the data are consistent with the stated administrative procedures of Carrera Magisterial. That is, do states adhere to the cutoff of 70 points when allocating promotions? We assess this question by conducting locally weighted regressions of promotion to level A (a dichotomous outcome) on the final points received by teachers or principals. We begin with the case for teachers and then follow with the case for principals.

---

91. Three schools appear to have more than one principal. However, they constitute a negligible proportion of the total sample.

Table 7.5. Descriptive Statistics for Principals

Variable	Mean	Minimum	Maximum	Description
Education	8.40 (1.62)	0	15	Points awarded for educational degrees
Experience	7.78 (2.25)	0	10	Points awarded for years of experience
Peer review	9.09 (1.44)	0	10	Points awarded for peer review by principals' colleagues
Federal training	0.89 (2.53)	0	11.11	Points awarded for participation in federal-level training courses
State training	2.78 (2.41)	0	5	Points awarded for participation in state-level training courses
Principal test	17.33 (3.71)	5	28	Points awarded for principal knowledge test
Initial points	46.27 (7.25)	9.8	74.31	Sum of the previous 7 variables
Initial points < 50	0.74	0	1	
Initial points 50–70	0.25	0	1	
Initial points ≥ 70	<0.01	0	1	
School performance	11.73 (1.79)	5.76	20	Points awarded for mean score of students and teachers in school
Final points	58.00 (7.79)	16.8	85.91	Sum of initial points and school performance
Final points ≥ 70	0.07	0	1	
Promoted	0.04	0	1	Promoted to level A
Attempts	3.40 (2.37)	1	9	Number of attempts at promotion to level A, including current attempt
Male	0.65	0	1	
Morning	0.77	0	1	School meets in the morning
Afternoon	0.23	0	1	School meets in the afternoon

(Continued)

Table 7.5. Descriptive Statistics for Principals (*Continued*)

Variable	Mean	Minimum	Maximum	Description
Evening	<0.01	0	1	School meets in the evening
Year 9	0.39	0	1	9th year of Carrera Magisterial (1999/2000 school year)
Year 10	0.26	0	1	10th year of Carrera Magisterial (2000/01 school year)
Year 11	0.35	0	1	11th year of Carrera Magisterial (2001/02 school year)
Number of principals	5,055			
Number of schools	5,051			

Note: Standard deviations are in parentheses for nondummy variables.
Source: Carrera Magisterial databases and authors' calculations.

Teachers

Figure 7.1 graphs the fitted values against final points for various samples (sample sizes are available in table 7.4). Panel A includes the sample from 3 later years of the program. It suggests that the probability of being promoted to level A is essentially zero for teachers scoring below 70. For teachers scoring above 70, the probability sharply rises to just below 0.8, and it appears quite steady regardless of the score. Similar results are obtained when dividing the sample by year (see panels B, C, and D).

Similar results were obtained by estimating a linear probability model, in which promotion was regressed on the final point score and its square, as well as on a dummy variable indicating whether the score is 70 or higher. The coefficient on this last variable is reported in the first row of table 7.6, and it suggests that the probability of promotion rises by 0.73 for teachers above the cutoff. In other specifications, which are not reported here, we conditioned on other observable teacher variables, including gender, grade level, and session of instruction, but their coefficients were not statistically significant.[92]

---

92. Because the final allocation of promotions really occurs at the state level, the previous results might occur if 32 states applied 32 different—but deterministic—cutoffs above 70 (for example, Chiapas applying a cutoff of 74, above which 100 percent of teachers are promoted, and so on). Thus, we conducted the exercise in figure 7.1 again, dividing the sample by each year and state. The results (which are not reported here) suggested that teachers in individual states almost always experience a sharp rise in the probability of promotion above 70, but that the probability is rarely 1 for such teachers.

Figure 7.1. Fitted Values of Promotion on Final Points, by Year, for Teachers

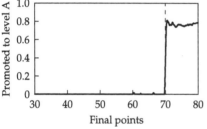

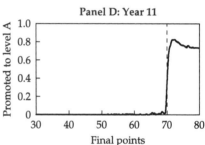

Note: Bandwidth is 0.01.

Table 7.6 also reports the regressions conducted within each state. They suggest that teachers experience wide differences in their probability of promotion to level A, depending on the state in which they work. Marginal probabilities of promotion for teachers scoring above 70 range from a low of 0.27 in Tlaxcala to a high of 0.97 in Morelos—both geographically small and similarly wealthy states near the capital. In fact, there appears to be little relationship between the estimated probabilities and a state's wealth. We regressed the estimated marginal probabilities from table 7.6 on a state-level index of well-being constructed by the National Institute of Statistics, Geography, and Information (Instituto Nacional de Estadística, Geografía e Informática, or INEGI). The results, which are not reported here, suggested a very small and statistically insignificant relationship.

Principals

Following the same empirical approach, we calculated promotion probabilities for school principals. Results are shown in figure 7.2 and suggest that the probability of being promoted to level A is small for principals scoring below 70 (see panel A). For principals scoring above 70, the probability

Table 7.6. Determinants of Teacher Promotion, by State

Sample	Coefficient on final points ≥ 70	Standard error	N	R^2
Full sample	0.73	(0.01)	76,567	0.69
State subsample (> 0.73)	0.83	(0.01)	37,283	0.80
State subsample (< 0.73)	0.63	(0.02)	39,284	0.59
Aguascalientes	0.92	(0.06)	657	0.88
Baja California	0.61	(0.05)	2,696	0.60
Baja California Sur	0.57	(0.11)	283	0.73
Campeche	0.95	(0.05)	698	0.95
Chiapas	0.80	(0.10)	2,008	0.70
Chihuahua	0.88	(0.03)	2,289	0.84
Coahuila	0.88	(0.05)	1,589	0.86
Colima	0.75	(0.10)	389	0.62
Distrito Federal	0.57	(0.04)	5,648	0.51
Durango	0.71	(0.08)	1,648	0.69
Guanajuato	0.74	(0.04)	5,200	0.74
Guerrero	0.71	(0.07)	4,500	0.71
Hidalgo	0.85	(0.06)	1,557	0.82
Jalisco	0.69	(0.04)	4,453	0.65
State of Mexico	0.80	(0.02)	11,529	0.78
Michoacán	0.82	(0.05)	2,696	0.82
Morelos	0.97	(0.03)	773	0.97
Nayarit	0.76	(0.10)	526	0.72
Nuevo León	0.87	(0.03)	2,787	0.84
Oaxaca	0.89	(0.06)	2,313	0.87
Puebla	0.66	(0.09)	4,343	0.63
Querétaro	0.70	(0.11)	653	0.75
Quintana Roo	0.48	(0.06)	835	0.46
San Luis Potosí	0.72	(0.08)	1,446	0.64
Sinaloa	0.58	(0.06)	2,557	0.59

(Continued)

Table 7.6. Determinants of Teacher Promotion, by State (*Continued*)

Sample	Coefficient on final points ≥ 70	Standard error	N	R^2
Sonora	0.68	(0.07)	1,510	0.67
Tabasco	0.90	(0.07)	1,086	0.89
Tamaulipas	0.59	(0.05)	2,004	0.68
Tlaxcala	0.27	(0.10)	514	0.37
Veracruz	0.63	(0.05)	5,170	0.59
Yucatán	0.82	(0.06)	1,186	0.77
Zacatecas	0.62	(0.09)	1,024	0.60

Notes: Robust standard errors are corrected for school-level clustering. Each row reports a coefficient from a separate regression. Regressions also control for the final points variable and its square.

Figure 7.2. Fitted Values of Promotion on Final Points, by Year, for Principals

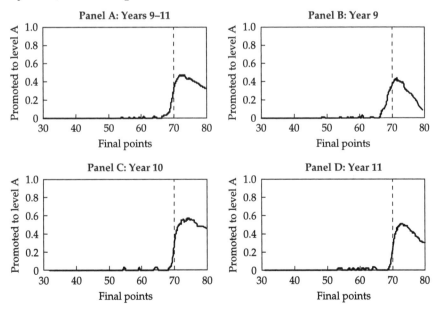

Note: Bandwidth is 0.05.

sharply rises to just below 0.6. Similar results are obtained when dividing the sample by year (see panels B, C, and D). Table 7.7 suggests that the probability of promotion rises by 0.44 for principals above the cutoff.

Table 7.7 also includes regression results divided by state. They suggest that principals experience wide differences in their probability of promotion to level A, depending on the state in which they work. Marginal probabilities of promotion for principals scoring above 70 range from a low of zero in Campeche, Tlaxcala, and Zacatecas to a perfect probability in Nayarit. All of those states rank in the middle or lower end of the wealth distribution. As with teachers, there is little relationship between the estimated probabilities and a state's wealth. We again regressed the marginal probabilities from table 7.7 on a state-level index of well-being. The results, which are not reported here, suggested a small and statistically insignificant relationship.

Empirical Strategy

This section describes two empirical strategies that will be used to estimate whether the incentives offered by Carrera Magisterial to teachers and principals were related to any changes in student or school performance. To simplify the exposition, we will fully describe the strategies for the teacher case only. However, in the last part of this section, we note differences that arise in the analysis of principals.

Incentives in Carrera Magisterial

The objective of this chapter is to assess whether Carrera Magisterial caused increases in the mean of classroom achievement, perhaps by improving teachers' incentives to exert effort in the classroom. The data contain observations only on teachers who have consented to be assessed in a given year. However, we argue next that subgroups of teachers— which are often quite large—experienced weaker incentives to improve their classroom's mean achievement. Those teachers will serve as the needed counterfactual.

As we previously described, 70 points are determined by the teacher's background characteristics, such as formal education, experience, training courses, and teacher's test score. Another 10 points are determined by peer review, but those ratings are generally high (the sample mean is 9.2). All of those factors are assessed in advance of collecting the students' test scores. The scoring procedure is well publicized through materials distributed to teachers and through national and state-level Web sites.[93]

---

93. See http://www.sep.gob.mx/wb2/sep/sep_617_carrera_magisterial.

Table 7.7. Determinants of Principal Promotion, by State

Sample	Coefficient on final points ≥ 70	Standard error	N	R^2
Full sample	0.44	(0.01)	5,055	0.34
State subsample (> 0.44)	0.67	(0.02)	1,939	0.54
State subsample (< 0.44)	0.29	(0.02)	3,116	0.22
Aguascalientes	0.98	(0.20)	28	0.67
Baja California	0.41	(0.10)	133	0.29
Campeche	0.00	—	31	—
Chiapas	0.26	(0.05)	138	0.25
Chihuahua	0.45	(0.12)	98	0.31
Coahuila	0.69	(0.10)	125	0.44
Colima	0.51	(0.16)	45	0.35
Distrito Federal	0.41	(0.05)	452	0.34
Durango	0.25	(0.07)	114	0.18
Guanajuato	0.27	(0.07)	169	0.4
Guerrero	0.43	(0.04)	398	0.27
Hidalgo	0.79	(0.05)	135	0.83
Jalisco	0.15	(0.05)	228	0.09
State of Mexico	0.72	(0.03)	1,076	0.61
Michoacán	0.34	(0.05)	341	0.19
Morelos	−0.23	(1.00)	10	0.14
Nayarit	1.00	—	23	—
Nuevo León	0.99	(0.11)	65	0.68
Oaxaca	0.37	(0.05)	244	0.36
Puebla	0.02	(0.11)	174	0.1
Querétaro	0.03	(0.12)	43	0.69
Quintana Roo	0.53	(0.11)	41	0.52
San Luis Potosí	0.37	(0.09)	83	0.25
Sinaloa	0.26	(0.07)	156	0.24
Sonora	0.29	(0.14)	35	0.16

(*Continued*)

Table 7.7. Determinants of Principal Promotion, by State (*Continued*)

Sample	Coefficient on final points ≥ 70	Standard error	N	R^2
Tabasco	0.77	(0.08)	94	0.75
Tamaulipas	0.54	(0.10)	158	0.46
Tlaxcala	0.00	—	33	—
Veracruz	0.17	(0.04)	297	0.14
Yucatán	0.6	(0.11)	51	0.53
Zacatecas	0.00	—	31	—

Notes: Robust standard errors are corrected for school-level clustering. Each row reports a coefficient from a separate regression. Regressions also control for the final points variable and its square.

Given the large number of teachers promoted, even within particular schools, it is likely that teachers share information about procedures and outcomes. Finally, there is anecdotal evidence that teachers are aware of their position in the scoring process; therefore, many suffer from a malady referred to as "point-itis."[94]

In this context, let us consider how the program might alter teachers' incentives to improve student achievement. The final assessment score (the final points received) can be expressed as $f(X, A)$, where X is a vector of the teacher's background characteristics and A is the mean achievement of the teacher's students. Likewise, $A = a(X, Z, e)$, where Z is a vector of students' background characteristics (such as parental schooling) that determine achievement and e is the chosen effort of each teacher. Additional effort is presumed to be costly for teachers.

A substantial portion of teachers' scores is determined before students' test scores are collected. These are the initial points received. Assume that teachers possess sufficient knowledge to calculate the initial points as $f(X, 0)$, or the score they would receive when $A = 0$. From this calculation, it is apparent that some teachers face weak incentives to improve their students' achievement. If the initial points are greater or equal to 70, then teachers already fall above the promotion cutoff and have no additional incentive to exert costly effort over the course of the year. Similarly, if the initial points are below 50, then teachers cannot be promoted, even if they obtain the full 20 points awarded for students' test scores. Again, their incentives to exert additional effort to improve those test scores are weak.

---

94. Ortiz Jiménez (2003) refers to the issue disapprovingly in an official publication of Carrera Magisterial that was distributed free of charge to all teachers.

Table 7.4 suggests that the first group is quite small. The mean of the dummy variable initial points greater than or equal to 70 is less than 0.01. The group was larger in earlier years of the program, when more experienced and highly educated teachers vied for promotion. In contrast, the second group constitutes the majority of the sample (the mean of the dummy variable of initial points below 50 is 0.85). The essential premise of this paper is to show that teachers were unlikely to exert effort toward the pursuit of an unattainable reward.

When initial points are between 50 and 70, teachers may face stronger incentives to improve their students' test scores. More specifically, they are assumed to choose a level of effort, e^*, so that their final points are $f(X, a(X, Z, e^*)) = 70$. As teachers' initial points cross the 50-point threshold, one would anticipate a tipping point in effort. Such teachers would move from minimum effort to maximum effort. This hypothesis forms the basis of the first empirical strategy, which is akin to a regression-discontinuity design.

Empirical Strategy 1

Panel A in figure 7.3 portrays a stylized version of this approach. In the absence of Carrera Magisterial, there would likely be a positive relationship between the initial points—an index of teacher observables—and the mean classroom test score of teachers. This relationship is portrayed with a straight line in panel A, although the functional form is indeterminate. One source of this relationship is the causal effect of teacher attributes on student outcomes. It is also rooted in correlations between observable teacher attributes and unobserved teacher or student attributes. For example, one might anticipate that better teachers—gauged by their degrees or experience—sort into the classrooms of higher-achieving students, as measured by socioeconomic status. Although this sorting would alter the functional form of the relationship, one would still anticipate a smooth relationship.

As teachers cross the 50-point threshold, they face incentives to substantially increase their achievement and, hence, their effort. This situation would be evidenced by a break in the relationship between their initial points and test scores, which is illustrated by the dotted line segment. As teachers' initial points increase, however, the additional achievement and effort required to reach the promotion cutoff becomes progressively smaller. Eventually, close to 70, the achievement and effort required to reach the promotion cutoff is minimal, and there will be little break, if any.

The magnitude of the break at 50 will likely vary across teachers, who surely recognize that some classroom achievement will result from their own background characteristics (the X's) and the characteristics of their students (the Z's). Thus, some teachers whose initial points equal 50 will

Figure 7.3. Stylized Portrayal of Empirical Strategy

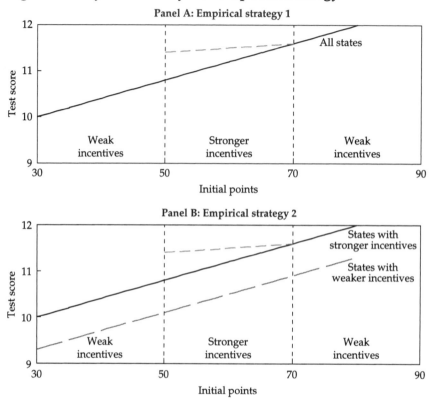

find that less effort is required to reach 70 (for example, those with higher socioeconomic status and higher-achieving students). Others will find that substantial effort is required (such as those with lower socioeconomic status and lower-achieving students).

As an initial test, we will estimate

$$(7.1) \quad Testscore_i = \beta_0 + \beta_1 Initialpoints_i + \beta_2 (50 \leq Initialpoints < 70)_i + \varepsilon_i$$

where the points from the classroom test score of the ith teacher are a function of the initial points, a dummy variable indicating a value between 50 and 70, and an error term. Further specifications will divide the 50–70 interval into a smaller series of dummy variables (in which the dummy variable indicating the leftmost interval should capture the break). We will also add controls for a limited number of observed teacher variables, as well as school fixed effects that control for unobserved school, teacher, and student variables that are constant within schools.

As a sharper test of the presence of a break in classroom test scores around the discontinuity, we will further estimate

$$(7.2) \quad Testscore_i = \beta_0 + \beta_1 Initialpoints_i + \beta_2 (Initialpoints \geq 50)_i + \varepsilon_i$$

within subsamples of teachers whose values of the initial points fall within successively narrower bands around 50. Again, additional specifications will control for observed teacher variables and school fixed effects.

A plausible explanation for a discontinuous relationship between the initial points and the test scores—gauged by β_2—would be a program effect. Yet it is possible that a sharp break would not be observed, even in the presence of an effect for many individual teachers. Suppose that some teachers whose initial points equal 50 will derive substantial disutility from the effort required to obtain higher test scores; thus, the expected award would not outweigh the disutility. Such teachers would need to attain a higher value of initial points (thus exerting a smaller e^*) before the disutility of effort was outweighed. In the extreme, some teachers might find the required effort so onerous that they would exert no effort at any value of initial points between 50 and 70. If a teacher's preferences regarding effort are heterogeneous, then the dotted segment in panel A may resemble a hump-like spline.

It would be difficult to convincingly attribute a smooth relationship (albeit a curiously nonlinear one) to the effects of Carrera Magisterial. An alternative explanation, for example, is that the nature of student and teacher sorting intensifies at higher values of initial points. Perhaps higher-achieving students in a school opt into the classrooms of better teachers—in part, because the latter are observed to exert more effort. Anecdotally, at least, parents have little control over classroom assignment in the Mexican public school system. However, it would still be desirable to corroborate any program effect (or lack thereof) with another empirical strategy.

Empirical Strategy 2

The evidence on the state-level allocation of promotions provides one alternative. Recall that teachers receiving a final score of 70 or above had different probabilities of being promoted, depending on their state of residence. Thus, the expected value of the awards was different. We will assume that teachers in states with higher probabilities face relatively stronger incentives to exert effort than their counterparts in states with lower probabilities. Nonetheless, teachers in all states whose initial points are lower than 50 are assumed to face weak incentives.

The empirical strategy is illustrated in panel B of figure 7.3. It adds a dashed line, representing states where teachers face lower probabilities of promotion (and weaker incentives) below the solid line that now represents states where teachers have higher probabilities of promotion (and stronger incentives). The former serves as a counterfactual for the latter in a difference-in-differences framework. If we observe a hump between 50 and 70 in the strong-incentive group, the same relationship should be attenuated in the counterfactual group. The empirical strategy rests on the assumption that the functional form of relationship of the strong-incentive group would be the same as the weak-incentive group in the absence of the incentive difference. We estimate the difference-in-differences in a regression framework:

$$Testscore_i = \beta_0 + \beta_1 Initialpoints_i$$
$$+\beta_2 (50 \leq Initialpoints \geq 70)_i + \beta_3 (Highprob)_i$$
$$+\beta_4 (50 \leq Initialpoints < 70)_i * (Highprob)_i + \varepsilon_i$$

where *Highprob* is a dummy variable indicating that the *i*th teacher lives in a state with relatively higher promotion probabilities. The coefficient on the interaction (β_4) identifies the effect of the differential incentives between the two groups. Other specifications are further conditioned on teacher observables and school fixed effects.

Differences in Empirical Strategy in the Principal Case

Similar to our case of teachers, we argue in the case of principals that subgroups experienced weaker incentives to improve their classrooms' mean achievement. Those principals will serve as the needed counterfactual.

Also similar to our case of teachers, if the principals' initial points are greater than or equal to 70, then the principals already fall above the promotion cutoff and have no additional incentive to exert costly effort over the course of the year. If their initial points are below 50, principals cannot be promoted, even if they obtain the full 20 points awarded for school performance. Again, their incentive to exert additional effort to improve those scores is weak. Table 7.5 suggests that the group of principals facing stronger incentives is quite small. The mean of the dummy variable of initial points ≥ 70 is again less than 0.01. The group of principals facing weaker incentives constitutes the majority of the sample (the mean of the dummy variable of initial points < 50 is 0.74).

As we described, 70 points are determined by the principal's background characteristics, such as formal education, experience, training courses, and a principal test score. Another 10 points are determined by supervisor evaluations, but those ratings are generally high (the sample mean is 9.1). All of those elements are assessed in advance of collecting the students' test scores. Unlike the case for teachers, however, a portion of the principal's 20-point school performance score is assessed at the same time that principals are obtaining part of their initial points score. Specifically, half the school performance points are awarded for teacher-specific test scores, which are collected each year in March. Thus, the principals have a year-long incentive (or at least one lasting until March) to encourage teachers to prepare better for their own test scores. Thus, it will be difficult to determine whether any effects for principals stem from efforts to improve students' achievement or from efforts to improve teachers' test scores. Unfortunately, our school performance data are not broken down into the two 10-point components.

Results for Teachers

Empirical Strategy 1

Figure 7.4 reports preliminary evidence that can be used to visually identify an effect. We performed locally weighted, smoothed regressions of test scores on initial points at various bandwidths. Panel A graphs the fitted values obtained from a bandwidth of 0.01, whereas panels B, C, and D use successively wider ones. There is a positive and apparently linear relationship between the index of teacher observables and test scores. However, there is little evidence of a discontinuity in the relationship when initial points equal 50. A very small hump is observed between 50 and 55,

Figure 7.4. Fitted Values of Classroom Test Scores on Initial Points, by Bandwidth for Teachers

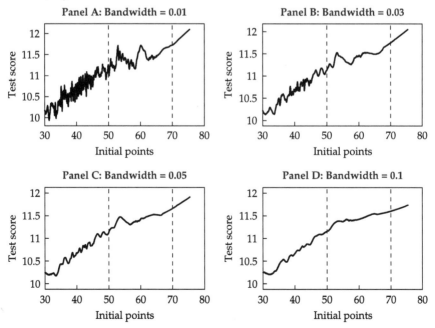

most notably in panels B and C. If one attributes this hump to a program effect—and we do not hazard such an interpretation—it would be quite small. The "effect" appears roughly equal to 0.2 test score points for a classroom in this narrow range of initial points, equivalent to less than 0.1 standard deviations.

Table 7.8 reports regression evidence on these points. Column 1 regresses test scores on initial points and initial points between 50 and 70. All other controls are omitted, providing the best analogue to the previous visual evidence. The statistically significant coefficient on initial points (0.04) implies that a one standard deviation increase will lead to a 0.12 standard deviation in classroom test scores. The dummy variable is positive, though small and statistically insignificant. It represents an average across all individuals in this interval. Column 2 adds more controls for teacher observables as well as state-level dummies, but the results are quite similar. Column 3 further controls for school-level dummies, relying on within-school variation that appears to be substantial. The coefficient on initial points falls by more than half, although it is still significant. This result suggests that school-level fixed effects are absorbing some variation in teacher or student unobservables that are correlated with teacher observables.

Columns 4 through 6 control for initial points between 50 and 55, in an effort to better capture any perturbation in the functional form. The coefficients on the dummy variables are small though statistically significant in the first two specifications, roughly consistent with figure 7.4. However, the effect disappears upon controlling for school fixed effects. One might be concerned that this result occurs simply because little variation exists within schools, but this absence does not appear to be the case. Overall, 46,209 teacher observations are made in a school where all teachers have initial points below 50 and 2,248 are made in a school where all teachers have initial points greater than or equal to 50. The remaining 28,110 observations are from schools with teachers on either side of 50.

Columns 7 through 9 report less restrictive specifications, splitting the 50–70 interval into four dummy variables. There is an even smaller, marginally significant coefficient on initial points between 50 and 55 that again disappears on the inclusion of school dummies. The other coefficients are not statistically significant (although the thinness of the sample, especially when initial points are greater than 65, does not suggest that we would be able to precisely estimate these coefficients).[95]

Table 7.9 reports estimates of equation 7.2 that focus more intently on the vicinity of the hypothesized discontinuity. The samples are limited to teachers whose initial points are close to 50—within 10, 5, and 3 points, respectively. Panel A reports coefficients on a dummy variable that is equal to 1 when initial points are above 50 (all regressions also control for a con-

---

95. Only 204 observations have values of initial points above 65.

Table 7.8. Teachers' Initial Points and Classroom Test Scores

				Dependent variable: test score					
	(1)	(2)	(3)	(4)	(5)	(6)	(7)	(8)	(9)
Initial points	0.043** (0.002)	0.037*** (0.002)	0.016*** (0.003)	0.042** (0.002)	0.036*** (0.001)	0.017*** (0.002)	0.044** (0.002)	0.038*** (0.002)	0.015*** (0.003)
Initial points 50–70	0.026 (0.042)	0.020 (0.039)	0.013 (0.054)	—	—	—	—	—	—
Initial points 50–55	—	—	—	0.129** (0.042)	0.083** (0.040)	-0.012 (0.054)	0.090* (0.045)	0.060 (0.043)	0.008 (0.058)
Initial points 55–60	—	—	—	—	—	—	-0.104 (0.062)	-0.063 (0.058)	-0.002 (0.079)
Initial points 60–65	—	—	—	—	—	—	-0.158 (0.107)	-0.085 (0.101)	0.224 (0.139)
Initial points 65–70	—	—	—	—	—	—	-0.284 (0.231)	-0.189 (0.225)	0.264 (0.357)
R^2	0.02	0.13	0.56	0.02	0.13	0.56	0.02	0.13	0.56
Controls?	No	Yes	Yes	No	Yes	Yes	No	Yes	Yes
State fixed effects?	No	Yes	No	No	Yes	No	No	Yes	No
School fixed effects?	No	No	Yes	No	No	Yes	No	No	Yes

Note: The total number of regressions is 76,567. *** indicates statistical significance at 1 percent, ** at 5 percent, and * at 10 percent. Robust standard errors are in parentheses, adjusted for school-level clustering. Controls include Male, Afternoon, Evening, Year 10, Year 11, Grade 4, Grade 5, and Grade 6.

Table 7.9. Teachers' Initial Points and Classroom Test Scores, within Narrow Bands

| | ±10 points from cutoff | | | ±5 points | | | ±3 points | | |
	(1)	(2)	(3)	(4)	(5)	(6)	(7)	(8)	(9)
Panel A									
Initial points ≥ 50	0.015	-0.051	-0.129	-0.021	-0.028	-0.122	-0.086	-0.095	-0.179
	(0.062)	(0.058)	(0.097)	(0.089)	(0.084)	(0.216)	(0.117)	(0.111)	(0.434)
	[43,491]	[43,491]	[43,491]	[18,134]	[18,134]	[18,134]	[10,162]	[10,162]	[10,162]
Panel B									
Initial points ≥ 51.2	0.006	-0.031	-0.115	0.086	0.063	-0.039	-0.048	-0.066	-0.154
	(0.065)	(0.061)	(0.107)	(0.093)	(0.089)	(0.242)	(0.120)	(0.114)	(0.427)
	[38,273]	[38,273]	[38,273]	[15,720]	[15,720]	[15,720]	[8,994]	[8,994]	[8,994]
Panel C									
Initial points ≥ 54.1	-0.180*	-0.086	-0.027	-0.176	-0.087	-0.003	-0.166	-0.085	-0.124
	(0.076)	(0.072)	(0.146)	(0.110)	(0.104)	(0.307)	(0.141)	(0.133)	(0.570)
	[25,830]	[25,830]	[25,830]	[11,283]	[11,283]	[11,283]	[6,852]	[6,852]	[6,852]
Panel D									
Initial points ≥ 55.4	-0.227**	-0.158**	0.041	-0.277*	-0.296***	-0.227	-0.045	-0.119	-0.589
	(0.084)	(0.079)	(0.173)	(0.119)	(0.113)	(0.363)	(0.154)	(0.147)	(0.642)
	[21,513]	[21,513]	[21,513]	[9,683]	[9,683]	[9,683]	[5,822]	[5,822]	[5,822]
Controls?	No	Yes	Yes	No	Yes	Yes	No	Yes	Yes
State fixed effects?	No	Yes	No	No	Yes	No	No	Yes	No
School fixed effects?	No	No	Yes	No	No	Yes	No	No	Yes

Notes: *** indicates statistical significance at 1 percent, ** at 5 percent, and * at 10 percent. Robust standard errors are in parentheses, adjusted for school-level clustering. The N of each regression is in brackets. All regressions control for a continuous measure of initial points. Additional controls include Male, Afternoon, Evening, Year 11, Grade 4, Grade 5, and Grade 6.

tinuous measure of initial points. None of the results from successively narrower bands around 50 suggest the existence of a sharp difference in test scores around 50. The results do not change when teacher observables or school fixed effects are added. In other specifications, which are not reported here, we added a quadratic term of initial points, but the results were similar.

The absence of results could be explained by the fact that the "true" discontinuity is higher. Teachers whose initial points equal 50 may not perceive that obtaining 20 points from classroom test scores is feasible. Panel A in figure 7.5 reports a kernel density on test score. Few teachers in the sample obtain the full 20 points. Panel B reports evidence that corroborates the previous regression findings, by reestimating kernel densities for teachers that are above and below 50 points. The distribution of teachers scoring above 50 is shifted very slightly to the right, which may result from the direct effect of higher values of initial points on test scores. When we restrict the samples to teachers whose scores fall within narrower bands—in panels C and D—the distributions essentially overlap.

Figure 7.5. Kernel Densities of Test Score for Teachers

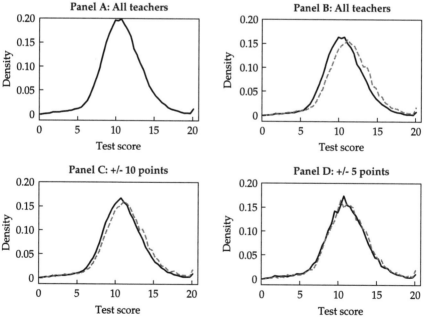

Notes: The interval width is 0.1 point for all densities. In panels B, C, and D, the solid line includes teachers with initial points below 50; the dotted line includes teachers with initial points equal to or above 50. Panels C and D limit the sample to teachers with values of initial points that are ± 10 points and ± 5 points, respectively, from 50.

Teachers might implicitly consider a higher discontinuity. To explore this possibility, we note that the 99th, 95th, and 90th percentiles in the test score sample are 18.8, 15.9, and 14.6, respectively. The three values imply discontinuities of 51.2, 54.1, and 55.4, respectively. Panels B, C, and D in table 7.9 report additional regression results using these discontinuities, but none of the coefficients are positive and significant. The same results hold when we control for a quadratic term of initial points.

One might also posit that teachers, in assessing the "maximum" value of classroom test scores that is feasible, rely on their knowledge of the state distribution in test scores, rather than on their knowledge of the national one. Thus, we repeated the previous exercise by estimating the 99th percentile of test scores within each of Mexico's states. Then, we constructed a dummy variable equal to 1 if a teacher's value of initial points fell above the discontinuity implied by the state-specific test score. This variable was used in the same regressions reported in table 7.9. The same exercise was repeated for the 95th and 90th percentiles. None of the results suggested that teachers scoring above discontinuities, however defined, would obtain higher classroom test scores.

Empirical Strategy 2

The first strategy did not turn up positive and robust effects. However, the lack of a sharp break could result from heterogeneous teacher preferences. To examine this possibility, we identified two groups of teachers: (a) those working in states where scoring above 70 increases the probability of promotion by 0.73 or more (the estimated probability in the full sample) and (b) those working in states with probabilities of less than 0.73. The probabilities for each group, estimated separately, are 0.83 and 0.63, respectively (see table 7.6). The difference of 0.2 implies that the expected value of scoring above 70 is 32 percent higher for teachers in the first group. Hence, we dub the two groups the "stronger-incentive" and "weaker-incentive" groups.

We repeat the previous section's visual exercise by obtaining separate fitted values for each group (see figure 7.6). The solid and dashed lines in each panel indicate the strong- and weak-incentive groups, respectively. When initial points are below 50, we surmise that both groups face weak incentives and should have similar functional forms. That similarity seems to be the case in all panels, and it is also the case in a formal test.[96] Above 50, one might anticipate a divergence in the lines in the presence of a program

---

96. We limited the samples to observations with initial points below 50. We then regressed the test score variable on (a) the initial points variable, (b) a continuous variable containing the state-specific probability, and (c) the interaction between the two variables (with robust standard errors adjusted for school-level clustering). We could not reject the null that the coefficient on the interaction is zero.

Figure 7.6. Fitted Values of Classroom Test Scores on Initial Points, by Bandwidth and State, for Teachers

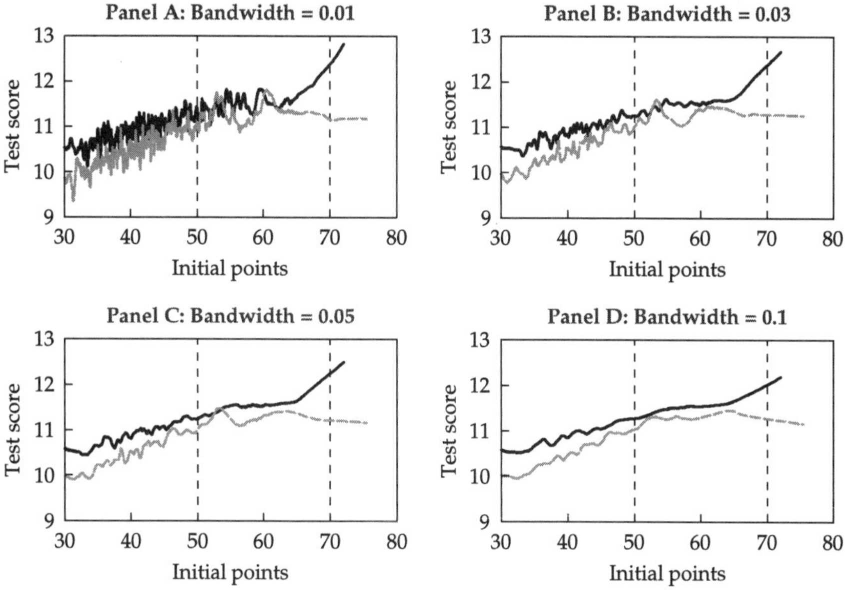

Note: Solid lines include states in which the probability of promotion is 0.73 or more (see table 7.6). Dashed lines include states in which the probability is less than 0.73.

effect. At first glance, that divergence appears to be the case in the upper reaches of the 50–70 interval. However, less than 1 percent of the sample has initial points above 65. In panel D, where we use a larger bandwidth and greater smoothing, much of this pattern dissipates. It appears that the hump-like pattern in the lower reaches is accounted for by teachers in the weaker-incentive group. One might have anticipated a similar, or even more pronounced, pattern among the stronger-incentive group, but this is not the case.

Table 7.10 estimates the difference-in-differences via regression analysis. The variable for high probability is dichotomous, indicating whether teachers work in higher- or lower-probability states. (Note that its coefficient is not estimated in columns 2 and 3, given controls for state-level and school-level dummies.) The key coefficient is the interaction between falling within the 50–70 interval and working in a higher-probability state. These coefficients are uniformly negative and statistically significant across all specifications. However, the practical magnitude is small, less than 0.1 standard deviations. The results are not substantively altered by further controlling for a quadratic term of initial points or by specifying high prob-

Table 7.10. Teachers' Initial Scores and Classroom Test Scores: Difference-in-Differences

	Dependent variable: test score		
	(1)	(2)	(3)
Initial points	0.042***	0.037***	0.016***
	(0.002)	(0.002)	(0.003)
Initial points 50–70	0.141***	0.094*	0.118*
	(0.052)	(0.049)	(0.067)
Higher probability	0.404***	—	—
	(0.029)		
(Initial points 50–70) × (Higher probability)	−0.213***	−0.142**	−0.204**
	(0.063)	(0.059)	(0.082)
Controls?	No	Yes	Yes
State fixed effects?	No	Yes	No
School fixed effects?	No	No	Yes

Notes: The N of all regressions is 76,567. Robust standard errors are in parentheses, adjusted for school-level clustering; *** indicates statistical significance at 1 percent, ** at 5 percent, and * at 10 percent. Additional controls include Male, Afternoon, Evening, Year 10, Year 11, Grade 4, Grade 5, and Grade 6.

ability as a continuous variable—measuring state-specific probabilities—rather than a dichotomous variable.

One might further posit that, in some states, the probabilities are more stable across time, perhaps suggesting that such teachers are more responsive to such information in determining their level of effort. We identified a subset of 15 states in which three estimated probabilities—estimated separately across each year of data—were never more than 0.2 apart. The regression results were similar.

Robustness Checks

Thus far, the results do not indicate that teachers with stronger incentives produce higher achievement than teachers with weaker incentives. This section probes this conclusion further by carrying out a number of robustness checks.

First, it is possible that effects are heterogeneous across groups of teachers. We reestimated the regressions from the discontinuity specification in columns 4–6 of table 7.9 and from the difference-in-differences specification in columns 1–3 in table 7.10. The regressions were estimated within subsamples defined by year of the sample (9, 10, and 11); by the teacher's gender; by the teacher's educational level; and by the socioeconomic index of the community where the school is located.[97] None of the coefficients were positive, and they were statistically significant at 5 percent.

Second, it is possible for teachers to reenter the assessment process in subsequent years, even if they are denied promotion in the current year. About one-third of our sample is attempting promotion for the first time, while the rest are appearing for the second time or more. The latter group is older and, hence, more likely to fall within the 50–70 interval. That fact may lead to higher or lower achievement among their students, perhaps because of experience or demoralization. Thus, we reestimated the same specifications as in the previous paragraph, while including a series of dummy variables that control for promotion attempts (ranging from the second to the tenth attempt, relative to the first). In other regressions, we limited the sample to first-timers. None of those results altered the previous conclusions.

Third, one might question whether all components of the initial points that a teacher receives are exogenous. The most likely candidate is the teachers' test that is administered in March, which contributes 28 points to the score. Suppose that teachers can allocate their effort across two activities: (a) classroom teaching and (b) "cramming" for the teachers' test, which is based on subject matter. If cramming is a successful strategy, then one might expect that teachers who retake the test—as described in the last paragraph—would experience test score gains.[98] To test this hypothesis, we regressed the teacher test data on a series of dummy variables that control for promotion attempts (again, ranging from the second to the tenth attempt), in addition to dummy variables indicating the assessment year and teacher fixed effects. None of the coefficients on the promotion attempt dummy variables were statistically significant. This result provides some limited evidence that—at least among a subsample of teachers who took the test multiple times—that teachers' test scores are relatively stable.

Nonetheless, imagine that additional effort might influence one's own test score. In such a case, the relevant initial points measure, from the teacher's perspective, would include all the previous components except for the teachers' test. The outcome variable would now be the sum of the students' test score and the individual teacher's test score (ranging from 0 to 48). The relevant discontinuity, in this case, is 22. Teachers scoring below 22 face weak incentives, because they cannot score above 70, even

---

97. We defined three levels of education: (a) no higher-education degree, (b) a teacher's college degree or equivalent, and (c) a university degree or higher. The socioeconomic index is by INEGI. It is at the community level and is based on a range of variables, including illiteracy, utility access of homes, and income. We divided the sample into three groups, which are based on terciles of the index.

98. In a similar vein, Vigdor and Clotfelter (2003) demonstrate gains on SAT scores among students who take the test multiple times, perhaps because of learning or greater familiarity with the test format.

with the full 48 points on the tests for teachers and students. If their scores are above 22, teachers allocate their efforts across teaching effort and cramming effort. To assess that possibility, we reestimated all regressions with the revised dependent and independent variables, but there was still no evidence of a positive effect.

Discussion

In a program as large and costly as Carrera Magisterial, it is important to ask why there is no apparent effect. There are several possible explanations. First, teachers may perceive that the mean test score of their class is a noisy measure. Analyses of test score data in the United States and Chile suggest that the error variance of school-level mean test scores is substantially larger when the school enrollment is smaller, because of sampling variation (Chay, McEwan, and Urquiola 2003; Kane and Staiger 2001). In the present case, individual classroom means are assessed. The smaller samples imply relatively noisier measures. The original Carrera Magisterial data do not contain either class sizes or school enrollments, but we obtained the pupil–teacher ratio of each school in grades 3–6 (the grades corresponding to our sample) in program year 10. We then graphed the test score of each classroom against its school's pupil–teacher ratio (see figure 7.7). A pattern emerges, as in prior research, in which mean performance is more variable in smaller classrooms (as proxied by the pupil–teacher ratio). Of course, the vast majority of observations are drawn from schools with pupil–teacher ratios of less than 50.

Suppose teachers perceive that the mean test score in a given year is indeed a noisy measure that fluctuates widely from year to year. Because teachers are allowed to participate in the assessment more than once—and points received from other factors appear stable—teachers may simply decide that it is better to reduce costly effort and to wait for a year in which their class receives a transitorily high mean score.

Second, it is possible that the disutility of additional effort always outweighs the expected utility of receiving an award. Nevertheless, the extraordinarily generous awards—more than 20 percent of subsequent career wages—render this argument somewhat less plausible.

Third, it is possible that teachers do not have a clear understanding of the classroom production technology. They may be willing to increase effort but are unsure of how to fruitfully expend effort toward improving their students' test scores. This scenario might be likely if the teachers are not aware of the content of the student test. However, the tests are grade specific and are designed to reflect the content of the existing curriculum and textbooks (Ortiz Jiménez 2003). Another possibility is that there is not enough time—in the 2 to 3 months between the teacher test (when teachers more or less can calculate their "exogenous" score) and the

Figure 7.7. Test Scores and Pupil–Teacher Ratios in Year 10 for Teachers

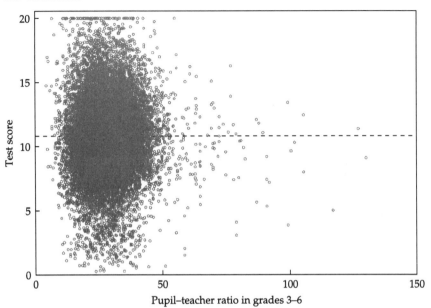

Note: The horizontal line is located at the sample mean (10.8).

student test—for them to be able to substantially improve their students' performance, even with high levels of effort.

Results for Principals

Empirical Strategy 1

Figure 7.8 reports evidence that can be used to visually identify an effect. Panel A graphs the fitted values obtained from a bandwidth of 0.01, whereas panels B, C, and D use successively wider ones. There is a positive and apparently linear relationship between the index of observables for principals and school performance scores. However, there is little evidence of a discontinuity in the relationship when initial points equal 50. A small hump is observed just before 60, roughly equal to 0.4 test score points for a classroom in this narrow range of initial points, which is equivalent to less than a quarter of a standard deviation.

Table 7.11 reports regression evidence on these points. Column 1 regresses test scores on initial points and on initial points between 50 and 70. All other controls are omitted, providing the best analogue to the previous visual evidence. The statistically significant and positive coefficient on ini-

Figure 7.8. Fitted Values of Classroom Test Scores on Initial Points, by Bandwidth for Principals

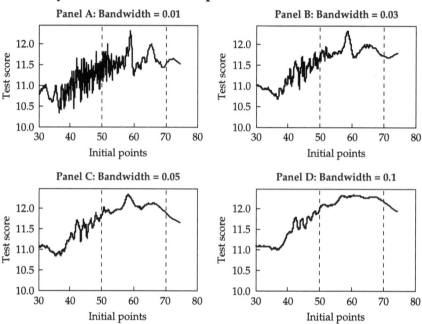

tial points (0.044) implies that an increase of one standard deviation in initial points (7.25 units) is associated with an increase of close to one-fifth of a standard deviation in the school performance variable. The dummy variable for the 50–70 interval is positive, though small and statistically insignificant. Column 2 adds more controls for observables of principals, as well as for state-level dummies, but the results are quite similar. Column 3 further controls for school fixed effects, which are, in fact, individual fixed effects. The coefficient on initial points becomes insignificant as fixed effects absorb most of the variation between principals and, as expected, explain a large proportion (0.82) of the variation in school performance scores. Columns 4–6 report less restrictive specifications, splitting the 50–70 interval into four dummy variables. There is a larger, albeit negative, coefficient on initial points between 60 and 65.

Empirical Strategy 2

We next identified two groups of principals: (a) those working in states where scoring above 70 increases the probability of promotion by 0.44 or more (the estimated probability in the full sample), and (b) those working in states with probabilities of less than 0.44. The probabilities for each group, estimated separately, are 0.67 and 0.29, respectively (see table 7.7).

Table 7.11. Principals' Initial Points and School Performance Scores

	Dependent variable: school performance					
	(1)	(2)	(3)	(4)	(5)	(6)
Initial points	0.044**	0.037***	0.011	0.050**	0.043***	0.012
	(0.005)	(0.005)	(0.009)	(0.006)	(0.005)	(0.01)
Initial points 50–70	0.06	0.074	−0.092	—	—	—
	(0.083)	(0.081)	(0.119)			
Initial points 50–55	—	—	—	0.059	0.07	−0.085
				(0.086)	(0.084)	(0.121)
Initial points 55–60	—	—	—	0.062	0.077	−0.124
				(0.128)	(0.125)	(0.191)
Initial points 60–65	—	—	—	−0.370*	−0.363**	−0.333
				(0.174)	(0.17)	(0.297)
Initial points 65–70	—	—	—	−0.472	−0.507*	0.176
				(0.272)	(0.266)	(0.494)
R^2	0.04	0.10	0.82	0.04	0.10	0.82
Controls?	No	Yes	Yes	No	Yes	Yes
State fixed effects?	No	Yes	No	No	Yes	No
School fixed effects?	No	No	Yes	No	No	Yes

Notes: The N of all regressions is 5,055. *** indicates statistical significance at 1 percent, ** at 5 percent, and * at 10 percent. Standard errors are in parentheses. Controls include Male, Afternoon, Evening, Year 10, and Year 11.

The difference of 0.38 implies that the expected value of scoring above 70 is more than 130 percent higher for principals in the first group. Hence, we dub the two groups the "stronger-incentive" and "weaker-incentive" groups.

We repeat the previous section's visual exercise, obtaining separate fitted values for each group (see figure 7.9). The solid and dashed lines in each panel indicate the strong-incentive and weak-incentive groups, respectively. When initial points are below 50, we surmise that both groups face weak incentives and should have similar functional forms. That similarity seems to be the case in all panels, and it is also the case in a formal test.[99] When the initial points are above 50, one might anticipate

---

99. We limited the samples to observations with initial points below 50. We then regressed the test score variable on (a) the initial points variable, (b) a continuous variable containing the state-specific probability, and (c) the interaction between the two variables (with robust standard errors adjusted for school-level clustering). We could not reject the null that the coefficient on the interaction is zero.

Figure 7.9. Fitted Values of Classroom Test Scores on Initial Points, by Bandwidth and State

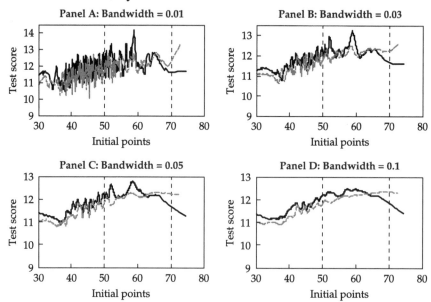

Note: Solid lines include states in which the probability of promotion is greater than 0.44 (see table 7.7). Dashed lines include states in which the probability is less than 0.44.

a divergence in the lines in the presence of a program effect. At first glance, that divergence appears to be the case close to 50 (where most of the sample is concentrated). In panel D, which uses a larger bandwidth and greater smoothing, much of this pattern dissipates.

Table 7.12 estimates the difference-in-differences via regression analysis. The variable for high probability is dichotomous, indicating whether principals work in higher- or lower-probability states. (Note that its coefficient is not estimated in columns 2 and 3, given controls for state-level and school-level dummies.) The key coefficient is the interaction between falling within the 50–70 interval and working in a higher-probability state. The coefficients are positive, but they are small in magnitude and statistically insignificant across all specifications.

Overall, the results do not suggest that principals improved school performance in their promotion years. In addition, there is limited evidence to suggest that after reaching an initial point score of 60, principals tend to be associated with lower school performance. Those results include an important caveat, however. A more thorough analysis of those and other possibilities would necessitate more data to be able to separate the school performance score into its two components: the students' scores and the

Table 7.12. Principals' Initial Scores and Classroom Test Scores: Difference-in-Differences

	Dependent variable: school performance		
	(1)	(2)	(3)
Initial points	0.043***	0.037***	0.01
	(0.005)	(0.005)	(0.009)
Initial points 50–70	0.061	0.024	–0.217
	(0.095)	(0.094)	(0.146)
Higher probability (dichotomous)	0.224***	—	—
	(0.059)		
(Initial points 50–70) × (Higher probability)	0.038	0.122	0.265
	(0.117)	(0.116)	(0.193)
Controls?	No	Yes	Yes
State fixed effects?	No	Yes	No
School fixed effects?	No	No	Yes

Notes: The N of all regressions is 5,055. Standard errors in parentheses; *** indicates statistical significance at 1 percent. Additional controls include Male, Afternoon, Evening, Year 10, and Year 11.

teachers' scores. It might be that principals have somewhat more control (or power to affect) teachers' scores than students' scores. For example, principals could give teachers time to prepare for the Carrera Magisterial tests or could provide guidance and training. The possibility must also be considered that principals exert control over which teachers participate in any given year. In so doing, they may be able to select higher-scoring teachers or teachers with the highest-scoring students. This chapter has not investigated that possibility.

Conclusions

This chapter has provided empirical evidence on the student and school performance effects of Mexico's Carrera Magisterial program for teachers and principals. In estimating the effects, we relied on the fact that some participating teachers and principals face weaker incentives, because they face insurmountable barriers to promotion in a given year or simply because they live in a state where high-scoring participants face a lower probability of promotion. For both teachers and principals, the chapter did not find robust evidence that Mexican teachers facing stronger incentives actually improved student achievement in the year in which they were assessed.

These results have several potential implications. First, an essential premise of this chapter is that many Mexican teachers and principals—

85 percent and 74 percent of our sample respectively—faced weaker incentives, even when participating in the Carrera Magisterial assessment. Even disregarding the subsequent empirical findings, this conclusion is sobering. It suggests that a revised assessment process could restrict eligibility to groups of participants that are most likely to face strong incentives (thus incurring savings from a reduced assessment burden). Similarly, one might place increasing weight on students' test scores in the promotion formula (for both teachers and principals), thus expanding the "treated" range of initial points beyond the 50–70 interval.

Second, one could imagine a scenario under which student test scores did improve in the case of teachers or where evidence of improvements in school performance was much stronger. Even under this optimistic scenario, the cost of a one-shot gain in students' test scores or school performance is clearly high. After receiving their promotions, particularly at the highest level, teachers and principals once again face weak incentives to improve the achievement of later student cohorts.[100] Yet they continue to receive substantial monetary rewards throughout their careers. It is unclear, for example, why Mexico should not simply invest in a relatively cheap tutoring program and obtain a 0.2 standard deviation gain, as was done in Chile (Chay, McEwan, and Urquiola 2003).

Third, it would be appropriate to base a permanent and costly promotion on more than a single classroom's test scores or on the average scores of participating Carrera Magisterial teachers in the school, which in some years can mean only one or two teachers. On the one hand, combining various years' test scores might diminish the noise of a mean test score measure that is based on a small sample of students or teachers. On the other hand, it would provide added incentives for participants to exert effort in more than the particular year in which they are being considered for promotion.

Fourth, it is possible that large and permanent wage increases have succeeded in attracting a more qualified pool of teacher applicants (and perhaps teacher hires) in the past decade, in part because they link teacher wages to teacher test scores.[101] That research question was not addressed in this chapter. Even if this possibility were the case, however, it might have been accomplished at a lower administrative cost by simply implementing across-the-board wage increases or by modifying the wage schedule to place greater weight on teacher competencies.

---

100. Teachers may, however, decide to participate each year so they can obtain a high score that they can use later for promotion. However, once a teacher or principal obtains a sufficiently high score in any given year, the incentive to keep participating in the program (and thus to improve in the school or classroom) diminishes.

101. Teachers' test scores generally have more demonstrable links to student achievement in Mexico and elsewhere (see, for example, Hanushek 2002; Santibáñez 2003). We are interested here only in the effects on the teacher applicant pool, because all public school principals in Mexico must be first hired as teachers.

References

Bossert, S. T., D. C. Dwyer, B. Rowan, and G. V. Lee. 1982. "The Instructional Management Role of the Principal." *Educational Administration Quarterly* 18(3): 34–64.

Chay, K. Y., P. J. McEwan, and M. Urquiola. 2003. "The Central Role of Noise in Evaluating Interventions That Use Test Scores to Rank Schools." NBER Working Paper 10118. National Bureau of Economic Research, Cambridge, Mass.

Courty, P., and G. Marschke. 2004. "An Empirical Investigation of Gaming Responses to Explicit Performance Incentives." *Journal of Labor Economics* 22: 23–56.

Cullen, J. B., and R. Reback. 2002. "Tinkering toward Accolades: School Gaming under a Performance Accountability System." University of Michigan, Ann Arbor. Processed.

Eberts, R. W., and J. A. Stone. 1988. "Student Achievement in Public Schools: Do Principals Make a Difference?" *Economics of Education Review* 7(3): 291–99.

Education Week. 2004. *Quality Counts 2004.* Bethesda: Editorial Projects in Education.

Figlio, D. N. 2002. "Can Public Schools Buy Better Teachers?" *Industrial and Labor Relations Review* 55: 686–99.

Figlio, D. N., and L. S. Getzler. 2002. "Accountability, Ability, and Disability: Gaming the System." Working Paper 9307. National Bureau of Economic Research, Cambridge, Mass.

Figlio, D. N., and J. Winicki. Forthcoming. "Food for Thought: The Effects of School Accountability Plans on School Nutrition." *Journal of Public Economics* 89(2): 381–94.

Gates, S. M., J. S. Ringel, L. Santibáñez, K. E. Ross, and C. H. Chung. 2003. *Who Is Leading Our Schools? An Overview of School Administrators and Their Careers.* Santa Monica, Calif.: Rand.

Glewwe, P., N. Ilias, and M. Kremer. 2003. "Teacher Incentives." Working Paper 9671. National Bureau of Economic Research, Cambridge, Mass.

Hallinger, P., and J. Murphy. 1986. "Instructional Leadership in Effective Schools." *Elementary School Journal* 86: 217–47.

Hanushek, E. A. 2002. "Publicly Provided Education." In A. J. Auerbach and M. Feldstein, eds., *Handbook of Public Economics* (vol. 4). Amsterdam: North-Holland.

Hanushek, E. A., and M. E. Raymond. 2002. "Improving Educational Quality: How Best to Evaluate Our Schools?" In Y. K. Kodrzycki, ed., *Education in the 21st Century: Meeting the Challenges of a Changing World.* Boston: Federal Reserve Bank of Boston.

Jacob, B. A., and S. D. Levitt. 2003. "Rotten Apples: An Investigation of the Prevalence and Predictors of Teacher Cheating." *Quarterly Journal of Economics* 118: 843–78.

Kane, T. J., and D. O. Staiger. 2001. "Improving School Accountability Measures." Working Paper 8156. National Bureau of Economic Research, Cambridge, Mass.

Lavy, V. 2002. "Evaluating the Effect of Teachers' Group Performance Incentives on Pupil Achievement." *Journal of Political Economy* 110(6): 1286–317.

Murnane, R. J., and D. K. Cohen. 1986. "Merit Pay and the Evaluation Problem: Why Most Merit Pay Plans Fail and a Few Survive." *Harvard Educational Review* 56: 1–17.

Ortiz Jiménez, M. B. 2003. *Carrera Magisterial: Un proyecto de desarrollo profesional.* Cuadernos de Discusión 12. Secretaría de Educación Pública, Mexico City.

Prendergast, C. 1999. "The Provision of Incentives in Firms." *Journal of Economic Literature* 37 (March): 7–63.

Presidency of the Mexican Republic. 1992. *Decreto para la celebración de convenios en el marco del acuerdo nacional para la modernización de la educación básica* (ANMEB). Diario Oficial de la Federación, May 19.

Santibáñez, L. 2003. "Why We Should Care if Teachers Get A's: Teacher Characteristics and Student Achievement in Mexico." RAND, Santa Monica. Processed.

SEP (Secretaría de Educación Pública). No date. *Cronograma de actividades para la operación de Carrera Magisterial, décimatercera etapa (ciclo escolar 2003–2004)*. Mexico City.

———. 2003. *Informe de labores 2003*. Anexo 3. Mexico City.

Vigdor, J. L., and C. T. Clotfelter. 2003. "Retaking the SAT." *Journal of Human Resources* 38: 1–33.

Zigarelli, M. A. 1996. "An Empirical Test of Conclusions from Effective Schools Research." *Journal of Educational Research* 90(2): 103–10.

8

Decentralization of Education, Teacher Behavior, and Outcomes

The Case of El Salvador's EDUCO Program

Yasuyuki Sawada

and Andrew Ragatz
University of Tokyo

El Salvador's model for decentralized schools, Educación con Participación de la Comunidad (Education with Community Participation, or EDUCO), presents a unique opportunity to evaluate the effect of decentralization on education. This chapter builds on a study by Jimenez and Sawada (1999) that measured the effects on student outcomes of decentralizing educational responsibility to communities and schools. It further explores the effect of decentralization, this time focusing on how it affects administrative processes and teacher behavior, and on how those changes affect student achievement and the quality of education.

In our empirical implementations, we control for school, community, and school participant (teacher, director, student) characteristics. We also control for sample selection bias using two methods. First, we use propensity score matching in an attempt to eliminate selection bias. Then we use a standard sample selection model to determine whether the level of bias in our model resulting from unobserved variables is significant. The results indicate that, interestingly, most administrative processes in EDUCO have not shifted to the local level, if we compare it to traditional schools, but that certain key administrative activities such as hiring and firing decisions do, in fact, differ significantly between EDUCO and traditional schools.

The more striking finding is that school associations tend to feel they have greater influence in virtually every administrative activity. Our results also indicate that decentralization may have a positive influence on teacher behavior. Although certain concerns exist in ability to measure

We would like to thank all the participants of the World Bank workshop on April 22, 2004. The many insightful comments we received were helpful in bringing out key messages and greatly improved the content of our paper.

the abstract concept of teacher behavior, there does seem to be a statistically significant "EDUCO effect." This effect, in turn, may have a positive influence on student performance.

Teachers play a central role in education. From a financial standpoint, teachers account for a large share of the total educational budget. From a quality of education standpoint, a talented, motivated teacher can have a positive effect on students. Conversely, a teacher who does not put much effort into creating a positive learning environment or who is frequently absent can have a detrimental effect on student outcomes. Many studies have demonstrated that, controlling for differences in students' socioeconomic background, teachers constitute the most important determinant of student achievement.[102] Creating an environment and providing incentives that promote positive teacher behavior, then, can be a critical component of improving education.

Many developing countries have recently adopted various models of decentralized school management, where communities play a larger role in running the school (Bardhan 2002; Conning and Kevane 2002; Rai 2002; Stiglitz 1999; World Bank 2003). Theory suggests that decentralization can ease the problem that results from imperfect information, enable the poor to amplify their voice in policymaking and strengthen the incentives for providers to serve effectively (World Bank 2003).[103] This model of schooling could potentially have a significant influence on teacher behavior and motivation. El Salvador's decentralized school management program, EDUCO, provides a unique opportunity to explore the issue of teacher behavior in a decentralized schooling model. This chapter examines the EDUCO program in an attempt to better understand how the schooling model has affected teacher motivation and behavior, as well as how those behavioral changes have affected student achievement.

This chapter builds on the study by Jimenez and Sawada (1999) that measured the effects on student outcomes of decentralizing educational responsibility to communities and schools. We compare administrative activities and teacher behavior in EDUCO schools to those in traditional schools. We control for school, community (socioeconomic), and participant (teacher, director, and student) characteristics. We also control for sample selection bias, using both propensity score matching and an exogenously determined formula for targeting EDUCO schools as an instrumental variable.

Interestingly, the results indicate that many administrative processes in EDUCO have not dramatically shifted to the local level when compared with traditional schools. Yet, selective administrative activities such as hir-

---

102. For recent examples, see Ehrenberg and Brewer (1995); Monk (1994); and Rivkin, Hanushek, and Kain (forthcoming).

103. In practice, in many centrally run government programs, the employees might become accountable not to local beneficiaries but to central authorities. Because compensation of teachers and doctors usually is not linked to their performance, their work incentives are likely to be weak. As a result, salaried teacher absenteeism and tardiness are prevalent in many developing countries, especially in rural areas (Lockheed and others 1991, p. 101).

ing and firing decisions do, in fact, differ significantly between the two systems. But striking decentralization differences emerged when measuring perceived amount of influence. School associations in EDUCO tend to feel they have greater influence in virtually every administrative activity, even though many of those processes may still be carried out primarily at the national level.

The results also indicate (a) that decentralization may have had a positive effect on teacher behavior, with teachers tending to show more motivation in EDUCO schools, and (b) that this increased motivation may, in turn, have had a positive effect on student performance, as measured by mathematics and Spanish achievement test scores and by school attendance.

The chapter is organized as follows. In the next section, we describe the background of the EDUCO program and give a simple comparison of EDUCO and traditional schools. Then we make an empirical study of the EDUCO program. The section shows empirical evidence on how decentralization has changed the process for teacher management, how decentralization changes have affected teacher behavior, and to what extent changes in teacher behavior have affected the educational outcome. Finally, we conclude with a brief discussion of the policy implications of our empirical findings.

The Case of El Salvador's EDUCO Program

Background

The EDUCO program is based on an inventive decentralized schooling model that evolved during El Salvador's civil war. In the 1980s, many rural communities were cut off from, or had only limited access to, the traditional education system. In many areas, the communities themselves took responsibility for providing educational opportunities for their children. By the late 1980s, the national government saw the community model that had emerged as having great potential for efficiently and effectively providing education, particularly to isolated rural communities. With the support of international agencies, the national government implemented the EDUCO program in 1990. The program is for both pre-primary and primary education and aims at decentralizing education by strengthening direct involvement and participation of parents and community groups (Jimenez and Sawada 1999, 2001; Reimers 1997; World Bank 2003).

The EDUCO program was designed to achieve several goals. A primary goal was to provide access to schools in the country's poorest and most-isolated rural communities. Other goals included supporting and encouraging community participation in education, improving the quality of pre-primary and primary schooling, and improving school-level management and administration by allowing the communities—who best know their own schooling needs—to create and manage school priorities.

In EDUCO schools, the Community Education Association (Asociación Comunal para la Educación, or ACE) plays a central role in school administration and management. The selection process of ACE members is democratic: ACE members are selected by votes of parents of all students at a biannual general assembly. ACEs are contracted by the Ministry of Education (MINED) to deliver a given curriculum to an agreed number of students. ACEs are then responsible for contracting and removing teachers by closely monitoring teachers' performance and for equipping and maintaining the schools. In short, the ACE members have power to decide the allocation of school resources and employment of teachers (figure 8.1). The partnership between MINED and ACEs is expected to improve school administration and management by reflecting local demand needs more appropriately than that of traditional public schools. Conversely, a parents' association (*sociedad de padres de familia*, or SdPF) in centrally managed traditional public schools has little or no administrative capability over school personnel or budget.[104]

The initial indications are that the EDUCO program has accomplished its primary goal of rapidly expanding access to education in remote rural areas by using the demonstrated community interest as a platform (World Bank 1997). One concern is whether this rapid expansion using a decentralized model has come at the expense of quality of education as the system moves away from traditional programs that provide education centrally. The theory favoring the decentralized model is that education quality will improve because communities can better identify needs of the school and can quickly respond. This increased sense of ownership could also foster pride and greater dedication to ensuring that the school operates properly.

Similar to other decentralization studies in Latin America, a 1997 study of the EDUCO program found that student achievement was positively affected by decentralization (World Bank 1997). Jimenez and Sawada (1999) concluded that student achievement has not been adversely affected by the rapid deployment of EDUCO schools.

An area that is still not well understood for this type of decentralization model is how it influences teacher behavior. This chapter focuses specifically on differences in administrative processes and teacher behavior, as well as on how teacher behavior affects student outcomes.

Data

The data were collected in October 1996 by MINED of El Salvador with the assistance of the World Bank and the U.S. Agency for International

---

104. In 1996, School Management Councils (Consejos Directivos Escolares, or CDEs) were introduced to the traditional schools in order to increase participation and democracy in school management. The council is composed of a school director, teachers, parents of students, and students. Since 1998, CDEs have become legally mandatory for all traditional schools. In the future, MINED intends to introduce community management into all traditional schools through CDEs.

Figure 8.1. Comparison of EDUCO
and Traditional Governance Structures

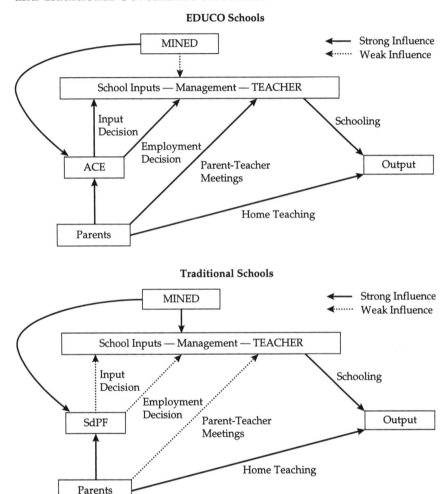

Source: Author's illustration.

Development. The data set includes 311 primary schools, with data of 1,555 students, and 596 ACE committee members, which were randomly sampled from the 3,634 primary schools (Jimenez and Sawada 1999).[105] The surveys focused on third-grade sections for each school.

---

105. The survey was conducted again in 1998, with slightly different questionnaires and different respondents. In the 1998 survey, the students in the 1996 survey were interviewed as well. See Jimenez and Sawada (2001).

The survey covered 162 of El Salvador's 262 municipalities. Those municipalities share responsibility with the central government for the delivery of social services. The original sample was selected to capture data for four types of schools—EDUCO, traditional, "mixed" (having some school sections under the EDUCO system and other sections under the traditional system), and private. In this study, we dropped samples for private schools and traditional public schools located in urban areas because those samples are not comparable with rural EDUCO schools. To have the clearest distinction possible between EDUCO and traditional systems, we also dropped the mixed schools. We were left with 37 pure EDUCO schools and 96 pure traditional rural schools.

The survey is composed of five questionnaires: student, parents, school director, teacher, and parents' association. In addition, we use various municipality-level socioeconomic indicators, such as municipality-level poverty indices, infant mortality rates, and illiteracy rates.

Variables and Descriptive Statistics

Following are simple statistics that present a general picture of the differences between EDUCO and traditional schools.

The selection criteria used for placing EDUCO schools target primarily the poorest, most isolated rural communities. A comparison of municipality's socioeconomic characteristics in table 8.1 reflects these criteria. In every category, community characteristics for the EDUCO schools show higher poverty and lower education characteristics, with the exception of overage students in grades 7–9. This difference is most likely because in most of the poorest communities schooling is not even offered for grades 7–9, so most students in those communities do not continue their education.

The descriptive statistics in table 8.2 show household socioeconomic characteristics to be much better for traditional school students than for EDUCO students. The parents of traditional school students have more education than those of EDUCO students, with 54 percent of mothers or female guardians of traditional students having basic education, compared with 50 percent for EDUCO students. The same is true of the fathers' education. The educational differences are reflected also in the asset indicators. Fewer EDUCO parents have access to home ownership, electricity, sanitary services, and running water. These data all suggest that EDUCO students come from poorer backgrounds than traditional school students. Therefore, the EDUCO program has been successful in targeting poorer segments of the population.

Basic school characteristics found in table 8.3 are consistent with the pattern for the socioeconomic characteristics of students and households. Although the availability of sanitation is similar in both types of schools, fewer EDUCO schools have access to electricity or piped water.

Table 8.1. Means and Standard Deviations of Municipality-Level Socioeconomic Variables

Variable definitions	EDUCO schools	Traditional schools	All schools
Poverty decile (1–10, with 1 being poorest decile)	3.59 (1.77)	4.82 (2.00)	4.48 (2.01)
Mortality rate (%)	38.44 (17.45)	34.68 (14.57)	35.72 (15.45)
Illiteracy rate (%)	35.49 (11.41)	29.66 (10.75)	31.28 (11.21)
Improvisational housing (%)	46.01 (9.52)	39.6 (11.72)	41.38 (11.48)
Education rate, grades 1–6 (%)	38.42 (10.92)	46.04 (13.93)	43.92 (13.56)
Education rate, grades 7–9 (%)	17.35 (9.08)	20.41 (10.78)	19.56 (10.39)
Overage students, grades 1–6 (%)	53.00 (5.62)	50.37 (8.72)	51.10 (8.05)
Overage students, grades 7–9 (%)	49.45 (8.45)	51.20 (12.61)	50.71 (11.6)
Rural population (%)	71.96 (21.3)	67.74 (19.82)	68.94 (20.26)
Number of observations	37	96	133

Note: Standard deviations in parentheses.
Source: Author calculations using data from the 1996 MINED survey.

Data on teachers' characteristics indicate that EDUCO teachers are more likely to have finished a university education but are less experienced because EDUCO teachers typically are relatively young recent graduates. Although EDUCO teachers earn less without controlling for any differences in age, experience, or educational level, they tend to receive more benefits than traditional school teachers.

As for classroom characteristics, there are no differences in accessibility to textbooks in the two types of schools, but an EDUCO classroom typically has fewer pupils and a larger number of books in the classroom library than a traditional school classroom has. Moreover, a multigrade setting is found more frequently in EDUCO schools than in traditional schools.

Regarding community participation issues, parents of EDUCO students participate more in school affairs. ACE members in EDUCO schools visit classrooms about four times more often than their traditional counterparts.

Table 8.2. Means and Standard Deviations of Child and Household Variables, by School Type

Variable definitions	EDUCO schools	Traditional schools	All schools
Gender (female = 1)	0.51	0.51	0.51
Child's age (years)	11.01	10.44	10.58
	(1.97)	(1.66)	(1.76)
Live without parent(s) = 1	0.16	0.13	0.14
Child had respiratory illness/ flu in the last 2 weeks = 1	0.63	0.59	0.60
Number of siblings (ages 4–15)	2.11	1.98	2.01
	(1.50)	(1.56)	(1.54)
Mother enter basic education = 1	0.50	0.54	0.53
Mother's education missing = 1	0.06	0.09	0.08
Father enter basic education = 1	0.38	0.40	0.39
Father's education missing = 1	0.03	0.04	0.04
Own house = 1	0.68	0.73	0.72
Electricity available = 1	0.28	0.67	0.58
Sanitary service available = 1	0.06	0.22	0.18
Water available = 1	0.01	0.08	0.06
Number of observations	142	464	606

Note: Standard deviations in parentheses.
Source: Author calculations using data from the 1996 MINED survey.

At the parental association meetings, 80 percent and 79 percent of ACEs discussed teacher discipline and attendance of school personnel, respectively, whereas corresponding figures for SdPFs are 62 percent and 38 percent, respectively. Less teacher absenteeism and more frequent meetings with parents in EDUCO schools might reflect the effectiveness of implicit or explicit teacher monitoring by parental associations in those schools.

Empirical Analysis of the EDUCO Program

In this section, we evaluate the EDUCO program in an attempt to answer the three following questions:

1. How has decentralization changed the process for managing teachers?
2. How has decentralization changed the behavior of teachers?
3. How do differences in teachers' behavior affect students' achievement?

Table 8.3. Means and Standard Deviations of School, Teacher, Classroom, and Community Variables, by School Type

Variable definitions	EDUCO schools	Traditional schools	All schools
School variables:			
Teacher–pupil ratio (school level)	0.05 (0.09)	0.03 (0.041)	0.04 (0.056)
If sanitation or latrine is available at school = 1	0.89	0.94	0.93
If electricity is available at school = 1	0.30	0.80	0.68
If piped water is available at school = 1	0.12	0.38	0.32
Teacher and classroom variables:			
If teacher finished a university education = 1	0.75	0.37	0.46
Years of teaching experience	4.37 (2.71)	8.89 (6.87)	7.83 (6.44)
Monthly base salary of teacher (colon)	2,919.23 (269.40)	3,070.71 (574.84)	3,035.21 (523.38)
If teacher receives bonus = 1	0.74	0.61	0.64
If all students have math textbook = 1	0.58	0.62	0.61
If math textbook information is missing = 1	0.25	0.07	0.11
If all students have language textbook = 1	0.59	0.59	0.59
If language textbook information is missing = 1	0.28	0.07	0.12
If teacher teaches in multigrade classroom = 1	0.39	0.20	0.24
If multigrade information is missing = 1	0.04	0.00	0.01
Number of books in classroom library	114.63 (272.84)	61.98 (166.42)	74.32 (197.59)
If classroom library information is missing = 1	0.24	0.54	0.47
Community participation variable:			
Number of ACE or SpDF visits to classroom	5.65 (6.59)	1.56 (3.63)	2.52 (4.82)
Number of observations	31	102	133

Note: Standard deviations in parentheses.
Source: Author calculations using data from the 1996 MINED survey.

Each question is a logical progression that builds on the results of the previous one. If one first better understands how EDUCO administrative processes differ from those of traditional schools, then teacher behavior differences can be analyzed with a clearer lens, especially when evaluating the effects on student achievement.

In each section, we first form hypotheses, driving the structure of the model used. Those hypotheses are discussed in more detail within each section, but here we provide a brief summary. First, EDUCO has the charter of decentralizing administrative processes. Our hypothesis in analyzing administrative processes, then, is that they would be more decentralized in EDUCO schools and that participants at the local level would feel they have more influence. Second, for teacher behavior, our hypothesis is based on the principal–agent model. In a more decentralized school, the teacher (agent) is being closely monitored by the school association (principal) rather than by a centralized body, as is the case in traditional schools with the Ministry of Education. The hypothesis is that this close monitoring in EDUCO schools would lead to more-motivated teacher behavior. Finally, regarding student achievement, our hypothesis is that more motivated teachers will have a positive effect on student achievement.

How Has Decentralization Changed the Process of Teacher Management?

To evaluate the effect of EDUCO program on teacher behavior, one must first understand how administrative processes differ between EDUCO and traditional schools. The surveys of director, teacher, and school association members contain questions covering 29 administrative processes. For each process, the interviewees were asked whether they believe the major influence level of the process is at the national, departmental, or school level and how much influence they believe they have in the process, allowing for a comparison of perspectives by the different key participants (table 8.4). The former question gives an imperfect but supportive measure of decentralization, while the latter question gives a subjective assessment of one's own influence in administrative processes.

Our hypothesis is that administrative processes in EDUCO schools are more decentralized than in traditional schools and that participants in EDUCO schools, particularly school association members, feel they have more influence. Although this shift in influence is expected to be primarily from the central to the local level, we also hypothesize that gains in influence by one group within the schools (particularly school associations) could take away influence from other school members (particularly directors).

The survey questions give nice insights into perspectives of different school members and can create a clearer picture of how the EDUCO and

Table 8.4. The Format of Questions on the Administrative Process

Q1. The major influence of the process j is at what level?

1. National
2. Departmental
3. School

Q2. How much influence do you (as director, teacher, or association member) have in the process j?

1. None
2. A little
3. Some
4. A lot

Source: 1996 MINED Survey.

traditional systems operate differently, but some issues should first be noted. First, the responses are subjective. The fact that we have responses from three different perspectives allows a more objective picture to emerge, but subjective responses are generally not as reliable as hard data. Second, the question of *major influence* does not give an accurate measure of level of decentralization. For example, a process that takes place at the national level, such as determining teacher salary, may be answered as "national" by both traditional and EDUCO respondents. It may be, however, that the schools in one system do, in fact, have much more influence in the process, even though the final decision is made at the national level. This difference would not be captured in the *decentralization-level* question but might be reflected more in the *amount of influence* question. Finally, although the surveys are comprehensive and allow us to control for many variables, it is still likely that bias exists from unobserved characteristics. The issue of sample selection and unobserved bias, as well as how we address it, is discussed in detail in subsequent sections.

The Model of Administrative Process Measurement

The models of EDUCO and traditional schools are structured so that the administrative processes between the two systems may function differently and that the roles of different participants—directors, teachers, and school associations—may also differ. To compare differences between EDUCO and traditional schools, we first start with the following simple model:

$$(8.1) \qquad Y_{ij} = \delta D_i + Z_i\beta_z + X_i\beta_x + u_i,$$

where Y_{ij} is the decentralization measure by school i in an administrative process j; D is an indicator variable of school type, where D equals 1 for an EDUCO school and D equals 0 for a traditional school; Z denotes a vector of observed physical school-level characteristics; X represents a vector of characteristics of employees within the school; and C is a vector of municipality m's specific variables. In equation 8.1, the estimated coefficient δ captures the "EDUCO effect" after controlling for observed differences between EDUCO and traditional schools in school-level, employee, and community characteristics. The coefficient can be interpreted as the unobserved effect in EDUCO schools generated by the difference in school governance, organization, and resulting incentive mechanism, which are identified by Hanushek (1995) and Kremer (1995) as important factors in producing education.

This simple ordinary least squares (OLS) model may suffer from sample selection and unobserved variable bias. To address that issue, we used two techniques: propensity score matching and endogenous sample selection.

Propensity Score Matching[106]
In equation 8.2, denote that Y_1 and Y_0 represent outcome with and without treatment, respectively. Because an individual cannot be in both states, we cannot observe both Y_1 and Y_0. Instead, what we observe is

$$(8.2) \qquad Y \approx D \, Y_1 + (1 - D)Y_0$$

To measure the effect of treatment, the literature focused on the following two quantities: average treatment effect (ATE) and average treatment effect on the treated (ATT). The ATE and ATT, respectively, are

$$(8.3) \qquad E(Y_1 - Y_0 | Z_i, X_i, C_m)$$

$$(8.4) \qquad E(Y_1 - Y_0 | D = 1, Z_i, X_i, C_m)$$

There are several approaches to quantify the treatment effects. In this chapter, we use the propensity score matching method for the ATT and the sample selection method for the ATE.[107]

In the propensity score matching method, the comparison group is matched to the treatment group on the basis of propensity score, where *propensity score* is defined as the conditional probability of receiving a treatment given pretreatment characteristics (Woodridge 2002). The propensity score is estimated by using the probit model. Then we use a matching method called weighted nearest-neighbor matching. Under this method, each treated unit is matched with the control unit with the closest propensity score.[108]

---

106. This section is based on Becker and Ichino (2002) and Woodridge (2002).

107. Other methods include randomized experiments that became extremely popular in development economics (Angrist and others 2002; Kremer 2003; Miguel and Kremer 2004; Schultz 2004).

108. We also use kernel matching, under which all treated units are matched with a weighted average of all control units with weights that are inversely proportional to the distance between the propensity scores of treated units and controls. The results are not presented in this chapter but are available upon request from the authors.

Endogenous Sample Selection

Placement of EDUCO schools is not randomly determined. Program participation is affected by the targeting procedure in EDUCO schools. From the beginning of the program in 1991–1992 to the time of the survey, the established policy is that the EDUCO schools function exclusively in the most distant, inaccessible rural areas. The government established a priority list of municipalities that were to receive an EDUCO program according to poverty and education deficiency characteristics. To open a new EDUCO school, the community needed to have a student population at the preschool and first-grade level, and the location of the new school could not have another school within at least 4 kilometers. Finally and more important, the community had to show interest in participating in the administration of the school.

This endogenous placement procedure might generate an endogeneity bias if we estimate the model of equation 8.2 by using only OLS. For example, it is likely that a community highly motivated in educating its children received an EDUCO school. In that case, the error term of equation 8.2 and an unobserved factor affecting placements are likely to be positively correlated.

Hence, we also model explicitly the endogenous placement of EDUCO schools as follows:

$$(8.5) \qquad\qquad D_i^* = W_i\gamma + v_i$$

$$(8.6) \qquad\qquad D_i = \begin{cases} 1 & if\, D_i^* > 0 \\ 0 & if\, D_i^* > 0 \end{cases}$$

where D^* is a latent variable of the propensity of EDUCO placement. The econometric model of equations 8.2, 8.5, and 8.6 is called "treatment effects model" in the literature (Greene 2003, pp. 787–89).[109]

Suppose that the error terms in equations 8.2 and 8.5 follow a joint Normal distribution with $var(u) = \sigma 2$, $var(v) = 1$, and $cov(u, v) = \lambda$. Let the functions, $\phi(\bullet)$ and $\Phi(\bullet)$ represent density and cumulative density functions, respectively, of standard Normal distribution. Then there are several ways to estimate the model of equations 8.2, 8.5, and 8.6. We apply James Heckman's two-step estimation method to estimate the following augmented regression model:[110]

---

109. A generalized version of the model is also called self-selection model (Lee 1978), switching regression model (Maddala 1983, pp. 117–22), Type 5 Tobit model (Amemiya 1985), and the model with dummy endogenous regressor (Angrist 1999).

110. We adjusted and estimated the consistent variance–covariance matrix because OLS estimation of the second step in the two-step procedure does not provide the consistent variance–covariance matrix. We can also use the nonlinear least squares method to estimate equation 8.7.

$$(8.7) \; Y = \delta D + Z\beta_z + X\beta_x + C_m\beta_c + D\lambda\frac{\phi(W\hat{\gamma})}{\Phi(W\hat{\gamma})} + (1-D)\lambda\frac{\phi(W\hat{\gamma})}{1 - \Phi(W\hat{\gamma})} + \tilde{u}$$

When we estimate equation 8.7, we use estimated γ by the first-step probit model of equations 8.5 and 8.6.

In equation 8.2, the critical focus is on the coefficient δ on the EDUCO dummy variable, D, where—controlling for community, school, and employee characteristics—the effect of the EDUCO model on the given administrative process Y can be measured relative to the traditional school model. A crucial point to keep in mind is that the D gives an account of how EDUCO schools compare for the given administrative process relative to traditional schools but *does not* show to what extent the process has been decentralized in absolute terms.

Variables Used in Analysis

We use the first question in table 8.4 to quantify the degree of decentralization for each school. The questions on major influence were answered separately by the three participants (directors, teachers, and association members). We combine those responses by school to make an integrated indicator of decentralization for each school.[111] The coefficient on the EDUCO dummy variable is interpreted to be the degree of decentralization in EDUCO schools compared with traditional schools.

We use the second question in table 8.4 to quantify how much influence the group or individual has on the process. The range of options is from 1 (no influence) to 4 (a lot of influence).[112] In the regressions, a positive coefficient in the EDUCO dummy variable indicates that in EDUCO schools the amount of influence is greater than in traditional schools, whereas a negative coefficient indicates that the influence is greater in traditional schools.

Table 8.5 shows mean and standard deviation for both level of decentralization and perception of influence. The numbers allow for comparison between EDUCO and traditional schools, as well as show magnitudes of the responses. For example, *determine salary* is extremely low for both EDUCO and traditional schools, indicating that the activity occurs primarily at the national or departmental level in almost all cases, whereas *spend school money* occurs primarily at the school level in almost all cases for both school systems.

---

111. We constructed two indicators of the degree of decentralization. First, the administrative process takes place at the school level or not at the school level, so that if a response of national or department is given, then it receives a value of 0, whereas a response of school level receives a value of 1. We take the average of this binary indicator over three participants.

112. The survey originally used 1 = a lot of influence to 4 = no influence, but we flipped the responses so that a higher number would represent more influence.

Table 8.5. Means and Standard Deviations of Decentralization and Perceived Influence Variables

| | Decentralization | | | Amount of perceived own influence | | | | | | | | |
| | Weighted average | | | Association | | | Director | | | Teacher | | |
	EDUCO	Traditional	Total	EDUCO	Traditional	Total	EDUCO	Traditional	Total	EDUCO	Traditional	Total
Determine salary	0.14 (0.24)	0.06 (0.15)	0.08 (0.18)	3.00 (0.84)	2.89 (0.78)	2.96 (0.80)	1.05 (0.23)	1.36 (0.94)	1.27 (0.82)	1.28 (0.81)	1.17 (0.62)	1.20 (0.68)
Determine teacher incentives	0.42 (0.35)	0.34 (0.31)	0.36 (0.32)	2.44 (1.08)	1.83 (1.03)	1.99 (1.07)	2.26 (1.26)	2.17 (1.32)	2.20 (1.30)	2.00 (1.31)	1.40 (0.84)	1.55 (1.00)
Evaluate teacher	0.44 (0.33)	0.53 (0.31)	0.51 (0.32)	2.61 (1.11)	1.65 (0.86)	1.91 (1.02)	3.08 (1.09)	3.35 (1.00)	3.27 (1.03)	1.84 (1.13)	1.66 (1.05)	1.70 (1.07)
Give teacher incentives	0.35 (0.33)	0.37 (0.32)	0.36 (0.32)	2.41 (1.00)	1.91 (1.05)	2.05 (1.06)	2.13 (1.31)	2.28 (1.32)	2.24 (1.32)	1.85 (1.22)	1.39 (0.79)	1.50 (0.93)
Hire and fire administration	0.47 (0.32)	0.24 (0.31)	0.30 (0.33)	2.35 (1.17)	1.45 (0.86)	1.71 (1.04)	1.63 (0.97)	1.57 (0.99)	1.59 (0.98)	1.21 (0.57)	1.30 (0.85)	1.27 (0.78)
Hire and fire director	0.45 (0.37)	0.14 (0.24)	0.22 (0.31)	2.76 (1.02)	1.52 (0.89)	1.87 (1.08)	1.18 (0.64)	1.30 (0.81)	1.27 (0.77)	1.06 (0.25)	1.21 (0.69)	1.17 (0.61)

(Continued)

Table 8.5. Means and Standard Deviations of Decentralization and Perceived Influence Variables (Continued)

| | Decentralization | | | | | | Amount of perceived own influence | | | | | |
| | Weighted average | | | Association | | | Director | | | Teacher | | |
	EDUCO	Traditional	Total	EDUCO	Traditional	Total	EDUCO	Traditional	Total	EDUCO	Traditional	Total
Hire and fire teacher	0.51 (0.36)	0.07 (0.17)	0.20 (0.31)	2.79 (1.13)	1.52 (0.91)	1.88 (1.13)	1.30 (0.74)	1.40 (0.84)	1.37 (0.81)	1.19 (0.54)	1.18 (0.63)	1.18 (0.60)
Spend school money	0.94 (0.14)	0.99 (0.07)	0.97 (0.09)	3.47 (0.84)	3.18 (0.92)	3.26 (0.90)	3.28 (1.11)	3.30 (0.91)	3.30 (0.96)	2.66 (1.23)	2.36 (1.14)	2.43 (1.17)
Observe teachers' association relations	0.38 (0.31)	0.54 (0.35)	0.49 (0.35)	2.36 (0.99)	1.89 (1.00)	2.03 (1.02)	2.45 (1.20)	2.91 (1.24)	2.79 (1.24)	1.88 (1.16)	2.16 (1.25)	2.08 (1.23)
Observe teacher supervision	0.38 (0.28)	0.51 (0.33)	0.47 (0.32)	2.39 (1.00)	1.57 (0.76)	1.81 (0.91)	3.19 (0.91)	3.28 (1.09)	3.26 (1.04)	1.81 (1.20)	1.71 (1.15)	1.74 (1.16)
Number of observations	37	95	132	33	79	111	31	91	122	34	89	123

Notes: Standard deviations in parentheses. *For decentralization:* The possible range for decentralization is from 0 to 1, with 1 representing that the activity occurs primarily at the school level and 0 indicating that the activity occurs primarily at the departmental or national level. The decentralization number is a weighted average of director, teacher, and association responses, each given one-third value. *For influence:* The possible range is from 1 to 4, with 4 being "A lot," 3 "Some," 2 "A little," and 1 "None."

Source: Author calculations using data from the 1996 MINED survey.

In the regressions on administrative processes, we used various control variables. A list of those variables can be found in table 8.6, along with descriptive statistics for the EDUCO and traditional models.

The control variables highlight some key differences between EDUCO and traditional schools. First, directors at traditional schools on average

Table 8.6. Means and Standard Deviations of Control Variables Used in Administrative Process Regressions

Variable Definitions	EDUCO	Traditional	All schools
School characteristics:			
Student-teacher ratio in 1996	44.32	40.61	41.64
	(20.16)	(16.25)	(17.42)
Whether the school operates with alternative classrooms	0.34	0.20	0.23
	(0.48)	(0.40)	(0.43)
Whether the school has latrines (1 = yes, 0 = no)	0.89	0.95	0.93
	(0.31)	(0.20)	(0.23)
Whether the school electricity (1 = yes, 0 = no)	0.29	0.82	0.67
	(0.46)	(0.38)	(0.46)
Whether the school a phone (1 = yes, 0 = no)	0.00	0.09	0.06
	0.00	(0.29)	(0.25)
Whether the school is in good condition (1 = yes, 0 = no)	0.30	0.41	0.38
	(0.46)	(0.49)	(0.49)
Students have desks (1 = <25%, 2 = 25%–50%, 3 = 51%–75%, 4 = >75%)	3.16	3.36	3.31
	(1.12)	(0.98)	(1.02)
What turn the school operates (1 = morning, 0 = afternoon)	0.46	0.56	0.53
	(0.51)	(0.50)	(0.50)
The distance of the next closest school (kilometers)	3.41	2.85	3.00
	(2.71)	(1.71)	(2.03)
Participation in school programs:			
Library program (1 = yes, 0 = no)	0.76	0.52	0.58
	(0.43)	(0.50)	(0.49)
Interactive radio program (1 = yes, 0 = no)	0.76	0.90	0.86
	(0.43)	(0.31)	(0.35)
Food program (1 = Yes, 0 = No)	0.59	0.31	0.39
	(0.50)	(0.47)	(0.49)

(Continued)

Table 8.6. Means and Standard Deviations of Control Variables Used in Administrative Process Regressions (*Continued*)

Variable Definitions	EDUCO	Traditional	All schools
Health program (1 = yes, 0 = no)	0.57	0.33	0.40
	(0.50)	(0.47)	(0.49)
Canasta program (1 = yes, 0 = no)	0.81	0.91	0.88
	(0.39)	(0.29)	(0.33)
Model school program	0.00	0.09	0.07
(1 = yes, 0 = no)	0.00	(0.29)	(0.25)
Director characteristics:			
Director has university level	0.68	0.52	0.56
education (1 = yes, 0 = no)	(0.47)	(0.50)	(0.50)
Years of experience of the director	2.45	6.56	5.42
	(1.70)	(6.87)	(6.18)
Years of experience of the	8.82	89.78	67.14
director squared	(12.36)	(184.20)	(160.40)
Director's age	29.45	38.02	35.62
	(6.71)	(8.79)	(9.10)
Director's gender	0.51	0.46	0.47
(1 = female, 0 = male)	(0.51)	(0.50)	(0.50)
The school has a sub-director	0.65	0.80	0.76
(1 = yes, 0 = no)	(0.48)	(0.40)	(0.43)
Community characteristics:			

All municipality socio-economic characteristics listed in Table 1 are used as control variables in the administrative process regressions.

Number of observations	37	96	133

Note: Standard deviations in parentheses.
Source: Author calculations using data from the 1996 MINED survey.

have more than 4 additional years of experience than EDUCO directors have, but the former have lower levels of education. The directors also tend to be female more often in EDUCO than in traditional schools. With school programs, EDUCO schools tend to participate more in the library, food, and health programs, which tend to target poverty more, whereas traditional schools tend to participate more in the interactive radio, *canasta básica* and model school programs.

The condition of EDUCO schools tends to be worse, with fewer having electricity, latrines, or phones. EDUCO schools also have more students without desks. Overall subjective rating of school condition reflects those results, with the school condition tending to be lower in EDUCO schools. EDUCO schools tend to be in more isolated areas, with the next-closest school tending to be farther away.

Although the results are controlled for in the regression analysis, the poorer conditions of EDUCO schools would most likely have a negative effect on administrative processes, as well as on teacher behavior and student achievement. In this sense, a downward bias in unobserved variables may exist when measuring the EDUCO effect.

Empirical Results for Administrative Processes

The results for administrative processes are broken out into three separate sections. First, a summary of the results for degree of decentralization (whether the major influence level is at the school, departmental, or national level) is given. Second, a summary of the results for perception of own influence for directors, teachers, and school associations is presented. Third, the main conclusions of the administrative analysis are summarized.

Because of the large number of regressions, the full regression results could not be easily shown.[113] To focus on one common and important result of all the regressions, we presented the OLS coefficient found on the EDUCO dummy variable, δ, in equation 8.1. In most of the following tables and figures, we show OLS coefficient of δ and indicate which coefficients are statistically significant. To conserve space in the main body of this chapter, we focus on only the 10 administrative processes that are most likely to influence a teacher's behavior.

Degree of Decentralization

The results for the degree of overall decentralization are mixed, with a fairly even distribution of positive and negative coefficients. Of the 29 administrative processes, only 7 are statistically significant. Those results on the level of decentralization do not confirm the hypothesis that EDUCO schools are more decentralized than traditional schools when measured by major influence. For many administrative processes, the major decisions are still made at the national or departmental level for both EDUCO and traditional schools.

Figure 8.2 illustrates the OLS coefficient values of the 10 administrative processes most likely to affect teacher behavior.

When one looks at administrative processes as a whole, EDUCO schools do not seem much more decentralized when compared with traditional schools, but one administrative process that could arguably have the most

---

113. Detailed regression results are available from the authors upon request.

Figure 8.2. OLS Estimated Coefficients on the EDUCO Variable for Major Influence Level of Key Administrative Processes

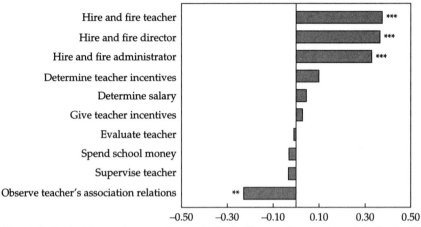

*** statistically significant at 1 percent; ** statistically significant at 5 percent; * statistically significant at 10 percent.
Source: Author calculations using data from the 1996 MINED survey.

effect on teacher behavior—hiring and firing of teachers—does stand out as significantly decentralized. The framework of EDUCO schools assigns ACEs (school associations) the authority for hiring and firing. The results verify that EDUCO schools truly are decentralized in this area. Hiring and firing teachers has a particularly large and positive coefficient and *t*-statistic.

One other interesting result emerges. The administrative process of teachers' association relations has a negative and statistically significant coefficient. This finding is puzzling in that it indicates teachers' association relations are more decentralized in traditional schools. This result may be caused by the fact that in EDUCO schools this relationship is formally established at the national level, department level, or both, but that in traditional schools there is no formal policy. It may also indicate that teachers' associations tend to be stronger in traditional schools, possibly because the teachers have been teaching at the same school for a longer period of time and see their role at the school as more permanent. EDUCO teachers, in contrast, may have a harder time organizing because of a variety of factors. They are typically younger, and their future at the school tends to be less clear. In addition, EDUCO schools are relatively new and some typical school organizations may have not had time to take root.

PERCEPTION OF OWN INFLUENCE
The perception of one's own influence gives a strong indication of whether directors, teachers, and school associations feel they are participating in the process, and to what degree. This perception by key participants pro-

vides a good indication of whether a process is relatively decentralized in EDUCO compared with traditional schools. At the same time, because the perspectives are subjective rather than hard data, there is the potential that respondents understood the questions differently or may have had reason to respond according to what they felt they should say rather than their giving a truthful answer. Even looking at the responses with a skeptical eye, we see some interesting results emerge.

Figure 8.3 summarizes the results of the perception of own influence for director, teacher, and school association for the 10 processes that are most likely to influence a teacher's behavior. The figure illustrates the following key findings:

- First, the most striking results of influence come from the school association responses. Of the 29 questions related to administrative processes, all estimated coefficients were positive, and 26 were statistically significant (note that *determine salary* was dropped because almost all responses were "national"). The reduced graph of the 10 key administrative processes is illustrative of the overall results, indicating that associations in EDUCO schools tend to feel that they have significantly more influence than associations in traditional schools.

Figure 8.3. Estimated Coefficients for EDUCO Perceived Amount of Influence Compared with Traditional Schools

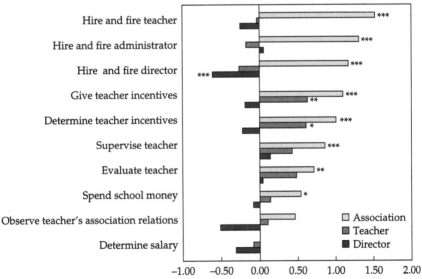

*** statistically significant at 1 percent; ** statistically significant at 5 percent; * statistically significant at 10 percent.
Source: Author calculations using data from the 1996 MINED survey.

- Second, the results for director influence tend to be negative but are not statistically significant except for the administrative process of hiring and firing of director. Those negative coefficients may indicate that directors in EDUCO schools tend to feel that they have less influence than their traditional counterparts. This finding could be the result of some responsibility in administrative processes shifting toward the school associations.
- Third, teacher responses tended to be positive, though often not statistically significant, with 16 of the 29 processes having a positive coefficient. This finding brings up an interesting aspect of the EDUCO school system: although teachers act as agents in the EDUCO structure—with their activities being monitored and hiring and firing decisions being made by the ACE—the results indicate that teachers in EDUCO schools may also feel that they can influence the processes more than their traditional counterparts.

Addressing Bias Issues

As mentioned earlier, there is a strong likelihood of selection bias and unobservable variable bias. A few key areas of concern include the following:

- *Likelihood of sample selection bias to exist:* Because part of the selection process for placement of EDUCO schools includes a demonstration of interest from the community, EDUCO schools are more likely to be placed in more-motivated communities. This motivation factor may play an important role in the operation of the school, in teachers' behavior, and in students' achievement. This form of bias would result in overstating the EDUCO effect.
- *The newness effect:* The fact that EDUCO schools tend to be newer could create both positive and negative unobserved effects. A newer school may receive more attention and care from the community. EDUCO schools, thus, may benefit from what is known as the "Hawthorne" effect—schools that have more recently entered the program have staff and students who are motivated and ready to undertake more reforms. However, this enthusiasm may wane over time.
- *Negative aspect of the newness effect:* On the flip side, newer schools may struggle if administrative processes are not well established or if parents are not as capable of operating the school. This weakness could have a negative effect on teachers' behavior, administrative process, and, ultimately, students' achievement.

Many of the control variables that are used will help to capture some of those factors, but there is a high likelihood that bias still exists. To check whether the sample selection or unobservable bias is serious, we use two econometric methods: propensity score matching[114] and Heckman's model of endogenous sample selection.[115]

Results and Interpretation of the Propensity Score and Treatment Effects

The propensity score and treatment effects model look at the bias issue from different angles. In this case, both arrive at the same conclusion that the OLS model, in general, does not suffer from serious bias. First, the propensity scores are similar to the OLS results. There are a few OLS results, however, that are statistically significant, but that the propensity score, treatment-effects model, or both have identified as containing bias.

Two exceptions stand out for the results in level of decentralization. First, the hiring and firing of administration has strong statistical significance in the OLS model. However, that significance disappears in the propensity score model, indicating that this administrative process is, in fact, not more decentralized in EDUCO schools. Second, the determination of teacher salaries was not statistically significant using OLS, but it becomes statistically significant using propensity score matching.

One striking result emerges for the influence results. In the OLS model, teachers had statistically significant results for determining teacher incentives and giving teacher incentives. The statistical significance disappears with propensity score matching. This finding seems to indicate that teachers do not tend to feel they have more influence in EDUCO schools.

In table 8.7 and table 8.8, in the Heckman two-step model columns, z-stat and λz-stat represent z-statistics of EDUCO coefficient and t-statistics of λ in the case of the Heckman's two-step estimation procedure. The treatment effects model does not have any statistically significant λz-statistics for the decentralization level results, which indicates that the model does not suffer from serious sample selection bias. For influence level, three λz

---

114. Propensity score matching helps address the selection bias problem by "correcting" the estimation of treatment effects. It does so by controlling for the existence of unobserved characteristics that are based on the idea that the bias is reduced when the comparison of outcomes is performed using treated and control subjects who are as similar as possible.

115. To implement this technique, we used the treatment-effects model command, *treatreg*, using the Heckman two-step option. A critical factor in using the treatreg command is to be able to identify the ingredients that go into deciding which schools receive the treatment (become EDUCO schools). We used community-specific, socioeconomic, and school distance variables as instruments for the endogenous sample selection for equation 8.5, because those characteristics are used in determining the placement of EDUCO schools. Using this technique, we can determine whether bias exists in our model.

Table 8.7. Level of Decentralization: Comparison of OLS Results to Propensity Score and Treatment Effects Results

	OLS		Propensity score matching		Heckman two-step treatment effects model			
	Coefficient	t-statistic	ATT	t-statistic	Coefficient	z-statistic	λ coefficient	λz-statistic
Determine salary	0.05	0.92	0.10	(1.88)*	0.14	(1.60)	−0.05	(1.06)
Determine teacher incentives	0.10	(1.03)	−0.05	(0.51)	−0.04	(0.22)	−0.08	(0.79)
Evaluate teacher	−0.01	(0.11)	−0.05	(0.50)	0.14	(0.88)	−0.09	(0.97)
Give teacher incentives	0.03	(0.27)	0.05	(0.59)	0.09	(0.52)	−0.02	(0.23)
Hire and fire administration	0.33	(3.57)***	0.08	(0.68)	0.31	(1.90)**	0.01	(0.80)
Hire and fire director	0.37	(4.25)***	0.39	(4.37)**	0.30	(2.04)**	0.04	(0.51)
Hire and fire teacher	0.37	(5.87)***	0.36	(5.02)**	0.30	(2.70)**	0.05	(0.80)
Spend school money	−0.03	(1.37)	0.01	0.39	−0.60	(1.40)	0.20	(0.81)
Observe teachers' association relations	−0.23	(2.36)**	−0.18	(1.74)*	−0.10	(0.60)	−0.08	(0.74)
Observe teacher supervision	−0.03	(0.37)	−0.02	(0.15)	−0.15	(0.89)	−0.76	(0.84)

* = statistically significant at 10 percent; ** = statistically significant at 5 percent; and *** = statistically significant at 1 percent.

Notes: Results are a weighted average of teacher, director, and association member responses for a given question, with one-third weighting for each group. The coefficient measure has a range of −1 to 1, with 1 indicating a high decentralization in EDUCO schools relative to traditional schools and −1 indicating a high decentralization in traditional schools relative to EDUCO schools. This table summarizes only the results on the EDUCO variable, but various school and community-level characteristics are controlled for. Absolute values of *t*-statistics, *z*-statistics, and λ*z*-statistics are in parentheses.

Source: Author calculations using data from the 1996 MINED survey.

Table 8.8. Influence Level by Group: Comparison of OLS Results to Propensity Score and Treatment Effects Results

	OLS		Propensity score matching		Heckman two-step treatment effects model			
	Coefficient	t-statistic	ATT	t-statistic	Coefficient	z-statistic	λ coefficient	λz-statistic
School association:								
Determine salary	Dropped	(.)	0.09	(0.38)	1.38	(3.34)***	−0.26	(1.05)
Determine teacher incentives	1.01	(3.43)***	0.28	(1.28)	2.00	(3.63)***	−0.64	(1.99)**
Evaluate teacher	0.72	(2.32)**	0.88	(3.16)***	1.46	(2.86)***	−0.35	(1.16)
Give teacher incentives	1.10	(3.42)***	0.77	(2.68)***	1.63	(3.10)***	−0.37	(1.19)
Hire and fire administration	1.31	(3.60)***	0.95	(3.59)***	0.99	(1.98)**	0.20	(0.64)
Hire and fire director	1.17	(3.77)***	1.23	(4.74)***	1.67	(3.16)***	−0.31	(0.98)
Hire and fire teacher	1.53	(5.08)***	1.38	(4.49)***	1.51	(3.12)***	0.01	(0.03)
Spend school money	0.54	(1.81)*	0.41	(1.53)	0.95	(1.80)*	−0.25	(0.80)
Observe teachers' association relations	0.47	(1.34)	0.71	(2.91)**	0.67	(1.15)	−0.13	(0.38)
Observe teacher supervision	0.86	(3.07)***	0.88	(3.73)***				
Director:								
Determine salary	−0.31	(1.46)	0.33	0.94	−0.32	(0.89)	0.01	(0.04)
Determine teacher incentives	−0.22	(0.58)	−0.26	(0.91)	−0.27	(0.45)	0.05	(0.14)
Evaluate teacher	0.04	(0.14)	−0.01	(0.04)	0.06	(0.12)	−0.01	(0.03)
Give teacher incentives	−0.19	(0.45)	−0.40	(0.93)	−0.48	(0.64)	0.26	(0.57)
Hire and fire administration	0.06	(0.18)	−0.52	(1.46)	0.53	(1.09)	−0.29	(0.98)
Hire and fire director	−0.61	(2.67)***	−0.13	(0.66)	0.05	(0.13)	−0.37	(1.62)

(Continued)

Table 8.8. Influence Level by Group: Comparison of OLS Results to Propensity Score and Treatment Effects Results (Continued)

	OLS		Propensity score matching		Heckman two-step treatment effects model			
	Coefficient	t-statistic	ATT	t-statistic	Coefficient	z-statistic	λ coefficient	λz-statistic
Hire and fire teacher	−0.25	(0.92)	−0.37	(1.26)	−0.42	(0.96)	0.10	(0.38)
Spend school money	0.07	(0.22)	−0.30	(0.96)	0.31	(0.61)	−0.16	(0.53)
Observe teachers' association relations	−0.51	(1.30)	−0.88	(2.40)**	−0.75	(1.12)	0.10	(0.25)
Observe teacher supervision	0.15	(0.43)	−0.33	(1.00)	−0.09	(0.15)	0.21	(0.59)
Teacher:								
Determine salary	−0.08	(0.40)	0.16	0.66	0.67	(1.84)*	−0.44	(2.08)**
Determine teacher incentives	0.61	(1.89)	0.00	0.01	0.97	(1.88)*	−0.19	(0.63)
Evaluate teacher	0.48	(1.53)	0.13	0.35	−0.09	(0.17)	0.31	(0.96)
Give teacher incentives	0.63	(2.18)**	0.21	0.75	−0.54	(0.95)	0.72	(2.23)**
Hire and fire administration	−0.17	(0.79)	−0.29	(1.17)	0.00	(0.01)	−0.11	(0.55)
Hire and fire director	−0.26	(1.53)	−0.22	(1.05)	0.00	(0.01)	−0.16	(0.91)
Hire and fire teacher	−0.03	(0.19)	0.14	0.83	0.23	(0.76)	−0.15	(0.86)
Spend school money	0.14	(0.40)	0.20	0.55	−0.66	(1.01)	0.53	(1.39)
Observe teachers' association relations	0.11	(0.27)	−0.44	(1.19)	0.38	(0.58)	−0.17	(0.45)
Observe teacher supervision	0.43	(1.28)	0.32	0.80	0.08	(0.14)	0.20	(0.60)

* = statistically significant at 10 percent, ** = statistically significant at 5 percent, and *** = statistically significant at 1 percent.

Notes: The coefficient measure has a range of −1 to 1, with 1 indicating a high decentralization in EDUCO schools relative to traditional schools and −1 indicating a high decentralization in traditional schools relative to EDUCO schools. This table summarizes only the results on the EDUCO variable, but various school and community-level characteristics are controlled for. Absolute values of t-statistics, z-statistics, and λz-statistics in parentheses.

Source: Author calculations using data from the 1996 MINED survey.

results are statistically significant: *evaluate teacher* for school association and *determine salary* and *give teacher incentives* for teacher. In this case, the rule is to use the z-statistic and coefficient of the treatment effects model in place of OLS. The z-statistics for the school association *evaluate teacher* and teacher *determine salary* are similar to the OLS result, so no change is made, but the result for teacher *give teacher incentives* becomes statistically insignificant.

Overall Conclusion of Administrative Processes

When we compare EDUCO and traditional schools from the perspective of where decisions primarily occur (at the school, departmental, or national level), the overall results suggest that the EDUCO program does not enhance the degree of decentralization as much as might be expected in a decentralization program. Still, significant decentralization does emerge in the area of hiring and firing decisions. When comparing EDUCO and traditional schools from the perspective of perceived influence, much more distinct differences emerge between the two programs. Actually, associations in EDUCO schools feel they have greater influence than their traditional counterparts. For some of those processes, teachers, directors, and association members in EDUCO schools all feel they have more influence than in traditional schools, signaling more decentralization. For processes where associations feel they have more influence, directors tend to feel they have less influence. This finding indicates that there may be a reallocation of influence, where associations have been given more power in areas traditionally performed by the director.

The check for sample selection bias using propensity score matching and the treatment effects model uncovered some areas where the OLS results appeared to be statistically significant but, in fact, contained sample selection bias, unobservable variable bias, or both. We can be more confident that the results that survived both the propensity score and the treatment effects check capture an "EDUCO effect."

Of the results that emerged, two points are critical for analysis in the following sections. First, school associations in EDUCO schools do tend to feel they have significantly more influence in virtually every administrative process. Second, although we did not find it to be the case that all administrative processes have shifted to the school level under the EDUCO model, hiring and firing authority does seem to be much more decentralized in EDUCO schools. This variable could arguably be the biggest potential influence on teacher behavior because teachers are closely monitored by school associations and because teachers realize their contract renewal depends on the decision of the school associations. Those two points lead to the argument that EDUCO schools do, in fact, represent a classical principal–agent model, which could address some of

the moral hazard and information problems faced by microdevelop-
ment programs.[116]

How Has Decentralization Changed Teachers' Behavior?

The results from the previous section indicate that EDUCO administrative processes show some marked differences from those of traditional
schools. EDUCO associations tend to feel they have more influence in
almost all administrative matters examined. A key administrative process
that could influence teacher behavior—hiring and firing of teachers—
seems to be much more decentralized in EDUCO when compared with
traditional schools. With this understanding, what sort of effect does the
EDUCO model have on teachers' behavior?

A comparison of the EDUCO and traditional models presents a classic
example of the principal–agent economic model. The teachers in this case
are the agents. In EDUCO schools, the ACE plays the role of principal,
whereas in traditional schools the principal is typically at the departmental or national level. Economic theory suggests that because the principal,
who plays a role in evaluating and determining the agent's incentives
and future employment, is much closer to the agent in the EDUCO model
and can closely monitor the agent's activities, the agent will be motivated
to work harder. The following section analyzes how the more-decentralized
EDUCO model affects teacher behavior.

The Model of Endogenous Teacher Effort

Teachers in EDUCO schools are selected and dismissed according to their
teaching performance by the community associations drawn from the
parents of the students (ACEs). Therefore, we can plausibly suppose that
the "principal" is either the Ministry of Education in traditional schools or
the community association in EDUCO schools, and the "agent" is a teacher.

In El Salvador's traditional public primary schools, specific government
regulations (Escalafón Magisterial) ensure a teacher's job stability, and
teachers' wage levels are determined by MINED (World Bank 1994, 1995).
Hence, we can model the teacher wage scheme in traditional schools as
basically a fixed-wage system. In contrast, the ACEs supervise and evaluate EDUCO teachers according to their performance (World Bank 1995).
Teachers in EDUCO schools receive yearly contracts and their contract

---

116. Moral hazard is the risk that one party to a contract can change his or her behavior
to the detriment of the other party once the contract has been concluded. In this case, the
moral hazard is that a teacher who does not feel that poor performance on her or his part will
lead to firing (or that good performance will be rewarded) lacks incentive to work hard. The
more secure contract of a traditional school teacher and the inability of the national government to observe the teacher's activities could lead to poor performance.

renewal depends on their performance (MINED 1999). Hence, we can plausibly represent that a teacher, particularly an EDUCO school teacher, will be paid according to the "observed" level of teaching effort, which is estimated by the principal. The model constructed in this section follows Sawada (1999), who constructed a standard principal–agent model with a linear compensation scheme (Hart and Holmström 1987; Holmström and Milgrom 1991).

If we denote the observed effort level of a teacher as OE, then we can represent the teacher payment scheme by a linear function of the observed effort level as follows:[117]

$$(8.8) \qquad\qquad W = a_1 + a_2\, OE$$

where W is the present value of a teacher's expected wage rate. Note that $a_2 > 0$ denotes a de facto piece-rate contract of EDUCO schools, while a case of $a_1 > 0$ and $a_2 = 0$ can be interpreted as a fixed-wage contract in traditional schools.

The community association can observe an imperfect indicator, OE, of the true teacher effort, e, where OE provides some information about the teacher's effort but is contaminated by random events beyond the control of the teacher. Formally, we can write

$$(8.9) \qquad\qquad OE = e + z$$

where z indicates a measurement error with $E(z) = 0$. Although the principal cannot observe e and z separately, a more-involved community association allows the observation of teacher effort with higher precision through close and frequent monitoring of a teacher's behavior. This consideration can be represented as $\text{var}(z) = \sigma_z^2$, which theoretically is smaller for EDUCO schools than for traditional schools.[118]

Suppose that a teacher is risk-averse with the coefficient of absolute risk aversion, γ. Then, we obtain the following incentive compatibility constraint of a teacher from the first-order condition of a teacher's utility maximization problem:

$$(8.10) \qquad\qquad a_2 = \frac{\partial CS(e)}{\partial e}$$

---

117. Although we can simply interpret the linearity with respect to effort level as an approximation of a general nonlinear wage-payment formula, the linear compensation scheme is shown theoretically to be adequate and optimal (Hart and Holmström 1987).

118. This variance, $V(z)$, can be interpreted as the inverse of the precision of estimating teachers' efforts, thereby reflecting the monitoring technology adopted by the community association.

where the cost created by effort, CS, is assumed to be a convex function of effort level, e. Accordingly, we have the optimal level of effort as a function of the slope of the wage scheme parameter, that is, $e^* = e\,(a_2)$, where it is easily verified that $\partial e^*/\partial a_2 > 0$.

THE ROLE OF COMMUNITY IN DESIGNING AN OPTIMAL TEACHER PAYMENT SCHEME

If the community association has full administrative and management ability, the coefficient, a_2, is determined endogenously by the community association in order to "discipline" teachers. The community association will be concerned with the social benefit of education, which is measured by a weighted average of students' educational achievements and of a teacher's benefit. A community association maximizes the sum of the certainty equivalent incomes of the principal (community association) and the agent (teacher), subject to the incentive compatibility constraint. Then, we obtain the following optimal intensity of incentives condition, that is, the optimal slope of the wage compensation scheme as a function of σ_z^2 and other parameters (Milgrom and Roberts 1992, pp. 221–23):

(8.11) $$a_2{}^* = g(\sigma_z^2)$$

where it is easily verified that $\partial a_2{}^*/\partial(\sigma_z^2) < 0$.[119]

Equation 8.11 indicates the important role of community monitoring. In EDUCO schools, intensive community participation improves the precision of measuring teacher effort. When a teacher's performance is easy to identify, strong incentives are likely to be optimal. Under the centralized system, in contrast, community participation is minimal and thus the precision-of-effort estimation is quite low. When effort measure is highly imprecise, it is unfruitful to use a wage incentive scheme. As a result, the fixed teacher compensation scheme in traditional schools can be rationalized.

Finally, combining equation 8.10 with equation 8.11, we have the optimal level of effort as a function of the level of community participation and school type:

(8.12) $$e^* = e[g(\sigma_z^2)]$$

where $\partial e^*/\partial(\sigma_z^2) < 0$. Equation 8.12 represents that in EDUCO schools— where the precision of monitoring teacher behavior is higher (σ_z^2 is smaller) than that in traditional schools—teacher effort level is higher. In

---

119. This optimal intensity of incentives condition indicates that the community association will choose a_2 optimally to induce the teacher to set the marginal cost of effort equal to its marginal social value of effort.

a typical case, the slope of equation 8.8 is higher for EDUCO schools than for traditional schools because EDUCO schools have lower σ_z^2. From these results, we can hypothesize that the level of teacher effort is systematically higher in EDUCO schools than in traditional schools because of the difference in the intensity of community participation. This theoretical gap in the level of teacher effort suggests the moral hazard problem of teacher effort in traditional schools.

ESTIMATING TEACHER EFFORT

According to equation 8.10, the de facto piece-rate payment scheme in EDUCO schools is thought to enhance teacher effort. Moreover, the choice of payment scheme should be related to the intensity of community participation according to the optimal intensity of incentives condition (equation 8.11). Hence, the observed level of teacher effort must be a function of the precision of monitoring the teachers' behavior (equation 8.12).

To investigate this mechanism empirically, we estimated a linearized version of the teacher-effort function along with teacher-specific variables. By combining equations 8.9 and 8.12, we have

(8.13) $$OE = e^* \left(\sigma_z^2\right) + z$$

By linearizing equation 8.13, we get an estimation model of the observed effort level:

(8.14) $$OE_j = \alpha_0 + \alpha_1 D_j + X_j \beta + z_j$$

where D is a dummy variable that takes one if the school is an EDUCO school and zero otherwise, and where X is a set of other control variables. Thus, we focus on the major difference in σ_z^2 between EDUCO and traditional schools, because we take the EDUCO dummy as a proxy variable for σ_z^2.

In equation 8.14, the observed measure of teacher effort, OE, is not observed by the econometrician. Therefore, we have used various measures to quantify it. If the estimated coefficient, α_1, of equation 8.14 is positive and statistically significant, the finding indicates that—with the higher degree of community participation—the teacher effort measure in EDUCO schools is better than that in traditional schools. This result can be interpreted as finding that community participation enhances the teacher effort level, possibly through designing an appropriate wage compensation scheme for teachers.

Moreover, in EDUCO schools, teacher candidates are interviewed by ACE. Then ACE determines who is hired on a 1-year contract. Hence, unobserved factors affecting teacher assignments or self-selection to EDUCO schools might be correlated with unobserved factors in determining

teacher behavior. This endogeneity of teacher assignments might generate an endogeneity bias if we estimate the model of equation 8.14 by using
OLS. We also model the endogenous assignment of teachers to EDUCO
or traditional schools as follows:

(8.14') $D_{s_i}^* = W_i^s \gamma_s + v_{s_i}$

(8.14") $D_{S_i} = \begin{cases} 1 & if\ D_{s_i}^* > 0 \\ 0 & if\ D_{s_i}^* < 0 \end{cases}$

where D_S^* is a latent variable of the propensity of becoming an EDUCO
teacher. As before, we can estimate the model of (8.14), (8.14'), and (8.14")
by using Heckman's two-step estimation procedure.

Survey Questions Related to Teacher Behavior
Teacher behavior is an abstract concept that is extremely difficult to quantify or measure. The survey questions cover behavior that can be measured
to a certain extent and that, although not perfect measures of a teacher's
motivation level, can give an indication of how teachers tend to behave
as a result of working within the different school systems.

To determine what effect the EDUCO program has had on teacher performance, we used 19 questions that may provide insights into teacher
behavior and effort. The following is a brief explanation of the data, as well
as an explanation of how it relates to the hypothesis of how monitoring
influences teacher behavior.

First, a more-motivated teacher would tend to spend more time interact-
ing with other members of the school, including students, other teachers, the
director, and the parents. Hence, we use the following five meeting time
variables to quantify this aspect: separate meeting hours with (a) students,
(b) parents, (c) teachers, and (d) a director, plus (e) total meeting hours.

Second, if a teacher is increasingly motivated, she or he might demonstrate an effort by dedicating more time to teaching. Hence, we use three
variables of (a) hours preparing for class, (b) hours grading homework,
and (c) hours teaching.

Third, a more-motivated teacher would tend to be more concerned and
responsive when students are not participating in education, including
extended absences. The survey included a question about what the teacher
does when a student is absent for an extended period of time. Possible
responses were (a) visiting family, (b) meeting with family, (c) talking to
students, and (d) talking to the director.

Fourth, a more-motivated teacher would tend to miss fewer days of
school. Therefore, we include days missed by students because of the
teacher's absence as one of the dependent variables.

Finally, a more-motivated teacher would tend to have the desire to get more training, which could help him or her be a more-effective teacher. Hence, we include the following training-related variables: training hours, plus various binary variables on participation in different trainings for program, evaluation, community relations, teaching, and materials.

Statistics on those variables are presented in table 8.9.

Table 8.9. Means and Standard Deviations of Variables Used to Measure Teacher Behavior

	EDUCO	Traditional	Total
Hours per week in teaching activities:			
Hours teaching	22.66	20.30	20.92
	(7.31)	(7.34)	(7.38)
. Hours in class	4.63	4.08	4.22
	(1.66)	(1.14)	(1.31)
Hours preparing	8.46	8.19	8.26
	(4.98)	(5.30)	(5.20)
Hours grading homework	5.71	5.17	5.31
	(4.59)	(3.82)	(4.03)
Total hours	36.83	33.67	34.49
	(11.1)	(11.5)	(11.4)
Hours per week in meeting activities:			
Meetings with students	1.63	2.89	2.56
	(1.98)	(8.50)	(7.39)
Meetings with parents	4.69	2.94	3.40
	(3.01)	(2.40)	(2.68)
Meetings with other teachers	3.20	1.83	2.19
	(5.91)	(2.13)	(3.55)
Meetings with director	3.91	3.12	3.33
	(4.38)	(2.61)	(3.17)
Total hours meeting	20.74	17.27	18.18
	(13.8)	(13.3)	(13.5)
Response when student absent:			
Visit family (1 = Yes, 0 = No)	0.69	0.40	0.47
	(0.47)	(0.49)	(0.50)
Meet family (1 = Yes, 0 = No)	0.50	0.79	0.72
	(0.50)	(0.40)	(0.45)

(Continued)

Table 8.9. Means and Standard Deviations of Variables Used to Measure Teacher Behavior (*Continued*)

	EDUCO	Traditional	Total
Talk to student's friends (1 = Yes, 0 = No)	0.92	0.93	0.93
	(0.27)	(0.25)	(0.25)
Talk to the Director (1 = Yes, 0 = No)	0.62	0.74	0.71
	(0.49)	(0.44)	(0.45)
Teacher absence according to parent			
Days of school missed due to teacher absence	1.19	1.40	1.35
	(1.15)	(1.43)	(1.36)
Training variables:			
Training hours	7.77	9.12	8.77
	(11.2)	(12.1)	(11.9)
Training—program	0.86	0.69	0.73
	(0.35)	(0.46)	(0.44)
Training—evaluation	0.91	0.95	0.94
	(0.28)	(0.22)	(0.23)
Training—community relations	0.63	0.41	0.47
	(0.49)	(0.49)	(0.50)
Training—materials	0.60	0.43	0.48
	(0.49)	(0.49)	(0.50)
Training—teaching	0.79	0.64	0.68
	(0.84)	(0.74)	(0.77)
Total observations	35	99	134

Note: Standard deviations in parentheses.
Source: Author calculations using data from the 1996 MINED survey.

The measures of teacher behavior are certainly not ideal measures and must be looked at in context. First, the responses were given by the teachers themselves. The responses may be subjective or the teacher may attempt to give the response that she or he believes is best to give. Very often the responses are on an amount of time spent over a given period. It is unlikely that teachers keep precise records, so there is a risk that the answers are not completely accurate. One exception is the measure of a teacher's absence, for which parents say how often their children miss school because the teacher is absent. This response is potentially more objective, but parents may not keep accurate records of actual days of absence.

But the argument can also be made that because EDUCO and traditional teachers have no reason to give different answers (that is, one should not exaggerate more than the other), then the overall results should give a fairly reasonable picture of level of effort and motivation.

Control Variables Used in Regressions
The analysis controlled for various teacher, school, and community characteristics. Table 8.10 gives descriptive statistics of the control variables used.

Results of Empirical Analysis
The OLS results for teacher behavior are presented in table 8.11. A number of teacher behavior measures tend to indicate that there may be an EDUCO effect on teacher behavior. When addressing bias issues through propensity score matching and Heckman two-step procedures, some of the statistically significant OLS results are weeded out, but many statistically significant results remain.

Addressing Bias Issues
We estimated the model by considering possibilities of the endogenous sample selection. Here, we explicitly model a teacher's choice of EDUCO or traditional schools by a system of equations 8.14, 8.14′, and 8.14″. We estimate this model by using Heckman's two-step procedure. Estimation results are represented in table 8.11. Most of the z-statistics of the sample selection coefficient, λ, are not statistically significant. This finding indicates that potential bias generated by endogeneity of teacher assignments is not serious. Two exceptions are the school program and the community relations training. For these variables, the λ is statistically significant, indicating that we should use the Heckman result rather than the OLS. The EDUCO dummy variables for those measures are statistically significant using OLS but become insignificant under Heckman.

In running the propensity score matching, we were unfortunately not able to get results using our full regression. Because we used 42 different control variables and had a total of only 134 observations with Stata,[120] our results were unable to satisfy the balancing check in order to do nearest-neighbor matching. Although we believe this problem is caused by the large number of control variables used, we must also consider the possibility that Stata could not find neighbors because the control and treatment groups are too different. In running the regression after removing 10 of what seemed to be the least-important control variables and leaving the 32 most important, Stata was able to complete the nearest-neighbor matching. This option is certainly second-best, but we considered that having imperfect results will give more insight than having no results.

---

120. Stata is a statistical analysis program that was used in performing the regression analysis for this study.

Table 8.10. Means and Standard Deviations of Control Variables Used in Teacher Behavior Regressions

Variable definitions	EDUCO schools	Traditional schools	All schools
Teacher characteristics:			
Years of experience	3.91	9.46	8.01
	(2.64)	(7.05)	(6.66)
Years of experience squared	22.14	138.86	108.37
	(29.68)	(216.18)	(193.15)
Years of experience at school where currently teaching	2.17	6.17	5.15
	(1.29)	(5.69)	(5.24)
Teacher who has a university education level (1 = yes, 0 = no)	0.74	0.30	0.41
	(0.44)	(0.46)	(0.49)
Wage of teacher (salary and bonus)	3,815.00	4,002.00	3,947.00
	(251.00)	(559.00)	(494.00)
One who teaches in alternative classroom (1 = yes, 0 = no)	0.35	0.19	0.23
	(0.48)	(0.39)	(0.42)
Number of students in classroom	20.80	28.00	26.10
	(7.71)	(11.10)	(10.80)
Teacher's age	27.37	34.41	32.57
	(4.47)	(7.83)	(7.74)
Teacher who has class in morning (1 = morning, 0 = afternoon)	1.62	1.46	1.50
	(0.49)	(0.50)	(0.50)
Teacher's gender (1 = female, 0 = male)	1.37	1.27	1.29
	(0.49)	(0.44)	(0.45)
Teacher's residence (1 = town, 2 = different town in municipality, 3 = other municipality but same department, 4 = other department)	2.68	2.46	2.52
	(1.05)	(0.95)	(0.97)
Time it takes to commute to school (1 = 30 min, 2 = 30 min–1 hour, 3 = more than 1 hour)	2.08	2.10	2.09
	(0.88)	(0.82)	(0.83)
Frequency of commute to school per week (1 = daily, 2 = weekly)	1.28	1.12	1.16
	(0.45)	(0.32)	(0.37)
Incentives received by teacher in past year:			
Diploma (1 = yes, 0 = no)	0.31	0.16	0.20
	(0.47)	(0.36)	(0.40)
Raise (1 = yes, 0 = no)	0.00	0.16	0.11
	0.00	(0.36)	(0.32)

(Continued)

Table 8.10. Means and Standard Deviations of Control Variables Used in Teacher Behavior Regressions (*Continued*)

Variable definitions	EDUCO schools	Traditional schools	All schools
Scholarship (1 = yes, 0 = no)	0.02 (0.16)	0.02 (0.14)	0.02 (0.14)
Economic (1 = yes, 0 = no)	0.14 (0.35)	0.11 (0.31)	0.11 (0.32)
Benefits received by teacher:			
Life insurance (1 = yes, 0 = no)	0.57 (0.50)	0.90 (0.28)	0.82 (0.38)
Medical (1 = yes, 0 = no)	1.00 0.00	0.93 (0.23)	0.95 (0.20)
Vacation (1 = yes, 0 = no)	0.94 (0.23)	0.94 (0.22)	0.94 (0.22)
Housing (1 = yes, 0 = no)	0.88 (0.32)	0.80 (0.39)	0.82 (0.37)
School characteristics:			
School is part of library program (1 = yes, 0 = no)	0.74 (0.44)	0.48 (0.50)	0.55 (0.49)
School is part of interactive radio program (1 = yes, 0 = no)	0.62 (0.49)	0.79 (0.40)	0.75 (0.43)
School is part of Canasta program (1 = yes, 0 = no)	0.74 (0.44)	0.84 (0.36)	0.82 (0.38)
School is part of food program (1 = yes, 0 = no)	0.54 (0.50)	0.35 (0.48)	0.40 (0.49)
School is part of health program (1 = yes, 0 = no)	0.57 (0.50)	0.31 (0.46)	0.38 (0.48)
School is part of model school program (1 = yes, 0 = no)	0.00 0.00	0.12 (0.32)	0.08 (0.28)
Number of visits per month by departmental director	3.85 (6.76)	4.72 (6.63)	4.50 (6.65)

Community characteristics:

All municipality socioeconomic characteristics listed in table 8.1 are used as control variables in the administrative process regressions.

Number of observations	35	99	134

Note: Standard deviations in parentheses.
Source: Author calculations using data from the 1996 MINED survey.

Table 8.11. Comparison of OLS Results to Treatment Effects and Propensity Score Matching Results

Output variable	Original OLS with 42 dependent variables		Heckman two-step procedure				Revised OLS with 32 dependent variables		Propensity score with 32 dependent variables	
	Coefficient	t-statistic	Coefficient	z-statistic	λ coefficient	λz-statistic	Coefficient	t-statistic	Coefficient	t-statistic
Meeting time (hours/week):										
With students	-1.07	(0.78)	-0.92	(0.40)	0.03	(0.02)	-0.45	(0.48)	-1.65	(0.50)
With parents	2.20	(2.44)**	4.25	(0.53)	-0.92	(0.78)	2.31	(3.53)***	1.97	(2.10)**
With other teachers	4.24	(2.21)**	5.65	(1.76)*	-0.96	(0.46)	2.87	(2.23)**	1.09	(1.48)
With director	1.26	(0.79)	3.97	(1.20)	-1.59	(0.89)	2.15	(1.96)*	-1.24	(1.38)
Total meeting time	13.12	(1.99)**	22.27	(2.33)**	-6.32	(0.77)	11.29	(2.48)**	1.42	(0.29)
Teaching activities (hours/week):										
Classroom teaching	3.06	(0.91)	10.13	(1.84)*	-4.70	(1.09)	3.51	(1.31)	5.79	(1.91)**
Preparation for class	1.49	(0.66)	-4.75	(0.67)	3.04	(1.16)	0.75	(0.46)	1.95	(0.99)
Grade homework	2.18	(1.35)	-0.36	(0.08)	1.69	(0.94)	1.54	(1.30)	1.93	(1.21)
Total hours	6.73	(1.49)	5.01	(1.19)	0.02	(0.00)	5.80	(1.52)	9.66	(2.29)**
Response to student absence:										
Visit family (1 = yes, 0 = no)	-0.04	(0.12)	-0.81	(1.40)	0.50	(1.63)	0.19	(0.77)	0.27	(1.63)
Meet family (1 = yes, 0 = no)	-0.32	(1.02)	0.11	(0.73)	-0.10	(0.39)	-0.14	(0.65)	-0.08	(0.54)

DECENTRALIZATION OF EDUCATION 293

Talk to friends (1 = yes, 0 = no)	0.15 (0.78)	0.69 (0.70)	-0.26 (1.49)	0.10 (0.83)	0.12 (1.62)
Visit director (1 = yes, 0 = no)	-0.07 (0.22)	0.20 (0.42)	-0.08 (0.29)	0.03 (0.17)	-0.30 (1.99)*
Teacher absence:					
Days missed	-1.37 (1.95)**	-0.51 (0.64)	-0.55 (0.63)	-1.12 (2.26)**	-0.79 (1.86)*
Training:					
Total hours	2.99 (0.48)	7.94 (1.67)*	-3.89 (0.54)	4.23 (1.03)	-3.91 (0.87)
School program (1 = yes, 0 = no)	0.36 (1.74)*	-0.44 (1.25)	0.52 (1.88)*	0.47 (3.56)***	0.44 (3.12)***
Evaluation (1 = yes, 0 = no)	0.13 (1.31)	0.43 (2.02)**	-0.20 (1.63)	0.07 (0.94)	0.02 (0.29)
Community relations (1 = yes, 0 = no)	0.38 (1.67)*	-0.49 (1.20)	0.52 (1.76)*	0.33 (2.02)**	0.37 (2.15)**
Materials (1 = yes, 0 = no)	0.48 (2.14)**	0.36 (0.11)	0.08 (0.31)	0.38 (2.32)**	0.24 (1.34)
Teaching (1 = yes, 0 = no)	0.32 (0.83)	0.46 (0.29)	-0.37 (0.81)	-0.14 (0.61)	-0.52 (1.94)*

* = statistically significant at 10 percent, ** = statistically significant at 5 percent, and *** = statistically significant at 1 percent.
Notes: The reduced OLS contains the same control variables as the original OLS, except for health program, Canasta program, model school program, transit frequency, life insurance benefits, vice director, municipal mortality, municipal percent rural, phone, electricity, and latrine. Absolute values of t-statistics, z-statistics, and λz-statistics in parentheses.
Source: Author calculations using data from the 1996 MINED survey.

The results for propensity score matching indicate that there is bias in the OLS results for a few measures. The measures of meeting with other teachers, meeting with the director, total meeting time, and teaching materials training were statistically significant under OLS but were insignificant with propensity score matching. Conversely, the results for time teaching total hours and for student absent—talk to director were insignificant using OLS, but become significant under propensity score matching.

So what are we left with? For meeting time, some statistically significant OLS meeting variables become only marginally significant, but the measure of meeting with parents remains strong through all tests. EDUCO teachers do tend to dedicate more time to meetings.

The strong statistical significance that emerges for time dedicated to teaching (particularly with propensity score matching) indicates that teachers may also dedicate more time to teaching. The propensity score results have a coefficient indicating 9.7 hours more per week.

The teacher absence variable also stays statistically significant through all tests, indicating that EDUCO teachers may be absent less than traditional school teachers. Because teacher absence is a big issue in rural communities and can potentially have a negative effect on students' learning, this result is important.

A few statistically significant results emerge about how the teacher responds to a student's extended absence, but those results seem invalid. For example, while one teacher may answer that she or he visits the student's family, another may respond that she or he talks to the director. Is one really better than the other? Because no strong differences emerged in this area, it seems better not to draw any conclusions from the results.

Finally, with respect to training, although OLS had many statistically significant results indicating that EDUCO teachers are more motivated to get training, the Heckman and propensity score matching results indicate that they are, in fact, not statistically significant. No strong differences emerge in the area of training.

Overall Conclusions on Teacher Behavior
As mentioned earlier, the measures used here for teacher behavior are imperfect indicators because behavior and motivation are difficult concepts to capture statistically and because it is difficult to know whether responses to questions asking amount of time dedicated to activities actually are accurate. Those limitations should be kept in mind, but some interesting results do emerge, indicating that teacher behavior and motivation may be influenced by differences between the EDUCO and traditional school programs.

Simple OLS showed many statistically significant results, all indicating that EDUCO teachers are more motivated and active than teachers in traditional schools. Some of the results proved to be caused by sample selection or unobservable bias, but many key measures survived the bias tests, including meeting with parents, teacher absence, and hours dedicated to teaching.

Although we have to be careful not to jump to conclusions, the results indicate that community participation seems to enhance the teacher effort level, possibly because of intensive monitoring of teacher behaviors and the implicit threat that exists because hiring and firing of teachers occurs at the community level. The measures used are directly observable to both teachers and parents by nature. Thus, teachers might be interested in improving them. Close teacher monitoring by communities rather than by external supervisors can be less costly than teacher evaluations by external supervisors. Even in a small rural school with only one teacher, frequent and close teacher monitoring becomes possible if the supervisor is drawn from the same community.

Moreover, teachers may become accountable to the community group that monitors, supervises, and evaluates their performance. Accordingly, when members of the community association are elected from the parents of the students, inconsistency between the teachers' behavior and the welfare objective of the beneficiaries is likely to disappear. Community participation not only uses relevant information that outside government agencies are not likely to have, but also imposes commitment on teachers, which leads them to exert greater effort.

How Do Differences in Teacher Behavior Affect Student Achievement?

Although the previous analysis helps to shed light on the effects of decentralization on teacher behavior, the second-order effects on student achievement and learning are not necessarily clear. We would expect that positive teacher behavior would result in positive student outcomes. In practice, this link is extremely difficult to establish. Our teacher behavior measures—such as time spent meeting with parents and other teachers, decreased teacher absence, and working hours—are not perfect measures of teacher behavior and can at best be linked tentatively to student outcome. If we think of the teacher behavior variables as representing the more-general unobservables of teacher behavior, however, and of a teacher demonstrating those observable characteristics as being more likely to be motivated, we can attempt to link teacher behavior and student outcomes. Although imperfect, this approach may shed some light on teacher behavior and student outcome.

In an attempt to get a complete picture of this link, we approach our analysis from various angles. First, we estimate student outcomes—as measured by student absence and student test scores in math and Spanish—without including teacher behavior variables but controlling for child and household characteristics. (Those control variables can be found in table 8.2.) Then we bring in teacher behavior characteristics. We use some characteristics that emerged as statistically significant in the previous section—teacher absence, teacher working hours, and teacher meeting time with parents. Those variables are first treated as exogenous and then as endogenous. By looking at student achievement from the different angles, we hope to capture the effects of teacher behavior on student outcomes. In all cases, the EDUCO dummy is included to separate the interaction between EDUCO and teacher behavior, as well as to separate the teacher behavior effect from the program effects.

Measure of Student Achievement

For measurement of student outcomes, the achievement tests for various subjects were applied by MINED in October 1996 with the assistance of the Intercultural Center for Research in Education (MINED 1997). The tests were applied nationally in the third, fourth, and sixth grades. We use the third-grade results, and we focus only on the results for the mathematics and Spanish tests in the analysis.[121]

According to table 8.12, the average student was able to master 3.70 out of 10 subjects in mathematics, but only 1.75 out of 9 in languages. The results are comparable to national averages (MINED 1997). Between EDUCO and traditional schools, no statistically significant difference exists in the test scores in spite of the poorer background of EDUCO students. This finding suggests an advantage for community participation in education. In days of child absence, there is no difference between EDUCO and traditional schools.

The Model of Teacher Behavior Effects on Educational Outcomes

To examine the complex interaction in the schooling process of the behaviors of various agents such as students, groups of parents, teachers, and administrators in creating educational output (Glewwe 2002; Hanushek 1995), we use a reduced-form of an education production function. With respect to the output measure, we focus on student scores on standardized achievement tests.[122] Suppose that the educational achievement, Q_{ij}, of a child i, who is studying at a school j in municipality m, can be represented by the following production function:[123]

---

121. The mathematics test is composed of 30 questions on 10 key subjects—that is, three items for each subject. A student passed a subject if she or he answered two out of three questions right. For the Spanish test, there are 36 questions on nine subjects—that is, four items each. A student has passed a subject if she or he answered three out of four questions right.

122. Most studies measure educational output by students' achievement scores, school attendance rates, repetition rates, and school continuation or dropout rates, which are thought to capture prospects of future earnings in the labor market (Hanushek 1995).

123. Gaynor and Pauly (1990) called this function the "efficient" or "maximum (observed) effort" production function.

Table 8.12. Means and Standard Deviations of Student Achievement Test Scores

Variable definitions	EDUCO schools	Traditional schools	All schools
Output variables:			
Achievement test score, math	3.59	3.73	3.70
(number of subjects taken)	(2.77)	(2.47)	(2.54)
Achievement test score, language	1.73	1.76	1.75
(number of subjects taken)	(1.85)	(1.67)	(1.71)
Days of child absence from school	0.95	0.95	0.95
in the past 4 weeks	(0.11)	(0.10)	(0.10)

Note: Standard deviations in parentheses.
Source: Author calculations using data from the 1996 MINED survey.

$$(8.15) \qquad Q_{iji} = f(X_i, C_m, D_j, Z_j, e_j^*)$$

where X represents a vector of student and household characteristics, C is a vector of municipality m's specific variables, and D is an indicator variable of school type attended by a student, where $D = 1$ for an EDUCO school and $D = 0$ for a traditional school.

We estimate a linear approximated version of the reduced-form function of education production of equation 8.15 as follows:

$$(8.16) \qquad Q_{ij} = X_i\beta + C_m\gamma + \alpha_1 D_j + \alpha_2 OE + v_{ij}$$

where v represents a well-behaved error term with assumptions of $E(v_i) = 0$ and $\text{var}(v_i) = \sigma_v^2$. We assume that the term C_m represents municipality-specific variables.

We also control for endogeneity of teacher-effort variables and for sample selection bias. We have used all the exogenous variables, the amount of government transfers, and the community participation variables as instruments for teacher-effort variables.

In some cases, it is possible for parents to select either a nearby EDUCO school or a traditional school for their child's schooling. Hence, we also model the endogenous assignment of teachers to EDUCO or traditional schools as follows:

$$(8.17) \qquad D_{pi}^* = W_i^s \gamma_p + v_{pi}$$

$$(8.18) \qquad D_{p_i} = \begin{cases} 1 \text{ if } D_{p_i}^* > 0 \\ 0 \text{ if } D_{p_i}^* < 0 \end{cases}$$

where D^*_{Pi} is a latent variable of the propensity of selecting an EDUCO school. As before, we estimate the model of equations 8.16, 8.17, and 8.18 by using Heckman's two-step estimation procedure to control for school selection of students (parents). For the selection equation, we have used household and school characteristics, as well as densities of EDUCO and traditional schools as identifying instruments.

Results of the Empirical Analysis

Tables 8.13, 8.14, and 8.15 represent the estimation results of production function 16 for mathematics test score, Spanish test score, and days of absence, respectively. All tables contain the following four different specifications. In specification 1, we use the propensity score matching method. In specification 2, we estimate the model without teacher behavior variables, controlling for the child and household characteristics in table 8.2. In specification 3, we treat two variables as exogenous, and we control for

Table 8.13. Estimated EDUCO Effects on Mathematics Scores

	Specification 1	Specification 2	Specification 3[a]	Specification 4[b]
	Coefficient (z-statistic)	Coefficient (z-statistic)	Coefficient (z-statistic)	Coefficient (z-statistic)
Estimation method	Propensity score	Sample selection (2 stage)	Sample selection (2 stage)	Sample selection (2 stage) instrumental variable
Coefficients on:				
EDUCO dummy	0.165 (0.401)	0.253 (0.19)	0.04 (0.03)	0.447 (0.21)
Teacher's absence days (past 2 weeks)			0.039 (0.75)	0.052 (0.03)
Working hours (per day)			0.214 (1.90)*	−0.235 (0.13)
Hours meeting with parents (per month)			0.06 (0.95)	0.569 (1.67)*
Lambda		−0.342 (0.42)	−0.305 (0.38)	−0.631 (0.52)

* = statistically significant at 10 percent
Note: Absolute values of t-statistics reported in parentheses.
a. Specification 3: Treating three variables of teacher behavior as exogenous and controlling for child and household characteristics.
b. Specification 4: Treating three variables of teacher behavior as endogenous and controlling for child and household characteristics.
Source: Author calculations using data from the 1996 MINED survey.

Table 8.14. Estimated EDUCO Effects on Spanish Scores

	Specification 1	Specification 2	Specification 3[a]	Specification 4[b]
	Coefficient (z-statistic)	Coefficient (z-statistic)	Coefficient (z-statistic)	Coefficient (z-statistic)
Estimation method	Propensity score	Sample selection (2 stage)	Sample selection (2 stage)	Sample selection (2 stage) instrumental variable
Coefficients on:				
EDUCO dummy	0.021	2.481	2.357	2.498
	(0.081)	(2.71)**	(2.57)**	(1.78)*
Teacher's absence days (past 2 weeks)			−0.042 (1.15)	0.159 (0.12)
Working hours (per day)			0.074 (0.94)	0.159 (0.12)
Hours meeting with parents (per month)			0.027 (0.60)	0.457 (1.93)**
Lambda		−1.331 (2.49)**	−1.303 (2.43)**	−1.528 (2.00)**

* = statistically significant at 10 percent, and ** = statistically significant a 5 percent.
Note: Absolute values of *t*-statistics reported in parentheses.
a. Specification 3: Treating three variables of teacher behavior as exogenous and controlling for child and household characteristics.
b. Specification 4: Treating three variables of teacher behavior as endogenous and controlling for child and household characteristics.
Source: Author calculations using data from the 1996 MINED survey.

child and household characteristics listed in tables 8.2 and 8.3. Finally, in specification 4, we treat two variables as endogenous, controlling for child and household characteristics in tables 8.2 and 8.3.

According to tables 8.13, 8.14, and 8.15, most of the coefficients are in line with our theoretical predictions, but the results are not particularly strong. The Spanish score findings in table 8.14 do have some strong results where the coefficients that are based on the sample selection methods are all statistically significant. There seem to be positive EDUCO effects, a part of which can be explained by positive effects of teacher effort on educational outputs. The results for mathematics and Spanish test scores that are based on specification 4 show the statistically significant positive effects of teacher–parent meetings. The results tend to support the theoretical hypothesis that EDUCO program governance leads to better effort of teachers, which improves educational outcome, even after controlling for observed student, household, and community characteristics, as well as

Table 8.15. Estimated Effects on Days of Absence

	Specification 1	Specification 2	Specification 3[a]	Specification 4[b]
	Coefficient (z-statistic)	Coefficient (z-statistic)	Coefficient (z-statistic)	Coefficient (z-statistic)
Estimation method	Propensity score	Sample selection (2 stage)	Sample selection (2 stage)	Sample selection (2 stage) instrumental variable
Coefficients on:				
EDUCO dummy	0.021 (0.081)	−0.896 (0.86)	−0.766 (0.73)	−0.201 (0.18)
Working hours (per day)			−0.111 (1.27)	−0.640 (1.30)
Hours meeting with parents (per month)			−0.043 (0.83)	0.018 (0.14)
Lambda		−0.321 (0.51)	0.299 (0.47)	0.102 (0.18)

Note: Absolute values of *t*-statistics reported in parentheses.
a. Specification 3: Treating three variables of teacher behavior as exogenous and controlling for child and household characteristics.
b. Specification 4: Treating three variables of teacher behavior as endogenous and controlling for child and household characteristics.
Source: Author calculations using data from the 1996 MINED survey.

possible endogeneity and sample selection biases. Yet, we do not obtain robust results for the statistical significance. Particularly, the propensity score matching estimations do not give us significant results. Hence, the findings are only suggestive and are by no means conclusive.

As for sample selection aspects, we observe a significantly negative sample selection at the student or household level in the case of the Spanish test scores (table 8.14). These negative coefficients suggest that those who select EDUCO schools have unobserved characteristics that lead to systematically lower Spanish test scores. Poor family background of EDUCO students might be captured by these negative coefficients.

Conclusions

In this chapter, we investigated the effects of decentralization of an education program by closely examining the example of El Salvador's EDUCO program, which was designed to rapidly expand rural education following the country's civil war. Our focus was on how decentralization alters administration processes and teacher behavior and how those changes might affect the quality of education.

We compared administrative activities and teacher behavior in EDUCO schools with those activities and behaviors in traditional schools, controlling for characteristics of school, community, and school participants (teacher, director, and student). We also attempted to control for sample selection bias, using an exogenously determined formula for targeting EDUCO schools as an instrumental variable. As an additional step in addressing bias issues, we also used propensity score matching techniques to evaluate the EDUCO program effects.

The results indicate that, interestingly, most of administrative processes in EDUCO schools have not yet shifted to the local level. Nevertheless, selective administrative activities, such as hiring and firing decisions, do differ significantly between EDUCO and traditional schools. A large difference is seen when observing perceptions of amount of influence. Key players in the EDUCO schools—especially school associations—tend to feel they have greater influence in many of the administrative activities.

The results also indicate that decentralization has possibly had a positive effect on teacher behavior. Although some results that seemed statistically significant under the OLS model disappeared when other techniques were used to control for sample selection and unobservable bias, many key measures survived. There are indications that EDUCO teachers may have more motivation, as measured (a) by spending more time meeting with parents and other school members, (b) by being absent less, and (c) by dedicating more time to teaching. Although it is difficult to directly link teacher motivation and student outcomes, the increased motivation may have had a positive effect on student performance. Such results indicate that decentralized management programs, when designed correctly, may be able to provide an incentive structure that leads to greater teacher motivation and performance.

Policymakers should consider three important issues carefully when they apply our analysis in practice. First, the optimal form of community-managed development programs is specific to the development level of a country (Conning and Kevane 2002, p. 389).

Second, we should resist the temptation to romanticize the value of the local community as a social and economic organization (Bardhan and Udry 1999). In reality, mere decentralization does not guarantee the successful community-based management. One of the more serious problems lies in program implementation caused by a distant, uncoordinated, and corrupt bureaucracy (Bardhan and Udry 1999, pp. 149–50). In that case, even if the government aims at allocating its budget to alleviate poverty, aid does not reach the real poor. Moreover, the superior information and monitoring technologies in the hands of communities also means that there are potential information rents to be captured (Conning and Kevane 2002, p. 383). Therefore, there is a risk that the local rich can "capture" the local community institutions (Reinikka and Svensson 2004).

Finally, regarding efficiency, there could be a major tradeoff between the need for central policy coordination because of externalities or scale economies and the need for local information and accountability (Bardhan 2002, p. 190). With externalities across communities, decentralization leads to underprovision of public goods. With strong economies of scale, the central government can play an important role. For example, it is better to let the government construct infrastructure such as electric power generation and telecommunication facilities. In primary education, the government has an absolute advantage in designing curricula and in preparing textbooks. But as the results of this study suggest, decentralization of certain education management functions has advantages over a centralized model and can have positive effects on important factors such as teacher behavior and student performance.

In any case, further research on this theme should be directed toward modeling the complicated incentive problems in micro-development programs to derive structures of appropriate governance of such programs. At the same time, serious efforts should be made in evaluating the effect of various ongoing experiments of micro-development programs by using micro data.

References

Amemiya, T. 1985. *Advanced Econometrics*. Cambridge, Mass.: Harvard University Press.

Angrist, J. 1999. "Estimation of Limited Dependent Variable Models with Dummy Endogenous Regressors: Simple Strategies for Empirical Practice." *Journal of Business and Economic Statistics* 19(1): 2–16.

Angrist, J., E. Bettinger, E. Bloom, E. King, and M. Kremer. 2002. "Vouchers for Private Schooling in Colombia: Evidence from a Randomized Natural Experiment." *American Economic Review* 92(5): 1535–58.

Bardhan, P. 2002. "Decentralization of Governance and Development." *Journal of Economic Perspectives* 16(4): 185–205.

Bardhan, P., and C. Udry. 1999. *Development Microeconomics*. Oxford, U.K., and New York: Oxford University Press.

Becker, S. and A. Ichino. 2002. "Estimation of Average Treatment Effects Based on Propensity Scores." *Stata Journal* 2(4): 358–77.

Conning, J., and M. Kevane. 2002. "Community-Based Targeting Mechanisms for Social Safety Nets: A Critical Review." *World Development* 30(3): 375–94.

Ehrenberg, R. G., and D. J. Brewer. 1995. "Did Teachers' Verbal Ability and Race Matter in the 1960s? Coleman Revisited." Economics of Education Review, 14(1): 1–21.

Gaynor, M., and M. V. Pauly. 1990. "Compensation and Productive Efficiency in Partnerships: Evidence from Medical Group Practice." *Journal of Political Economy* 98(3): 544–73.

Glewwe, P. 2002. "Schools and Skills in Developing Countries: Education Policies and Socioeconomic Outcomes." *Journal of Economic Literature* 40(2): 436–82.

Greene, W. 2003. *Econometric Analysis*. 5th ed. Upper Saddle River, N.J.: Prentice Hall.

Hanushek, E. A. 1995. "Interpreting Recent Research on Schooling in Developing Countries." *World Bank Research Observer* 10(2): 227–46.

Hart, O., and B. Holmström. 1987. "The Theory of Contract." In T. Bewley, ed., *Advances in Economic Theory—Fifth World Congress*. Cambridge, U.K.: Cambridge University Press.

Holmström, B., and P. Milgrom. 1991. "Multitask Principal–Agent Analyses: Incentive Contracts, Asset Ownership, and Job Design." *Journal of Law, Economics, and Organization* 7: 24–52.

Jimenez, E., and Y. Sawada. 1999. "Do Community-Managed Schools Work? An Evaluation of El Salvador's EDUCO Program." *World Bank Economic Review* 13(3): 415–41.

———. 2001. "Does Community Management Help Keep Kids in Schools? Evidence Using Panel Data from El Salvador's EDUCO Program." Paper presented at the Economists Forum 2001, World Bank, Washington, D.C.

Kremer, M. R. 1995. "Research on Schooling: What We Know and What We Don't—A Comment on Hanushek." *World Bank Research Observer* 10(2): 247–54.

———. 2003. "Randomized Evaluations of Educational Programs in Developing Countries: Some Lessons." *AEA Papers and Proceedings* 93(2): 102–6.

Lee, L.-F. 1978. "Unionism and Wage Rates: A Simultaneous Equation Model with Qualitative and Limited Dependent Variables." *International Economic Review* 19: 415–33.

Lockheed, M., A. Verspoor, and others. 1991. *Improving Primary Education in Developing Countries*. New York: Oxford University Press.

Maddala, G. S. 1983. *Limited-Dependent and Qualitative Variables in Econometrics*. Cambridge, U.K.; New York; and Sydney: Cambridge University Press.

Miguel, E., and M. Kremer. 2004. "Worms: Identifying Impacts on Education and Health in the Presence of Treatment Externalities." *Econometrica* 72(1): 159–217.

Milgrom, P., and J. Roberts. 1992. *Economics, Organizations and Management*. Englewood Cliffs, N.J.: Prentice-Hall.

MINED (Ministerio de Educación), El Salvador. 1997. "Informe de evaluación del rendimiento en 3o, 4o, 6o grado de educación básica en lenguaje, matemática, estudios sociales y ciencia, salud y medio ambiente basado en la aplicación nacional de pruebas de octubre de 1996." Dirección Nacional de Evaluación e Investigación, San Salvador.

———. 1999. "Orientaciones para el trabajo de las ACE." San Salvador.

Monk, D. H. 1994. "Subject Area Preparation of Secondary Mathematics and Science Teachers and Student Achievement." *Economics of Education Review* 13(2): 125–45.

Rai, A. 2002. "Targeting the Poor Using Community Information." *Journal of Development Economics* 69: 71–84.

Reimers, F. 1997. "The Role of the Community in Expanding Educational Opportunities: The EDUCO Schools in El Salvador." In J. Lynch, C. Modgil, and S. Modgil, eds., *Education and Development: Tradition and Innovation: Equity and Excellence*. Vol. 2. London: Cassell.

Reinikka, R., and J. Svensson. 2004. "Local Capture, Evidence from a Central Government Transfer Program in Uganda." *Quarterly Journal of Economics* 119(2): 679–705.

Rivkin, S. G., E. A. Hanushek, and J. F. Kain. Forthcoming. "Teachers, Schools, and Academic Achievement." *Econometrica*.

Sawada, Y. 1999. Community Participation, Teacher Effort, and Educational Outcome: The Case of El Salvador's EDUCO Program." Davidson Institute Working Paper Series 307. University of Michigan Business School, Ann Arbor.

Schultz, T. P. 2004. "School Subsidies for the Poor: Evaluating the Mexican Progresa Poverty Program." *Journal of Development Economics* 74: 199–259.

Stiglitz, J. 1999. "Incentives and Institutions in the Provision of Health Care in Developing Countries." Paper presented at International Health Economics Association Meetings, Rotterdam, Netherlands, June 7, 1999.

Woodridge, J. M. 2002. *Econometric Analysis of Cross Section and Panel Data.* Cambridge, Mass.: MIT Press.

World Bank. 1994. "El Salvador: Community Education Strategy: Decentralized School Management." Country Report 13502-ES. Washington, D.C.

———. 1995. "Staff Appraisal Report El Salvador Basic Education Modernization Project." IBRD Report 14129-ES. Washington, D.C.

———. 1997. "El Salvador's EDUCO Program: A First Report on Parents' Participation in School-Based Management." Working Paper Series on Impact Evaluation of Education Reforms Paper No. 4. Washington, D.C.

———. 2003. *World Development Report 2004: Making Services Work for Poor People.* Washington, D.C.

9
Teacher Effort and Schooling Outcomes in Rural Honduras

Emanuela di Gropello
World Bank

and Jeffery H. Marshall
Stanford University

In recent years, community school programs have been expanded in a number of developing countries. Part of the justification for empowering parents and local communities is simply to expand access. In Central America, this objective has clearly been met. Hundreds of remote and isolated communities throughout the region now have a school, thanks to initiatives like the EDUCO program (Programa de Educación con Participación de la Comunidad, or Education with Community Participation Program) in El Salvador; PRONADE (Programa Nacional de Autogestión para el Desarrollo Educativo, or National Program for Educational Self-Management) in Guatemala; and PROHECO (Proyecto Hondureño de Educación Comunitaria, or Honduran Community Education Project) in Honduras. In addition to expanding access, community schools are frequently touted as being more efficient than "traditional" public schools. Given the nonrandom nature of selection for those schools, the task of evaluating the relative quality of each school is a difficult one. However, the initial work—coming mainly from the EDUCO experience—is generally favorable (Jimenez and Sawada 1999; Sawada 1999). This chapter continues in this vein by analyzing a new and extensive data set collected in Honduras with the purpose of assessing the effect of the PROHECO community schools. The sample includes more than 200 rural schools from all regions of the country, divided between PROHECO community schools and regular public schools during the 2002 and 2003 school years.

The authors want to thank the participants who attended the World Bank's April 22 workshop on teachers' incentives for their comments, which helped improve the first draft of this paper.

Using a variety of statistical techniques, we compare PROHECO and non-PROHECO schools along two general dimensions. The first considers "first-order" differences in teaching and learning environments and relies heavily on simple comparisons of means between control and treatment (PROHECO), although multivariate analysis on the determinants of measures of teacher effort is also presented. We then ask how those observed differences translate into improvements in second-order outcomes like student learning. To answer the question, we bring in multivariate analysis and make use of extensions to the basic linear model that account for sample selection bias.

The chapter proceeds as follows. In the next section, we detail our analytical framework, beginning with a hypothetical model of the mechanisms that improve efficiency in community schools, as well as explaining the data and econometric methods we used to test those ideas. Then, we present the results for the comparisons of PROHECO and non-PROHECO schools, beginning with the first-order differences in teaching and learning environments and then showing the indirect (second-order) effects of PROHECO involvement on student learning and grade promotion. The final section summarizes the findings and provides additional policy analysis.

Analytical Framework

Below, we detail a hypothetical model of the mechanisms that improve efficiency in community schools and then explain the data and empirical methodology we used to test this model.

Model of an Effective Community School with Testable Hypotheses

Why should we expect community schools to be better run than their regular, public school counterparts? The mere fact of hiring teachers locally would generate (a) more efficiency by introducing a simpler payment model, (b) more accountability by making use of fixed-term contracting, and (c) more responsiveness to local conditions by using local information. Additionally, community schools are expected to operate as if in an education market because the producers (namely, the teachers) are more responsive to the consumers (namely, parents and students), given the latter's ability to hire and fire teachers. The expectation is that clearer signals between producer and consumer will improve the quality of the product. More specifically, increasing parents' participation maximizes the use of local information and leads to greater involvement of participants in the way that the educational process is actually carried out. This participation, in turn, can lead to a better use of school capacity, to higher teacher effort through higher teacher accountability to the parents, and to teacher selection and pedagogical techniques that are more suitable and responsive to local needs and characteristics.

Figure 9.1 provides a simple overview of this process, together with some of the proximate mechanisms linking (in theory) community schooling with improved student outcomes. For now, only three components are included: management processes, classroom processes, and student outcomes. When parents are empowered, the school is managed differently compared with the average public school that is run by a school director who answers directly to district supervisors and indirectly to parents. Parents, parental councils, or both are more actively involved in the day-to-day operation of the school and are responsible for monitoring teacher performance. For example, parent councils can keep records of days and hours worked or can note complaints registered by students or other parents. Parents may also be more attuned to environmental problems in the school, the community, or both and may take actions to improve the school climate in general.

With greater parental involvement—especially through monitoring—teacher effort is expected to increase. Working more and longer days are two obvious examples, but teacher effort has many dimensions, such as the use of homework, meetings with parents and students, and incorporation of more "active" and personalized teaching methodologies. Parents may also instigate changes in the curriculum. Examples include indigenous communities demanding more instruction in Spanish or the indigenous language, plus school activities that are more relevant to the daily lives of the residents.

Community schools are also expected to use a more efficient business model simply because of the benefits that decentralization confers. Teachers are paid directly at the school level, so they do not have to travel to state or municipal capitals to retrieve paychecks.[124] Teachers are more accountable because they are hired locally, their contracts are renewable, and their pay scale is set by the school. Local hiring also makes it possible to select the teacher who is best suited for the job.

By fundamentally altering the management structure of the school, community school initiatives are expected to affect classroom processes. In figure 9.1, the "first-order" effects are readily apparent and take the form of teachers working more days, having more dynamic classrooms, teaching locally determined curricula, and having better preparation. But the purpose of decentralized control is not only to create a better school but also to improve student learning. Given those changes in classrooms, the

---

124. It is not uncommon for teachers in isolated areas to be given days off to retrieve and cash their paychecks (Marshall and White 2002). However, note that, although community school pay plans may reduce the necessity to go and pick up one's check, they do not necessarily reduce the need to go somewhere to cash or deposit it.

Figure 9.1. Model of Effective Community School, With (Some) Testable Hypotheses

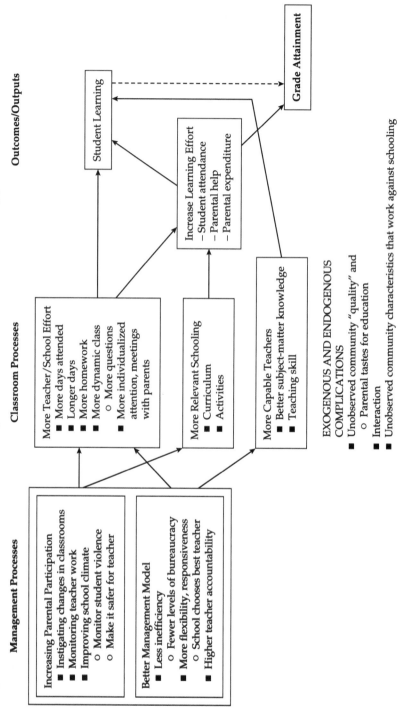

second-order effects come naturally and include increased student effort, more learning, and higher grade-level attainment. Those outcomes are, from the standpoint of the communities and funding agencies, the most important ones. But from the standpoint of evaluators, the identification of first-order changes is important to fully understand any observed differences between schools with respect to student outcomes.

The processes depicted in figure 9.1 are an idealized version of reality. As evaluators, we have to consider a less-than-ideal world for three reasons. First, decentralization initiatives are likely to be affected by the methods used to implement them and by the larger, national, institutional, and political settings. Simply stated, the devolution of control to parent councils and communities either may not go as smoothly as figure 9.1 may imply or may be carried out to achieve goals other than maximizing teacher efficiency. Other possible constraints may be related to the design of the model itself. Some evidence from Central America (Fuller and Rivarola 1998, for Nicaragua) indicates that unintended consequences can result from decentralization. A related concern is capacity. It is common in education circles to think of capacity as being a teacher issue, a school director issue, or both. But parental capacity is an important—if rarely discussed—component of the educational process. The need for parental capacity becomes especially true when parent councils are given more power to run schools. In many of those communities, educational levels are low, which raises questions about the ability of parents to instigate positive changes in some dimensions of schooling (such as teaching methodologies).

Finally, evaluating the true effect of community schools is greatly complicated by nonrandom selection that, in turn, raises the possibility of selection bias. For example, if a community with highly motivated parents starts a community school and if those motivated parents have succeeded in improving other aspects of life in the community, then observed differences in teaching behaviors or student learning may not necessarily be attributable to the community school structure per se. Conversely, community schools that are located in communities with unobserved characteristics that are especially pejorative to learning may appear to be much less effective than they really are.

Data and Sample

The Unidad de Medición de la Calidad Educativa (UMCE) evaluation project has created two samples to conduct PROHECO-control comparisons. The first is based on a survey conducted in October 2003 in 120 schools with roughly 1,100 third-grade students. Teachers were asked to complete a questionnaire detailing their personal characteristics (age, gender, experience), education, form of teaching contract, and a range of dimensions of their professional experience (working conditions, teaching strategies, and so forth). Students were given exams in Spanish, mathematics, and science, and they answered questions on family background and schooling histories as part of a questionnaire. Additional data came from questionnaires completed by school directors about the school and community.

Because of a lack of accurate information about PROHECO schools and, therefore, about the control schools during the sample design, the resulting sample of control schools (in 2003) appears not to be the best possible match for the PROHECO sample. This issue is addressed in more detail in the following sections. To address these concerns about the 2003 control group of schools, we matched an additional group of schools from the 2002 UMCE data application with PROHECO schools from 2003 (in other words, we conducted an ex post matching exercise). Because those schools, as a group, are a better match with the PROHECO schools, they are also included in the comparisons. But the data collected in 2002 contain less information than the 2003 questionnaires and are from a different year, which raises some concerns with respect to validity. Overall, however, we will see consistency in the multivariate analysis that was conducted using those two control groups.

Empirical Methodology

The data analysis proceeded in two stages. In the first, simple t-tests were used to compare teacher answers with a range of questions about working conditions, teaching strategies, personal characteristics (and qualifications), and so forth. This approach was an imperfect way to measure the extent of first-order differences in classroom environments in PROHECO schools when compared with public schools. But in the absence of observational data, they are the main tools we had available. By comparing differences in socioeconomic status between the various groups of schools (PROHECO, Control 2002, Control 2003), we could also begin to assess the comparability of the various samples. Multivariate analysis was also conducted to analyze the determinants of measures of teacher effort.

In the second stage, we used multivariate analysis to isolate a causal effect of PROHECO participation on student outcomes such as achievement. Our most basic model of the PROHECO effect took the form of

$$(9.1) \qquad A_{ij} = \alpha_j + \beta'_x X_i + \beta(PROHECO) + \varepsilon_{ij}$$

where achievement for student i on test subject j is measured as a function of a vector of individual and family characteristics X (student gender, age, parental education, and so forth) and a single 0–1 control for whether or not the school is in the PROHECO program. This approach was hardly sufficient, however, for two reasons. First, if the PROHECO schools are significantly affecting academic achievement when controlling for student background, then the model in equation 9.1 provides no information about the mechanisms.

A more complete model of the form

$$(9.2) \qquad A_{ij} = \alpha_j + \beta'_X X_i + \beta'_S S_{ij} + \beta(PROHECO) + \varepsilon_{ij}$$

enabled us to identify characteristics of PROHECO schools that explain the differences. For example, a 10-point value for the PROHECO dummy in equation 9.1 may become much smaller in equation 9.2 once the variables that account for the first-order changes in PROHECO schools (teacher attendance, teaching methodology, and so forth) are controlled. This approach not only provided a more valid assessment of the PROHECO program but also provided policymakers with important information about the kinds of factors that affect student achievement. This strategy can be extended by estimating separate equations (such as equation 9.2) for PROHECO and control schools (without the PROHECO dummy) and by breaking down the total differences in achievement into means and slopes.

However, even the more complete model in equation 9.2 did not guarantee a causal argument. The principal problem, already referred to, was selection bias. The nature of this bias is far from certain. Three possibilities deserve mention.

First, if PROHECO schools are being targeted in poor communities where parental tastes for education are low and low levels of education are correlated with other environmental problems in the community (crime, isolation, and so forth), then the PROHECO school effect is likely to be underestimated. With additional controls in equation 9.2 for community characteristics such as average levels of parental education or the presence of services, those unobserved components of poverty can be controlled. Second, a more troubling kind of selection bias involves poor communities that are particularly motivated to have a school and improve the lives of their children, for whatever reasons. Again, with additional controls for community characteristics such as the presence of services, it may be possible to measure the degree of community "activeness."

The main econometric solution to these two forms of selection bias, especially the second variety, is to use a two-equation model. In the first-stage equation, the probability that the individual is enrolled in a PROHECO school is modeled as (a) a function of all of the exogenous variables in equation 9.2 and (b) an identifying instrument that predicts attending a PROHECO school but is uncorrelated with the error term in equation 9.2. The second-stage equation is now identical to equation 9.2, only instead of a 0–1 PROHECO dummy, a transformed measure of the probability of participation is used as a regressor. The challenge for this method is finding suitable instruments.

Finally, a third form of selection bias that has received very little attention in the literature can also affect the test score equation in equation 9.2. If PROHECO schools have done a better job of retaining students, then the PROHECO achievement effect may be washed out by a positive PROHECO attainment effect. In other words, by retaining students who may otherwise drop out, the average achievement of those students that remain may be lower. The converse is also possible, of course, because either PROHECO schools may enroll fewer students in the community initially or more students may leave prematurely. Marshall (2003) shows that the PRONADE schools in rural Guatemala have higher promotion and retention rates. Furthermore, schools that have higher rates of retention, ceteris paribus, score lower on standardized exams. Controlling this form of bias can be done with data taken from school rolls on enrollment, passing rates, and desertion rates. Even better for this purpose is information on households that is taken from census data.

Results

We present below a comparison of preexisting differences between PROHECO and non-PROHECO schools, followed by an analysis of first-order differences in the teaching and learning environment and second-order differences in educational achievement and student flows.

Preliminary Comparisons: "Preexisting" Differences among Schools and Students

Before moving on to comparisons of teaching behaviors and student learning among the various groups of schools, some preliminary comparisons are in order. In this section, we provide a brief overview of the sample schools, as well as the characteristics of their respective "clientele." We will see that, in spite of the effort that was made, there really is no corresponding group of non-PROHECO schools with characteristics identical to those of PROHECO, a condition that made multivariate analysis essential.

By comparing things like parental education and household socioeconomic status, we can begin to assess the "equalness" of the various school groupings. How important is it that the PROHECO schools have similar student and community characteristics when compared with the 2002 and 2003 control groups? In the next section, we proceed as if we had experimental data by comparing the means of teacher and student responses to various questions. However, the validity of those comparisons may be called into question if the background characteristics of the respective samples are very different. For the multivariate analysis in later sections, the existence of observable differences among the various categories for things like parental education is less problematic if we assume that those variables capture all of the systematic differences between the various categories of schools. This assumption is probably strong, but given the nature of PROHECO participation, it is impossible to construct a sample of PROHECO and control schools that allows for a "clean" comparison between the two groups.

In table 9.1, we summarize the schools by geography. All departments have at least one school in the three school groupings (PROHECO, Control 2002, and Control 2003), except for Atlántida where the only schools in the sample are in the Control 2003 sample. For logistic reasons, the Bay Islands (Islas de la Bahía) and Gracias a Diós are not included in any of the samples. The departments that have the most students and schools in the sample come from Choluteca, El Paraíso, Intibuca, and Olancho.

One result that stands out is the high number of students per school in the Control 2003 sample. This high number is an indication that the control schools in this year are different from the PROHECO "treatment" schools that appear to be (much) smaller. The second result that stands out is the similarity between the Control 2002 and PROHECO samples, at least in terms of their respective distributions by department. This similarity is not surprising because the Control 2002 sample was created post hoc to match the PROHECO sample. Even so, once again, we see that the PROHECO schools are comparatively small because their total number of students is less than the Control 2002 total, despite the fact that they have four more schools with student data (91 versus 87).

The data in table 9.1 provide some useful information, but to really assess the comparability of the samples, we need to do more. In table 9.2, we present a series of t-tests comparing the PROHECO schools from 2003, first with the Control 2003 sample and then with the Control 2002 sample. The t-test scores refer to comparisons of the PROHECO sample mean with only one category at a time, which means that the asterisks in the Control 2003 and Control 2002 columns refer to individual comparisons between each control sample and the PROHECO schools.

The results in table 9.2 highlight the difficulty of matching PROHECO schools with control schools serving similar kinds of students. For the Control 2003 sample, the problems—already referred to—were related to the accuracy of information available during the sample design. Ministry data were not always accurate. For the Control 2002 sample, a post hoc sample was created where several variables—collected by UMCE and not the ministry data files—were used to match PROHECO and control schools. In both cases, in spite of the effort to select similar schools, the control schools serve relatively affluent populations compared with PROHECO, especially in the Control 2003 sample. This result is not that surprising because we know that community schools frequently spring up in the communities that are most needy and poor. In other words, there really is no corresponding group of non-PROHECO schools with identical characteristics.

**Table 9.1. Sample Overview: Number of Students
and Schools (in Parentheses), by Department**

Department	PROHECO	Control 2003	Control 2002	Total
Atlántida	0 (0)	35 (3)	0 (0)	35 (3)
Choluteca	82 (11)	14 (0)	100 (10)	196 (21)
Colón	9 (1)	37 (3)	5 (1)	51 (5)
Comayagua	41 (5)	51 (3)	75 (5)	167 (13)
Copan	39 (6)	24 (1)	63 (6)	126 (13)
Cortés	50 (6)	47 (3)	99 (5)	196 (14)
El Paraíso	55 (9)	25 (1)	86 (9)	166 (19)
Francisco Morazán	49 (5)	33 (3)	32 (5)	114 (13)
Intibucá	60 (8)	37 (2)	80 (8)	177 (18)
La Paz	26 (3)	28 (3)	31 (2)	85 (8)
Lempira	51 (7)	25 (2)	67 (7)	143 (16)
Ocotepeque	23 (3)	45 (1)	29 (2)	97 (6)
Olancho	86 (13)	45 (3)	106 (13)	237 (29)
Santa Barbara	26 (3)	46 (3)	19 (3)	91 (9)
Valle	18 (2)	22 (2)	10 (2)	50 (6)
Yoro	64 (9)	25 (1)	103 (9)	192 (19)
Total	679 (91)	539 (34)	905 (87)	2,123 (212)

Source: UMCE (2003).

Table 9.2. Comparisons of Student and Family Characteristics among PROHECO and Control Samples

Variable	PROHECO	Control 2003	Control 2002
Student characteristics:			
Female	0.51	0.52	0.52
Age in years	10.60	9.80***	10.10***
Did not attend preschool	0.65	0.49***	0.53***
Has ever repeated grade	0.51	0.45*	0.44**
Is currently repeating	0.07	0.07	0.08
Commute time in minutes	21.80	19.50**	—
Does homework alone	0.79	0.67***	0.73***
Wants to go to secondary	0.89	0.88	—
Works outside of home	0.26	0.30	0.79***
Household characteristics:			
Home has dirt floor	0.61	0.34***	0.56*
Average physical condition	2.77	2.83***	—
Ratio of people to rooms	4.62	3.88***	4.68
Mother's education in years	2.51	3.43***	—
Mother can read	0.65	0.79***	0.76***
Father's education in years	2.60	2.95**	—
Father can read	0.67	0.73**	0.76***
Mother works	0.46	0.39**	0.54***
Sum of household items	1.95	3.40***	2.33***
Household has books	0.43	0.64***	0.21***
Number of books in home	2.05	3.71***	—
SES factor 1	−0.35	0.53***	—
SES factor 2	−0.25	0.73***	−0.22

SES = socioeconomic status.
Notes: Asterisks refer to significance (two-tail) for *t*-test comparisons of independent sample means assuming equal variances (* = significant at 10 percent; ** = significant at 5 percent; *** = significant at 1 percent). For Control 2002, the applied questionnaires were not as complete as in the Control 2003 sample, so it is not always possible to compare their means with PROHECO.
Source: UMCE (2003).

Of the two control samples, the 2002 sample is generally a better reference group because the means are generally closer to PROHECO for the various student and family characteristics. In most cases, the differences are still statistically significant, but the size of the difference when using the 2002 sample is generally smaller than the 2003 control sample.

One very important difference that will be returned to again and again in this paper concerns class size. This issue is a commonly debated policy lever in the policy environments of both developing and industrialized countries. The results here are consistent with those detailed elsewhere, and they show that community schools have lower ratios of students to teachers. This finding could have important implications for comparisons of efficiency later on.

Table 9.3 considers some other dimensions of the PROHECO–non-PROHECO comparison. We see that the PROHECO and Control 2002 schools are a better fit in terms of size because the two data sets show no significant differences in total enrollment, even though both control groups show no significant differences for school type (which is encouraging). The control schools are generally better equipped. Because the PROHECO schools are very new (most were built after 1998) their physical condition is significantly better. Finally, we see no significant differ-

Table 9.3. Comparisons of School Characteristics between PROHECO and Control Samples

Variable	PROHECO	Control 2003	Control 2002
School type:			
Single teacher	0.34	0.29	0.34
Two teachers	0.45	0.34	0.44
More than two teachers	0.22	0.37	0.22
Total enrollment	68.70	98.50**	77.20
Average student-teacher ratio	29.70	37.60***	37.60***
School library size	1.07	2.71***	—
Sum of classroom materials	2.38	3.00*	—
Sum of school services	1.75	3.78***	4.51***
Physical condition	2.66	2.40***	2.52*
Sum of community services	0.91	2.10***	1.01

Notes: Asterisks refer to significance (two-tail) for t-test comparisons of independent sample means assuming equal variances (* = significant at 10 percent; ** = significant at 5 percent; *** = significant at 1 percent). For Control 2002, the applied questionnaires were not as complete as in the Control 2003 sample, so it is not always possible to compare their means with PROHECO.
Source: UMCE (2003).

ences between the sum of community services (water, post office, and so forth) for PROHECO communities and Control 2002 communities.

First-Order Effects: Teaching and Learning Processes

In the previous section, some preliminary descriptive and comparative statistics were used to help set up the work we are most interested in: comparing teachers' behaviors and students' outcomes between PROHECO and non-PROHECO schools. We now turn to this first group of variables relating to the teaching and learning environment. How valid are simple comparisons of means when we know from the previous sections that the various school categories are significantly different in many aspects? Caution is clearly necessary, but as we stated earlier, it is impossible to find a group of schools in rural Honduras that will have student, family, and community characteristics identical to PROHECO. Furthermore, because both control school samples come from comparatively affluent communities, we are, in effect, "raising the bar" in terms of expectations for the PROHECO schools.

Table 9.4 shows that PROHECO teachers are different from their control-school counterparts. PROHECO teachers have much less experience and, not surprisingly, are younger. They are also much less likely to

Table 9.4. Comparisons of Teachers Characteristics

Variable	PROHECO (N = 90)	Control 2003 (N = 38)	Control 2002 (N = 107)
Teacher is female	0.62	0.66	0.63
Teacher age	27.80	34.90***	30.10***
Teacher experience (years)	2.20	11.50***	7.60***
Teacher attended normal school	0.40	0.70***	0.93***
Teacher attended UPN	0.04	0.30***	0.05
Teacher did not attend normal school	0.55	0.00***	0.04***
Teacher is from area	0.56	0.53	—
Teacher is currently studying	0.45	0.60	—

Notes: Sample sizes at top refer to the number of teachers who are in each school type and who answered the questions. Those totals vary only by one or two teachers per variable. Unless otherwise noted, all variables are 0–1 where 1 indicates Yes. The p-values refer to t-test comparisons of independent sample means assuming equal variances. Asterisks refer to significance (two-tail) for t-test comparisons of independent sample means assuming equal variances (*** = significant at 1 percent).
Source: UMCE (2003).

have attended a normal school or to have obtained a tertiary degree from the national teachers college (Universidad Pedagógica Nacional, or UPN). The remaining category for teacher training (teacher did not attend normal school) refers basically to those who attended a regular high school that was not specialized in teaching. Hence, along two of the most commonly analyzed dimensions of teachers (experience and preservice education), we see considerable variation between the two groups of teachers.

With table 9.5, we move from basic school and teacher characteristics to more complicated indicators of teacher activities. However, before detailing those variables, we must state that data quality for tables 9.5 and beyond is questionable for two reasons. First, teachers simply do not always understand the questions or, even if they do understand them, they do not always answer honestly. UMCE has been applying questionnaires

Table 9.5. Comparisons of Teacher Work Hours and Absences

Variable	PROHECO (N = 94)	Control 2003 (N = 38)	Control 2002
Hours of Spanish per day	1.18	1.04	—
Hours of math per day	1.18	1.07	—
Total hours of class	5.64	5.55	—
Weekly hours preparing classes	5.57	6.48	4.55
Weekly hours teaching	21.66	21.67	23.00
Weekly hours grading	5.26	4.54	4.07
Weekly hours administrative	1.73	2.99**	2.05
Weekly hours meeting with parents	1.74	3.33**	1.28**
Total weekly hours	36.40	39.70	34.40
Absences because of studying	2.04	2.18	—
Absences because of health	3.23	2.39	—
Absences because of training	4.78	2.32***	—
Absences because of personal reasons	0.96	0.84	—
Absences because of union issues	0.95	3.50***	—
Total absences	17.40	13.90	—

Notes: Sample sizes at top refer to the number of teachers who are in each school type and who answered the questions. Those totals vary only by one or two teachers per variable. The p-values refer to t-test comparisons of independent sample means assuming equal variances. Asterisks refer to significance (two-tail) for t-test comparisons of independent sample means assuming equal variances (** = significant at 5 percent; *** = significant at 1 percent).
Source: UMCE (2003).

of this kind for almost 10 years, and with each successive data collection, the process is improving. But the reality is that a culture of evaluation does not exist in Honduras (or in many places), and teachers may feel the need to tailor their responses to what they think they "should" be saying. Or they may simply not answer, which will become more apparent as, for some kinds of questions, more missing cases arise. Again, UMCE has made great strides in reducing the quantity of missing answers. Compared with most data collection projects, the number of missing student and teacher answers is not large. But if certain kinds of teachers are not answering the questions, or are falsifying their answers, then those kinds of comparisons will have little validity, hence the difficulty of relying on teacher responses instead of observing actual actions.

A commonly cited justification for empowering parental councils is that teachers' effort will increase with greater parental participation. Table 9.5 shows mixed results for this rationale. PROHECO teachers report spending more time teaching the basic subjects (math and Spanish), but the differences are not statistically significant, and their overall reported class time is identical. The same is true with overall weekly hours; the Control 2003 school teachers actually report more time spent in the school (but the differences are insignificant). However, the individual time categories show some interesting differences. First, Control 2003 school teachers spend almost twice as much time as PROHECO teachers in administrative tasks. So the image of a more "streamlined" delivery in PROHECO finds support. However, PROHECO teachers report significantly less time each week meeting with parents compared with Control 2003 and significantly more time than Control 2002 teachers. Table 9.2 showed that mothers work more in the Control 2002 sample, which may, in turn, have affected their ability to meet with teachers.

Do PROHECO teachers work more days? The tentative answer is no, but the breakdown of teacher absences (available only with the 2003 data) shows some important differences.[125] PROHECO teachers appear to miss more days because of training. This finding is perhaps not unexpected, given their comparatively low levels of preservice education. Not surprisingly, Control 2003 teachers miss almost four times as many days because of meetings with their union. Unfortunately, the most valid comparison of teacher attendance requires data on unexcused absences that are not likely to be reported by teachers in these kinds of questions. Unexcused absences appear to be a severe problem in rural Honduras (Bedi and Marshall 2002), and with a payment schedule based on days worked, it would seem that PROHECO schools are well equipped to reduce these kinds of absences.

---

125. The 2002 teacher questionnaire has data on teachers' absences, but it uses a different measurement scale so it cannot be compared with the data collected in 2003 for PROHECO.

The fact that the data in table 9.5 imply otherwise should not be taken too literally because the absences in table 9.5 are probably restricted to the ones the teacher is comfortable reporting. We will return to this issue below when we compare student responses about teacher absences.

An imperfect way of assessing teacher quality and parental valuation of school quality is by comparing teachers' salaries in PROHECO and the control school (in 2003 only). The results in table 9.6 show that Control 2003 teachers earn significantly more than PROHECO teachers. This finding is not surprising when considering their higher levels of education and experience, although it should be pointed out that only about half of the control teachers responded to this question. Interestingly, PROHECO teachers report more problems with receiving their pay than do control teachers. This statistic does cast some doubt on the effectiveness of the PROHECO business model, at least in terms of payment delivery. In both school types, teachers report late pay in about half of the cases, but in the PROHECO schools, the delays are much longer.

With multivariate analysis, we can make even more specific comparisons between PROHECO and Control 2003 teachers' salaries. The results in table 9.7 show that, when controlling experience and education, PROHECO teachers earn about 10 percent less than their counterparts. Again, because less than half of the control school teachers responded, this comparison may be meaningless in reality. But the result is intriguing. First, it suggests that PROHECO parents are not necessarily interested in recruiting the best teachers available. Or, because of supply-side restrictions (namely, teacher availability), the teachers they do get to work in their communities are of lower quality. The difference in quality (as defined by salary) becomes even greater between PROHECO teachers and control

Table 9.6. Comparisons of Teacher Salaries and Payment "Issues"

Variable	PROHECO (N = 90)	Control 2003 (N = 17)	Control 2002
Teachers' salary in school	3,046.10	3,846.60***	—
Teachers' salary outside school	867.70	1,302.10	—
Salary ever arrived late	0.50	0.53	—
How many days late?	26.60	4.70***	—

Notes: Sample sizes at the top of the table refer to the number of teachers who are in each school type and who answered the questions. Those totals vary only by one or two teachers per variable. Unless otherwise noted, all variables are 0–1 where 1 indicates Yes. The p-values refer to t-test comparisons of independent sample means assuming equal variances. Asterisks refer to significance (two-tail) for t-test comparisons of independent sample means assuming equal variances (*** = significant at 1 percent).
Source: UMCE (2003).

Table 9.7. Teacher Earnings Equations

Variable	PROHECO teachers	Control 2003 teachers
PROHECO school	−0.10 (−1.99)**	−0.12 (−2.27)**
Teacher is female	0.01 (0.77)	0.01 (0.53)
Teacher is from area	0.03 (1.55)	0.02 (1.12)
Teachers' experience (months)	0.001 (3.55)***	0.001 (3.69)***
Teacher has post in school	−0.04 (−0.87)	−0.04 (−0.85)
Teacher attended normal school	0.15 (7.14)***	0.15 (6.34)***
Teacher attended UPN	0.17 (4.76)***	0.18 (4.61)***
School is single teacher	0.05 (1.98)	0.05 (1.76)*
School is double teacher	0.06 (2.85)***	0.06 (2.42)***
State fixed effects?	No	Yes (1.29)
Sample size	96.00	96.00
R^2	0.69	0.76

Notes: Dependent variable is natural log of monthly (teacher reported) salary in lempiras. Two teachers who reported 0 were dropped from this sample. Teacher attended normal school and UPN dummies are interpreted in relation to non-normal and non-UPN teachers. Single and double teacher school dummies are interpreted in relation to multidocente schools. Asterisks refer to significance (two-tail) for t-test comparisons of independent sample means assuming equal variances (* = significant at 1 0 percent; ** = significant at 5 percent; *** = significant at 1 percent). Figures shown in parentheses are t-statistics. For the estimation of state fixed effects, the number in parentheses is the F-test for significance of state effects ($p = 0.23$).
Source: UMCE (2003).

teachers if we consider the possibility that those communities are more difficult places to work. This assumption may not hold, for any number of reasons.[126] However, if it is true, then those communities will, in theory, have to pay more to get the same level of quality.

Making inferences about teacher quality on the basis of salary is purely speculative at this point, and more important issues remain. Note that teacher quality in Honduras is determined more by bureaucratic fiat than by performance, as demonstrated in table 9.7 by the returns to variables like experience and education that may in reality have little to say about quality. The data analysis of student outcomes will, presumably, shed more light on teacher quality. Furthermore, by transforming the manage-

---

126. Very likely, the PROHECO communities are, on average, more isolated than traditional school locations. But teachers may see those jobs as more attractive along other dimensions such as nonpecuniary remuneration (meals and so forth) or safer living arrangements.

ment process, the PROHECO schools may be more efficient, which would result in equal learning for less money. This outcome, of course, echoes Friedman's original argument for school choice in which he found the resulting system will be cheaper if not necessarily better. PROHECO parents may not be looking to build the best schools in Honduras; they may simply want the most efficient schools. Finally, these data say nothing about class size. Because PROHECO schools are keeping the student–teacher ratio low (see table 9.3), one could argue that the overall workload for teachers is lower and that less quality is needed overall. In other words, the total per pupil expenditure on quality may be more equal than what is implied by the results.

One of the most challenging aspects of comparing teachers concerns the methodologies they use in the classroom. Observational data on teaching processes are time-consuming data to collect and are very difficult to work into multivariate analysis (for example, see Marshall 2003). So instead, most researchers ask teachers to describe their methods. UMCE efforts have achieved some success using student responses about teaching strategies (UMCE, UPN, and SE 2003), and these data are also incorporated here (see table 9.8). Table 9.8 begins this line of analysis by comparing teacher responses about teaching methods from PROHECO and Control 2003 samples. The results reveal few significant differences. PROHECO teachers indicate that they use circles rather than groups (or rows) more frequently than control teachers, but the importance of this result is not clear. As for teaching strategies (for example, the frequency they have students working in pairs, by themselves, with worksheets, and so forth), no significant differences were found between the two groups of teachers.

Table 9.9 also reveals few differences in teaching processes between PROHECO and control samples. In general, teachers base their plans on the textbooks and the learning objectives. The only significant difference is for real-life situations, where the control group teachers indicate they are more likely to use examples from real life in their planning. The remaining variables are nearly identical for both groups.

In table 9.10, we continue the comparisons of teaching behaviors, as reported by teachers. In the first exercise, each teacher was asked to rank from 1 (most frequent) to 7 (least frequent) the methods they most frequently use in the classroom. Therefore, the lower the mean, the more frequently teachers use the strategy. The results show that PROHECO teachers report more dictation (p-value = 0.15), give fewer examples, and are less likely to use a learning dynamic (definition is uncertain). Those data are hardly sufficient for making sweeping conclusions about classroom processes. But they do not paint a picture of more active teaching strategies. Previous UMCE data have shown that teachers who use more dictation appear to be less effective. PROHECO teachers also continue to report less interaction with parents, although this difference is statistically insignificant. In addition, they do not report giving more homework.

Table 9.8. Comparisons of Teaching Strategies

Variable	PROHECO (N = 94)	Control 2003 (N = 38)	Control 2002
Does the teacher—			
Organize students in rows?	0.11	0.11	—
Organize students in circle?	0.18	0.00***	—
Organize students in groups?	0.71	0.89**	—
Frequency teacher has students—			
Work alone	0.81	0.94	—
Work alone with help from teacher	1.53	1.44	—
Listen to teacher	1.66	1.64	—
Work in pairs	0.88	1.06	—
Work in pairs with help from teacher	1.66	1.60	—
Work with worksheets	0.96	1.06	—
Have contests	1.17	1.35	—

Notes: Sample sizes at the top of the table refer to the number of teachers who are in each school type and who answered the questions. Those totals vary only by one or two teachers per variable. The p-values refer to t-test comparisons of independent sample means assuming equal variances. For frequency, the options are coded 0 (Never), 1 (Sometimes), 2 (Always). Asterisks refer to significance (two-tail) for t-test comparisons of independent sample means assuming equal variances (** = significant at 5 percent; *** = significant at 1 percent).
Source: UMCE (2003).

The only other differences in means that approach statistical significance are for the frequency with which teachers let students grade homework (more in PROHECO) and the frequency with which teachers use short answer tests (more in PROHECO).

How do PROHECO teachers compare with control school teachers in terms of their evaluation of the work environment? Table 9.11 presents data about teacher opinions, although it should be noted once again that a large group (about 20) of Control 2003 teachers did not respond. If those who did not respond chose not to participate because they are generally unhappy with teaching, then the comparisons have no meaning. The results once again reveal few significant differences. It is interesting that PROHECO teachers report getting along better with parents (the definition of this question is not exact), which would appear to contradict the earlier data indicating less frequent contact. However, the two things are not necessarily the same. The only significant difference is related to pay;

Table 9.9. Comparisons of Teacher Planning Strategies, Part 1

Variable	PROHECO (N = 94)	Control 2003 (N = 38)	Control 2002
Does teacher base plans on—			
Their own studies?	0.11	0.13	—
Work of colleagues?	0.06	0.05	—
Textbooks?	0.26	0.21	—
Official learning objectives?	0.57	0.61	—
Frequency teacher bases plans on—			
Real-life situations in context	1.24	1.53**	—
Only on content	1.12	1.16	—
What is easiest to teach	1.11	0.92	—
Goal to cover all topics	1.67	1.51*	—
What is most useful	1.67	1.63	—
Student's ability	1.78	1.69	—
What is required	1.67	1.63	—

Notes: Sample sizes at the top of the table refer to the number of teachers who are in each school type and who answered the questions. Those totals vary only by one or two teachers per variable. The *p*-values refer to *t*-test comparisons of independent sample means assuming equal variances. For frequency, the options are coded 0 (Never), 1 (Sometimes), 2 (Always). Asterisks refer to significance (two-tail) for *t*-test comparisons of independent sample means assuming equal variances (* = significant at 10 percent; ** = significant at 5 percent).
Source: UMCE (2003).

in both groups of schools, teachers are generally unhappy with the level of pay, but in PROHECO schools, there is even more concern about the pay level. This result is indirectly confirmed by the teacher earnings equations in table 9.7, and it raises some important questions about the dynamics of school operation. This issue will be returned to in later discussion.

In table 9.12, we conclude the comparison exercise with some more data about teacher opinions concerning the work environment. For the first group of questions, the sample is restricted to those teachers who work in schools with directors. The results show that PROHECO and Control 2003 teachers are equally content with school directors. A larger group of teachers—although, once again, missing a significant group of control teachers—answered questions about their degree of influence over various components of school life. On average, they report less control, but in only one case is the difference significant and, furthermore, they

Table 9.10. Comparisons of Teaching Strategies, Part 2

Variable	PROHECO (N = 83)	Control 2003 (N = 35)	Control 2002
Frequency (1 = most, 7 = least) with which the teacher			
Dictates to class	3.94	4.63	—
Reviews with class	3.63	3.74	—
Gives examples	4.11	3.31**	—
Uses chalkboard	4.20	4.22	—
Uses learning dynamic	4.14	3.19**	—
Uses exercises	4.64	4.44	—
Uses questions	4.73	4.44	—
Frequency of parent meetings	2.49	2.67	—
Frequency with which teacher gives homework	2.75	2.68	—
Frequency (0 never, 1 = sometimes, 2 = always) with which the teacher			
Records homework	1.97	2.00	—
Grades homework	1.58	1.58	—
Reviews homework	1.71	1.78	—
Lets students grade homework	1.46	1.29	—
Focuses on errors from homework	1.66	1.58	—
Uses homework in grading	1.56	1.67	—
Frequency with which teacher bases evaluation on			
Standardized tests	0.54	0.57	—
Short answer tests	1.60	1.43*	—
Classroom observations	1.90	1.84	—
Classroom questions	1.76	1.76	—
Homework	1.54	1.78*	—
Multiple-choice tests	1.68	1.73	—

Notes: Sample sizes at the top of the table refer to the number of teachers who are in each school type and who answered the questions. Those totals vary only by one or two teachers per variable. The p-values refer to t-test comparisons of independent sample means assuming equal variances. For frequency, the teachers were asked to rank the seven options from 1 (most frequent) to 7 (least frequent), so higher values mean this strategy is less frequently incorporated in the classroom. Asterisks refer to significance (two-tail) for t-test comparisons of independent sample means assuming equal variances (* = significant at 10 percent; ** = significant at 5 percent).
Source: UMCE (2003).

Table 9.11. Comparisons of Teacher Attitudes, Part 1

Variable	PROHECO (N = 87)	Control 2003 (N = 16)	Control 2002
In this school—			
My work is valued	2.67	2.56	—
The work conditions are adequate	2.11	1.94	—
I am close with the parents	2.43	2.18*	—
The parents collaborate	1.86	1.82	—
Students respect me	2.71	2.65	—
Teachers work well together	2.58	2.62	—
I get along with the director	2.69	2.65	—
I feel safe	2.53	2.35	—
I am happy with the pay	1.33	1.65**	—
Discipline is adequate	2.48	2.47	—
Average of scores in above 10 rows	2.31	2.25	—
Teacher thinks majority of students			
Have learning problems	0.37	0.35	—
Are poorly motivated to learn	0.30	0.29	—
Have nutrition problems	0.61	0.71	—
Are frequently absent	0.41	0.41	—
Average of scores in above 4 rows	0.46	0.45	—

Notes: Sample sizes at the top of the table refer to the number of teachers who are in each school type and who answered the questions. These totals vary only by one or two teachers per variable. The p-values refer to t-test comparisons of independent sample means assuming equal variances. For the first group of questions ("In this school"), the responses are coded 1, "I disagree"; 2, "I agree"; and 3, "I strongly agree." For the second group, the teacher answers are 0 = No, 1 = Yes. Asterisks refer to significance (two-tail) for t-test comparisons of independent sample means assuming equal variances (* = significant at 10 percent; ** = significant at 5 percent).
Source: UMCE (2003).

generally seem to feel they have a fair amount of control over those aspects. Interestingly, the aspect for which PROHECO teachers report the least amount of control is school priorities, and the mean difference is statistically significant. Without more information on how teachers' perceptions of priorities differ from those of the parental council, the importance of this difference is difficult to interpret. It is certainly consistent with a manage-

Table 9.12. Comparisons of Teacher Attitudes, Part 2

Variable	PROHECO (N = 43)	Control 2003 (N = 11)	Control 2002
Teacher appraisal (1 = inefficient, 4 = very good) of school director's management of			
Materials	3.19	2.82	—
Teacher training	2.51	2.64	—
Coordination	3.14	3.00	—
Organization of school	2.86	2.80	—
Conflicts	3.02	3.00	—
Commissions	3.32	3.45	—
Average of scores in above 6 rows	2.99	2.98	—
Teacher assessment (1 = little, 2 = some, 3 = a lot) of control over			
Teaching methodology	2.64	2.82	—
Use of materials	2.41	2.59	—
School priorities	2.19	2.59**	—
Decisions	2.72	2.66	—
Rules	2.64	2.76	—
Planning	2.64	2.71	—
Average of scores in above 6 rows	2.54	2.66	—
Would you leave teaching if given the opportunity?	0.15	0.22	—

Notes: Sample sizes at the top of the table refer to the number of teachers who are in each school type and who answered the questions. Those totals vary only by one or two teachers per variable. The p-values refer to t-test comparisons of independent sample means assuming equal variances. Asterisks refer to significance (two-tail) for t-test comparisons of independent sample means assuming equal variances (** = significant at 5 percent).
Source: UMCE (2003).

ment framework where parents are empowered. But knowing more about the kinds of priorities that teachers think are important would be interesting, especially in terms of how they differ from what priorities parents think are important.

For most of the comparisons made in this section, we have relied on the teacher questionnaire. However, as mentioned before, there are some reasons to be suspicious about the validity of teacher responses. Another way of getting at teaching and learning environments is by aggregating student responses concerning some of these dimensions. Table 9.13 presents the results of comparisons among the three types of schools (when possible), using several questions that appear on the student interview. The results reveal some interesting differences. First, according to students, Control 2003 teachers were more frequently absent in 2003 than the PROHECO teachers. Results also seem to indicate that PROHECO teachers make more use of dictation and chalkboard examples when teaching. Student responses corroborate the teachers and show that Control 2003 school teachers make more use of homework, but given the differences in socioeconomic status between Control 2003 and PROHECO, this finding may simply reflect students' ability to do homework rather than teachers' effort. Control 2003 students also report more physical problems with classrooms and school environments than do students in PROHECO schools, which is consistent with previous comparisons. However, a surprising finding is that the Control 2002 students actually report fewer problems. Finally, for 2003, we see

Table 9.13. Comparisons of School Environments According to Students

Variable	PROHECO	Control 2003	Control 2002
How frequently is the teacher absent?	1.54	1.94***	—
Predominant teaching methodology:			
Dictation	0.23	0.20**	0.19**
Teacher works at chalkboard	0.44	0.37***	0.41
Students work in groups	0.10	0.15***	0.14***
Question and answer	0.07	0.09	0.25***
Other	0.17	0.20	0.01
Frequency of homework:			
In Spanish	3.38	3.47**	—
In mathematics	3.50	3.58**	—
Number of problems in classroom	0.93	1.14***	0.80***
Frequency of fights with students	0.16	0.31***	—

Notes: Sample sizes at the top of the table refer to the number of teachers who are in each school type and who answered the questions. Those totals vary only by one or two teachers per variable. The p-values refer to t-test comparisons of independent sample means assuming equal variances. For frequency, the options are coded 0 (Never), 1 (Sometimes), 2 (Always). Asterisks refer to significance (two-tail) for t-test comparisons of independent sample means assuming equal variances (** = significant at 5 percent; *** = significant at 1 percent).
Source: UMCE, 2003.

that PROHECO school environments are less chaotic; PROHECO students report fewer fights with other students. Previous work in Central America (Marshall 2003) has identified student violence as a significant predictor of grade attainment and has found that PRONADE schools in Guatemala had less violence among students. The result in table 9.13 suggests that one mechanism that may link community schooling with better student outcomes is an increased awareness of how students are getting along.

First-Order Effects: Teacher and School Effort

The previous section showed little evidence that teacher effort in PROHECO schools is greater than in the control schools. But this data point is a very difficult one to measure, so we should be wary of making sweeping conclusions. Furthermore, given the differences between treatment and control in this sample, we also cannot rule out the possibility that real differences exist. In this section, we continue this discussion, first with additional simple comparisons using the Director questionnaire and then in a more demanding framework using multivariate analysis.

Table 9.14 concludes the comparisons of means analysis with the director responses. Once again, we have the problem of "equalizing" the data between two years, and the result is that, for 2002, only some of the data are available. Table 9.14 shows some interesting differences. Not surprisingly, directors in control schools are more likely to have university degrees, and the control schools receive more frequent visits from district supervisors. Not many differences are apparent in directors' use of time.

Another unsurprising finding is that PROHECO schools are closed less frequently for work stoppages than control schools, although the averages are about even for the remaining categories. Work stoppages can occur because of lack of teachers, teachers' absences, teachers' strikes, and so forth. Our evidence shows that fewer work stoppages occur in PROHECO schools, that work stoppages do not translate into school closings, or both. Fewer work stoppages may be attributed to the fact that teachers are hired directly by the school, that they are hired according to yearly renewable contracts (with, therefore, the threat not to be rehired), and that communities are involved in the monitoring of the school. Fewer school closings after work stoppages may be attributed to community "activeness" that makes sure an absent teacher is replaced. In any case, PROHECO schools gain some work days.

PROHECO directors report significantly less autonomy than Control 2002 directors. This finding is an interesting one, but it is not inconsistent with what teachers indicated earlier. In PROHECO schools, the parents have more responsibility (in theory), and this dynamic appears to retard the degree of autonomy felt by school personnel.

Table 9.14. School Characteristics According to Directors

Variable	PROHECO	Control 2003	Control 2002
Director has a university degree	0.06	0.28***	0.08
Frequency district supervisor visits	1.16	1.71**	1.71**
Percentage of time director spends			
Administrating issues	10.9	9.9	16.1***
Organizing activities	15.7	12.8*	18.7
Meeting with community	5.1	5.5	9.6**
Meeting with teachers	9.2	8.7	10.2
Meeting with parents	13.4	11.2	12.8
Teaching	41.7	44.7	43.5
Number of school closings because of			
Holidays	6.1	6.9	—
Bureaucratic processes	2.2	2.3	—
Work stoppages	0.4	6.2***	—
Union meetings	2.1	3.2	—
Training sessions	4.5	4.1	—
Parties	0.6	0.7	—
SEP	0.7	2.0***	—
Total closings	20.5	29.5***	—
Average director autonomy	1.3	1.2	1.7***
Average parental capacity and involvement	1.7	1.7	—
Frequency of parent meetings	1.7	2.6***	—

Notes: The p-values refer to t-test comparisons of independent sample means assuming equal variances. Asterisks refer to significance (two-tail) for t-test comparisons of independent sample means assuming equal variances (* = significant at 10 percent; ** = significant at 5 percent; *** = significant at 1 percent).
Source: UMCE (2003).

Finally, a particularly surprising finding is that Control 2003 schools report more frequent parent meetings. Some caution is urged here, however, because a large group (about 20) of control schools reported no data for this question. So we cannot rule out the possibility that the only ones who reported are the ones with the most active parent associations. An additional problem—already referred to with teachers—is definitional. PROHECO directors may not consider the PROHECO parent associations to be associations per se; they may use a different terminology than that used in the public system. It seems hard to believe that parents in PROHECO schools have fewer meetings. Nevertheless, this issue has already been raised earlier, and we cannot discard the possibility that PROHECO schools are run by parent councils that are not necessarily more involved in day-to-day operations than control school parents.

We now turn to the multivariate analysis of teacher and school effort. This analysis is an important component of this study, because we expect the mechanism linking PROHECO with improved student outcomes to be a more efficient workplace environment. In other words, existing capacity should be better maximized in PROHECO schools. Unfortunately, the results from these analyses (presented in table 9.15) reveal little in the way of a significant systematic relationship between PROHECO participation and outcomes of teacher and school effort. Caution is urged when drawing conclusions from those estimations, however, because of the measurement problems with most of the dependent variables and the small sample sizes.

The results in table 9.15 include a total of 11 different outcomes chosen from the student, teacher, and director questionnaires. The only parameter that is presented is for the PROHECO dummy. Interested readers can obtain the full results on request, but the reality is that very few variables of any kind are significant predictors of those outcomes. For example, the independent variable for frequency of parental meetings (according to the director) is never a significant predictor of any of the dependent variables for teacher or school effort. The only indicator of accountability that approaches significance in at least some of the estimations is the variable for the frequency of district supervisor visits. So given the insignificance of the other predictors and the quantity of outcomes considered (13 dependent variables with three models), those other variables are excluded from table 9.15.

All data are taken from the 2003 data collection, and each of the dependent variables is detailed in the previous section when we compared means. Three models are estimated for each outcome. The first includes only the PROHECO dummy and basic teacher (when it is a teacher-specific outcome) and school characteristics such as experience, gender, and school type (single teacher, and so forth). In the second model, we add additional school characteristics such as the frequency of district supervisor visits, parental meetings (when the outcome is not parental meetings), and school size. Finally, in model 3, the department dummies and socioeconomic controls are added. All estimations are done at the school or teacher level, which involves sample sizes of between 95 and 130. Those are very small samples from which to obtain efficient and robust parameters.

Table 9.15. PROHECO Parameter in Regressions of Teacher and School Effort on Various Groupings of Variables

Outcome		Model 1	Model 2	Model 3
(1)	Teacher-reported hours per week (OLS)	−8.30* (1.73)	−4.17 (0.66)	−3.23 (0.44)
(2)	Teacher-reported teaching hours per week (OLS)	−3.34 (0.49)	1.43 (0.20)	−0.88 (1.24)
(3)	Teacher-reported administrative hours per week (OLS)	−2.06** (2.77)	−3.16*** (1.45)	−1.81 (2.43)
(4)	Teacher-reported parent meeting hours per week (OLS)	−2.12** (2.54)	−2.97** (1.89)	−2.37* (2.58)
(5)	Teacher-reported homework assigned	0.42 (1.87)	0.82* (0.04)	0.03 (1.22)
(6)	Average student-reported Spanish homework (OLS)	−0.08 (0.09)	−0.01 (0.57)	0.10 (0.61)
(7)	Average student-reported fights (OLS)	−0.05 (0.70)	−0.05 (0.06)	−0.01 (0.87)
(8)	Average student classroom problems (OLS)	−0.28 (1.44)	−0.38 (0.90)	−0.23 (1.56)
(9)	Teacher-reported absences (OLS)	3.88 (0.86)	4.19 (0.72)	3.92 (1.15)
(10)	Average student-reported teacher absence frequency (OLS)	−0.28 (0.49)	−0.16 (0.54)	−0.17 (0.90)
(11)	School closings (OLS)[a]	−8.83*** (1.11)	−3.95 (0.55)	−2.37 (2.85)

Notes: Reported parameters are the point estimates for the PROHECO school dummy with *t*-statistics in parentheses below. Model 1 includes basic teacher and school controls (experience, gender, school type). Model 2 adds indicators of work environment such as frequency of district supervisor visits and parental meetings (when applicable). Model 3 adds the remaining socioeconomic controls and also adds department fixed effects. Full results available on request. Asterisks refer to significance (two-tail) for *t*-test comparisons of independent sample means assuming equal variances (* = significant at 10 percent; ** = significant at 5 percent; *** = significant at 1 percent).
a. In the case of school closings, the differences in the PROHECO effect going from model 1 to models 2 and 3 can be explained by the number of observations that are lost when the parental meetings variable is introduced and not by the interaction between the newly included variables and the PROHECO dummy.
Source: UMCE (2003).

As mentioned earlier, table 9.15 provides little in the way of systematic evidence to link PROHECO participation with increased teacher effort, although some evidence indicates a positive PROHECO effect. Worth mentioning is that those dependent variables are very difficult to measure. The significant parameters are in both directions. For example, PROHECO teachers report fewer hours of work per week. Not surprisingly, they report significantly fewer hours per week in administrative duties. But they also report significantly less time devoted to meetings with parents. This issue has already been addressed, and it seems surprising that PROHECO teachers have less interaction with parents. One explanation may be that, instead, PROHECO teachers interpret the term *parent meeting* differently. Nevertheless, this issue is an open question that deserves more attention in the future. On the positive side, PROHECO students report fewer problems in the classroom than non-PROHECO students, although the point estimates only approach statistical significance. Additionally, PROHECO teachers report more homework, with point estimates that reach significance in model 2. Finally, evidence confirms that the PROHECO schools are associated with fewer closings according to the director.

Taken together, the results in table 9.15 highlight the importance of collecting more and better data on first-order, procedural outcomes in Honduran schools. This emphasis is not to say that the UMCE data are inappropriate for evaluating the effect of PROHECO. But the real challenge in identifying the effect of a program like PROHECO lies in explaining differences in classroom and school environments because those are, in theory, the mechanisms that link increased parental participation with improvements in student outcomes.

Second-Order Effects: Academic Achievement and Student Flows

We review below second-order effects of PROHECO schools. In the first two subsections, we provide an analysis of academic achievement levels and variance decomposition. In the third subsection, we analyze academic achievement while controlling for selection bias. Finally, we analyze the effect of PROHECO schools on student flows.

Academic Achievement

If PROHECO schools have succeeded in transforming the teaching and learning environment, then we should expect second-order—or indirect—effects to turn up in student outcomes. Test scores are the most commonly used measure of school production, in addition to pass rates and desertion. With multivariate analysis, as detailed in the methodology section, we can begin to form a causal argument relating PROHECO participation with student outcomes. The previous section relied largely on simple *t*-tests, but bivariate comparisons are problematic if other factors are different between PROHECO and control schools. In this section, we fit econometric models of student learning to those same kinds of data.

According to the UMCE tests, the PROHECO schools are scoring significantly higher on standardized exams (see table 9.16). This finding is important because we know that PROHECO schools come from the poorest communities in the sample. So we have a positive "PROHECO effect" to explain. But is there a causal effect of PROHECO on student learning in the UMCE sample? Tables 9.17, 9.18, and 9.19 present the results from the multivariate analysis for Spanish, mathematics, and science achievement. Four models are estimated separately for each year (2002 and 2003). The first regresses the student's test score onto the gender control and the 0–1 measure for PROHECO during that year. In the second estimation, the student, family, and community controls for socioeconomic status (SES) are added. In the third estimation, we add teacher experience and school size. Finally, in the fourth estimation, we add the measures that we consider to be indicative of teacher and school effort.

The intuition behind this setup (shown in tables 9.17, 9.18, and 9.19) is as follows. In the first estimation, we get the most basic—and naive—measure of PROHECO effectiveness. By adding controls for SES in estimation 2, we sharpen this measure because we already know that PROHECO schools come from relatively poorer communities. This estimation is, in many ways, our cleanest measure of the PROHECO effect (subject to selection concerns, of course). Then in estimations 3 and 4, we begin to measure the mechanisms that explain whatever differences are found in estimations 1 and 2. Estimation 4 is crucial to our analysis, because it is here that we measure capacity use—a big issue in decentralization—and its effect on student learning.

Table 9.16. Summary of Test Scores

Variable	PROHECO	Control 2003	Control 2002
Spanish Exam	38.0	37.0	35.2***
	(15.6)	(14.7)	(14.7)
Math Exam	46.1	42.5***	43.3**
	(18.5)	(15.6)	(17.3)
Science Exam	39.3	35.8***	36.6***
	(16.9)	(15.2)	(15.7)

Notes: Test scores measured in percentage correct (0–100). Standard deviations in parentheses. The *p*-values refer to *t*-test comparisons of independent sample means assuming equal variances. Asterisks refer to significance (two-tail) for *t*-test comparisons of independent sample means assuming equal variances (* = significant at 10 percent; ** = significant at 5 percent; *** = significant at 1 percent).
Source: UMCE (2003).

Table 9.17. OLS Estimates of Determinants of Spanish Achievement, 2002 and 2003

Variable	2002 estimations				2003 estimations			
	(1)	(2)	(3)	(4)	(1)	(2)	(3)	(4)
PROHECO school	3.19 (1.73)*	3.21 (1.75)*	2.99 (1.41)	2.27 (0.90)	1.35 (0.69)	2.63 (1.04)	3.08 (1.05)	1.47 (0.46)
Student and family characteristics								
Student is female	0.50 (0.57)	0.66 (0.76)	0.66 (0.76)	0.96 (1.16)	0.36 (0.30)	-0.50 (0.40)	-0.49 (0.40)	-0.61 (0.51)
Person–room ratio	—	-0.53 (3.02)***	-0.53 (2.97)***	-0.56 (3.20)***	—	-0.55 (2.14)**	-0.55 (2.12)**	-0.57 (2.29)**
Student age in years	—	-0.03 (0.08)	-0.03 (0.10)	0.14 (0.42)	—	0.25 (0.67)	0.26 (0.71)	0.44 (1.19)
Student works	—	—	—	—	—	-4.00 (2.73)***	-4.03 (2.73)***	-4.09 (2.88)***
Community characteristics								
Average SES factor	—	0.22 (0.16)	0.38 (0.25)	-0.55 (0.32)	—	1.81 (1.11)	1.72 (0.96)	0.76 (0.42)
Municipal poverty	—	-0.001 (0.01)	-0.004 (0.04)	0.03 (0.29)	—	-0.06 (0.70)	-0.06 (0.70)	-0.07 (1.40)
School–teacher effort								
Teacher work hours	—	—	—	0.06 (1.72)*	—	—	—	0.09 (1.74)*

(Continued)

Table 9.17. OLS Estimates of Determinants of Spanish Achievement, 2002 and 2003 (Continued)

Variable	2002 estimations				2003 estimations			
	(1)	(2)	(3)	(4)	(1)	(2)	(3)	(4)
Average class size	—	—	—	-0.12 (0.77)	—	—	—	-0.11 (1.07)
Frequency of homework	—	—	—	—	—	—	—	4.82 (1.69)*
School closings	—	—	—	—	—	—	—	-0.01 (0.12)
Remaining controls								
Teacher experience	—	—	-0.02 (0.13)	0.01 (0.06)	—	—	0.06 (0.22)	0.06 (0.23)
Total enrollment	—	—	-0.003 (0.27)	-0.002 (0.17)	—	—	0.01 (0.40)	0.02 (0.27)
PROHECO dummy after removing outliers[a]	—	—	—	—	1.07 (0.56) [1]	— [0]	2.88 (1.04) [7]	0.54 (0.17) [37]
Fixed effects p-value	0.000	0.000	0.000	0.000	0.000	0.000	0.000	0.000
Sample size	1,257	1,257	1,257	1,257	975	975	975	975
R^2	0.050	0.058	0.058	0.073	0.097	0.125	0.125	0.153

Notes: Asymptotic *t*-statistics in parentheses are based on robust standard errors. All estimations use fixed effects at department level. Asterisks refer to significance (two-tail) for *t*-test comparisons of independent sample means assuming equal variances (* = significant 10 percent; ** = significant at 5 percent; *** = significant at 1 percent).

a. Parameter for the PROHECO dummy together with the *t*-statistic and number of dropped cases (in brackets).

Source: UMCE (2003).

Table 9.18. OLS Estimates of Determinants of Mathematics Achievement, 2002 and 2003

Variable	2002 estimations				2003 estimations			
	(1)	(2)	(3)	(4)	(1)	(2)	(3)	(4)
PROHECO school	2.88 (1.35)	4.03 (2.67)***	4.62 (1.79)*	4.05 (1.48)	2.66 (1.17)	3.80 (1.50)	6.06 (1.84)*	5.73 (1.57)
Student and family characteristics								
Student is female	0.12 (0.13)	0.28 (0.29)	0.22 (0.23)	0.48 (0.51)	-0.21 (0.18)	-0.75 (0.63)	-0.75 (0.64)	-0.74 (0.64)
Person–room ratio	—	-0.69 (3.34)***	-0.73 (3.51)***	-0.77 (3.79)***	—	-0.51 (2.16)**	-0.49 (2.09)**	-0.58 (2.46)**
Student age in years	—	-0.08 (0.23)	-0.03 (0.08)	0.12 (0.32)	—	-0.01 (0.01)	0.04 (0.10)	0.19 (0.42)
Student works	—	—	—	—	—	-2.40 (1.54)	-2.56 (1.63)*	-2.72 (1.85)*
Community characteristics								
Average SES factor	—	4.03 (2.67)***	2.80 (1.53)	1.89 (0.98)	—	2.33 (1.48)	1.81 (1.14)	0.89 (0.55)
Municipal poverty	—	-0.34 (2.56)***	-0.32 (2.41)**	-0.29 (2.13)**	—	-0.36 (2.74)***	-0.36 (2.77)***	-0.33 (2.64)***
School–teacher effort								
Teacher work hours	—	—	—	0.07 (1.47)	—	—	—	0.10 (1.64)*

(Continued)

Table 9.18. OLS Estimates of Determinants of Mathematics Achievement, 2002 and 2003 (Continued)

Variable	2002 estimations				2003 estimations			
	(1)	(2)	(3)	(4)	(1)	(2)	(3)	(4)
Average class size	—	—	—	-0.10 (0.95)	—	—	—	0.02 (0.11)
Frequency of homework	—	—	—	—	—	—	—	6.05 (1.92)*
School closings	—	—	—	—	—	—	—	0.01 (0.11)
Remaining controls								
Teacher experience	—	—	0.33 (1.31)	0.36 (1.49)	—	—	0.28 (1.68)*	0.31 (1.86)*
Total enrollment	—	—	0.01 (0.87)	0.01 (0.94)	—	—	0.01 (0.55)	0.02 (1.07)
PROHECO dummy after removing outliers[a]	—	—	—	—	1.49 (0.52) [1]	2.98 (1.14) [1]	7.42 (2.27)** [7]	5.08 (1.37) [34]
Fixed effects p-value	0.000	0.000	0.000	0.000	0.000	0.000	0.000	0.000
Sample size	1,253	1,253	1,253	1,253	952	952	952	952
R^2	0.083	0.131	0.140	0.150	0.159	0.198	0.205	0.234

Notes: Asymptotic t-statistics in parentheses are based on robust standard errors. All estimations use fixed effects at department level. Asterisks refer to significance (two-tail) for t-test comparisons of independent sample means assuming equal variances (* = significant at 10 percent; ** = significant at 5 percent; *** = significant at 1 percent).
a. Parameter for the PROHECO dummy together with the t-statistic and number of dropped cases (in brackets).
Source: UMCE (2003).

Table 9.19. OLS Estimates of Determinants of Science Achievement, 2002 and 2003

Variable	2002 estimations				2003 estimations			
	(1)	(2)	(3)	(4)	(1)	(2)	(3)	(4)
PROHECO school	2.33 (1.22)	2.00 (1.06)	2.16 (0.94)	1.00 (0.41)	4.64 (2.31)**	5.74 (2.45)***	6.99 (2.32)**	2.35 (0.76)
Student and family characteristics								
Student is female	0.87 (0.86)	1.09 (1.10)	1.03 (1.05)	1.42 (1.46)	-0.10 (0.09)	-0.63 (0.54)	-0.62 (0.54)	-0.86 (0.77)
Person–room ratio	—	-0.58 (2.95)***	-0.60 (3.02)***	-0.65 (3.30)***	—	-0.60 (2.47)***	-0.60 (2.46)**	-0.56 (2.28)***
Student age in years	—	0.35 (0.89)	0.34 (0.89)	0.59 (1.59)	—	0.40 (1.02)	0.43 (1.44)	0.56 (1.50)
Student works	—	—	—	—	—	-2.52 (1.76)*	-2.60 (1.83)*	-3.06 (2.23)**
Community characteristics								
Average SES factor	—	0.96 (0.62)	1.15 (0.69)	-0.19 (0.11)	—	1.68 (1.23)	1.41 (1.06)	0.41 (0.28)
Municipal poverty	—	-0.11 (1.16)	-0.12 (1.26)	-0.07 (0.78)	—	-0.16 (1.78)*	-0.16 (1.79)*	-0.14 (1.60)
School–teacher effort								
Teacher work hours	—	—	—	0.07 (1.95)**	—	—	—	0.09 (1.80)*

(Continued)

Table 9.19. OLS Estimates of Determinants of Science Achievement, 2002 and 2003 *(Continued)*

Variable	2002 estimations				2003 estimations			
	(1)	*(2)*	*(3)*	*(4)*	*(1)*	*(2)*	*(3)*	*(4)*
Average class size	—	—	—	-0.18	—	—	—	-0.28
				(1.59)				(2.64)***
Frequency of homework	—	—	—	—	—	—	—	3.57
								(1.60)
School closings	—	—	—	—	—	—	—	-0.07
								(1.95)**
Remaining controls								
Teacher experience	—	—	0.14	0.18	—	—	0.15	0.11
			(0.63)	(0.84)			(0.88)	(0.63)
Total enrollment	—	—	-0.02	-0.02	—	—	0.01	0.02
			(1.34)	(1.13)			(0.44)	(1.07)
PROHECO dummy after removing outliers[a]	—	—	—	—	3.15	—	7.32	1.84
					(1.43)		(2.45)**	(0.60)
					[1]	[0]	[8]	[35]
Fixed effects *p*-value	0.000	0.000	0.000	0.000	0.000	0.000	0.000	0.000
Sample size	1,257	1,257	1,257	1,257	974	974	974	974
R^2	0.061	0.072	0.077	0.100	0.122	0.143	0.146	0.178

Notes: Asymptotic *t*-statistics in parentheses are based on robust standard errors. All estimations use fixed effects at department level. Asterisks refer to significance (two-tail) for *t*-test comparisons of independent sample means assuming equal variances (* = significant at 10 percent; ** = significant at 5 percent; *** = significant at 1 percent).
a. Parameter for the PROHECO dummy together with the *t*-statistic and number of dropped cases (in brackets).
Source: UMCE (2003).

Teacher work hours and school closings are obvious measures of effort at different levels. Class size is included as an indirect measure of teacher effort, although this measure is subject to some criticism.[127] The frequency of homework is another problematic indicator of teacher effort, because it may instead be capturing unmeasured components of student ability, dedication, or family background. Those problems highlight the limitations of this analytical framework (and data) because what is really needed is a fully endogenized setup where teacher and school effort is treated as an outcome and its effect on student learning is modeled in a recursive setup. But this avenue is simply not available with those data, especially in the absence of good measures of community involvement in the school. So the reduced-form approach—warts and all—is used instead.

With three subjects, two years of comparisons, and four sets of variables, the three tables present a lot of results to peruse. But for the research query that drives this paper, the story is generally very similar in each case. The naive estimates of the PROHECO effect in estimation 1 are positive and marginally significant or approach significance in all estimations. With the inclusion of the student, family, and community controls in estimation 2, as well as the school and teacher controls in estimation 3, the PROHECO effect generally increases both in size and significance.

The interesting finding occurs in estimation 4 when the teacher and school effort controls are added. In every estimation—six in all—both the size and significance of the PROHECO dummy are reduced when we control for capacity use. Taken together, those results provide some important clues into understanding the dynamics of decentralization and community schooling in Honduras. PROHECO schools have much smaller class sizes, which, in turn, help explain why their students do better on exams (especially in science). But they also generally get more out of their existing capacity in the form of teacher work hours, school closings, and frequency of homework. Those results are particularly well illustrated by the 2003 science regression where, after including the four school–teacher efforts variables (all significant or very close to significance) in the regression, the PROHECO effect falls dramatically. Note that, although the link between PROHECO and teacher work hours could not be made in the first-order analysis, the evidence here indicates that the PROHECO effect is sensitive to including this variable (suggesting a positive correlation between the two variables) once a larger sample (at the student level now) and a more complete set of socioeconomic controls are included.

---

127. The workload of teachers who use very traditional, frontal teaching methods may be unaffected by the number of students in the classroom. This possibility is especially the case if little preparation is undertaken outside of class in the form of activity planning, homework grading, and so forth

What about the issue of parental involvement in the school, which occupies a more central role in other analyses of community schools (for example, Sawada 1999)? As detailed earlier, our measures of parent-teacher and parent-school interaction suffer from missing values and possible measurement error because of definitional issues about parent groupings. The regressions in tables 9.17–9.19 were also estimated (for 2003) using the frequency of parent association meetings as a covariate. The estimations were insignificant in all cases and resulted in losing 20 percent of the cases.

Our inability to capture parental involvement in the school—directly—is a weakness that needs to be addressed in future work. But the significance of this data omission should not be overstated. We have other measures—namely, teacher hours and school closings—that are likely to be affected by the degree of parental "activeness" in the school. And although it would have been nice to show that parent involvement predicts those variables that, in turn, predict better student outcomes, we can at least tell part of the story with what we do have.

Another omission in tables 9.17–9.19 is for teacher education. It was already noted in the comparisons of means that PROHECO teachers are less likely to have attended a university and are more likely to report non-normal school certification. However, UMCE personnel have some concerns about the measurement of those variables during the data collection because PROHECO teachers may have misunderstood the categories, and all teachers in the sample may have confused current enrollment in the UPN with a degree from the UPN. Furthermore, the breakdown of those various categories reveals that all teachers with non-normal school formations are in PROHECO, and all teachers with university are in non-PROHECO. The result is that the addition of those variables introduces some sensitivity to the analysis, especially for the parameter we are most interested in (the PROHECO dummy). So the safest course of action is simply to drop the education dummies altogether. As expected, lower educated teachers generally do worse, and there is a larger marginal effect of the PROHECO dummy to be explained.

The results shown in tables 9.17–9.19 are subject to the criticism that, because of small school sample sizes (especially the control group in 2003), the resulting comparisons are likely to be sensitive to outliers. For the 2003 estimations, this hypothesis was tested using Hadi's (1992) outlier detection formula.[128] At the bottom of each table is the parameter for the PROHECO dummy, together with the t-statistic and number of dropped cases (in brackets) after analyzing the data for outliers. Overall, the results change very little, although we should note that it was not possible to carry

---

128. "Hadimvo" command in Stata Version 8.

out the hadimvo command using the department dummies because of col-inearity problems.

Another issue that has not been addressed is interaction. If PROHECO schools have succeeded in creating a different work environment, then we may expect more than just "differences in means" between the various school categories. With interaction terms, we can test this proposition more directly, although with small sample sizes and collinear regressors, the challenges are considerable. For 2002, two interaction terms were constructed for PROHECO*work hours and PROHECO*class size. For 2003, the days-closed variable was also interacted with the PROHECO dummy. The resulting point estimates, in all four models for each subject, revealed little in the way of systematic interaction according to those interaction terms.

Academic Achievement Variance Breakdown

With the results from the various production functions, we are beginning to form a picture of why PROHECO schools have marginally higher scores on UMCE exams. All of this analysis is, of course, subject to concerns about selection bias, which are dealt with (very imperfectly) in the next section. For now, we will pause and try and will put the findings in tables 9.17–9.19 into some policy context.

Table 9.20 presents the results from a simple breakdown exercise. The process has two parts. In the first (not presented), separate production functions taken from estimation 3 in tables 9.17–9.19 are conducted separately by PROHECO and Control 2003 schools. For now, Control 2002 is left out of the exercise because of the similarity between the results by year and the limited data available in 2002. In the second stage of the analysis, the mean difference between PROHECO and Control 2003 for each variable is multiplied by the coefficients taken from each of these two first-stage regressions. We use two sets of coefficients, taken from McEwan and Marshall (2004), because of sensitivity in the first-stage regressions by school type.

The best behaved results are for science, where the school sector-specific regressions are very similar. How are the data interpreted? For example, for the SES factor, the mean difference is −1.01, so when this figure is multiplied by the coefficient for SES in the production functions, it predicts between 1.3 points and 2.3 points lower. In other words, PROHECO schools lose between 1.3 points and 2.3 points relative to the Control 2003 schools because of their lower levels of SES.

For each group of variables—SES and School–teacher effort—the individual variables are summed to create a group total. This total is then divided (at the bottom) by the standard deviation of the subject to get an idea of how big the difference is. In most cases, the differences in SES predict lower scores for PROHECO schools whereas the opposite is true for the School–teacher effort variables. The biggest predictors are the SES

Table 9.20. Breakdown of PROHECO and Control School Achievement Differences, 2003

Variable	Raw mean difference	Spanish Control coefficient	Spanish PROHECO coefficient	Math Control coefficient	Math PROHECO coefficient	Science Control coefficient	Science PROHECO coefficient
Raw achievement difference		0.69		1.42		2.64	
1. SES controls:							
Student age	0.79	-0.26	0.59	-0.67	0.56	-0.20	0.90
Person–room ratio	0.72	0.06	-0.57	-0.11	-0.48	-0.16	-0.37
Student works	-0.06	0.32	0.19	0.21	0.20	0.21	0.24
SES factor	-1.01	0.62	-2.24	-0.38	-3.47	-1.32	-2.34
Total	—	0.63	-1.83	-2.00	-0.89	-2.93	-2.77
2. School-teacher effort:							
Teacher hours	0.98	-0.02	0.14	0.10	0.17	-0.03	0.08
Average class size	-5.49	0.93	0.60	3.02	-0.88	1.37	1.92
Frequency of homework	-0.04	0.18	-0.20	0.08	-0.26	0.09	-0.26
School closings	-12.74	0.89	-1.40	2.04	-0.38	1.53	1.02
Total	—	1.98	-0.86	5.24	-1.35	2.96	2.76
1. Total/standard deviation	—	4.0	12.0	11.6	5.1	17.5	16.6
2. Total/standard deviation	—	12.9	5.6	30.3	7.8	17.7	16.5

Notes: Raw mean difference is calculated by subtracting the Control 2003 average from the PROHECO average for each variable (negative values indicate PROHECO is lower). The remaining data in the table are calculated by multiplying the mean difference by two sets of coefficients. Control coefficients are the coefficients from the production function, which are estimated using only control schools, whereas PROHECO coefficients are taken from the PROHECO specific production function. Those first-stage regression results are available from the authors on request. Positive coefficients in the breakdown refer to gains by PROHECO whereas negative results indicate gains by control schools. For each group of variables, the totals are calculated at the bottom. For SES, the variables for female and municipal poverty are included in the total but are not shown here. Finally, at the bottom of the table, the total effects for the SES controls (group 1) and School–teacher effort (group 2) are calculated as a percentage of one standard deviation in each subject. *Source:* UMCE (2003).

factor (favoring Control 2003), class size (favoring PROHECO), and school closing (also favoring PROHECO). How big are the effect sizes? For Spanish and math, the pronounced differences in the first-stage regressions make it hard to comment on the size (and, to a lesser extent, even the direction). But in science, we see that the differences in socioeconomic status between PROHECO and Control schools predict between 16.6 percent and 17.5 percent of a standard deviation in the overall sample science average. The size of the School–teacher effort group is nearly identical.

Academic Achievement, Controlling for Selection Bias

Few issues are more vexing when assessing the causal effects of projects like PROHECO than sample selection bias. In this section, we discuss three extensions to the basic production function approach presented previously. Those extensions include (a) adding more controls for community characteristics to capture unmeasured components of community "activeness," (b) adding more controls for child enrollment ratios to control for cohort selection bias, and (c) conducting additional econometric estimations using two-stage Heckman style and propensity score matching correction techniques.

We were unable to track down additional data on community activeness using the national census. However, it was possible to address the second extension. Using the national census from 2001, it was possible to construct enrollment ratios for children aged 6–10 in about 60 percent of the communities (*aldeas*) that appear in the 2003 UMCE sample. The aldeas that did not appear in the census data file were assigned the municipality average for enrollment. This approach is problematic if the aldeas that are most likely to be missing in the census file are very small communities, which seems likely. The results for the various achievement production functions did not change when this control for enrollment was added. As expected, in most cases, the percentage of children enrolled was negatively associated with achievement, but not in a significant way. More important, the PROHECO dummy was completely unaffected by the inclusion of this control, suggesting no evidence that PROHECO schools do a better or worse job of enrolling children who would otherwise choose to stay home. Because of this result and the concerns that surround the measurement, these results are not presented here.

We also explored econometric solutions to correcting for selection bias. Table 9.21 presents the results from the first-stage selection equation where a 0–1 PROHECO dummy is regressed onto the student, family, and community variables only. How can we identify selection into PROHECO? Few UMCE variables would appear to be ideal candidates for identifying instruments because a variable that predicts whether or not a student attends PROHECO is likely also to predict test scores. We used the presence of potable water in the community for 2002 and the sum of commu-

Table 9.21. First-Stage Equations: Binary Probit Estimates of PROHECO Participation, 2002 and 2003

Variable	2002 estimations		2003 estimations	
	(1)	(2)	(1)	(2)
Student and family characteristics				
Student is female	0.02	0.06	0.04	−0.07
	(0.30)	(0.9)	(0.38)	(0.60)
Student age	0.13	0.13	0.11	0.12
	(3.93)***	(3.98)***	(2.66)***	(2.62)***
Person–room ratio	−0.01	−0.02	−0.008	0.006
	(0.57)	(0.76)	(0.31)	(0.23)
Average SES factor	0.18	0.01	−0.88	−0.64
	(0.91)	(0.05)	(3.95)***	(3.06)***
Municipal poverty	−0.002	−0.04	−0.01	−0.01
	(0.22)	(0.36)	(0.62)	(0.08)
Student works	—	—	−0.21	−0.42
			(1.06)	(1.99)**
Identifying instrument				
Sum of services	—	—	−0.11	−0.20
			(0.86)	(1.78)*
Community has potable water	−0.57	−0.38	—	—
	(2.00)**	(1.33)		
Department fixed effects?	Yes	No	Yes	No
Sample size	1,280	1,280	976	976
Pseudo R^2	0.073	0.030	0.324	0.271

Notes: Coefficients are unstandardized probit estimates. Dependent variable = 1 if student attends PROHECO school in that year, it is 0 otherwise. The t-statistics in parentheses are based on robust standard errors. Asterisks refer to significance (two-tail) for t-test comparisons of independent sample means assuming equal variances (* = significant at 10 percent; ** = significant at 5 percent; *** = significant at 1 percent).
Source: UMCE (2003).

nity services for 2003 as identifying instruments for PROHECO participation. In both cases, those variables are largely orthogonal to student achievement when they are included in the achievement production functions (with and without the PROHECO dummy), and they are moderately significant predictors of attending PROHECO. Because we have only one identifying instrument for each estimation, it is not possible to cannot do a better job of assessing instrument validity (such as incorporating a test for overidentification).

The results in table 9.21 highlight some of the difficulties involved in pursuing sexy econometric solutions to selection issues. Few parameters are significant predictors of PROHECO school attendance, although, in general, the parameter signs are in the right direction. In 2002, the proportion of explained variance is very low, which will have the effect of compressing the variance in the predicted parameter for PROHECO participation. The identifying instruments are generally significant but not very robust predictors. Finally, the results are somewhat sensitive to the inclusion of the department fixed effects, especially in 2003 when the PROHECO and Control samples were not equalized by geography.

Using the parameters from table 9.21, we calculated predicted probability of PROHECO attendance for each student. We then reestimated the production functions from tables 9.17, 9.18, and 9.19 using this predicted parameter. The full results do not change much, so to save space, the only parameters that are presented in table 9.21 are the PROHECO coefficients.

The results in table 9.22 are underwhelming. In general, the value of the predicted PROHECO parameter is larger than the actual parameter taken from the (nearly) identical estimations in tables 9.17–9.19. This finding implies that selection bias is an issue, and the nature of the bias is to underestimate the true effect of PROHECO. In other words, the

Table 9.22. Comparison of PROHECO Achievement Effect Using Predicted and Actual Measure of PROHECO Participation, 2002 and 2003

Variable	2002		2003	
	Predicted	Actual	Predicted	Actual
Spanish	6.71	3.21	5.54	2.63
	(0.63)	(1.75)	(0.25)	(1.04)
Mathematics	10.05	4.03	11.17	3.80
	(0.95)	(2.67)	(0.46)	(1.50)
Science	2.97	2.00	17.72	5.74
	(0.30)	(1.06)	(1.10)	(2.45)

Notes: PROHECO parameter taken from regression with individual and family controls only. Same estimations as estimation 2 in tables 9.17–9.19. Predicted refers to nontransformed (namely, inverse Mills ratio) predicted probability of being PROHECO school taken from estimations presented in table 9.21. Asymptotic t-statistics in parentheses are based on robust standard errors.
Source: UMCE (2003).

characteristics of students who attend either PROHECO or the schools themselves are negatively correlated with unobservable factors that lead to better outcomes. The key implication from table 9.22 is that, with more data measuring other influences, the effect of PROHECO on achievement should increase.

Those estimates using selection correction techniques represent a first cut at this issue. The sample sizes are small, the identifying instruments are not particularly convincing, and the results are fairly sensitive to the inclusion of the department dummies. Nevertheless, despite these concerns, these results do provide some support for interpreting the significant PROHECO parameters in tables 9.17–9.19 as indicators of PROHECO effectiveness.

In addition to doing the sample selection bias analysis using Heckman-style correction techniques, we conducted additional analyses using propensity score matching. The propensity score method proceeds in two stages. In the first stage, the 0–1 treatment is regressed onto control variables, and the cases are then put into blocks that are based on ranges of the propensity to be treated. The key to this phase is the balancing, where for each block, roughly equal numbers of treatment and control group cases must be included. Conditional on being balanced, the first-stage regression creates a variable that is the propensity score, which is included in the second-stage analysis of average treatment effect (ATE). For this second phase, a series of estimators is available to match treatment and control cases that are based on their propensity scores, including nearest neighbor, kernel matching, radius matching, and so forth. Because of small numbers of matching cases, bootstrapped standard errors are sometimes necessary, especially with small samples (like ours).

The results from our analysis for 2002 and 2003 in all three subjects are supportive of a positive treatment in PROHECO. This finding is consistent with our other analyses, including the Heckman-style model, although the size of the PROHECO effect is generally smaller and less significant than what was found elsewhere. However, the propensity score treatment method does not appear to be the best "fit" for our particular treatment analysis. Why? The main problem is that, because of the balancing requirement in the first-stage regression, we are left with a very narrow comparison to be made in the second-stage ATE analysis. To achieve balancing, we found it necessary to restrict the first-stage propensity score generation to a very small group of independent variables—even smaller than what was used in the Heckman model. In effect, this restriction means that we interpreted the second-stage treatment analysis as the difference in achievement conditional on student gender, age, and some (not all) of the remaining household characteristics (including average SES for the school). None of the department dummies were included. As a result, this first-stage regression has little predictive power.

All of this explanation means that the PROHECO effect is a ceteris paribus treatment effect that is based on very little in the way of conditioning variables. So unsurprisingly, the treatment effect—though consistently positive—is not very big. By failing to control for other things that are different between PROHECO and control schools—like teacher education, experience, and so forth—our treatment effect, which we expect to be largely a function of teacher effort, is partly washed out by the other differences.

This description is one explanation, anyway. Because we are new to this particular technique, user error may be another factor. But it also seems plausible that, with small samples and collinear predictors, the propensity score analysis is simply too sensitive to allow us to base policy recommendations on it. For now, the conclusion we make here is probably the safest one to make.

Student Flows

We have more data to exploit on student outcomes than just test scores. For a program such as PROHECO, we need to recognize both the possibility that PROHECO schools affect things other than achievement and the possibility that those other differences confound our analysis of test scores. Those possibilities and the way they might affect our analysis have already been referred to in the discussion on selection bias and in the previous section. Here, we turn to some of those additional student outcomes as dependent variables.

Table 9.23 details the determinants of student absences. In estimation 1 for each year, the basic student and family SES controls are included as predictors (and are presented). For estimation 2, the full model corresponding to the earlier production function work for achievement is estimated (but is not presented). All models include controls for the departments. In both 2002 and 2003, students were asked how many days they had missed during the school year. Their responses are grouped into an ordered categorical variable. As a measure of student attendance, this grouping is problematic because students may feel a need to underestimate the number of days they have missed. We also know nothing about how many days the school was open, which forces us to treat the absences as being the same in percentage terms.

We used an ordered probit model, given the ordered nature of the dependent variable. The results do not change much when we use ordinary least squares regression. One limitation of the ordered probit is that the resulting coefficients are very hard to interpret and depend on the densities in each of the categories.

No evidence indicates that PROHECO schools have succeeded in reducing student absences. The results in table 9.23 show that not much

Table 9.23. Ordered Probit Estimates of Student-Reported Absences, 2002 and 2003

Variable	2002 estimations		2003 estimations	
	(1)	(2)	(1)	(2)
PROHECO school	−0.07	0.08	0.06	0.24
	(0.61)	(0.50)	(0.58)	(1.34)
Student and family characteristics				
Student is female	−0.04	−0.05	−0.03	−0.02
	(0.61)	(0.72)	(0.34)	(0.23)
No preschool	0.08	0.13	0.04	0.05
	(0.99)	(1.38)	(0.68)	(0.95)
Repeating grade	0.12	0.14	0.16	0.17
	(1.06)	(1.21)	(1.44)	(1.40)
Commuting time	—	—	0.005	0.004
			(2.31)**	(2.17)**
Homework help	0.10	0.09	0.21	0.20
	(1.31)	(1.05)	(2.41)**	(2.24)**
Person–room ratio	−0.008	−0.02	0.006	0.008
	(0.43)	(0.75)	(0.39)	(0.48)
SES factor	0.11	−0.11	−0.05	−0.05
	(2.12)**	(2.27)**	(1.07)	(1.02)
Student works	—	—	0.18	0.16
			(1.85)*	(1.63)
Community characteristics				
Average SES factor	−0.07	−0.12	0.07	0.04
	(0.83)	(1.26)	(0.88)	(0.38)
Remaining school–teacher controls?	No	Yes	No	No
Department fixed effects?	Yes	Yes	Yes	Yes
Sample size	1,203	1,203	939	939
Pseudo R^2	0.026	0.035	0.027	0.033

Notes: Dependent variable is an ordinal measure of student-reported absences. Asymptotic *t*-statistics in parentheses are based on robust standard errors. All estimations use fixed effects at department level. Asterisks refer to significance (two-tail) for *t*-test comparisons of independent sample means assuming equal variances (* = significant at 10 percent; ** = significant at 5 percent).
Source: UMCE (2003).

of anything significantly predicts this particular outcome, which is not very surprising given the difficulty of getting clean data on attendance. Some interesting results do occur, however, namely, that commuting time, student work, and family SES significantly affect absences (in the expected direction).

Our final outcome is a more direct measure of student flow rates and uses the school-reported information on repetition and dropout rates. For those outcomes, the data are collected by grade and then are pooled for each school, which results in more than six observations for each unit (school).

The results in table 9.24 show that, in 2002, PROHECO has no significant effect on student repetition, but for dropout, PROHECO has a moderately significant (negative) effect. Of the two control years, 2002 is clearly the most problematic because those data refer to the 2002 school year and not the 2003 year. We have the same problem with test scores, of course, because the exams were applied in different years. But an intertemporal effect for those outcomes seems more likely.

So the focus should probably be on 2003. The results are encouraging for PROHECO because they show improvements in repetition and dropout rates, even if the point estimates are not really significant. The remaining parameters are generally in the expected direction. Because we pooled the data, it is necessary to include intercept controls for each grade, and the results corroborate what is already known about inter-grade variation in the outcomes: With each successive grade, less repetition and dropout occurs. But we know nothing about interyear dropout with those data, so we urge some caution.

Conclusions

Three general conclusions are supported by the empirical work conducted in this paper. First, PROHECO schools are different from their public-school counterparts. Those differences are generally consistent with what we should expect, although not on all accounts. For example, PROHECO schools appear to be open more frequently and have people working more hours. Other differences, however, are less "positive." In particular, we have found that PROHECO teachers have fewer educational qualifications and complain about delays in payments, which suggests that the teacher management model is not leading to a better-suited teacher selection approach or to a more efficient payment model—in contrast to what we may have expected.

Additionally, we did not uncover substantial differences in either classroom processes or teaching and learning environments. Those are, to be sure, very difficult data to collect and measure with accuracy. Yet the

Table 9.24. OLS Estimates of Determinants of School Average Repetition and Dropout Rates, 2002 and 2003

	2002 estimations		2003 estimations	
Variable	Repetition	Dropout	Repetition	Dropout
PROHECO school	−0.26	−2.91	−3.52	−1.89
	(0.27)	(1.77)*	(1.68)*	(1.32)
Grade (grade 1 excluded)				
Grade 2	−8.01	−2.95	−8.55	−2.56
	(4.77)***	(2.02)**	(5.11)***	(1.35)
Grade 3	−12.80	−4.69	−13.10	−3.31
	(8.56)***	(3.08)***	(8.28)***	(2.18)**
Grade 4	−15.13	−2.74	−16.36	−3.29
	(9.28)***	(1.61)	(9.52)***	(1.80)*
Grade 5	−17.31	−4.78	−17.23	−5.07
	(11.28)***	(2.91)***	(10.41)***	(3.02)***
Grade 6	−18.81	−5.03	−19.05	−5.42
	(13.24)***	(2.68)***	(12.47)***	(3.58)***
School and community characteristics				
Single teacher school	−2.28	1.58	0.68	0.96
	(1.28)	(0.38)	(0.34)	(0.42)
Two teacher school	−2.50	2.10	−0.81	0.69
	(1.66)*	(0.72)	(0.38)	(0.39)
Total enrollment	−0.007	0.008	0.002	−0.007
	(0.74)	(0.56)	(0.18)	(0.76)
Average class size	−0.07	0.20	−0.14	−0.08
	(1.88)*	(1.91)*	(2.29)**	(1.71)
Physical deficiencies	0.45	1.85	1.40	2.17
	(0.49)	(1.36)	(1.22)	(1.99)
Community characteristics				
Average SES factor	−0.55	2.70	−0.58	−0.45
	(0.71)	(1.54)	(0.72)	(0.54)
Sum of services	0.16	−0.35	−0.31	−0.02
	(0.25)	(0.37)	(0.48)	(0.03)
Department fixed effects?	Yes	Yes	Yes	Yes
Sample size	794	784	680	668
R^2	0.274	0.127	0.299	0.064

Notes: Dependent variable is measured between 0 percent and 100 percent. Asymptotic t-statistics in parentheses are based on robust standard errors. Asterisks refer to significance (two-tail) for t-test comparisons of independent sample means assuming equal variances (* = significant at 10 percent; ** = significant at 5 percent; *** = significant at 1 percent).
Source: UMCE (2003).

finding still deserves mention because it forces us to consider the mechanisms that will predict PROHECO school "success." The picture that is formed in our analysis is one of PROHECO schools making better use of existing capacity, mainly by having teachers work more and by limiting class sizes. According to our data, however, it is not the case that PROHECO teachers are more effective in the classroom.

Should we even expect differences in classrooms? In theory, the answer is yes because the community school's "responsiveness" to its users should turn up in differences in curriculum and teaching methods. Our data on this question are incomplete both in terms of qualitative processes and parental involvement. But we need to consider another scenario where community school parents limit their oversight to the most visible aspects of teacher effort—teachers' attendance and hours worked—without entering classrooms and instigating changes in teaching methodology and classroom management. In other words, community parent councils may not be striving to create the best schools; they may simply want the most efficient schools.

Our second main finding is that differences in PROHECO school capacity use explain a substantial proportion of the observed differences in academic achievement between PROHECO and control schools. In particular, PROHECO schools make better use of existing capacity, mainly by having teachers work more and by limiting class sizes, thereby confirming the existence of a link between community schooling and classroom process variables such as days attended, frequency of homework, and individualized learning.

This finding is subject to concerns about selection bias, which we address in the empirical work, although only imperfectly. Overall, our results show that selection bias is an issue, but that the nature of the bias is to underestimate the true effect of PROHECO. In other words, with more data measuring other influences, the effect of PROHECO on achievement should increase. Essentially, teacher and school selection tend to underestimate the PROHECO effect, providing support for interpreting the significant PROHECO parameters as indicators of PROHECO effectiveness. Additionally, we also find no evidence of cohort selection bias.

The link between capacity use differences and student outcomes is encouraging, and it provides prima facie support for PROHECO schooling on pure efficiency grounds. This support is especially true when we consider that PROHECO teachers are paid less and have fewer qualifications. Nevertheless, we should avoid concluding that PROHECO schools are more cost-effective, especially given the large differences in student–teacher ratios and unmeasured aspects of parental involvement. A calculation of the exact cost per student in PROHECO and non-PROHECO schools would allow us to make a cost-effectiveness comparison.

Our conclusion is actually less of a conclusion and more of an appeal. We need to know more about what parents want in community schools and how they go about making their desires reality. Data that will be available later in the year hold the promise of addressing those questions. It is easy to assume that parent councils want what is best for their children and then act accordingly. But what do we really know about what groups of rural Honduran parents want from the local school and schooling in general? Furthermore, how do they collect information about what is happening in their schools? We can get at those questions in an indirect way with quantitative data. Future efforts should improve the quantitative data framework while expanding qualitative investigations.

References

Bedi, A. S., and J. H. Marshall. 2002. "Primary School Attendance in Honduras." *Journal of Development Economics* 69(1): 129–53.

Fuller, B., and M. Rivarola. 1998. "Nicaragua's Experiment to Decentralize Schools: Views of Parents, Teachers and Directors." Working Paper on Impact Evaluation of Education Reforms 5. World Bank, Washington, D.C.

Hadi, A. S. 1992. "A New Measure of Overall Potential Influence in Linear Regression." *Computational Statistics and Data Analysis* 14: 1–27.

Jimenez, E., and Y. Sawada. 1999. "Do Community-Managed Schools Work? An Evaluation of El Salvador's EDUCO Program." *World Bank Economic Review* 13(3): 415–41.

Marshall, J. H. 2003. "School Attendance and Academic Achievement: A Simultaneous Equations Approach." Stanford University, Stanford, Calif. Processed.

Marshall, J. H., and K. A. White. 2002. "Academic Achievement, School Attendance, and Education Policy in Honduras." Stanford University, Stanford, Calif. Processed.

McEwan, P. J., and J. H. Marshall. 2004. "Why Does Academic Achievement Vary across Countries? Evidence from Cuba and Mexico." *Education Economics* 12(3): 205–17.

Sawada, Y. 1999. "Community Participation, Teacher Effort, and Educational Outcome: The Case of El Salvador's EDUCO Program." William Davidson Institute Working Paper 307. University of Michigan Business School, Ann Arbor.

UMCE (Unidad de Medición de la Calidad Educativa), Universidad Pedagógica Nacional Francisco Morazán (UPN), and Secretaria de Educación (SE). 2003. "Informe nacional de rendimiento academico 2002." Tegucigalpa, Honduras. Processed.

10
Teacher Incentives and Student Achievement in Nicaraguan Autonomous Schools

Caroline E. Parker
Education Development Center, Inc.

This chapter looks at Nicaragua's decentralization program, known as autonomy, through the lens of teacher incentives and student achievement. Although there have been numerous studies to date on Nicaraguan autonomy, most of them have focused on the decentralization of decision-making. Few studies have looked at what effects decentralization has on teacher behavior and whether changes in teacher behavior have an effect on student achievement. This chapter considers the following question: Have the changes in autonomy, particularly those related to teacher incentives, led to improved student outcomes?

To address that question, the chapter first describes the national context of Nicaragua's education reform, next considers the analytic framework and the methods of the study, and then answers the research question.

Nicaraguan Context

Nicaragua, a country of 5.3 million people, has 2.2 million children and youth of school age. The average age of Nicaraguans is 22 years, which has been rising for the past 10 years, but still ranks the country as having the youngest population in Latin America. The average total education for Nicaraguans is 4.6 years. Adult illiteracy rates range around 33 percent, and 36.8 percent of the adult population does not have a complete primary education; 71.5 percent of adults have not completed secondary education. Sixty percent of teenagers are not in the education system. Only 4.7 percent

I would like to thank Maria Martiniello, Patrick McEwan, Andrew Ballard Ragatz, Lucrecia Santibáñez, Yasuyuki Sawada, and Emiliana Vegas, for their comments, as well as the members of the April 22 Workshop. I would also like to thank Reyna López of the Nicaraguan Ministry of Education for providing valuable assistance.

of the adult population has university degrees (MECD 2003b). Thus, this
study of educational change and quality takes place in the context of less
than full access to all tiers of education. Nicaragua, like other developing
countries in the 21st century, must address issues of school quality con-
currently with addressing issues of access—a forbidding challenge
(Tedesco and López 2002).

Nicaragua also faces educational challenges amid long-term social and
political upheaval. Economically, although Nicaragua has been experi-
encing growth over the past 10 years, the slowness of the growth means
that many Nicaraguans continue to be poor: 46 percent live in poverty,
with 15 percent in extreme poverty (MIGOB 2003). Nicaraguans' per
capita income ranges around US$700 annually. Official unemployment is
11.3 percent, but of the employed, 64 percent are in precarious jobs (informal sector) and 33 percent are underemployed (MIGOB 2003). The country's generalized poverty means that both the government and individual
families have extremely limited resources to invest in education.

Nicaraguan Autonomy

Among the education reforms sponsored by the Nicaraguan Ministry of
Education, Culture, and Sports (MECD) during the past 15 years is a school-
based reform of management decentralization known as autonomy. Begun
in 1993, the school-based management model had three goals (Castillo
1998):

1. Increase community participation in educational administration.
2. Obtain financial resources for schools beyond government funding.
3. Increase efficiency in the use of human and financial resources for
   schools.

The decentralization began within a political framework of "returning
education to local communities" (Arcia and Belli 2001). However, a recent
qualitative analysis of autonomous schools found that the reform has not
reconstructed the social pact to increase parents' role in their children's
education. Instead, it has a "financial-administrative" focus (Asencio and
others 2001, p. 6). The MECD first decentralized the 20 largest secondary
schools in Managua, hoping that they would become a model of autonomy for other schools. The autonomy process continued to expand through
2000. There were experiments with municipal decentralization in rural
areas, and there continue to be various iterations of school-based management. In 2002, 37 percent (1,781) of all Nicaraguan primary and secondary
schools were autonomous (MECD 2004). Autonomous schools served 63 percent of students (501,000) and had 13,419 teachers (MECD 2004).[129] Of

---

129. These numbers differ slightly from numbers in other MECD data.

472 public secondary schools, 331 were autonomous (MECD 2003a). Of the 252,000 public secondary school students in 2002, only 42,000 were served outside the autonomous school system.

In the original autonomy reform, improving educational quality was not among the top three goals. The underlying assumption, however, was that by increasing community participation, improving a school's financial status, and improving efficiency, the final result would be higher-quality education. The following section carefully examines the history and current status of autonomy as background for answering the primary research question of whether students in autonomous schools perform better than those in centralized schools.

Community Participation

Autonomy, or school-based management, gives greater decisionmaking power to school directors, teachers, and parents. Autonomous schools form school councils made up of parents, teachers, the school director, and a nonvoting student representative. Parents and teachers are selected in various ways, ranging from general elections to appointment by a local mayor or MECD delegate (Gershberg 2003). The autonomous school council hires and fires teachers and the director; designs the annual plan; approves school rules; modifies the curriculum within Ministry of Education, Culture, and Sports standards; and authorizes the budget (Castillo 1998). In reality, school directors dominate school councils in many schools (Castillo 1998; Fuller and Rivarola 1998; King 1996), and parents and teachers have less participation than originally envisioned. Decentralization does appear to be related to greater local decisionmaking at autonomous schools, but evaluations have been mixed about the participation level on school councils. Neither parents nor teachers generally feel that they have much authority, but directors have said that they feel they have greater ability to make decisions (di Gropello 1997; King 1996). The extent of participation by stakeholders appears to depend on the leadership style of the school director (Asencio and others 2001; Asencio Florez and others 2001). Teacher participation appears to wane when teachers' financial incentives are smaller (Gershberg 2003; Gershberg and Winkler 2000).

Finance

The most contentious of the three goals in the autonomy process were the financial aspects (Gershberg 2003). Antidecentralization activists emphasized the privatizing characteristics of charging for public education. For many poor Nicaraguans, autonomy did, indeed, seem like another word for privatization. Although autonomy encompasses far more than simply the parent's financial commitment to a child's education, the monthly fee was foremost in parents' minds in Nicaragua's crisis economy (Fuller and Rivarola 1998). In 1995, the government determined, through a constitutional amendment, that autonomous primary schools could not charge obligatory fees, but secondary schools were allowed to charge up to a certain amount (about US$2 monthly) in obligatory fees (Castillo 1998; Fuller and Rivarola 1998). This resolution meant that all secondary schools could charge monthly fees, and critics continued to predict that the policy would exacerbate educational inequities. In 2002, however, new legislation, which for the first time legalized school-based management, eliminated the right to charge fees. Thus, by law, neither primary nor secondary schools may charge obligatory fees for attendance, although they may strongly encourage voluntary donations.

The MECD has two funding structures: one for nonautonomous (centralized) schools and one for autonomous schools. The ministry directly pays all the costs of the centralized schools. For the autonomous schools, it pays each school on a per student basis and on a sliding scale that was implemented in July 2002, by which smaller schools get more per student than larger schools. The monthly amounts range from about 78 córdobas (US$6) for small schools to 52 córdobas (US$4) per student for large schools (Morales 2002). Proactive directors can seek outside donations and get external funding from both national and international sources. Because schools may no longer charge obligatory fees, the ministry recognizes that one of its challenges is to make sure that no schools are prohibiting entrance on the basis of ability to pay fees. In addition to per student funding sent to each school, teachers get a twice-yearly bonus from the government. The bonuses are currently funded by the World Bank and depend on the number of students in each classroom. The bonus is supposed to encourage teachers to work hard on student retention. In 2003, 16,000 teachers in autonomous schools received the biannual bonus, among a total of 31,000 teachers in the entire system (autonomous and centralized). The bonus in 2003 averaged 800 córdobas (about US$52).

Centralized schools have a different funding structure. The ministry pays all their expenses—water bill, electric bill, teacher salaries, and so on. Less of a relationship exists between the number of students and how much a school receives. Teachers in autonomous schools can be let go if they do not have at least 35 students in their classroom, which is not the case in centralized schools. About 15,000 teachers are not in the autonomous system.

Many of the schools that initially chose autonomy convinced their teachers that it would lead to higher salaries, because the increased freedom to charge fees would improve their financial situation. In this way, the ministry saved money at the central level, and, theoretically, schools obtained more money for school improvements (Arnove 1995). Thus, whereas parents often equated autonomy with privatization, teachers often equated it with improved salaries (accompanied by less job stability).

When the MECD eliminated obligatory fees in 2002, some teachers interviewed described the change as the end of autonomy because it was the end of their monthly, school-based bonuses. In practice, many primary schools, especially those in poor and rural areas, had eliminated the obligatory fees well before 2002, and the financial benefits of autonomy had all but disappeared for teachers (Asencio and others 2001). In contrast, some secondary schools have continued charging fees despite the legal mandate against them (Asencio and others 2001).

In 2003, the annual educational budget reached US$100 million, which represents almost 4.5 percent of Nicaragua's gross domestic product. However, this figure averages only US$72 per student throughout the system. Of the budget, 76 percent goes toward teacher salaries. Almost 20 percent of the educational budget comes from foreign loans.

Efficiency

The third goal of Nicaraguan autonomy was efficiency. By transferring fiscal responsibility and decisionmaking to the school level, school directors, school councils, and teachers would become accountable directly to parents, thus increasing the ability of stakeholders to directly affect education. Among others are three ways in which improved efficiency can target, in particular, teacher behaviors: teacher incentives, increased resources, and professional development.[130]

Primary school teachers earn an average of US$111 monthly, about 70 percent of the government-determined market basket (MECD 2003b). They have, on average, 11 years of education, equivalent to a high school degree. Secondary school teachers have an average of 13 years of education and earn an average of US$117 monthly (MECD 2003b). Most primary school teachers are trained at normal schools, which are teacher training institutes. In 2000, 73.6 percent of teachers reported having the requisite teaching certificates from normal schools (MECD 2004). All newly hired teachers must have certificates. However, many rural schools do not have enough qualified teachers, and Normal Schools continue to be under enrolled, indicating that there will continue to be a shortage of qualified teachers.

Incentives

Teacher incentives have been an important element in decentralization from the beginning of the reform. For a school to become autonomous, 80 percent of teachers must vote in favor of autonomy. One of the biggest selling points for teachers was the promise of higher salaries through

---

130. Although decentralization of decisionmaking has been a key element of Nicaraguan autonomy, this data set does not include questions about decisionmaking.

bonuses and incentives. Teachers faced lower job security, however, because in autonomous schools the councils hire and fire teachers. Thus, teachers without at least 35 students in their classroom can be let go. Autonomous schools can give their teachers incentives from two sources. First, the World Bank funds an incentives program that is based on student attendance. Teachers receive biannual incentives tied to the number of students who are registered and who study in their class. Incentives average almost a month's salary. The second form of incentive depends on each school's individual resources. Teachers receive incentives drawn from monthly fees collected from students. Because autonomous schools kept 100 percent of all fees collected but centralized schools kept only 50 percent, becoming autonomous brought with it the prospect of increased income for schools and, therefore, increased incentives for teachers. In a recent survey of autonomous schools, monthly fees resulted in up to 5 percent additional revenue for the school. Generally, half of this revenue is given to teachers, half to school maintenance. Teachers in autonomous primary schools receive from 0 to 30 percent of their salary in bonuses, while in secondary schools they earn from 0 to 50 percent (Gershberg 2003).

Infrastructure and Material Resources
Because of their greater financial independence, autonomous schools also have potentially more resources and better-quality infrastructure. In the early years, autonomous schools often received government or international funding. The World Bank has funded a US$14 million education program that has targeted funds to autonomous schools. Directors of autonomous schools are encouraged to seek alternative sources of funding, both in the local community and through international contacts. Likewise, one of the school council's stated responsibilities is to diversify financial sources for the school. Thus, autonomous schools would be likely to have more resources than centralized schools.

Professional Development
Finally, teacher professional development has been recognized as a critical element in school improvement. Teachers' salaries are the single greatest expense for the MECD, and efficient use of those resources includes improving the quality of teaching through further education and training for those teachers. The initial stages of the autonomy reform did not emphasize professional development, and the MECD continues to provide professional development to all schools, centralized and autonomous. Autonomous schools have the potential to provide more and better-quality professional development, although no studies to date have identified whether they do so. In addition, autonomous schools may theoretically choose their own curriculum. However, they rarely do so in practice (Asencio and others 2001; Asencio Florez and others 2001).

Autonomy Today

School autonomy was institutionalized with the "Educational Participation" law of May 2002. The major elements of the new law include the following (MECD 2003c):

- No schools may charge obligatory fees (although schools continue to be responsible for all school finances).
- The name "autonomous schools" has been eliminated, and autonomous schools are now termed "schools of educational participation."[131]
- All schools must become schools of educational participation by May 2006 (although there are no funds for schools to implement decentralization, and there have been no new autonomous schools since 2001).
- There is a renewed emphasis on developing school councils and community councils. School councils administer all funds; they hire and fire teachers and principals.
- The decentralization structures, including the funding process, are a part of school structures.
- Autonomous schools receive per student funding.
- The school director and school council have financial and administrative responsibilities.
- Parents have an active role in decisionmaking through the school councils.
- Directors have academic development responsibilities.

A recent evaluation of autonomous schools found that "the Autonomous School is a concept that is not sufficiently understood" (Asencio and others 2001, p. 8). Throughout my study of the effects of decentralization on teacher practice, I have kept in mind that definitions of autonomy vary by school, that the implementation of autonomy varies by school, and that recent legislation has legalized some aspects of autonomy while changing others such as the name. Although school-based management may be clearly defined on paper, in practice there is great variation within Nicaraguan schools.

Previous Studies of Nicaraguan Autonomy

Nicaraguan autonomy has been studied from numerous angles. Some studies focus on governance issues and look at shifts in decisionmaking (Arnove 1995; Gershberg 1999a; King 1996; King, Ozler, and Rawlings 2000). Others focus on finance (Gershberg 2003; Gershberg and Meade 2003); on equity (Castillo 1998; di Gropello 1997; di Gropello and Cominetti

---

131. In my study, decentralized schools will be referred to as autonomous schools because the terminology continues to be in common use in Nicaragua. Nonautonomous schools are referred to as centralized schools.

1998); on parental involvement (Fuller and Rivarola 1998; Gershberg 1999a, 1999b); and finally, on student outcomes (King and Ozler 2000).

This chapter contributes to the literature on student outcomes. It attempts to address some of the methodological challenges faced by King and Ozler (2000) in their previous study of student outcomes (discussed in the Methods section that follows). It looks more closely than previous studies do at what teachers' characteristics are and at what happens in the classroom. It uses the first wave of an important new data set that is the most-comprehensive study of student achievement to date in Nicaragua.

The autonomy process has been a far-reaching reform that has touched many aspects of the educational process in Nicaraguan primary and secondary schools. However, any study of the effects of autonomy must remember the following:

- Overall funding for public schooling in Nicaragua continues to be very low, and there is a risk that it has not yet reached a threshold of spending that can significantly and positively affect student outcomes. With only US$72 per student, there may simply not be enough resources to provide professional development, materials, and infrastructure that will allow any school—whether decentralized or not—to improve student performance.
- Despite being a reform that is now 10 years old, autonomy has experienced several significant challenges that may affect its ability to improve student performance:

  - Proponents of autonomy spent many years fighting accusations of privatization and were placed in a defensive position rather than being able to promote community participation.
  - The initial emphasis on financial autonomy led many schools to focus almost exclusively on financial aspects, to the detriment of school improvement.
  - The new educational participation law in 2002 has led to some confusion because of the elimination of the term "autonomy." Although the law states that *all* schools will now have the decentralized characteristics of autonomous schools, the change is often interpreted as being the end of autonomy.
  - Studies have shown that there is generalized confusion over what autonomy is and what it is supposed to do for schools, teachers, and students (Asencio and others 2001).

In summary, although this study separates autonomous from centralized schools, fewer differences than expected may materialize between autonomous and centralized schools, even after 10 years of reform. In the context of Nicaraguan education, asking whether autonomy has led to improvements in student outcomes may be the wrong question. The correct question would identify which school characteristics are associated with improved student outcomes and would use that information for policy development. This study asks the first question and concludes with implications for the second.

Methods

Analytic Framework

This study uses impact evaluation methods, which involve establishing a counterfactual state (centralized schools) against which the current state (autonomous schools) will be compared. The research question considers the effect of school characteristics and teacher behavior on student achievement, in this case on Spanish and math scores. The multilevel model estimates the effect of the dummy variable autonomy (A) on student outcomes (Y) for student i in the classroom of teacher j. The model controls for observed characteristics of students (S) and for teacher characteristics (T). The relationship can be written as

$$Y_{ij} = \alpha_j + \beta_1(\text{Autonomous})_j + \beta_2 S_i + \beta_3 T_j + \varepsilon_{ij}$$

Although the multilevel model addresses the nesting issue and is able to identify the teachers' characteristics, it does not address the bias of sample selection. Previous analysis of data looking at student outcomes in Nicaraguan autonomy (King and Ozler 2000) has been subject to criticism because of its statistical procedures (Kaestner and Gershberg 2002). King and Ozler used panel data that matched autonomous and centralized schools, collected data on schools and individuals, and administered math and Spanish tests to a randomly selected group of students in the fourth grade and in the third year of secondary school. They faced two significant challenges with these data: a very large attrition rate of almost 50 percent (Kaestner and Gershberg 2002) and sample selection bias. Because schools are not randomly assigned to autonomous status and students are not randomly assigned to schools, any study of differences between autonomous and centralized schools can suffer from selection bias. Despite King and Ozler's use of instrumental variables estimation to address this challenge, the results have been open to criticism.

The data set used in my analysis does not have the problem of attrition, but it does face the same challenges of selection bias. Schools were not randomly chosen to be autonomous; thus, those schools that became autonomous may share certain characteristics beyond autonomy that contribute to student outcomes (some that have been suggested include student characteristics of socioeconomic status or parent education, or school characteristics of director skills or teacher quality). To address this potential bias, I have chosen propensity score matching using stratification and nearest-neighbor matching. There are two levels of selection bias. The first is at the school level, because certain types of schools may be more likely to become autonomous than others. The second is at the student level, because in areas where there are both autonomous and centralized schools, certain types of students may be more likely to attend autonomous schools over centralized schools.

Because I am interested in student outcomes, I have conducted the propensity score matching at the student level, including appropriate teacher-level variables. In addition, the variables that best contribute to developing a propensity score are those that can be expected to be associated both with participation and with the outcome. At the student level those variables are socioeconomic status and student age. At the school level, the variables could be teacher years of education and teacher experience, but neither of those variables is significantly different between autonomous and centralized schools in the studies. Other school-level variables that are significantly different include incentives, teachers' view of school conditions, and directors' provision of professional development. I argue that by using propensity score matching, I address the limitations of selection bias and that my outcomes reflect more accurately the differences between autonomous and centralized schools. I report results using multilevel modeling without correcting for selection bias, as well as results using stratification and nearest-neighbor matching with propensity scores.

Statistical Analysis

The model in this paper builds on the premise that autonomy has led to changes in teacher incentives; that the changes in teacher incentives have led to changes in teacher behavior; and that those changes, in turn, have led to improved student achievement. I test the hypothesis with the equation described in the Analytic Framework section earlier. The variables were placed into one of the following clusters: three control variable clusters—student-level characteristics, classroom characteristics, and school characteristics; and three question clusters—incentives, infrastructure and materials, and technical assistance. For both the third- and sixth-grade outcomes, each of the variable clusters was first tested independently. Then those variables that reached significance were kept in the model until a final model was obtained. The model tables include each of the initial models and the final model. The models were tested using both random effects and fixed effects. The fixed-effects model captures *all* differences by teacher, rather than just the variables included in the model. The fixed-effects models do not provide a coefficient for the difference between autonomous and centralized schools. Rather, they help us to see the overall differences between teachers, regardless of school type.

Because the multilevel model does not adequately account for selection bias, propensity score matching was done using both stratification and nearest-neighbor matching. The propensity score was determined by considering which variables contribute to both the treatment (being autonomous or not) and the outcome. After looking at propensity scores using variables from all of the clusters previously described, I chose the propensity score using the variables that remain in the final multilevel model. This choice makes sense substantively because the propensity score describes schools that are essentially similar on all the variables of interest and then tests for the difference in means between schools that share similar propensity scores.[132] The differences in results among the three different statistical processes are discussed later.

Data

The data were collected as part of a World Bank–funded project, the first national study of educational quality, which was administered in 2002 to a nationally representative sample of third- and sixth-grade students. Students were given tests in Spanish and mathematics. Students, teachers, parents, school directors, and school council members filled out questionnaires about their school. The schools were chosen using a stratified random sample by region, school type, urbanicity, and multigrade modality, thereby allowing analysis at various levels, including school type. All students in the third and sixth grades were tested (third- and sixth-grade samples were developed separately). The study encompassed all school types, including private schools that do and do not receive state funding.

Sample

This study uses information from the director, teacher, parent, and student interviews, as well as test results from both third- and sixth-grade students.[133] For the purposes of this study, the sample was restricted to only autonomous and centralized public schools in order to focus on differences between the two public school models.

Most student scores fall in the basic range. Fewer than 20 percent of students in any grade level or subject scored proficient. Those results include not only centralized and autonomous schools, but also private subsidized and private schools, which, on average, have higher scores than public schools. Overall achievement levels on the Spanish and math assessments

---

132. The propensity score matching details are available from the author upon request.

133. The socioeconomic status variable was built from the parent survey, and student data on gender and age were taken from the student data.

were low, and many students performed well below grade level (MECD 2003a). The tests were designed through extensive consultation with experienced teachers and in accordance with the national standards for Spanish and mathematics. Thus, the ministry staff considers them to be aligned to the curriculum. The generally low results indicate that students are not learning what teachers think they are teaching the students. The tests were scored using Item Response Theory (MECD 2003a). In the following sections, I first describe the results obtained using third-grade data, then follow with sixth-grade data.

Third-Grade Descriptive Statistics

There are 134 schools in the third-grade study: 52 percent autonomous and 48 percent centralized. Of the sections, 80 percent meet in the morning, 20 percent in the afternoon. Of the directors, 63 percent reported using multigrade classrooms. Among the schools, 71 percent are in rural areas; 29 percent are in urban areas. The sample is evenly divided between boys and girls.

The director and teacher interviews asked extensive questions related to incentives, infrastructure and materials, and professional development and classroom practice. This conformation permitted the development of a series of variables that describe director and teacher perceptions and practice.

As already described, certain uniform governance policies occur across autonomous schools, which include government funding formulas, fiscal responsibility, and the practice of hiring and firing of teachers and directors. Variations exist from school to school in the concrete implementation of autonomy, but this data set does not include a detailed study of decisionmaking patterns. Thus, the statistical analyses focus specifically on those school practices that could have a direct effect on teacher behavior, rather than on those governance practices that are most closely associated with autonomy.

Control Variables
The statistical analyses control for variables that may affect teacher behavior or student achievement but that are not part of the research question. Student controls include student age, student sex, and household socioeconomic status (SES). Teacher controls include class size, teacher's experience, teacher's years of education, section mean of household SES, section mean of age, student absences reported today and last week, and number of students repeating grade. School control variables include school type, total number of students in school, mean school SES, and urbanicity.

The students who attend autonomous schools differ significantly from those who attend centralized schools in a number of areas. On average, students in autonomous schools are younger than those in centralized schools. On average, students in autonomous schools are also wealthier than those in centralized schools.

Average student absences vary by school type. Teachers reported more absent students in autonomous schools (6.17) than in centralized schools (4.98). Table 10.1 provides descriptive information for all the control variables.

In addition to identifying schools as autonomous or nonautonomous, this study breaks down autonomous schools by the number of years each has been autonomous. Table 10.2 shows the breakdown by years.

Question Variables
Incentives
Although financial incentives in the form of teacher bonuses are the most common incentive, the questionnaire asked about eight different incentives (financial incentives, job promotions, scholarships for further study, honor roll, medals, school supplies, extra books, and teacher field trips). The question was asked of both the teacher and the director. For this study,

Table 10.1. Control Variables: Third-Grade Mean Values, by School Type

Variable	Centralized	Autonomous	Total
Student characteristics:			
Student age***	9.8	9.6	9.68
Student SES***	−0.308	−0.192	−0.242
Classroom characteristics:			
Classroom mean SES	−0.593	−0.531	−0.56
Mean age	10.2	10.1	10.15
Mean class size*	25.9	30.6	28.3
Teaching experience	11.7	11.3	11.5
Total years education	12.2	12.2	12.2
Number of students repeating this year	2.86	2.93	2.89
Students absent this week*	4.98	6.17	5.59
Students absent today	3.6	5.8	4.7
School characteristics:			
Total students***	381	916	686

Note: *$p < 0.05$, ***$p < 0.001$.
Source: Author's calculations.

Table 10.2. Years of School Autonomy, Third Grade

Years of autonomy	Frequency	Percentage
Not autonomous	64	48.0
1	9	6.7
2	0	0.0
3	3	2.24
4	29	21.64
5	3	2.24
6	11	8.21
7	15	11.19
Total	134	100.00

Source: Author's calculations.

the financial incentive variable was used in table 10.3 because it has been—and continues to be—the most common and popular of the incentives.

Both teachers and directors in autonomous schools report higher rates of financial incentives than the rates in centralized schools. However, it is interesting to note that although 74 percent of autonomous school directors say that teachers get incentives, only 67 percent of autonomous school teachers say they do (table 10.3).

Resources
Four variables address infrastructure and material resources. The first is the mean of 30 variables asking teachers about the condition of certain items at their school, ranging from chalk to computer labs. The last three variables focus on teaching resources: whether or not teachers have access to the curriculum standards and curriculum guides, and how

Table 10.3. Third-Grade Descriptive Statistics for Incentive Variables

Variable	Centralized schools (percent)	Autonomous schools (percent)
Teacher reports financial incentive***	22	67
Director reports teacher financial incentive***	36	74

Note: ***$p < 0.001$.
Source: Author's calculations.

Table 10.4. Third-Grade Descriptive Statistics for Infrastructure and Material Resources, by School Type

Resource	Centralized	Autonomous	Total
School condition according to teacher***	1.91	2.27	2.1
Years implementing standards	1.97	1.93	1.95
Has copy of curriculum standards*	62%	74%	
Has copy of curriculum guides	78%	87%	

Note: *$p < 0.05$, ***$p < 0.001$.
Source: Author's calculations.

long the school has been implementing the new curriculum standards (table 10.4).

Professional Development

Four variables address professional development: whether the director meets with teachers, whether the director provides technical assistance to teachers, whether the director gives Spanish workshops to teachers, and whether the director gives math workshops to teachers (table 10.5).

Outcome Variables

Student scores on the Spanish and math tests were used as outcome variables. As shown in table 10.6, third-graders in autonomous schools scored significantly better in both the Spanish and math tests.

Table 10.7 shows average school scores by years of autonomy.[134] Schools with more years of autonomy have, on average, higher average Spanish scores ($p < 0.10$). There is no significant difference by years of autonomy for math scores.

In conclusion, some characteristics of students and schools differ significantly by school type, but not as many as might be expected after 10 years of reform. Both teachers and directors report higher levels of incentives in autonomous schools, and those levels reach significance. More autonomous directors report giving technical assistance to their teachers. Autonomous schools are more likely to have copies of the curriculum standards. In general, autonomous schools appear to provide more incentives, resources, and professional development than do centralized schools. The statistical analysis attempts to provide a model for better understanding which of the characteristics contribute to the differences in scores between centralized and autonomous schools.

---

134. This table (as well as table 10.14) looks at the frequency of classrooms rather than at schools, which is why there are 152 observations rather than 134.

Table 10.5. Third-Grade Descriptive Statistics for Professional Development, by School Type

Variable	Centralized	Autonomous	Total
Director meets with third-grade teachers	1.96	2.12	2.05
Director gives technical assistance to third-grade teachers***	62%	94%	
Director gives Spanish workshops	44%	61%	
Director gives math workshops	54%	58%	

Note: ***$p < 0.001$.
Source: Author's calculations.

Table 10.6. Third-Grade Achievement Scores, by School Type

Variable	Centralized	Autonomous	Total
Spanish score*	241.6	245.8	243.9
Math score*	245.3	248.8	247.2

Note: *$p < 0.05$.
Source: Author's calculations.

Table 10.7. Third-Grade Spanish and Math Scores, by Years of Autonomy ($n = 152$)

Years of autonomy	Spanish score~	Math score	Frequency
Not autonomous	237.5	250.2	74
1	239.2	248.0	12
2			
3	241.1	259.2	3
4	249.3	257.9	32
5	265.7	255.6	5
6	242.1	249.6	10
7	246.1	257.9	16

Note: ~$p < 0.10$.
Source: Author's calculations.

Sixth-Grade Descriptive Statistics

The sixth-grade study covers 145 schools: 52 percent autonomous and 48 percent centralized. Of the sections, 62 percent meet in the morning and 38 percent in the afternoon. Among the directors, 64 percent reported using multigrade classrooms. Among the schools, 68 percent are in rural areas and 32 percent are in urban areas. In the sample, 53 percent are girls and 47 percent are boys.

Control Variables
Table 10.8 shows the student, classroom, and school variables that are controlled for in this study. Sixth-grade students resemble third-grade students in many ways. Teachers have similar years of teaching experience and education, and differences between autonomous and centralized schools are similar.

Sixth-grade students in autonomous schools are slightly younger than those in centralized schools, but the difference is not significant. On aver-

Table 10.8. Control Variables: Sixth-Grade Mean Values, by School Type

Variable	Centralized	Autonomous	Total
Student characteristics:			
Student age	12.84	12.74	12.78
Student SES***	−0.226	−0.111	−0.156
Classroom characteristics:			
Classroom mean SES*	−0.467	−0.289	−0.369
Mean student age	13.1	12.9	12.99
Mean class size***	26.0	33.5	30.0
Teaching experience	12.91	13.64	13.31
Total years education	12.9	12.9	12.9
Number of students repeating this year	0.739	0.64	0.684
Students absent this week**	3.03	5.53	4.44
Students absent today**	1.67	4.44	3.22
School characteristics:			
Total students	343.4	486.6	417.3

Notes: *$p < 0.05$, **$p < 0.01$, ***$p < 0.001$.
Source: Author's calculations.

Table 10.9. Years of School Autonomy, Sixth Grade

Years of autonomy	Frequency	Percentage
Not autonomous	69	47.59
1	15	10.34
2	1	0.69
3	2	1.38
4	31	21.38
5	3	2.07
6	9	6.21
7	15	10.34
Total	145	100

Source: Author's calculations.

age, students in autonomous schools are wealthier than those in centralized schools ($p < 0.001$). Mean classroom socioeconomic status differs significantly by school type. Class size in autonomous schools is significantly larger than in centralized schools. Autonomous schools have higher levels of student absence. No significant differences exist in teaching experience or educational levels by school type. Table 10.9 describes schools by years of autonomy.

Question Variables
Incentives
As for third grade, significant differences in incentives exist between autonomous and centralized schools. Both teachers and directors in autonomous schools report higher levels of incentives than do those in centralized schools. Whereas 87 percent of directors in autonomous schools report that teachers get financial incentives, only 64 percent of teachers report receiving incentives (table 10.10), an even greater gap than in third grade.

Table 10.10. Sixth-Grade Descriptive Statistics for Incentive Variables

Variable	Centralized	Autonomous
Teacher reports financial incentive***	27%	64%
Director reports teacher financial incentive***	38%	87%

Note: ***$p < 0.001$.
Source: Author's calculations.

Table 10.11. Sixth-Grade Descriptive Statistics for Infrastructure/Material Resources, by School Type

Resource	Centralized	Autonomous	Total
School condition according to teacher**	2.099	2.599	2.325
Years implementing standards	2.0	1.86	1.92
Has copy of curriculum standards	71%	81%	
Has copy of curriculum guides	89%	91%	

Note: **$p < 0.01$.
Source: Authors' calculations.

Resources

As seen in table 10.11, teachers in autonomous schools report significantly better school conditions than do teachers in centralized schools. No significant differences exist in the supply of curriculum standards and guides, although slightly more autonomous schools have both standards and guides.

Professional development

As with third grade, more professional development is reported in autonomous than in centralized schools, although only the levels of technical assistance from the director reach significance (table 10.12).

Outcome Variables

Individual math scores are higher in centralized schools (not significant), while no significant difference exists in Spanish scores (table 10.13). No significant difference in scores exists by years of autonomy (table 10.14).

Table 10.12. Sixth-Grade Descriptive Statistics for Professional Development, by School Type

Variable	Centralized	Autonomous	Total
Director meets with sixth-grade teachers	1.86	1.93	1.9
Director gives technical assistance to sixth-grade teachers*	76%	90%	
Director gives Spanish workshops	37%	46%	
Director gives math workshops	38%	51%	

Note: *$p < 0.05$.
Source: Authors' calculations.

Table 10.13. Sixth-Grade Achievement Scores, by School Type

Variable	Centralized	Autonomous	Total
Spanish score	241.9	242.2	242.1
Math score	248.0	245.5	246.5

Note: *$p < 0.05$.
Source: Authors' calculations.

Results

Third-Grade Results

The research question asks whether student outcomes differ by school type and which teacher or school characteristics are associated with those student outcomes. Multilevel models were built using student- and teacher-level variables. Table 10.15 shows the multilevel models for third-grade Spanish (appendix 10.A provides an expanded version of table 10.15).

When looking only at the difference between autonomous and centralized schools, one finds that autonomous schools, on average, score almost seven points higher on the third-grade Spanish assessment. However, when one controls student characteristics and the role of technical assistance, the coefficient drops to under five points and is no longer significant. As would be expected, student-level variables contributed to the final models. Student age and socioeconomic status are significantly associated with Spanish scores. In addition, girls, on average, score higher than boys. Interestingly, when directors give technical assistance, students score, on average,

Table 10.14. Spanish and Math Scores, by Years of Autonomy ($n = 152$)

Years of autonomy	Spanish score	Math score	Frequency
Not autonomous	237.6	247.0	95
1	232.7	244.4	18
2	237.6	210.1	1
3	239.0	249.0	4
4	238.7	248.7	42
5	233.2	226.9	5
6	236.1	249.3	14
7	245.4	245.3	33

Source: Authors' calculations.

Table 10.15. Third-Grade Spanish Achievement

Variable	Intercept only	Autonomous only	Final model	Fixed effects
Student SES			5.224***	4.617**
Student age			3.205***	3.133***
Student gender			−5.754***	−5.238**
School is autonomous		6.914*	4.576	Dropped
Director gives technical assistance to teachers			14.589**	Dropped
Constant	242.6***	239.0***	201.3***	217.3***
R^2	n.a.	n.a.	n.a.	0.1657
Log likelihood	−16,021.8	−16,019.9	−14,638.2	n.a.

n.a. = not applicable
*Note: *$p < 0.05$, **$p < 0.01$, ***$p < 0.001$.*
Source: Author's calculations.

15 points higher. This finding indicates an important role for onsite professional development in both centralized and autonomous schools.

The fixed-effects model describes the overall difference in scores between teachers. The scores do differ significantly by teacher, but the R^2 is 0.17, meaning that the model explains only 17 percent of the variation between teachers. This finding indicates that the variables used in the statistical analyses do not explain a large portion of the variation in scores between teachers.[135] Table 10.16 shows the multilevel modeling for mathematics.

On average, students in autonomous schools scored 3.9 points higher on mathematics than did students in centralized schools (not significant).[136] Like Spanish scores, mathematics scores are highly dependent on student characteristics. However, whereas girls score significantly higher than boys in the Spanish model, gender does not have a significant effect in mathematics. Similarly, socioeconomic status is not a significant predictor of mathematics outcomes. In contrast, age is a strong predictor of math scores. Older students tend to have higher math scores than younger students ($p < 0.0001$). The only classroom characteristic that contributes to third-grade math scores is the teacher's years of education, and it is negatively associated with math scores. Students, on average, have lower math scores in classrooms where their teachers have more education.

---

135. The final model was chosen after testing a large number of student-, teacher-, and school-level variables. This model had the greatest explanatory power.

136. Although this variable is significant in a simple regression model, it is not in the multilevel.

Table 10.16. Third-Grade Mathematics Achievement

Variable	Intercept only	Autonomous only	Final model	Fixed effects
Student SES			1.5	2.6~
Student age			3.01***	2.6***
School is autonomous		3.87	3.9	Dropped
Teacher years of education			−1.9**	Dropped
Constant	250.5***	248.5***	242.2***	222.1***
R^2	n.a.	n.a.	n.a.	0.15
Log likelihood	−17,491.6	−17,491.2	−17,073.5	n.a.

n.a. = not applicable.
Note: ~$p < 0.10$, **$p < 0.01$, ***$p < 0.001$.
Source: Author's calculations.

The fixed-effects model in mathematics is similar to that in Spanish. The model has an R^2 of 0.15. A significant difference exists in scores by teacher across the sample, but the model predicts only 15 percent of that difference.

Propensity Score Matching

Table 10.17 shows four different ways of calculating the mean difference in third-grade Spanish and math scores. The calculated mean difference in Spanish ranges from 1.8 to 4.6, depending on the method used. With propensity score matching, the average mean difference is smaller than in the multilevel model, indicating that the process has helped to resolve some of the selection bias problem. In contrast, there is almost no range

Table 10.17. Third-Grade Mean Difference in Scores between Autonomous and Centralized Schools, by Process

Variable	Spanish	Math
Multilevel with no variables	6.9*	3.9
Full multilevel model	4.6	3.9
Stratification matching	2.8 (1.5)~	3.9 (2.1)*
Nearest-neighbor matching	1.8 (0.7)	3.8 (1.4)~

Note: ~$p < 0.10$, *$p < 0.05$; t-statistics are in parentheses.
Source: Author's calculations.

of mean differences (3.8 to 3.9) in mathematics. Yet, in the propensity score, matching the mean difference does reach significance. From this finding, we can conclude that no significant difference exists between autonomous and centralized schools in third-grade Spanish, whereas there is a significant and positive effect of autonomy on third-grade mathematics.

Sixth-Grade Results

The sixth-grade results differ from the third-grade results (tables 10.18–10.20). For the sixth-grade Spanish scores (table 10.18), the final multilevel model shows that students in autonomous schools, on average, score between one and two points lower than students in centralized schools (this difference does not reach significance). The only school variable that reaches significance is the presence of curriculum guides (which was not significantly different by school type). On average, girls score better than boys, and younger students score better than older students. The fixed-effects model gives us an R^2 of 0.23, indicating that student characteristics of age and gender explain 23 percent of the differences in scores by teacher.

The sixth-grade math scores were the most difficult model to construct. Autonomy has a very small effect on the outcome, as can be seen in the small log likelihood difference between the first and second models in table 10.19. The difference is negative but does not reach significance. As with sixth-grade Spanish, the teacher and school characteristics do not contribute to

Table 10.18. Sixth-Grade Spanish Achievement

Variable	Intercept only	Autonomous only	Final model	Fixed effects
Student SES			1.9*	1.2
Student age			–3.9***	–4.0***
Student gender			–9.3***	–9.3***
Classroom mean age			–7.7***	Dropped
School has curriculum guides			11.4*	Dropped
School is autonomous		1.05	–1.59	Dropped
Constant	239.4***	238.8***	385.3***	197.3***
R^2	n.a.	n.a.	n.a.	0.23
Log likelihood	–28,959.8	–28,959.7	–28,844.0	n.a.

n.a. = not applicable.
Note: *$p < 0.5$, ***$p < 0.001$.
Source: Author's calculations.

Table 10.19. Sixth-Grade Math Achievement

Variable	Intercept only	Autonomous only	Final model	Fixed effects
Student SES			0.6	0.317
Student age			−2.65***	−2.7***
Student gender			4.2**	4.13**
School is autonomous		−2.12	−2.6	Dropped
Constant	246.2***	247.4***	280.8***	279.0***
R^2	n.a.	n.a.	n.a.	0.02
Log likelihood	−30,029.7	−30,029.4	−30,002.9	n.a.

n.a. = not applicable.
Note: **$p < 0.01$, ***$p < 0.001$.
Source: Author's calculations.

explaining the math scores; only student age and gender are significant. However, as shown in the fixed-effects model, the effect of those two variables is very small, with the model predicting less than 2 percent of the variation in math scores.

Propensity Score Matching

As for the third grade, propensity score matching was used to address the issues of sample selection bias. In Spanish, the mean difference in scores is negative and does not reach significance. In contrast, using propensity score matching, the mean difference in math scores is both negative *and* significant. Students in autonomous schools, on average, have

Table 10.20. Sixth-Grade Mean Difference in Scores between Autonomous and Centralized Schools, by Process

Variable	Spanish	Math
Multilevel with no variables	1.05	−2.1
Full multilevel model	−1.59	−2.6
Stratification matching	−1 (−.8)	−4.1 (−3.2)**
Nearest-neighbor matching	−1.9 (−1.1)	−3.7 (−2.1)*

Note: *$p < 0.05$, **$p < 0.001$; t-statistics are in parentheses.
Source: Author's calculations.

mathematics scores that are 3.7 to 4.1 points lower than students in centralized schools.

Conclusions

This study has not drawn a neat line between the process of decentralization, teacher change, and student achievement. It has shown that autonomous schools look different from centralized schools, particularly in terms of financial incentives, school resources, and professional development. In both third and sixth grades, autonomous schools are more likely to give financial incentives to teachers, schools have better resources and infrastructure, and teachers are more likely to receive direct technical assistance from the school director. In third grade, autonomous schools are also more likely to have curriculum materials. Class sizes, on average, are larger in autonomous schools. Autonomous and centralized schools differ in their student bodies as well. On average, both third- and sixth-grade students are wealthier in autonomous schools, and students are younger in autonomous schools.

This study has not shown, however, that those differences are linked to student outcomes. Multilevel modeling and propensity score matching have been used to better understand the differences between autonomous and centralized schools and the effect of those differences on Spanish and mathematics outcomes in third and sixth grades. Of the school and teacher characteristics that are more common in autonomous schools, only the presence of direct technical assistance contributes to Spanish scores and only in third-grade Spanish. Spanish scores are positively affected by technical assistance in third grade and by the presence of curriculum guides in sixth grade. These variables are not unique to autonomous schools, however. In neither third- nor sixth-grade Spanish was a treatment effect found for autonomy. In contrast, there is a treatment effect for autonomy in mathematics (positive in third grade and negative in sixth grade), but none of the teacher or school variables in the study contributed significantly to that difference.

Third-grade mathematics scores are not significantly affected by any type of teacher and school characteristics identified in this study. Interestingly, however, the propensity score matching process indicates that there *is* a positive and significant autonomy effect on the third-grade mathematics score of almost four points. Third-grade students in autonomous schools have higher average math scores than students in centralized schools, but the teacher and school characteristics in this study do not contribute to that difference. In sixth-grade mathematics, although there is a significant difference in average scores by school type (students in autonomous schools score 3.7 to 4.1 points lower than those in centralized schools), the model does not explain enough of the variation to have explanatory power. Although math scores were found to be higher in autonomous schools in third grade, they are lower in autonomous schools in sixth grade. This negative autonomy effect at higher levels deserves further investigation.

Although this study contributes to a better understanding of incentives, infrastructure, and professional development in autonomous schools compared to centralized schools, it has not shown clear differences in outcomes between centralized and autonomous schools. An initial hypothesis of this chapter was that the effects of decentralization contribute to changes in teacher behavior, with resultant changes in student outcomes. This study has not shown a clear relationship between the three.

In the Nicaraguan context, as described earlier in this chapter, decentralization takes many forms and is implemented in many different ways. A recent study of Nicaraguan autonomy found vastly different views of both the effects of autonomy and the definition of autonomy itself, indicating that there may be more differences between autonomous schools than between autonomous and centralized schools (Asencio and others 2001). Teachers no longer are assured of having school-based financial incentives. That factor may limit the role incentives play in producing change (in contrast, the World Bank–funded incentive tied to class size is more stable, and class sizes in autonomous schools are significantly higher than those in centralized schools). When incentives are unstable and do not depend on teacher behavior, it can be hypothesized that their effect on teacher behavior—and thus on student outcomes—is limited.

This study provides a context for future research on student achievement in Nicaragua. As more and more schools adopt the governance structures of autonomous schools (by law, all schools will be decentralized by 2006), it will become more imperative to continue to identify which aspects of school autonomy contribute to positive student outcomes. Onsite professional development by the school director appears to be one important variable, as does the availability of curriculum resources. If financial incentives for teachers become more stable and more clearly linked to teacher behaviors, they may also contribute to student outcomes. Those variables appear to have different effects on Spanish than on mathematics, however, and this finding deserves further investigation. Finally, given the difference in autonomy effects for third and sixth grade, longitudinal research will provide important information to better understand the learning experience of students across various grade levels.

References

Arcia, G., and H. Belli. 2001. *La autonomía escolar en Nicaragua: Reestableciendo el contrato social*. Managua: PREAL.

Arnove, R. F. 1995. "Education as Contested Terrain in Nicaragua." *Comparative Education Review* 39(1): 28–53.

Asencio Florez, C., R. Ruiz Carrión, V. Sequiera Calero, V. Castro, and A. Gershberg. 2001. *Lecciones aprendidas de la autonomía escolar Nicaragüense*. New York: New School University.

Castillo, M. 1998. "La descentralización de los servicios de educación en Nicaragua." Serie Reformas de Política Pública. Naciones Unidas Comisión Económica para América Latina y el Caribe, Santiago.

di Gropello, E. 1997. *Descentralización de la educación en América Latina: Un análisis comparativo*. Santiago: CEPAL.

di Gropello, E., and R. Cominetti, eds. 1998. *La descentralización de la educación y la salud: Un análisis comparativo de la experiencia Latinoamericana*. Santiago: Naciones Unidas.

Fuller, B., and M. Rivarola. 1998. "Nicaragua's Experiment to Decentralize Schools: Views of Parents, Teachers and Directors." Working Paper on Impact Evaluation of Education Reforms 5. World Bank, Washington, D.C.

Gershberg, A. I. 1999a. "Decentralization, Citizen Participation, and the Role of the State." *Latin American Perspectives* 26(4): 8–38.

———. 1999b. "Fostering Effective Parental Participation in Education: Lessons from a Comparison of Reform Processes in Nicaragua and Mexico." *World Development* 27(4): 753–71.

———. 2003. "Empowering Parents While Making Them Pay: Autonomous Schools and Education Reform Processes in Nicaragua." Paper written for the project Empowering Parents While Making

Them Pay: Autonomous Schools in Nicaragua, funded by the Tinker Foundation, New York.

Gershberg, A. I., and B. Meade. 2003. "Parental Contributions and School-Level Finances: An Analysis of Nicaraguan Autonomous School Budgets." Paper written for the project Empowering Parents While Making Them Pay: Autonomous Schools in Nicaragua, funded by the Tinker Foundation, New York.

Gershberg, A. I., and D. Winkler. 2000. Education Decentralization in Latin America: A Review of the Effects on the Quality of Schooling. In S. J. Burki, ed., *Decentralization and Accountability of the Public Sector: Proceedings of the 1999 Annual World Bank Conference on Development in Latin America*. Washington, D.C.: World Bank.

Kaestner, R., and A. I. Gershberg. 2002. "Lessons Learned from Nicaragua's School Autonomy Reform: A Review of Research by the Nicaragua Reform Evaluation Team of the World Bank." Paper written for the project Empowering Parents While Making Them Pay: Autonomous Schools in Nicaragua, funded by the Tinker Foundation, New York.

King, E. 1996. *Nicaragua's School Autonomy Reform: A First Look*. Washington, D.C.: World Bank.

King, E., and B. Ozler. 2000. "What's Decentralization Got to Do with Learning? The Case of Nicaragua's School Autonomy Reform." Working Paper Series on Impact Evaluation of Education Reforms. World Bank Development Research Group, Washington, D.C.

King, E., B. Ozler, and L. Rawlings. 2000. *Nicaragua's School Autonomy Reform: Fact or Fiction?* Washington, D.C.: World Bank.

MECD (Ministry of Education, Culture, and Sports). 2003a. "Evaluación del rendimiento académico de los estudiantes del 3ro y 6to grados de primaria: Informe de resultados 2002." Managua.

———. 2003b "Estado de la formación de la ciudadanía y recursos humanos: La educación en Cifras." Managua.

———. 2003c. "Ministry of Education Data." Ministry of Education, Department of Statistics, Managua.

———. 2004. "Autonomía Escolar." Managua. http://www.mecd.gob.ni/autonom.asp. Accessed April 4, 2004.

MIGOB (Ministry of Government). 2003. "National Development Plan Proposal." Government of Nicaragua, Managua.

Morales, A. 2002. "Colegios tendrán más fondos por menos alumnos." *La Prensa* (Managua), July 24, p. 3.

Tedesco, J. C., and N. López. 2002. "Desafíos a la educación secundaria en América Latina." *Revista de la CEPAL* 76: 55–69.

11

Political Economy, Incentives, and Teachers' Unions
Case Studies in Chile and Peru

Luis Crouch
Research Triangle Institute

> *The unionization of teachers and collective bargaining [is] likely to contribute to increasing rationalization. Unions will seek new rules and procedural safeguards, and management will counter with new rules and procedures of its own. . . . Major losers [in the struggle for power] will be teachers who will see their professional autonomy replaced by a bureaucratic conception of their role. The most tragic loss will be to the students who are cast as objects being prepared to assume their place in society.*
>
> —A. Wise

As other chapters in this volume show, in the past decade or so many countries in Latin America have introduced various incentive or incentive-like mechanisms to stimulate more, or better-directed, teacher effort and accountability. Those mechanisms range from formal incentive systems, such as some version of pay-for-performance (as in Chile), to informal or generalized incentives, such as those involved in community-based accountability (as in El Salvador or Honduras). Other chapters assess the effectiveness of the various incentives approaches using evaluation methodologies.

Instead, this chapter addresses issues related to the political economy of changes in teacher incentives regimes. What has made it possible to introduce and implement changes in incentives in some countries? What role have unions for teachers played in determining the nature and types of incentives that might be acceptable? What features of teacher unionism, or of the economics and political economy of incentives, have led to opposition in some cases and support in others? Most important, what lessons—

The epigraph to this chapter is drawn from Wise (1979, pp. 200 and 212).

either from the case studies, from other international experience, or from basic principles—can be learned for increasing support to teacher-incentive reforms in the future?

The chapter is based on some understanding and modeling of first principles from the literature and on two case studies: Chile and Peru. The case studies show quite different outcomes: Chile has managed to not only design but also implement incentives systems, whereas Peru has been much less successful with detailed, practical, and consistent (and, hence, implementable) design and implementation.

Because the chapter is based on only two cases, it does not propose easy generalizability of the lessons that emerge nor does it even pretend to test hypotheses. However, because the cases illustrate principles that appear fairly strong, some degree of generalizability should exist, at least with respect to the sorts of issues that should be considered as countries proceed to design or refine incentives systems. Valid pointers for how to proceed and how to think about the issues *do* emerge from the cases and from first principles, even if lessons about "what works" are less strong.[137] The intent of the chapter is not so much to provide generalizable lessons or to test hypotheses, as to point toward agendas for further analysis. After sufficient hypotheses are formulated, continentwide studies of the role of unionism might be feasible.

The chapter uses a document review and key-informant interviews. No primary data gathering or secondary data analysis was carried out.

Case Study of Chile: Reforms Designed and Implemented, Effect Yet to Be Seen

In the 1980s and 1990s, Chile has introduced some of the most extensive accountability and accountability-based incentive systems among middle-income countries—perhaps even among high-income countries. Some aspects of those systems and approaches were started, albeit in crude form, under the military government (1973–90), but serious education reforms started in 1980. A subset of those systems was continued under the democratic governments since 1990, but the democratic governments have added more sophistication to the accountability and incentive systems.

Many of the systems introduced after democratization began after consultation and negotiations with civil society, in particular with the teachers' union (the Colegio de Profesores de Chile, or CP). In some cases, particularly early in the democratization process, the consultations were fairly

---

137. Thus, generalizing good process and good use of basic principles related to unions and incentives is probably safe. Simply copying to other places the incentives that may have worked in one place, or may look as if they will work in one place, is probably not safe.

minimalist. More recently, consultations have become extensive and have, in fact, become co-design.[138] The reforms had political implications or required political compromises, and those issues were dealt with forthrightly, especially in recent years. How the compromises were generated is the main theme below. Before turning to this topic, however, three elements of background information are provided: (a) key elements of the reform created by the military government, (b) main aspects of the nature of teachers' unionism in Chile, and (c) a description of the basic incentives that have been negotiated.

Landscape under the Previous Government

The military government in Chile carried out several fundamental reforms that are germane to the issue of incentives and accountability:

- Education was "municipalized," which means public school teachers became municipal rather than central government employees, and schools came under municipal management, at least in a formal sense. School principals and municipal mayors were directly appointed by the central government. In this sense, the notion of municipalization being used was a rather peculiar one, and the centralist appointment of school principals had important consequences for the future.
- Funding was put on a per capita basis, and municipal public schools and private schools were put on the same funding basis to generate competition between schools within and between types. Funding of municipalities' educational responsibilities was put on a formula basis, with attendance as a key driver. This reform would also stimulate attendance and enrollment. The approach was expected to create a quasi-market in educational services, with built-in incentives for efficiency.[139]
- To provide market information and to create a metric for quality, which could thus inform the choices of parents as consumers of school services, a measurement system for results was created, the PER (Programa de Evaluación del Rendimiento). The logic of this approach was from its inception to provide accountability data to a market of consumers, rather than to provide suppliers with information on how to improve the services being offered.

---

138. As in the case of the new Sistema de Evaluación del Desempeño Profesional Docente—an individual, high-stakes, teacher evaluation system with high-incentive implications, not to be confused with the Sistema Nacional de Evaluación de Desempeño de los Establecimientos Educacionales (SNED), which confers group rewards.

139. In a sense, the principle is that government "buys" places for children in school, with parents as its agents. Those schools that cannot produce at the price the government is willing to pay are outcompeted. The efficient survive.

While those reforms were being carried out during the 1980s, however, total spending plus spending per student declined in real terms by about 25 percent (González 2003). Total enrollment in the public system or subsidized private system was essentially static, and there was some small growth in the private nonsubsidized system. The available data do not allow us to evaluate to what extent there were improvements in learning during this period.

A Few Key Characteristics of the Chilean Teachers' Union

Chile's powerful teachers' union, the CP, derives its power from a few factors:

- It is a largely monopolistic organization. A few other relatively minor teachers' associations exist, but the CP encompasses the overwhelming majority of unionized teachers. The CP was created by the military government in 1974, and constituted as a monopoly to which teachers had to belong, but the situation was liberalized in 1980. As a result, an alternative union sprang up, which was in a more traditional mold and did not owe its existence to a mandate from the government. In union elections for the CP in 1985, elements more friendly to a traditional union style won. The alternative union was disbanded, because, as of that election, the CP fulfilled the need for more traditional unionism (see Nuñez Prieto 2003). In an ironic sense, then, the military government may have been indirectly responsible for the power of this organization.
- The union formally encompasses teachers of all political views. On a scale of 1 to 10, with 1 being "left" and 10 being "right," teachers self-classify as very centrist or somewhat left-of-center. The average self-classification is 4.9. The current leadership, however, is identified with the Communist Party (the leadership affiliated with this party won 76 percent of the vote in the most recent election for which we have data). Interestingly, however (as will be seen later), since this leadership came to power, there has been more movement in the direction of individual evaluation with fairly high stakes (see Nuñez Prieto 2003).
- The union's bureaucratic and technical leadership is of high intellectual and organizational caliber. Advisers to the CP and its high-level technical leadership have considerable experience and have published scholarly and technical papers on many areas of educational quality. A casual review of the union's journal, *Docencia*, makes it clear that the intellectual level of the magazine is very high. Position notes and speeches of the CP are considerably more thoughtful than similar union documentation from other countries, and they focus on substantive matters of education policy, not simply on traditional union issues (see Assael Budnik and Urrutia 2002; Pavez Urrutia n.d.; Scherping 2003a, 2003b, 2003c; Verdugo 2004).

- The union's internal organization appears to be increasingly democratic, and its external positions are based on participatory development of positions. This trend is particularly seen after 1997, when the CP held its first major congress after the renewal of political democracy in Chile.
- The same 1997 congress induced the leadership, under pressure from the rank and file, to take more interest in educational and pedagogical issues, instead of bargaining and bread-and-butter issues. This shift led to changes in the internal emphasis of the CP, as well as in its offerings to its membership. It led, for example, to the emergence of a formal movement within the union, the "Movimiento Pedagógico," aimed at providing alternative ways of conceptualizing education.
- Both the union and the past-1990 government had been in the opposition during the military government from 1973 to 1990. Furthermore, from 1990 to 1995, the union was controlled by parties in the same political alliance as the government of the country. This connection was important, because it created an atmosphere of some trust and credibility. In the context of imperfect information about intentions that characterizes public sector bargaining (because the government is not a simple maximizer of a clear objective function), trust and credibility take on great importance.

Changes in Incentive Regimes since 1990

During the 1990s and early 2000s, there were massive increases in spending, in general, as "supply side" incentives, plus many innovations with performance-based incentives and competitive grants of various sorts. Total spending in the 1990s increased about 180 percent, and per student spending increased about 130 percent (González 2003). Most important, average teacher compensation increased substantially in real terms, again by about 150 percent in the 1990s (Mizala and Romaguera 2003). In addition to improving salaries, various incentive schemes have been negotiated, approved, and implemented. The following incentives stand out in chronological sequence:

- Collective performance-based incentives are related to measured student achievement. For instance, the Sistema Nacional de Evaluación de Desempeño de los Establecimientos Educacionales (National System of School Performance Assessment, or SNED) was negotiated in the mid-1990s and gives groups of teachers a salary bonus depending on performance of the whole school on the Sistema de Medición de la Calidad de la Educación (Education Quality Measurement System, or SIMCE) tests.
- The Asignación por Excelencia Pedagógica rewards individual teachers based on process criteria, not learning results. It was negotiated in 2000 and initiated in 2002, and teachers submit voluntarily.

- Under Law 19715 of 2001, if teachers are evaluated well in the Asignación por Excelencia Pedagógica, then the Red de Maestros de Maestros, may propose projects so they can mentor other teachers and receive financial incentives to do so.
- An increase in the size of the reward associated with the SNED was negotiated in 2003.
- Creation and approval of a Sistema de Evaluación del Desempeño Professional Docente, a nonvoluntary system (as opposed to the Asignación por Excelencia Pedagógica, which is voluntary) of performance review, made it possible for teachers to receive individual rewards (Asignación Variable por Desempeño Individual) that are based on peer-reviewed teaching ability (rather than student learning achievement). This upgraded incentive was negotiated in 2003 and is being applied to the first set of teachers during 2004. In a sense, it is the fulfillment of the obligatory individual performance review system mandated in the Estatuto Docente in the early 1990s, a system that took some 13 years to come to fruition.

In addition, many incentives exist that are not linked to performance, such as rurality incentives (or "difficult conditions" incentives) and rewards tied to administrative duties. Finally, there were many other major policy changes, such as the gradual elimination of double shifts, changes in how schools are funded (for example, the introduction of fees in public secondary schools, or the *financiamiento compartido* system), competitive school grant schemes, poverty-targeted programs, and curricular reforms.

In summary, Chile has managed to design and implement various performance incentive mechanisms throughout the 1990s. Some of those may have taken a long time and endless rounds of negotiation, but they are a reality. Nevertheless, as Mizala and Romaguera (2003) argue, the great variety and complexity of the incentives may dilute the messages they send. Moreover, the incentives may not be having the effect that was hoped for because teachers' ability to respond to the incentives may not be sufficiently strong. Such questions are for further empirical research. Nonetheless, the achievements are notable and raise the question as to how they were accomplished.

Factors Making the Changes Possible

Chile has created a far-ranging mix of individual and small-group incentives for teachers, including broad incentives related to overall improvements in salaries of teachers. The individual and small-group incentives are not typical of education sectors, especially in developing countries, and are often opposed by teachers' unions. As noted previously, Chile has an active and powerful teachers' union. How then was Chile able to set up such systems? The following reasons stood out in discussions and documents or are offered as original hypotheses in this report.

Leadership in the Ministry of Education

A first factor in explaining breakthroughs on incentives is the level of leadership in the education sector in Chile. "Leadership matters" is often taken by economists as a nonexplanation, or as a rather banal explanation, especially when it is implicitly defined circularly as a vague set of characteristics that are of people in formal leadership and that lead to results. If a good leader is someone who can deliver on reform results, then attributing reform results to good leadership is not very useful. But, in the case of Chile, one can assess the quality of leadership in quite objective terms: For example, in terms of education background and previous (or subsequent) experience in the Ministry of Finance or other high levels in the social and political structure.

Objectively, then, in terms of education background, four of seven ministers of education since 1990 have advanced degrees in economics (three Ph.Ds., one M.A.), specifically from Harvard and Duke. Another had a Ph.D. in education from Harvard University, but with economics and operations research emphases. Yet another had no advanced degree in economics, but did have a B.A. in the prestigious *Ingeniero Comercial* field in Chile. Similarly, in terms of previous or subsequent experience at high levels in Chilean society, two ministers, including the one who was perhaps the most important in negotiating the first breakthroughs in the incentives reforms, had cabinet-level experience in the Finance and Planning Ministries. Another went on to be president. One minister had plied his practical experience with public and private management in helping the CP solve internal financial problems, which helped create good relations with the CP.

All of these leadership factors are more or less objective and are not circularly defined with respect to reform success. The fact that such prominent people, who are well-qualified in statecraft, were ministers of education is likely a partial cause of the breakthroughs in incentives regimes. But the quality among leaders could also be, partly, a manifestation of the fact that government simply took education very seriously, and this general seriousness was the more-operant cause of breakthroughs than the appointment of very good leadership.

Role of the Ministry of Finance

The Ministry of Finance took an unusual level of interest in the education sector—unusual by both worldwide and Latin American standards. Many of the key reforms, such as the SNED, were initially sketched out in the mid-1990s in collaborative, technical sessions between key actors at the Ministry of Finance and at the Ministry of Education. The leadership from the Ministry of Finance that was crucial to this redesign then went on to lead the education sector, which may help explain why implementation was pursued after initial design. It also reaffirms the notion that the government tended to put economically minded leadership in the education sector. High-level formal and informal technical interactions between the Ministries of Finance and Education took place frequently during the mid-1990s. Even though this sort of collaboration put the economists in charge, it also meant that commitments to increase educational funding, which were tied to reforms, tended to be more credible.

Role of the Union

The quality of leadership extended to the CP as well. The CP has advisers who have worked independently (that is, not as part of their union or political affiliation) in education think-tanks and as consultants and advisers to private and nongovernmental organization (NGO) schools. Some of the leadership is involved in important roles in international initiatives, such as Education International, the Confederation of American Educators (Confederación de Educadores de América, or CEA), and PREAL (Programa de Promoción de la Reforma Educativa en América Latina, or Partnership for Education Revitalization in the Americas—a joint effort of the Inter-American Development Bank and the Inter-American Dialogue).[140] The leadership also has strong credentials in Chilean political life, given the members' background as militants in various parties in the opposition to the military regime and their decades of experience as union leaders. As noted previously, the writing of the leadership reflects serious thinking about education policy issues, well beyond typical union "militancy" issues. This focal point may be partly in response to pressure from rank-and-file teachers, but whatever the source of this pressure, the leadership has had the capacity to respond.

The high quality of leadership on all sides—the fact that many of the leaders were among the most experienced Chileans in the management of the state and the fact that so many of them had decades of negotiating experience—was a key determinant of the breakthroughs. The lesson appears fairly clear: if education is taken seriously, a good way to show it is to put the most-qualified people in the society in charge of the sector. Whether this positioning would always lead to good results is another story. However, the obverse, namely that good results are unlikely if the leadership is not of high quality, seems a safe conclusion.

The Logic of Collective Action and Generalized Salary Increases

The changes toward individual or small-group incentives in Chile took place (a) during a period of strong government commitment to general-

---

140. Information about PREAL can be found on the organization's Web site, http://www.preal.org/.

ized salary increases and (b) when government was delivering on its commitment in a way that was clear to all those concerned. Furthermore, the key breakthrough negotiation on small-group incentives (the SNED) took place only as part of a bargaining process that involved other key reforms, such as the possibility of eliminating redundant teacher posts (which the unions opposed), and against the background of generalized salary increases (which the unions favored). As reported by Mizala and Romaguera (2003), by the mid-1990s average and base salaries had already improved substantially (by at least 70 percent in real terms) since the lows experienced during the military government.

Resisting individual incentives until general or base salaries have improved has a certain commonsense logic and populist appeal. This factor was clearly operational in the union discourse in Chile, as summarized by observers (Belleï 2004; Nuñez Prieto 2003). The reality is that by 1990 the starting teacher salary was below the poverty line (Belleï 2004). A preoccupation with equality or equity is not peculiar to unions. In fact, most modern institutions (the World Bank, for example) generally favor some degree of nonmarket solutions to inequality, such as use of tax bases to generate redistribution through progressive spending incidence or poverty-targeted programs. The concern with equality is common to many institutions associated with "modernism," at least since the late 18th century. Although unions are certainly a prime example of this trend, they are hardly unique in this respect.

The resistance to individual incentives also has a much more practical and instrumental basis in the logic of union action and mobilization. That basis is related to the oft-observed phenomenon that the rank and file seem to be more accepting of merit pay than union leadership (see Ballou and Podgursky 1993 for an example). Seeking and achieving collective goals, such as improvements in base and average pay, requires collective mobilization. For example, the rank and file must be amenable to go on strike and not break strikes. Such action requires that the individual highly identify with the whole (Brimelow 2003). This collective identification is likely to be undermined if the reward structure emphasizes individual effort. Then, the returns to individual effort could become higher than the returns to collective effort, thus reducing incentives for collective effort to seek generalized improvements.[141]

It is not the case that any reward to individual effort will make the returns to individual effort higher than the returns to collective effort.

---

141. In the United States, this sort of reasoning (though not exactly this logic) is an accepted administrative principle. Brimelow (2003, p. 85) quotes the State Public Employees Relations Board of California, which issued the judgment that "The provision of benefits that are more than what is called for in a collective bargaining agreement is inherently destructive of a union's representation rights. It can be construed to give a message that unit employees would do better if they abandoned the union."

Given free-rider effects in collective efforts, it is clear that even fairly small returns to individual effort will tend to undermine the few—essentially nonmonetary—individual incentives for collective effort that do exist. Note that this is not the same as saying that individual rewards cannot vary or else collective identification is undermined. If individual rewards vary according to factors unrelated to individual effort, such as seniority, preservice training, or differential cost of living in certain areas, then the ability to make individuals identify with the collective group, so that they will press for overall improvements, is not undermined.

As a result, when collective goals, such as improvements in average pay, are seen as legitimate by the rank and file (for example, because base starting salaries for teachers are below the poverty line), then the rank and file may identify with the leadership's positions against pay for individual effort. A negative interpretation is that union leadership will find it easier to manipulate and control the rank and file—for self-seeking purposes—if the rank and file are all equal. Although this interpretation may be true in some unions, it need not be the case for the logic laid out here to be operational. The rank and file may well understand the implicit need for sameness in generating solidarity.

Simpler propositions suggest opposition to individualized incentives to effort and are based on median-voter analyses. For example, (a) if the individual teacher is risk-averse and does not know where he or she would fall in the distribution of ability to generate results in measured student achievement, and (b) if the increase in performance-related pay comes at the expense of existing generalized improvements (that is, if performance-related pay is seen as a redistribution of existing average pay, or as an alternative to a one-time increase in average pay), then the median voter in the rank and file would tend to oppose the introduction of performance-related pay. However, it is unlikely in the long run that this process would be a strong determinant if generalized increases are taking place at the same time the performance-related pay is introduced. Therefore, performance-related pay would not be seen as a zero-sum game. Individual rewards undermine collective effort even when average salaries are going up, whereas even a risk-averse individual might not be as opposed to individual rewards if the rewards were not a zero-sum game. Thus, if the real incentive or perceived need for collective mobilization is high, teachers will tend to oppose rewards for results that are based on individual effort.

Furthermore, as later discussion of union behavior will show, median-voter propositions do not fully explain union leadership behavior, even where unions are highly democratic and the leadership is not self-serving.[142]

---

142. Union leadership, at least where it has been studied, is not any more crudely self-serving than political leadership in any other area of democratic life in particular country contexts—see Freeman and Medoff (1984).

For example, rank-and-file teachers are often not opposed, in principle, to performance-related pay (see Ballou and Podgursky 1993; specifically for Chile, see Mizala and Romaguera 2003; for Peru, see Ministerio de Educación/IIPE-UNESCO 2002). Similarly, some evidence suggests that union leadership engages in more political activity and political activity of a different sort than the rank and file might want. Incidentally, union leaders may be more successful at the political activities they see as important than at the ones the rank and file might see as important (see Masters and Delaney 1987; Freeman and Medoff 1984). Instead, a "managerialist" approach to unions (Pemberton 1988)—where the dynamics between the leadership and the rank and file are assumed to be more complex than median-voter models suggest—might propose that the rank and file "delegate" any opposition to performance-based pay to the leadership. Such delegation would be a way of generating the solidarity needed to fight collectively for better average pay when seeking average increases is important to the rank and file and when winning such struggles seems possible. In fact, some analysts or commentators who have the deepest insider knowledge of unions, such as Lieberman (2000), place most of the burden for an explanation of why unions are opposed to most reforms on a managerialist rather than median-voter view of teacher unions. Those analysts observe that, where reforms such as vouchers or increased accountability to parents are seen as reducing the hold of union leadership on the rank and file, the reforms threaten access of the leadership to membership dues and the strike tool.[143]

In summary, because general salaries were increasing in Chile during the 1990s, individual teachers would not have to worry about an absolute decline in salary if they were found to be poor performers, and also because of the increase in general salaries, the need for collective allegiance to a fight for general salary improvements perhaps declined. For both reasons, in the case of Chile, improvements in general pay that were seen as likely to continue (because they were credible) probably favored breakthroughs in individualized or small-group incentives.

An important implication of Chile's experience is that, because *indefinite* generalized improvements in average pay are not likely in most countries but are probably available only during periods of catch-up, education sector leadership should take advantage of such periods to overcome the logical—and in many ways justified (in practical terms, if not necessarily in terms of ultimate justice)—resistance of teachers and unions to performance-related pay when average salaries are perceived to be too low.

---

143. Although these sorts of points of view are associated with critics of the unions, such as Brimelow (2003) and Lieberman (2000), there is no inherent reason why a more nuanced or neutral point of view, such as Moore (1976), who also attempts to explain uniformity in wages, should not prefer a managerialist viewpoint.

Social Accountability Pressure

As will be seen, in spite of dramatic increases in salaries and spending in the 1990s, results have not kept pace. Results of education reforms can take a long time to show up in achievement statistics or other indicators of objective results, and signs for the future are encouraging. It is also likely that the speed of quality response can be improved in Chile to shorten the gestation period of quality response to the reforms. But, for now, the point to be noted is that the media, civil society organizations, and general public opinion—not to mention finance ministers, cabinet, and legislatures—are unlikely to fully heed the gestation-period argument and to be as patient with reforms as educators would like them to be. The impatience of policymakers was already becoming evident in the mid-1990s and gained strength in the late 1990s. For that reason and because average pay was already increasing, it would have been less-and-less tenable for the CP to argue that there should not be some form of accountability for teachers. Their future as a professional organization willing to take accountability for the quality of education—as opposed to simple bread-and-butter issues—and their ability to speak collectively for teachers as professionals would have been undermined by a stance that refused to associate the results of the sector with individual or small-group work effort and creativity. In most other occupations considered to be "professional," considerable relationship exists between reward and individual effort, as well as considerable direct connection between professional worker and client. Thus, disassociating the union and teachers from this accountability pressure would have tended to undermine the union's stance that teachers should be treated as professionals.

Nevertheless, logic operates in most countries, even developing countries. Thus, this explanation cannot help us understand why that logic supported change in Chile, where two special circumstances had to be taken into account. First, much had already been done in terms of access to education. Certainly, by the early 1990s, a preoccupation with quality and achievement had set in. Clearly, quality improvements, as opposed to access improvements, require more work (or different work) from teachers. Second, in Chile as opposed to many other countries, recurrent reporting (at least to the government, later on to the public) of schooling results on a fairly objective basis was already common in the early 1990s and certainly by the mid-1990s. Furthermore, Chile participates willingly in international assessments, which are widely discussed in the media.[144]

---

144. It is important to note, however, that though the intertemporal comparability of the SIMCE results was, at best, suspect until the tests were improved in the late 1990s, the general public and opinion-makers were generally relatively immune to subtleties of this nature.

Therefore, the public and opinion-makers find it relatively easy to see whether results are improving at a pace that they believe is commensurate with spending increases and with improvements in teachers' conditions. This availability of information may lead to an impatience that is somewhat unjustified, again because in education there is a long lag between spending and results and because the sector was recovering from very low spending levels in the late 1980s. But, justified or not, the data availability and the public debate atmosphere that reigns in Chile certainly put pressure on both unions and the ministry to look for ways to create links between improvements in pay and results delivered, which, in turn, led to a serious consideration of individual or small-group incentives.

Attributability of Collective Results and Individual Process

Chile's incentives regime effectively tries to address key attributability problems. To explain why and how requires some digression.

Agency theory predicts that incentives matter most (a) if they are directed at actual results rather than at precursor processes or behaviors, and (b) if the results are relatively easily attributable to the agents enjoying the incentives.[145] The attributability aspect applies in two ways. First, the incentives have to apply to the set of agents that will create the results. Second, the agents have to actually be able to affect the results and have to be largely the *only* ones affecting the results. Those observations have two implications: first, to the degree that the results are generated collectively, the incentives have to be collective. Second, to the degree that one is encouraging results beyond the easily measurable ones and to the degree that one does not have an exact model of how each type of behavior leads to each type of result, then individual *or* group incentives have to focus on processes and precursors rather than on final results. Markets reward complex goods largely in this way. The price one pays for the experience of dining in a fine restaurant is not decomposable into rewards for easily measurable "components" of the dining experience. Thus, the problem arises when a bureaucracy tries to create bureaucratically driven incentives for results, but the incentives cannot be complex and general (the way the price of a meal in a fine restaurant is), because they have to be transparent and must yield to public accountability, and because the producer has no strong incentive to take prices into account and to put effort into assessing how to get the best price using complex trial-and-error methods, the way that, say, restaurant owners do. However, in the case of collective incentives, there is always a free-rider problem that is difficult to solve if the group is so large that free-riding is difficult to detect. If the

---

145. For a thoughtful review of agency theory, see Prendergast (1999).

group is too large, then incentives are unlikely to work well. Table 11.1 summarizes.[146]

The interesting cases are in the diagonal that goes from lower left to upper right in table 11.1. The upper-left-to-lower-right diagonal defines the ambit of pure market incentives or pure group loyalty (forced or spontaneous) and bureaucratic rules as opposed to incentives. Thus, this other diagonal is less relevant to the case at hand.

The more that process incentives (lower left-hand corner in table 11.1) are informed by sound professional judgment of direct practitioners (*if* they have an incentive to keep up the image of the profession), the better. Such direct practitioners, as opposed to bureaucratic managers, often have the most-subtle information on the precise precursor behaviors that will lead to the broader results. This is why codes of conduct that are determined by and enforced through professional associations can work—as long as the association has a real incentive to maintain its image and has effective sanction mechanisms to control the behavior of individuals who would free-ride on the image of the profession.[147] Peer-based evaluations in merit-pay systems have, therefore, been proposed and tried, although how well they really work is still debatable (see Brimelow 2003; Kerchner, Koppich, and Weeres 1997, 1998; Lieberman 2000).

The development of education incentives in Chile seems to wisely take into account the sorts of issues discussed above. This taking into account was partly determined by the technical ability of designers in the ministry and the CP, partly caused by bargaining by the CP in the design of incentives regimes, and, surely, partly caused by good luck.[148] The fact that bargaining and a sequence of reaction and counter-reaction played some role is evidenced in the original Estatuto Docente, which was crafted in 1991 and which called for individual evaluations that were not implemented because of teacher opposition. Teachers were against the notion of an evaluation system that did not involve their input in either design or execution. Ultimately, it would take some 12 or 13 years (1991–2003) to settle on a system of individual evaluation, which was codesigned by the CP, the Ministry of Education, and representatives of the municipalities

---

146. Note that these arguments do not define the issues as public or private goods. The arguments are about the nature of production by public or private bureaucracies, similar to the logic regarding the optimality of outsourcing. But the logic of excludability and rivalry, which are used in thinking about public goods, is similar to the logic of attributability and measurement.

147. Maintaining the professional image is less of an issue in teaching than in other professions that cater largely to the private sector without mediation by a public bureaucracy (such as accounting), because in teaching the union can blame problems on the government.

148. Apportioning between those factors is beyond the scope of this chapter but could be done with further research.

Table 11.1. Relationship of Incentives to Attributability of Results

	Measured results attributable to individuals	Measured results not attributable to individuals
Measurable key results	Incentives can be individual and results-based. However, in those cases, market or outsourced solutions to the production problem typically work well, so the problem does not really arise in bureaucratic management.	Group incentives are likely more fruitful. However, they cannot be used if the group is so large that free-rider detection is ineffective, or if social pressure cannot be used to supplement the incentives. Thus, small-group incentives are more likely to work, or a combination of group incentives and social pressure.
Many other unmeasurable results	Incentives can be individual. However, they most likely need to focus on processes and precursor behaviors, not just results.	Incentives are difficult to craft. Thus, pure group allegiance, command-and-control, ideology, or professionalism are often needed.

Source: Developed by the author.

(the contractual employers of the teachers). The individual evaluation system that emerged focuses largely on behaviors rather than on results, and it contains peer-review mechanisms.

Thus, the tension between collective and individual incentives was resolved in Chile, on the one hand, by making incentives that are based on measurable results collective (SNED) and, on the other hand, by making individual incentives (such as the Asignación Variable por Desempeño Individual, which is based on a system of evaluating teacher performance) that depend on processes and behaviors as evaluated by mutual collegial vigilance or peer review (*evaluación por pares*).

More measurement and better technology can help resolve some of these tensions. For example, tight yearly measurement on a value-added basis can relate child performance improvements to individual teachers, which might make it possible to create individual results-based incentives that line up individual results with individual efforts. However, such intense results-based evaluation may come at the cost of narrowing down what is taught in classrooms, and it requires sophisticated measurement capacity.

Tentative Lessons from Chile

The following lessons can be tentatively suggested as arising from the Chilean experience:

- The quality of leadership in the Ministry of Education, Ministry of Finance, and unions is important. Reforms are pushed and orchestrated by a few active leaders with technical imagination and an ability to collaborate.
- Individual or small-group incentives may be easier to negotiate when average salaries are increasing. Because average salary increases are unlikely to take place over very long periods and are most likely during a recovery from periods of salary depression (such as the Chilean salary recovery starting in 1990), governments interested in incentives should take advantage of periods of salary recovery. The timing of introduction of incentives may matter.
- Fine-tuning incentives to the basic problems of measurement and attributability might make sense. Incentives need to be related to what can truly be measured and is within the span of control of those presumably being motivated by incentives. Thus, collective incentives for group achievement on measured results (and with some degree of ex-post, measurement-based equalization of conditions), as in SNED, along with individual incentives for individual work behavior (and not student results), might make sense. However, either individual incentives for measured learning achievement in students or collective incentives for good process are less likely to be acceptable to unions or to have any significant effect, if acceptable. (Group incentives for good behavior unlinked to student results would always be acceptable, but it is hard to see why they would affect results. Group incentives of this sort are only a short step from generalized salary increases.)
- An alternative to both incentives schemes might simply be using more community or managerial discretion in rewarding teachers (as in the Nicaraguan autonomous schools) in more nuanced (less bureaucratic) fashions. Nonetheless, this system is difficult to use in Chile because school principals—many of whom are still appointees of the military government—are often not trusted by teachers. In other countries, more reliance on parental and managerial discretion, as opposed to bureaucratic and peer evaluation, might make some sense.
- Creating accountability pressure around value for money, or changes in measured results as compared to changes in expenditure, can create a favorable climate for performance-related incentives. This finding highlights the importance of measurement and assessments and of their dissemination to parents and communities, even if the measurement is

not to be used as a basis for individual accountability (as it perhaps should not be, unless it is a very sophisticated measurement).

- Incentives and accountability pressure, by themselves, might not work as quickly as one might hope. (But neither do generalized increases in spending nor generic training and teacher professionalism efforts.) Instead, it may be necessary to continue to improve schools' capacity to respond to incentives and accountability pressure, for example by showing teachers, very specifically, how to use learning assessment results to improve student achievement. This suggestion does not condone mechanistic "teaching to the test," but rather suggests that good testing materials be used to identify very specific conceptual gaps that teachers are leaving in students and to remedy those gaps with targeted and strategically managed programs, student by student and teacher by teacher, if necessary. Chile has no systematic approach for doing this, which may be one important reason for the slow improvement in learning scores. Thus, this lesson is, in some sense, a "negative" one.

Case Study of Peru: Incentive Reforms Underdesigned, Unimplemented

In Latin America, Chile is often considered as having the most innovative programs in various areas of education reform, including teacher incentives of various sorts. However, on paper, Peru may well be ahead of Chile, at least chronologically if not cumulatively. For example, by 1990, Peru already had a teacher statute (Ley del Profesorado, or Teacher Statute; Law Number D.S. 019-90-ED) that specified performance incentives. That law tied monetary rewards to increases in salary grade, and the salary grade changes were at least 50 percent driven by some measure of performance—in theory. In fact, there appear to be at least a dozen or more incentives and bonuses in Peru's teacher reward system. Many of them are oriented at eliciting behavior that everyone would agree is needed, and most of them do not contain major, obvious, unintended perverse consequences. Also, there have been various efforts to control the quality of teachers—efforts that have generated considerable interest (and tension), such as experiments in applying knowledge tests to candidates for permanent appointment, which, once attempted, have not been sustained.

At the end of all these experiments, Peru still has a remarkably flat teacher salary structure. The difference between level 5, the highest paid, and level 1, the lowest paid, is only 10 percent. The structure has become flatter with time. In 1980, there was a difference of 294 percent between the best-paid teachers and the worst paid. By 1990, the difference was 34 percent, which declined to today's difference of a mere 10 percent (Villarán 2003). Such a flat structure cannot be commensurate with stimuli related to the rest of the labor market or with eliciting or rewarding performance.

The basic thesis is that the problem in Peru is one of institutional ability to follow through with incentives systems. This institutional ability has various complex dimensions, many of which tend, at present, to undermine improvement efforts from the outset. Those complex dimensions will be explored next.

Context of Incentives and Accountability Changes in Peru

The context for reform in Peru in recent years has been very different from that in Chile. The following points summarize the landscape against which reforms have been tried in Peru:

- In Peru, teacher salaries increased at some points during the 1990s, but by the end of the 1990s, they were still 50 percent, in real terms, of what they were in the 1970s (Díaz and Saavedra 2000). In 2000, they were again 47 percent, in real terms, of what they had been in 1990. There is a widespread sense of salaries being low relative to the past and little sense of recovery. Similarly, spending on education, as a proportion of gross domestic product (GDP), is relatively low. It improved in the 1990s (from 2.2 percent of GDP in 1990 to 3.2 percent by 2000), but apparently not sufficiently to create a sense of strong commitment by the government to the sector—unlike the strong increases in Chile.
- Peru has a sample-based tool for assessing student learning, not a universal tool applied to all children. This tool may suffice for certain types of bureaucratic accountability, but it cannot drive local political or market-based accountability because the latter requires, in principle, results for each school. If the bureaucracy is weak, then bureaucratic accountability based on sample measurement is not likely to create much pressure for an improvement in teaching quality. Peru's participation in—and dissemination of—results of international assessments is weak compared with Chile's.
- Leadership in the Ministry of Education has changed frequently, particularly in the last few years. Although capable in many respects, ministers have typically not had a strong background in economics or in the economic ministries.
- The teachers' union devotes a large proportion of its time to traditional union issues as well as to partisan politics. The union and one particular political party of Maoist extraction are essentially conterminous with each other. The union's discourse, as can be judged from its publications, pays relatively little attention to professional development issues for teachers.

Many Incentives, in Theory

The argument that Peru already has a large array of various sorts of incentives—and even has no shortage of innovative proposals—is relatively easy to make. This section will be familiar territory to most Peruvians and to those familiar with Peru, but others may find it worth reading.

One way to very specifically and graphically gauge the incentive- or bonus-intensity of Peru's teacher rewards system is simply to look at a teacher's pay stub. In that pay stub, aside from the basic salary, one can count no less than 15 forms of extra pay, which does not include typical fringe benefits (health, life, or disability insurance; contributions to pension plan). Were one to add all forms of incentives and bonuses, such as rurality bonuses, there could well be another 5 or so items in a pay stub. Pay above the basic salary amounts to 95 percent of total pay in this example (it may well be more in other cases). Some items meriting an independent entry in the pay stub reward the teacher with about an extra 1 U.S. cent (0.04 soles at the March 2004 exchange rate). The structure of incentives includes items such as extra pay for preparing classes (received by everyone). Given this structure, teachers must find it confusing to define what they are paid for or why. Furthermore, it would be difficult for someone being paid in this manner to take his or her employer's policy and management capabilities, hence the running of the state, very seriously. This lack of credibility both undermines the possibilities for reform because there would seem to be little trust and, at the same time, makes reform all the more necessary.

The Ley del Profesorado

The Ley del Profesorado (Teacher Statute) was passed in 1984 and modified in 1990. The law created five salary grades, and salaries were pegged to the grades. Advancement between grades 1 and 2 was by seniority only, but beyond grade 2 advancement between grades was based on various promotion criteria, as shown in table 11.2.

This point allocation may not be perfect. One could argue that seniority weighs a bit too much (even then, it is only 15 percent) and that the responsibility of the post held weighs too little, especially relative to each other, and so forth. But the allocation clearly goes in the right direction, and it is, in theory, a good deal better than the usual salary structure common in, say, U.S. school systems. In fact, in actual practice, in large (and hence somewhat bureaucratic) private sector organizations, seniority weighs about this much in determining promotions.[149] This structure is

---

149. It could be argued that this weighting is justified in the private sector because experience leads to higher productivity, whereas in the public education sector it does not. But it would take more faith in econometrics than is probably healthy to take this argument very seriously.

Table 11.2. Promotion Criteria According to Ley del Profesorado

Criteria	Points
Professional background: 100 points	
Titles or degrees	30
Further course work and specialization, including in-service training	25
Seniority	30
Responsibility of post held	15
Professional performance: 60 points	
Efficiency on the job	30
Attendance and punctuality	15
Participation in community work	15
Merits: 40 points	
Official distinctions and honors	20
Intellectual output	20

Source: Chiroque 2004.

15 years old. Unfortunately, however, it is largely theoretical and is essentially without effect for several reasons.

First, no real regulation existed to give concretion to the abstractions in the law. To gauge "efficiency on the job" would have required effective regulatory or normative development and practice. But the regulation has never been developed, according to informants.[150]

Second, the performance points would have applied to basic salary. Given the overall inappropriate salary structure, where basic salaries are only about 5 percent of total pay, reasonable percentage improvements in basic pay between salary grades are essentially meaningless if they do

---

150. Lack of regulatory development subsequent to law is a common phenomenon in Latin America and in many developing countries. Moreover, when the regulatory development takes place, it is very often of quite poor quality. Peru's previous education law (the current one passed in 2004) is also from the 1980s, and some 4 or 5 years elapsed before its regulatory framework was developed. One reason regulatory development takes so long and is of such poor quality is that the laws are very abstract and skirt over the most controversial issues. Thus, key issues often get left to regulatory development in the executive body, which does not have the procedural capacity or accountability to deal with the sharp policy issues that the legislature avoided. All of these problems apparently existed in the Ley del Profesorado, given when it was negotiated and passed (late 1980s), and in the changes within government subsequent to its passage.

not drive other increases. So, even if there were mechanisms to apply the Ley del Profesorado, the monetary effect of the point system would be so small that it would constitute an ineffectual incentives system.

Third, promotions were largely frozen in the 1990s, for reasons that are not entirely clear (Chiroque 2004). This lack of promotion created a circular causality with the lack of good regulation for implementing the promotions: if there are no promotions, there is no need for a good regulation to implement them. But if a good regulation is deemed too difficult to create (bureaucratically and politically), or if promotions (as implied by the law) are deemed potentially fiscally dangerous by a new government, one way to prevent this source of fiscal pressure is to freeze promotions, which eliminates the need to create proper regulation. Thus, freezing promotions, on the one hand, and having no regulation with which to process promotions, on the other hand, are mutually reinforcing causes.

Hypotheses as to why promotions were frozen and, hence, why there was no need to develop implementing regulation were offered by interviewees in the background discussions leading to this chapter. One of them is that implementing the promotions would have been fiscally imprudent or, at any rate, was seen that way by the new government in the early 1990s. It is worth noting that the APRA (Alianza Popular Revolucionaria Americana, or American Popular Revolutionary Alliance) political party government that promoted the Ley del Profesorado had a record of fiscal management that was not the best, and the Fujimori government inherited a fiscal crisis. Another hypothesis is that attempting to promote on a merit basis and developing specific promotion criteria would have led to tension and difficulties, including politically undesirable comparisons between promotion criteria (and promotion amounts) in teaching and in other state services to which the government might have been giving more priority (albeit perhaps for valid reasons), such as the military. Which hypothesis is true is less important than the fact that all of the hypotheses offered (and, most likely, any that could be offered in addition to those) suggest basic problems in managing the state.

A Recent Experiment in Testing-at-Entry or Merit-Based Appointments

In 2001, the Ministry of Education inherited from a previous government the need to convert a large number of contract-based teachers (*contratados*) into permanent appointments (*nombrados*), because the process had already been started and was deemed irreversible. For Peruvian teachers, converting from a contract to an appointment represents a major step forward in job stability because permanent appointees are much more difficult to dismiss. The previous government had apparently based the process of transition between a *contrato* and a *nombramiento* on formal attributes and paper qualifications. The new ministry attempted to make the appointments merit-based through an open contest on the basis of an examination of substantive and pedagogical knowledge.

The process received various criticisms. For example, the tests were, it was suggested, excessively academic and inappropriate. Similarly, the *plazas* that were opened up included coveted urban postings, which were opened up only for *contratadado* teachers instead of being opened up also for rural teachers who were *nombrado* and perhaps should have been first in the queue for a similar post in an urban setting.[151] The process appears to have been somewhat rushed (although the rush may have been inevitable, given the need to act quickly in such situations).

Most of the opposition was to the notion of merit-based appointments as such, however, where powerful interests would have proposed simply going by order of length of time the *contratado* teachers had been waiting for a *nombramiento*. This opposition led to serious tensions with the Sindicato Único de Trabajadores de la Educación Peruana, or SUTEP (the teachers' union), including a 21-day hunger strike and widespread violence. Yet, in the end, SUTEP had to go along with the process because the rank-and-file teachers ultimately bought into the merit-based selection, leaving the union or its leadership little choice. Furthermore, although there may have been some valid criticisms relative to the technical or pedagogical quality of the process, no person interviewed for this research complained that the process had been corrupt or clientelist. Nevertheless, the experience has not been repeated or institutionalized. No evaluation of the experience was conducted.

Rurality Incentives

In Peru at present, two types of rurality incentives exist (see Cueto and Alcázar 2004; Díaz and Saavedra 2000): a general "difficult conditions" incentive and a specific rural incentive. But like most incentives in Peru, they seem to have little effect for several reasons. First, the general "difficult conditions" incentive is essentially inoperative because it is tied to the basic salary. As shown previously, the value of the basic salary has

---

151. This choice may not have been a technical oversight or design flaw, but the result of an unavoidable tradeoff. If the opportunity had been opened up to existing rural teachers with a *plaza*, it would have been consistent with the merit principle being applied to the *contrata* teachers if the rural *plaza* teachers had to pass the same test as the *contrata* teachers. If rural teachers could get the coveted urban posts before the *contrata* teachers and without an exam, the merit policy principle would have been undermined when the *contrata* teachers had to pass an exam to get the same posts. But to test existing rural teachers with *plazas* might have met truly serious opposition. So the ministry may simply have been confronted with an uncomfortable choice with no perfect solution.

been eroded. The rurality incentive is worth 45 soles, but this sum is still only about 5 percent of average total pay, which is unlikely to make much difference in anyone's attitude about anything—unless taken away. Second, teachers generally do not identify this component of pay as a specific incentive, which is understandable, given how complex the reward structure is and how small this incentive is as a percentage of total pay. Third, the incentive does not address the main concerns that teachers have with living in rural areas (see Alcázar and Cueto 2004; Instituto Apoyo 2001), which appear to have more to do with living conditions in general than with cost of living.[152] Fourth, the administrative infrastructure to apply these incentives is either weak or corrupt. Therefore, the incentive gets applied in areas that used to be rural but now have the basic services teachers seek, or it gets applied to teachers not teaching in rural areas, for example, because they have already transferred.[153] In short, although institutionalized, these so-called incentives are not real incentives in the sense that they may affect teacher behavior.

An Existing Incentives Proposal

Not only does Peru have a legacy of experiments and actual incentives, but also there is no lack of proposals for new teacher incentives. Chiroque (2001), in a survey, compiles at least 10 different sets of ideas that have been proposed and that have seriously entered public debate in the past decade or so. His own proposal has been floated to SUTEP. The union has neither endorsed nor rejected it. Furthermore, the proposal is associated with an institution that has a history of good relations with the union movement. Thus, the proposal could be considered somewhat union-friendly and is, in that sense, worth summarizing.

The proposal in Chiroque (2001) is for monetary and nonmonetary incentives, where incentives are defined as stimuli above and beyond basic pay. The proposal involves the following simple framework:

1. Incentives for performance
    a. Monetary
        (1) Group (school-level) incentives
        (2) Individual incentives for the two best teachers in any school
        Both types of monetary incentives would be based on measurements of learner and teacher performance by the Unidad de Medición de la Calidad Educativa (UMC) of the ministry. The

---

152. Incentives that are powerful enough to overcome a generalized dislike for living in rural areas might work, but they may need to be quite large.

153. This phenomenon is not exclusive of Peru. Urquiola and Vegas in this volume describe a similar situation that results in arbitrary variation in teachers' salaries in Bolivia.

group incentives would be about 80 percent of the performance incentive, and the individual incentives would be 20 percent. The incentive would go to about 2 percent of schools, and 15 percent of total remunerations would be reserved for such incentives.[154]

b. Nonmonetary
These incentives would be personalized distinctions to remarkable teachers, such as receiving certificates, having an opportunity for further study, having their practices disseminated to other teachers, and so on. The incentives could originate in the ministry, the municipality, or the civil society.

2. Incentives for work under difficult conditions
Service difficulty would be judged according to travel time, on foot, to the nearest city with urban facilities. Thus, this judgment determines a rurality incentive.

a. Access to improved services would include housing under certain conditions and access to a cluster-school nucleus with services such as telephone and library. They would be available only if teachers voluntarily cluster into networks.

b. Teachers volunteering for service under difficult conditions join the salary scale at level 2.

c. Incentives for those in rural areas upon stepping from level 2 to level 3 in the salary scale will consist of a 30 percent bonus over the level 3 base pay.

d. Extra points will be given in salary grade evaluations for teachers completing at least 5 years of service in a rural area.

Most important, the proposal includes sanctions for underperformance, which extend to the possibility of dismissal and which are relatively elaborate and comprehensive.

In sum, there are not only plenty of attempted reforms, but also plenty of existing proposals, most of them reasonable in key respects.

Reasons Why Reforms Fail to Take Hold

Many of the experiences listed previously explain some of the reasons that experiments with teacher incentives were not truly implemented or did not take hold in Peru. However, such specific explanations skirt the main issue of fundamental institutional weaknesses that go beyond those sug-

---

154. It is unclear whether the 15 percent applies to the remunerations *at the chosen schools.* Presumably it would, because dedicating 15 percent of all system remuneration to the 2 percent best-performing schools would be a very large incentive. In other places, the 15 percent seems to be devoted to all forms of incentive, including the rurality incentives.

gested in the narration of the specific experiences. The basic problem in Peru appears to be in the implementation capacity; policies are often designed but simply fail to be implemented. The knowledge that policies will tend not to be implemented may encourage a careless design, which creates a vicious cycle of poor design followed by lack of implementation, which then is an implicit excuse for poor design.

Peru has had 12 constitutions and 24 fundamental education laws since independence. Since 1990, Peru has had 17 ministers of education, each averaging some 10 months of tenure. As in much of Latin America and the developing world, laws generally are abstract and do not attribute responsibility to individual actors. The laws spend considerable time on abstractions (education) rather than concrete institutions (schools). Duties and powers of important actors are neither attributed to particular office-holders nor defined. Effective education laws, on the contrary (as in Malaysia, Singapore, or South Africa), contain implicit sets of job descriptions (the duties and powers) for the most important governance and management tasks performed by the most important actors in the sector. By attributing duties and powers specifically, they also contain an implicit organizational chart of the key relationships in the sector (but not of the institutions, naturally). Fortunately, the most recent education law in Peru appears to be a considerable improvement on this score.

The most basic governance and management systems fail. In Peru, it is not clear for example, how many teachers exist. The teachers' union finds this uncertainty upsetting and tends to mock the ministry on this score. However, the teachers' union itself does not have a list of paid-up members, and it is not even clear that such a concept exists. Contributions to the Derrama Educativa (a service organization controlled by SUTEP) are made on a presumptive basis. Similarly, "contracted" (as opposed to "appointed") teachers often go without pay for months, again a sign of the low degree of administrative and institutional regularity.

The union complains about clientelism and corruption in government (for example, as a principled reason for opposing performance evaluation of certain types), but it is not clear that it is free from clientelist practices itself. Commentators interviewed explained that, when the political party controlling the union has had the opportunity to govern (at subnational levels), it is hardly obvious that the party has done so without granting favoritism to clients.

Education laws in Peru are usually passed without much contemplation of the financial implications or of the necessary implementation mechanisms. For example, the Law on Public Investment in Education has stimulated the opening of hundreds of teacher training institutes without either the infrastructure to drive quality control and feedback in a market-based approach or the planning infrastructure to drive quantity and planning in a command-based approach. As a result, the system is producing some 17,000 new teachers per year, when only 5,000 to 8,000 are reportedly needed. This situation not only represents a waste, but also makes it difficult to institute evaluation systems without creating the suspicion that the evaluation system is meant to result in firings and layoffs. (For a change, the current development of a new law on the Carrera Pública Magisterial is one of the first that is being carried out with an explicit analysis of financial implications, which is a hopeful sign.)

In short, the development of incentives in Peru evidences serious institutional weaknesses. It is hard to apply a fair and efficient system of incentives in the presence of weak institutions. Moreover, when one is confronted with weak public institutions, it is also difficult to argue that incentives are the biggest problem facing the sector. But this situation presents a conundrum: in the face of weak institutions, a good system of incentives might at least offer some way forward in terms of actually reaching and teaching children; yet donors and governments would find it difficult to craft and apply such systems when the actors distrust (perhaps with good reason) the institutions that would manage the systems.

In terms of a comparison with Chile, essentially none of the factors that were present in Chile and that favored incentives reform were present in Peru. There was no universal testing in the country (there is sample-based testing), much less over a time series. Hence, one finds little basis for comparisons between individual schools or districts and little personal interest in accountability pressure. There has been little *reported* participation in international assessments (although this situation has changed). Ministers in Peru have changed often and did not generally have the background in economics or the interaction with economic ministries that ministers had in Chile. Teachers' salaries have not been on a generalized, significant, and undisputable improvement path, which in Chile both paved the way for ease among the rank and file with the notion of individual incentives and created an atmosphere of having to *rendir cuentas* (account for one's results). The teachers' union, either for objective or subjective reasons, is still relatively old-fashioned in terms of its vision and approach (perhaps justifiably so, at least in the view of its own rank and file, given average salary perceptions). The union's discourse is about bread-and-butter issues or very broad political militancy issues, even extending to international issues, with relatively less time and space devoted to a profound analysis of education policy in Peru or to the professional aspirations of teachers as individuals (for example, pedagogical skills). Finally, teachers are generally much less professionalized and are managed by less professional systems: they have lower levels of education, basic payroll and payment systems tend not to be fully reliable, and teachers more often have second jobs. Those factors, added to generalized apparent institutional weakness, created a situation where reform of incentives (or serious reform of other types) was not likely to flourish.

Some Suggestions for Progress

Peru has evidently attempted some and designed many incentive schemes or other accountability or merit-selection schemes. None has been fully or successfully implemented. This failure can be attributed to basic failures in state management. But this weakness does not mean that all efforts to craft improved incentives or improved accountability schemes are doomed. Two suggestions for improvement follow.

First, Peru is undergoing a process of policy reform redefinition under the leadership of the Consejo Nacional de Educación. This process is already well begun. Donors should consider providing sufficient support to this process so that it does not lead simply to a document that is published and is perceived as a fixed "reform proposal." Even if care is taken to make sure that the proposal emerges from a nonpartisan or multipartisan group, the group that eventually produces the report becomes, in some sense, a party or an identifiable group with an identifiable reform proposal. This partisan identification will be particularly strong if the proposal is, as it should be, quite specific and does not avoid the tough issues. Thus, in a country with a weak state, where new ministers and governments have to make their marketing points by coming up with their own proposals, all finite-end proposals—where the emphasis is on the proposal as such and its documents—tend to suffer the fate of being archived. Instead, donors should support the process so that it does a few things beyond writing down the key ideas.

The dialogue should be aimed at making sure the ideas that develop represent widespread opinion of many segments in society. This way, it is difficult for new governments to reverse the process. The basic points of the reform simply come to be part of the accepted intellectual landscape, without having to be formally adopted by the state (although to be implemented they must be). Most important, the more such ideas enter general parlance, the less they are identified with the ideas of a particular group and the less value there is in counterposing alternative proposals as a political market-differentiating strategy.

Donors should ensure that the process of marketing and discussing the ideas continues beyond the publishing of the report and, in fact, spans at least one significant change in government. This way social actors might start to see the possibility of a set of ideas spanning more than one government because the ideas have taken root in the minds of so many nonpolitical appointees in the bureaucracy and in civil society. In a sense, the ideas would tend to slowly start becoming the *política de estado*.

Leaders in the process should attempt to ensure strategic focus on a few key ideas rather than on the usual reformist laundry list. The issue of incentives or accountability mechanisms needs to be a central part of the process.

Donors could provide technical assistance, if needed. The aid would help resolve contradictions that arise when lack of technical imagination or experience results in problems being perceived as zero-sum games, which makes them more difficult to solve, or when it results in solutions that are much further from the optimum than would otherwise be possible.

Leaders should raise consciousness among participants in the process so that the whole point is to create an atmosphere whereby *políticas de estado* can emerge. That is, participants will not just carry out the process, but will carry it out in such a manner that the leadership is aware of the continuity between the process and the crafting of state policy.

Second, a need may also exist to create pilot experiences not only with incentives as narrowly defined, but also with the whole set of work conditions and work rules that determine low or high productivity in schools. Donors often tend to favor education projects that emphasize the traditional supply-side investments: teacher training, textbook provision, improvement of physical infrastructure, and so forth. Or, in response to such projects' lack of effect, donors shift to pure incentives and accountability, such as improving parental oversight in schools, choice-based alternatives, and so forth. Instead, or in addition, donors should perhaps consider funding experiences where a large set of schools is chosen; where their corresponding Unidad de Gestión Educacional Local or other higher-level entities are also chosen (possibly all the way to the ministry); and where the whole management and governance chain is improved, tested, and exercised in terms of both narrow (monetary or other) incentives. More important, the broader incentives must be related to governance and work rules, all of which help configure high-performance workplaces. This kind of project can demonstrate an empirically based way of creating the regulation and norms that the new education law—or the overall policy reform process—requires.

Regulation based on ex ante reasoning by academics or lawyers, or derived purely from the imagined administrative requirements of the law, can often be unimplementable. Regulation should instead be based on empirically observable and tested practice that yields results. But this approach is quite rare in Latin America. In implementing this approach, the union could be, ideally, involved in taking co-accountability for the process and its results. In this way, the norms that would evolve (and that could then be used to spread better norms to the whole system) would tend to be preapproved by the unions. Hence, there would be little or no excuse to fail to implement them later. At the same time, given the power of the union in Peru, attempting to improve on norms at the margin of the union is more likely to result in norms that are sabotaged or at least unimplemented later on—much as most incentives systems have been unsustained thus far, even under what might be considered "strong government" situations in the 1990s.

There are also current efforts and proposals to recraft teacher career and incentives systems that appear promising, including those proposed by

Chiroque (2001) as noted earlier and including those being worked on by consultants to the Ministry of Education.

Toward a Conclusion: Unions, Incentives, and Educational Progress in Latin America

We have seen that unions, or their leadership, have many reasons to oppose certain types of incentives that have the potential, in theory, to boost achievement. Are unions, therefore, "bad" for educational progress? Many analysts and commentators decry the role of unions in the education sector. Regardless of their empirically measurable effect, unions' oft-cited opposition to individualized incentives that are based on learner achievement gives rise to criticism. In addition, some analysts, especially in the United States and regardless of their stance on incentives for productivity, have concluded that incentives negatively affect the education sector, both by increasing costs and by lowering achievement. Their views are manifested in relatively popular works such as Brimelow (2003), academic work such as that of Hoxby (1996), and "insider" accounts such as that of Lieberman (2000). Other analysts, such as Eberts and Stone (1984), Grimes and Register (1990), Milkman (1997), and Stone (2000), find that although unions increase costs, they have an ambiguous or mildly positive effect on achievement. Others, such as Chambers (1976) and Hall and Carroll (1973), have found ambiguous effects in general (positive effect on salaries and negative effect on employment, leaving a neutral effect on total labor cost). Those findings are time-sensitive. Strong unionization in U.S. schools did not begin until the 1960s, and the effect of unions on costs did not start to be felt until the late 1970s (Baugh and Stone 1982; Eberts and Stone 1984).

Similar studies have not been systematically carried out in Latin America. An exception is Murillo and others (2002), which finds that, in Argentina, the measured effects of unions are generally somewhat ambiguous. For example, one of the effects identified was that greater degrees of unionization cause more days to be lost to strikes, or that teacher satisfaction decreases as unionization increases. Although some of this effect may be endogenous, unions may find it easier to unionize when there is dissatisfaction. There is also no doubt that "manufacturing dissatisfaction" is both a union tactic in a managerialist view of unions, as noted in Freeman and Medoff (1984), and a natural outcome of greater class consciousness. Further studies of this nature should be stimulated in Latin America.

The effect of unions appears ambiguous in most of the literature (see, for example, Jessup 1985; Johnson 1985; Mitchell and others 1981). Management is shown as able to adapt, partly by creating countervailing bureaucracy (which can increase transactions costs) and also simply by resorting to higher levels of informality. It can also create more appropriate mixes of informality and formality, through commonsense in management and, finally, through *better* formality, which can increase productivity. Such findings generalize to the economy as a whole—where it seems difficult to find strong evidence through large-scale quantitative assessment or through a combination of quantitative assessment and knowledge of how unions and management really interact—that unions systematically damage productivity (Aidt and Tzannatos 2002; Freeman and Medoff 1984).

To the extent that unions have had counterproductive effects on schooling, their effects are probably not the only concern. Rather, the struggle between unions—as monopolistic bureaucracies—and states or municipalities—as countervailing monopolistic bureaucracies—has a negative effect on schooling. Unions arose in the United States, partly as a form of countervailing power, to confront another monopolistic form of bureaucratic power, namely state provision of education. In the very early days, they arose partly as a way to defend professional autonomy from what was believed to be (by municipal governments and as part of the overall "good government" reforms) efficiency-enhancing bureaucratization of education in the early 20th century (Scarselletta Straut 1996). Such motivations appear to have continued well into the latter half of the 20th century (Jessup 1978). Unionization in the United States was also abetted by the fact that, over time, teachers came less and less from a generalized professional and middle-class background, and more and more from a lower-middle-class or working-class background (Cole 1968).

In Latin America, unions arose not only to support monopolistic state power in ideological terms (ideological support of the *Estado Docente*) but to also confront, or fight over, corruption and cronyism in state power that was seen (not just by unions) as inefficient, as centralist in theory yet particularistic in practice, and as too informal. Tenure for teachers, for example, arose partly as a form of protection against administrative venality and against political interference in the administrative function, whereby politicians would attempt to change even the village school teacher every time a change in government would come about.

In both the United States and Latin America, unions have themselves become monopolistic and bureaucratic. They have typically succeeded in increasing salaries beyond that which would be established by the market, through their competition between labor suppliers in selling to a monopolistic purchaser (the state in Latin America, municipal governments in the United States), as noted above. But, in so doing, they have used tactics that were borrowed (through the use of advisers and simple observation) from industrial unionism and that have typically not led to an improved sense of professionalism or autonomy. Instead, they have led to a simple shift of bureaucratic and collective allegiance from state to union (see Raelin 1989). This very deprofessionalization is generating internal pressures within unions, because the rank and file have professional and individual aspirations. However, the leadership frequently may prefer to work with a unified, collectivized mass that is easier to mobilize (in some cases to achieve collective goals that the rank and file themselves approve of).

The foregoing discussion suggests a few final pointers for possible ways forward regarding incentives and the role of unions (both in the narrow sense of pay for performance and in the broader sense of work and governance rules that determine high productivity) in improving education in Latin America.

First, the effect of incentives is complex, as is shown in the review of the literature on incentives presented elsewhere in this volume. Effects differ depending on the design, the circumstances, and the nature of the organization implementing them. It seems unlikely that incentives schemes that are implemented by monopolistic bureaucracies involved in contests with other monopolistic bureaucracies, will, by themselves, have a major effect on learning.

Second, as we have seen (at least in the case of Chile), unions themselves, or at least the rank and file, have some interest in professionalism, which ties increasingly well to the growing pressure for quality and for visible learning results in Latin America. This interest in professionalism is unlikely to translate into an easy acquiescence with, say, schemes tying teacher rewards to student achievement on standardized tests, but it does represent an opportunity. Unions are unlikely to become debureaucratized, just as governments are not about to. Thus, trends toward a "new unionism" are best viewed with some agnosticism, as union critics warn (see Brimelow 2003). Nevertheless, opportunities exist in the current concern with quality and with the interest of individual teachers in gaining professionalism.

Third, there are other models of accountability, different from the sorts of incentives typically being tried in Chile, for example. Some of those models are explored in this volume. The models may be necessary to reduce bureaucracy and monopolization of service provision. It may be useful to reduce bureaucratization and monopolization because incentives implemented under those conditions might have less effect. Accountability schemes, such as giving schools more autonomy and responsibility (in a context of measurement against standard), funding (or providing physical resources, if true funding is too difficult) on a per capita basis, involving parents in rewarding teachers both financially and with esteem and choosing teachers and their directors, plus other similar reforms, are all innovations that can be tried as alternatives to, or in addition to, bureaucratically driven and bureaucratically allocated monetary incentives. Nevertheless, teachers often fear local elite capture and local nepotism, and unions arose partly in response to such problems. Teachers are also often concerned about being evaluated by people who are less literate than they. In any case, it is not clear that demand about quality (say, actual learning), rather than simple precursors of quality (attendance of teachers), is so

easily orchestrated by communities. Polled teachers often prefer bureaucratic or peer evaluation (see Ministerio de Educación/IIPE-UNESCO
2002 in Peru). Thus, great care would have to be taken to create community influence systems that are not captured by local elites and are not
subject to local corruption, or that confuse parental governance with day-
to-day management. Such systems could, in principle, be tried on a pilot
basis, but they should be tried in pilots that make administrative sense—
allowing an exercise of the whole administrative system in geographically contiguous schools.

Fourth, in crafting such experiments, one may find it expedient to formally involve unions in developing the work rules and broad incentives,
and in monitoring, as long as they are willing to take formal, professional,
accountability for results. This inclusion may be expedient to minimize
the tendency of unions to block implementation after the experiments
are designed. It may be expedient, also, because ultimately teachers will
have good, applied ideas about school improvements. Their voiced suggestions may carry more implementation weight if they have been collectively vetted.

Fifth, the vicious cycle between poor legislation or policy and poor
implementation needs to be broken on a continuing basis, and donors
could play a role in this activity. Breaking the cycle is particularly important in countries with weaker institutional capacity such as Peru and is
particularly problematic in education and in education labor legislation.
Currently, legislation and policy are often poorly designed, because everyone knows the probability of implementation is low. Therefore, the skills
or political compromise capacity needed to make difficult decisions is not
sufficient. Thus, difficult decisions get left to the *reglamentación* stage,
where there is even less capacity to resolve difficult issues. But because the
laws are often so poorly designed, they are difficult to implement. A
vicious cycle thus exists between poor (unimplementable) policy design,
which leads to poor or no implementation, and the knowledge that there
will be low implementation, which becomes an excuse for poor policy
design and which makes implementation even more difficult. There seem
to be improvements in this area, as with the new education and education labor laws in Peru, but more could be done by providing more technical support in both legal and policy design and in consensus processes.

References

Aidt, T., and Z. Tzannatos. 2002. *Unions and Collective Bargaining: Economic Effects in a Global Environment.* Washington, D.C.: World Bank.

Assael Budnik, J., and J. P. Urrutia. 2002. "La experiencia del sindicalismo magisterial chileno de concertación y conflicto en el sector educativo." In M. V. Murillo, ed., *Carreras magisteriales, desempeño educativo y sindicatos de maestros en América Latina.* Facultad Latino-Americana de Ciencias Sociales. Sede Académica de Argentina.

Ballou, D., and M. Podgursky. 1993. "Teacher's Attitudes toward Merit Pay: Examining Conventional Wisdom." *Industrial and Labor Relations Review* 47(1): 50–61.

Baugh, W. H., and J. A. Stone. 1982. "Teachers, Unions, and Wages in the 1970s: Unionism Now Pays." *Industrial and Labor Relations Review* 35(3): 368–76.

Belleï, C. 2004. "La profesionalización docente desde los 90. Protección, apoyo, e incentivos." Ministry of Education, Santiago. Processed.

Brimelow, P. 2003. *The Worm in the Apple: How the Teacher Unions Are Destroying American Education.* New York: Perennial.

Chambers, J. 1976. "The Impact of Collective Bargaining for Teachers in Resource Allocation in Public School Districts." *Journal of Urban Economics* 4: 324–39.

Chiroque, S. 2001. "Sistema de incentivos al maestro Peruano." Documento de Trabajo al 15 de diciembre 2001. Instituto de Pedagogía Popular, Lima.

———. 2004. "Descongelar los niveles magisteriales." Informe 18. Instituto de Pedagogía Popular, Lima.

Cole, S. 1968. "The Unionization of Teachers: Determinants of Rank-and-File Support." *Sociology of Education* 41(1): 66–87.

Cueto, S., and L. Alcázar. 2004. "Informe final de análisis de datos de línea base plan piloto de bonificaciones especiales a docentes en zonas rurales." Lima, GRADE.

Díaz, H., and J. Saavedra. 2000. "La carrera del maestro del Peru: Factores institucionales, incentivos económicos y desempeño." Lima, GRADE.

Eberts, R. W., and J. A. Stone. 1984. *Unions and Public Schools: The Effect of Collective Bargaining and American Education.* Lexington, Mass.: Lexington Books.

Freeman, R., and J. Medoff. 1984. *What Do Unions Do?* New York: Basic Books.

González, P. 2003. "Estructura institucional, recursos, y gestión en el sistema educacional chileno." In C. Cox, ed., *Políticas educacionales en el cambio de siglo: La reforma del sistema escolar de Chile.* Santiago: Editorial Universitaria.

Grimes, P. W., and C. A. Register. 1990. "Teachers' Unions and Student Achievement in High School Economics." *Journal of Economic Education* 21(3): 297–306.

Hall, W. C., and N. E. Carroll. 1973. "The Effect of Teachers' Organizations on Salaries and Class Size." *Industrial and Labor Relations* 26(2): 834–41.

Hoxby, C. M. 1996. "How Teachers' Unions Affect Education Production." *Quarterly Journal of Economics* 111(3): 671–718.

Instituto Apoyo. 2001. "Plan de implementación de un programa de incentivos para docentes de zonas rurales y de condiciones especiales." Processed. Lima.

Jessup, D. 1978. "Teacher Unionization: A Reassessment of Rank and File Motivations." *Sociology of Education* 51(1): 44–55.

———. 1985. *Teachers, Unions, and Change. A Comparative Study.* New York: Praeger.

Johnson, S. M. 1985. *Teacher Unions in Schools.* Philadelphia: Temple University Press.

Kerchner, C. T., J. E. Koppich, and J. G. Weeres. 1997. *United Mind Workers: Unions and Teaching in the Knowledge Society.* San Francisco: Jossey-Bass.

————. 1998. *Taking Charge of Quality: How Teachers and Unions Can Revitalize Schools*. San Francisco: Jossey-Bass.

Lieberman, M. 2000. *The Teacher Unions: How They Sabotage Educational Reform and Why*. San Francisco: Encounter Books.

Masters, M., and J. T. Delaney. 1987. "Union Political Activities: A Review of the Empirical Literature." *Industrial and Labor Relations Review* 40(3): 336–53.

Milkman, M. 1997. "Teachers' Unions, Productivity, and Minority Student Achievement." *Journal of Labor Research* 18: 137–50.

Ministerio de Educación (Peru)/IIPE-UNESCO. 2002. *Magisterio, educación y sociedad en el Peru*. Lima.

Mitchell, D., C. Kerchner, W. Erck, and G. Pryor. 1981. "The Impact of Collective Bargaining on School Management and Policy." *American Journal of Education* 89: 147–88.

Mizala, A., and P. Romaguera. 2003. "Regulación, incentivos y remuneraciones de los profesores en Chile." In C. Cox, ed., *Políticas educacionales en el cambio de siglo: La reforma del sistema escolar de Chile*. Santiago: Editorial Universitaria.

Moore, G. A. 1976. "The Effect of Collective Bargaining on Internal Salary Structures in the Public Schools." *Industrial and Labor Relations Review* 29(3): 352–62.

Murillo, M. V., M. Tommasi, L. Ronconi, and J. Sanguinetti. 2002. "The Economic Effects of Unions in Latin America: Teachers' Unions and Education in Argentina." Research Network Working Paper R-463. Report for the Inter-American Development Bank, Washington, D.C.

Nuñez Prieto, I. 2003. "El profesorado, su gremio y la reforma de los noventa: Presiones de cambio y evolución de la cultura docente." In C. Cox, ed., *Políticas educacionales en el cambio de siglo: La reforma del sistema escolar de Chile*. Santiago: Editorial Universitaria.

Pavez Urrutia, J. No date. "Sobre el sistema nacional de evaluación de desempeño docente." Colegio de Profesores, Santiago, Chile. Processed.

Pemberton, J. 1988. "A 'Managerial' Model of the Trade Union." *Economic Journal* 98(392): 755–71.

Prendergast, C. 1999. "The Provision of Incentives in Firms." *Journal of Economic Literature* 37 (March): 7–63.

Raelin, J. A. 1989. "Unionization and Deprofessionalization: Which Comes First?" *Journal of Organizational Behavior* 10(2): 101–15.

Scarselletta Straut, D. 1996. "Full Circle: A Retrospective on Labor Relations and Educational Governance." Paper prepared for the American Education Research Association Annual Meeting, New York, April 8–12.

Scherping, G. 2003a. "Informe de participación en comisión SIMCE." Informal report to the Colegio de Profesores on position on SIMCE. Colegio de Profesores de Chile, Santiago. Processed.

———. 2003b. "Presentación, grupo de trabajo: El rol de la información en el sistema educacional Chileno: Información y calidad de la educación." Paper presented to Working Group. Colegio de Profesores de Chile, Santiago. Processed.

———. 2003c. "Propuesta." Discussion note on proposal by the Colegio de Profesores to the CUT to start an experimental technical-professional institute. Colegio de Profesores de Chile, Santiago. Processed.

Stone, J. A. 2000. "Collective Bargaining and Public Schools." In T. Loveless, ed., *Conflicting Missions? Teachers Unions and Educational Reform.* Washington, D.C.: Brookings Institution Press.

Verdugo, O. 2004. "Sueño compartido." Colegio de Profesores de Chile, Santiago. Processed.

Villarán, V. 2003. "Sindicato docente y gobiernos en el Perú, una mirada a la última década." Processed.

Wise, A. 1979. *Legislated Learning: The Bureaucratization of the American Classroom.* Berkeley: University of California Press.

Index

WITHDRAWAL